PC Magazine Guide to Professional Write Plus

PC Magazine Guide to Professional Write Plus

Gerry Litton

Ziff-Davis Press
Emeryville, California

Editor	Leslie Tilley
Technical Reviewer	Suzanne McGinn
Project Coordinator	Sheila McGill
Proofreader	Lysa Lewallen
Cover Concept	Gerard Kunkel
Cover Design	Gary Kaplow
Book Design	Laura Lamar/MAX, San Francisco
Page Layout	Peter Tucker and Tony Jonick
Technical Illustration	Tony Jonick, Cherie Plumlee, and Steph Bradshaw
Indexer	Richard Shrout

This book was produced on a Macintosh IIfx, with the following applications: FrameMaker, Microsoft® Word, MacLink*Plus*,® Aldus FreeHand, and Collage Plus™.

Ziff-Davis Press
5903 Christie Avenue
Emeryville, CA 94608

Copyright © 1991 by Ziff-Davis Press. All rights reserved. Printed and manufactured in the United States of America.

PC Magazine is a registered trademark of Ziff Communications Company. Ziff-Davis Press, ZD Press, and PC Magazine Guide To are trademarks of Ziff Communications Company.

All other product names and services identified throughout this book are trademarks or registered trademarks of their respective companies. They are used throughout this book in editorial fashion only and for the benefit of such companies. No such uses, or the use of any trade name, is intended to convey endorsement or other affiliation with the book.

No part of this publication may be reproduced in any form, or stored in a database or retrieval system, or transmitted or distributed in any form by any means, electronic, mechanical photocopying, recording, or otherwise, without the prior written permission of Ziff-Davis Press, except as permitted by the Copyright Act of 1976.

THE INFORMATION AND MATERIAL CONTAINED IN THIS BOOK IS PROVIDED "AS IS," WITHOUT WARRANTY OF ANY KIND, EXPRESS OR IMPLIED, INCLUDING WITHOUT LIMITATION ANY WARRANTY CONCERNING THE ACCURACY, ADEQUACY OR COMPLETENESS OF SUCH INFORMATION OR MATERIAL OR THE RESULTS TO BE OBTAINED FROM USING SUCH INFORMATION OR MATERIAL. NEITHER ZIFF-DAVIS PRESS NOR THE AUTHOR SHALL BE RESPONSIBLE FOR ANY CLAIMS ATTRIBUTABLE TO ERRORS, OMISSIONS OR OTHER INACCURACIES IN THE INFORMATION OR MATERIAL CONTAINED IN THIS BOOK, AND IN NO EVENT SHALL ZIFF-DAVIS PRESS OR THE AUTHOR BE LIABLE FOR DIRECT, INDIRECT, SPECIAL, INCIDENTAL OR CONSEQUENTIAL DAMAGES ARISING OUT OF THE USE OF SUCH INFORMATION OR MATERIAL.

ISBN 1-56276-027-0
10 9 8 7 6 5 4 3 2 1

**To Minnie
the terror**

CONTENTS AT A GLANCE

Introduction xxi

1. Introducing Professional Write Plus 1

2. Word Processing Basics 27

3. Controlling the Page Appearance 59

4. Sophisticated Editing Features 87

5. Working with Your Files 121

6. Using Styles 155

7. Styles and Templates 201

8. Customized Letters and Mailing Labels 229

9. About Printers, Typefaces, and Fonts 249

10. Using Frames 277

11. Working with Graphics 303

12. Grammar Checking and Electronic Mail 331

13. Creating Different Types of Documents 365

Appendix A. Installing Professional Write Plus 385

Appendix B. Customizing Professional Write Plus 389

Appendix C. Customizing for a New Printer 402

Appendix D. Troubleshooting 408

Index 411

TABLE OF CONTENTS

Introduction xxi

Chapter 1   Introducing Professional Write Plus 1

What You Need to Run Professional Write Plus 1
Starting Up Professional Write Plus 2
The Keyboard 2
    Keyboard Basics 2
    Special Keys 4
The Main Editing Screen 5
Using a Mouse 8
    Mouse Operations 8
    Mouse Terminology 9
    Mouse Maintenance 10
Using the Menus 10
    Using the Mouse to Select Menu Items 10
    Using the Keyboard to Select Menu Items 11
    Submenus 12
Using Dialog Boxes 13
    Using the Mouse in the Dialog Box 14
    Using the Keyboard to Make Selections 16
Scrolling Through Text 18
    Scrolling Vertically 18
    Scrolling Horizontally 19
Using the Side Bar Icons 19
Getting Help 20
    Using the Help Index 20
    Using Context-Sensitive Help 22
    Using Point-and-Click Help 23
Summary 24

Chapter 2   Word Processing Basics 27

Starting a New Document 27
Basic Text Editing 27

Entering Text 27
Moving the Text Cursor with the Mouse 29
Moving the Text Cursor with the Keyboard 30
Adding and Deleting Text 31
Using the Insert and Typeover Edit Modes 32

Saving a Copy of Your Document 32
Saving for the First Time 33
Saving Again 34
Other Types of Files 36

Printing Your Document 36

Starting Over 37

Working with a Previously Saved Document 38
Specifying the File You Want to Open 39

Using Different Display Modes 40
Using Different Layout Views 40

Working with Blocks of Text 41
The Clipboard 42
Selecting a Block 43
Moving a Block 45
Copying a Block 46
Deleting a Block 47
Undoing a Block Deletion 47
Block Operations Using Side Bar Icons and Speed Keys 48

Changing the Text Appearance 59
Using Special Text Attributes 49
Using Different Fonts 52

Changing the Page Appearance 54
Setting the Line Spacing 54
Aligning Text Horizontally 55

Ending a Professional Write Plus Session 57

Summary 57

Chapter 3   Controlling the Page Appearance 59

The Elements of a Page Layout 59

Setting Page Size and Orientation 59

Printing in Landscape Orientation 62
Setting the Margins for a Document 64
    Using Edit Boxes to Change Margins 64
    Using the Page Layout Tab Ruler to Change Margins 65
    Using Temporary Margins to Avoid Horizontal Scrolling 65
Working with Tabs 66
    Tab Types 66
    Using the Edit Screen Tab Ruler 67
    Using the Page Layout Dialog Box to Change Tabs 69
    Using Relative Tabs 70
    Changing Tab Settings 70
    Using Headers and Footers 72
    Inserting a Header or Footer 73
    Adjusting the Appearance of a Header or Footer 76
    Editing Headers and Footers 78
Numbering Your Pages 78
    Formatting the Page Numbers 80
    Editing and Deleting Page Numbers 80
Selecting the Number of Columns on the Page 81
Drawing Lines Around Pages 83
Summary 84

Chapter 4   Sophisticated Editing Features 87

Checking Your Spelling 87
    Spell Checking a Word or Block 88
    Spell Checking Larger Portions of a Document 89
    Handling Questionable Words 90
    Editing the Personal Dictionary 92
Using the Thesaurus 94
Finding and Replacing Words 96
    Finding a Word or Group of Words 97
    Finding a String 98
    Specifying Text Attributes and Capitalization 98
    Other Search Options 100
    Creating Bookmarks 101

Replacing One String with Another 102
Find-and-Replace Options 103
Using Wildcards to Locate and Replace Text 104
Searching for Special Characters 105
Tips on Find-and-Replace Operations 107

Adding Notes to Your Document 108
Entering a New Note 109
Displaying and Editing Notes 110
Deleting an Existing Note 112

Using a Document Description 112
Locating a Particular Document 113

Jumping to Different Parts of a Document 114
Repetitive Jumping 115

Recovering from Accidents 115
When Undo's Memory is Cleared 116

Using Insert Variables 117
Copying an Insert Variable into Your Document 118

Summary 118

Chapter 5   Working with Your Files 121

Selecting a Different Directory 121
Selecting the Files You Want Displayed 123

Making Backups 125
Using Automatic Timed Save 126
Using the Automatic Backup Feature 127
Saving to a Different File 128

Working with Several Documents at Once 128
Working with the Same Document in Two Windows 131
Transferring Text Between Documents 131
Appending One Document to Another 132

Importing Text from Other Programs 133
ASCII Files 133
Formatting Information 135
Importing a File 137

Exporting Files in Different Formats 141

        The Types of Files You Can Export 141
        Formatting Information 142
        Exporting a File 143
Using the File Manager 146
        Selecting the Directory to Access 146
        Selecting the File Names to Display 147
        Standard File Operations 148
        Exiting from the File Manager 151
Summary 152

Chapter 6   Using Styles 155

Introducing Paragraph Styles 155
        Features That Can Be Assigned Using Paragraph Styles 156
        Using the Default Template 158
        Using the Styles Box 159
        Assigning a Style to a Paragraph 161
Creating a New Paragraph Style 162
        Example: Creating a Style for Headings 163
        Using the New Style 166
        Adding Ruling Lines 167
        Adding Space Below the Heading 170
        Aligning the Heading 171
Modifying Paragraph Styles 172
Using Different Fonts 172
        Selecting the Typeface, Size, and Text Attributes 172
        Tips on Selecting Fonts 173
Indenting and Aligning Paragraphs 174
        Choosing the Paragraph Alignment 176
        Setting the Paragraph Indent 176
        Creating Common Types of Indents 177
Automatic Hyphenation 178
Customizing the Line and Text Spacing 179
        Setting the Line Spacing 180
        Adding Space Above and Below a Paragraph 180
        Specifying the Text Tightness 182

Controlling Page Breaks 182
    Example: Keeping a Heading with the Following Text 183
Creating Bulleted Lists 184
    Creating a Paragraph Style for Bulleted Lists 185
Creating Numbered Lists 187
    Single-Level Numbered Lists 188
    Multilevel Numbered Lists 190
    Documents with Several Multilevel Numbered Lists 191
Creating Introductory Text for Paragraphs 193
Using Ruling Lines 194
Special Applications for Styles 196
    Drawing Horizontal Lines 196
    Customizing the Document Spacing 196
Using Function Key Shortcuts 197
    Assigning Function Keys 197
    Keeping Your Styles Visible 198
Summary 198

Chapter 7 Styles and Templates 201

    Advantages of Style Templates 201
Using a Style Template 202
    Selecting a Different Template 203
Creating a New Template 204
Local and Global Styles 205
    How Styles Become Either Local or Global 206
Manipulating Paragraph Styles 206
    Deleting Paragraph Styles 206
    Creating New Styles 208
    Changing Style Types 208
    Renaming Paragraph Styles 211
Editing Paragraph Styles 211
    Editing a Style in a Template 212
    Reverting to the Original Style Options 214
Switching Paragraph Style Assignments 214

Templates and Page Layouts 215
    Changing the Current Document Layout 216
    Changing the Page Layout in a Template 216
Deleting a Template 217
Using Styles and Templates: Hints and Tips 218
    Switching Templates 218
    Manipulating Styles with Caution 220
    Remembering Page Layouts 220
    Recovering from an Accidental Style Deletion 220
Setting Template Defaults 221
    Selecting the Default Template Directory 221
    Selecting the Default Template 222
Including Text as Part of a Template 223
    Creating the Template 223
    Using the Template 223
Generating Rough Drafts 224
Using the Built-In Templates 225
Summary 226

Chapter 8   Customized Letters and Mailing Labels 229

Creating Customized Letters 229
    Creating a Data File 231
    Creating a Standard Letter 233
    Merging the Data and the Standard Letter 237
Using Data from Other Sources 239
    Merging Data from a File in Either Fixed or Comma Format 241
    Using Other ASCII File Formats 242
Mailing Labels 242
    Creating the Name-and-Address File 243
    Printing the Labels 245
Summary 246

Chapter 9   About Printers, Typefaces, and Fonts 249

Typeface, Font, and Other Vocabulary 249

Typefaces 249
Type Size 251
Text Attributes 252
Orientation 252
Fonts 252
Character Sets 253
Printer Capabilities 254
Print Quality 255
Tips on Optimizing Your Printer's Capabilities 256
The Types of Fonts Available 257
Fonts Built into Your Printer 257
Font Cartridges 257
Soft Fonts 258
Scalable Typefaces 259
Displaying the Available Fonts 261
Screen Fonts 262
Sources of Screen Fonts 263
Selecting Screen Fonts 264
Automating Font Changes 265
Special Print Options 266
Selecting the Options 266
Speeding Up Your Printout 268
Changing the Paper Size and Orientation 268
Working with More Than One Printer 269
Selecting the Active Printer 270
Assigning a Printer to a Document 272
What Happens When You Change the Assigned Printer 272
Getting Even Higher Print Quality 273
Summary 275

Chapter 10   Using Frames 277

Basic Frame Operations 277
Creating a Frame 278
Selecting a Frame 279
Resizing and Repositioning Frames 280

　　　　　　　Moving and Copying Frames 280
　　　　　　　Deleting Frames 281
　　　　　　　Locating Hidden Frames 282
　　　　Working with Multiple Frames 283
　　　　　　　Grouping Frames Together 283
　　　　　　　Overlapping Frames 285
　　　　Working with Text in a Frame 286
　　　　Setting the Frame Options 288
　　　　　　　Creating Borders 289
　　　　　　　Creating Lines Around a Frame 291
　　　　　　　Choosing a Frame Position 293
　　　　　　　Setting Tabs and Columns 294
　　　　　　　Adjusting the Frame Background 296
　　　　　　　Creating a Repeating Frame 297
　　　　　　　Setting Default Frame Options 298
　　　　Working with Frames 298
　　　　　　　Creating a Text Frame 298
　　　　　　　A Basic Newsletter Design 300
　　　　Summary 301

Chapter 11　Working with Graphics 303

　　　　The Types of Graphics Files You Can Import 303
　　　　　　　Bitmapped and Vector Graphics 303
　　　　　　　Usable Graphics Formats 304
　　　　General Notes About Importing Graphics 307
　　　　　　　Screen and Printer Output 307
　　　　Importing a Graphic Image 308
　　　　　　　Saving a Graphic with Your Document 309
　　　　Working with a Graphic Image 310
　　　　　　　Selecting a Frame Versus Selecting Its Contents 310
　　　　　　　Adjusting Image Size 311
　　　　　　　Cropping 313
　　　　　　　Deleting an Image 314
　　　　Fitting a Graphic Image into a Frame 314
　　　　　　　Fitting to a Frame of Specific Dimensions 314

Exact Cropping 316
Automatic Resizing 317
Techniques for Working with Frames 319
Adding a Caption to a Frame 319
Creating Shadowed Frames 321
Creating Thick Border Lines 322
Rotating and Inverting Graphics Frames 323
Rotating and Inverting Text 325
Summary 326

Chapter 12 Grammar Checking and Electronic Mail 331

Checking Your Grammar 331
Getting Started 332
Dealing with a Grammar Problem 333
Finishing Up 336
Other Methods of Proofreading 338
Protecting Your Documents 339
Strategies for Grammar Checking 340
Proofreading Other Documents 340
Displaying Statistical Output 341
Customizing the Grammar Checker 343
Using Electronic Mail 349
Logging in to E-Mail 350
Setting the Options 351
Transmitting the Current Document 352
Transmitting E-Mail Messages 355
Reading Your Mail 356
Using an E-Mail Address Book 362
Summary 363

Chapter 13 Creating Different Types of Documents 365

Selecting the Right Typeface 365
Page Design Tips 366
Technical Tips 367
Adjusting Text Spacing 367

Working with Multiple Frames 368
Letterhead 369
    Creating a Letterhead Template 369
    Using the Template 371
Business Cards 372
    Designing a Business Card 372
    Creating a Business Card 373
Greeting Cards and Invitations 374
Newsletters 376
    Designing Newsletters 376
    Creating a Newsletter 377
Summary 383

Appendix A Installing Professional Write Plus 385

Appendix B Customizing Professional Write Plus 389

Appendix C Customizing for a New Printer 402

Appendix D Troubleshooting 408

Index 411

ACKNOWLEDGMENTS

Just because my name appears on the cover of this book doesn't mean that I did it all alone. On the contrary, a large number of people were involved with its development. I just happened to write the original words, and tradition dictates that my name should be conspicuously placed.

Special thanks to Cindy Hudson, who was willing to listen to what seemed to be an idea ahead of its time. Cheryl Holzaepfel and Sheila McGill were instrumental in keeping things organized and running, and Leslie Tilley helped to make sense out of what was sometimes disorganized confusion. Thanks also to the many other folks who contributed to the total effort, including Collins Flannery for her fine eye for design, Dan Brodnitz for his help in working out screen image problems, and Howard Blechman and Kim Haglund for word processing.

INTRODUCTION

This book was written with two objectives. First, it guides you through all the features of the program in a systematic way, with the more commonly used features introduced in the early part of the book. The latter part of the text deals with more complex topics. To help you learn Professional Write Plus quickly, this book contains numerous step-by-step examples and screen illustrations that guide you through the process of mastering the program's many features. It's like having an expert at your side as you learn. You will also find helpful tips and hints throughout the book that alert you to information of special interest.

The second objective of the book is to provide a basic introduction to word processing, using Professional Write Plus as a vehicle. Even if you have no prior experience using a computer to create text, you can use the first part of the book to take a step-by-step guided tour through the basics of both Professional Write Plus and word processing.

You can use this book in several different ways. First, you can read through it from front to back, learning about the various features of Professional Write Plus. You can also skip around after reading the introductory chapters, to find information about whatever topic you need. Finally, you can use this book as a reference after you have become familiar with the program. Using the table of contents and the extensive index, you can quickly access information about any particular aspect of the program.

A Quick Tour Through the Chapters

PC Magazine's Guide to Professional Write Plus covers all of the features of Professional Write Plus and how to use them, from the very basics to the advanced techniques you need to master this word processing program. The 13 chapters and 4 appendices in this book cover the following topics:

Chapter 1: Introducing Professional Write Plus
Chapter 1 discusses the hardware you will need to run Professional Write Plus and introduces some of the program's basic features, such as menus, dialog boxes, and the extensive Help facility.

Chapter 2: Word Processing Basics
Chapter 2 illustrates the basic word processing techniques involved with creating attractive documents, including how to edit text, print your document, and use different fonts.

Chapter 3: Controlling the Page Appearance
Chapter 3 demonstrates how to customize your page layout by changing page size and orientation, creating headers and footers, setting page margins,

working with tabs, adding page numbers, selecting the number of columns per page, and drawing rules on a page.

Chapter 4: Sophisticated Editing Features
Chapter 4 expands on Chapter 2's discussion of editing techniques, showing how to perform such advanced editing tasks as using the built-in Spell Checker and Thesaurus and making global searches with the Find & Replace feature.

Chapter 5: Working with Your Files
Chapter 5 explores the tools Professional Write Plus provides to manage and organize your files. Topics include making backups, importing and exporting text, and using the File Manager feature.

Chapter 6: Using Styles
Chapter 6 introduces the concept of paragraph styles, a feature once restricted to desktop publishing programs, and teaches how to use paragraph styles in Professional Write Plus to change the appearance of your text by techniques such as altering paragraph alignment, controlling page breaks, and using automatic hyphenation.

Chapter 7: Styles and Templates
Chapter 7 demonstrates how to create and use *templates*—files that contain specific paragraph styles and page layout settings that you can apply to any document you create.

Chapter 8: Customized Letters and Mailing Labels
Chapter 8 shows how to perform mail merge operations in Professional Write Plus to create personalized letters and mailing labels.

Chapter 9: About Printers, Typefaces, and Fonts
Chapter 9 discusses the capabilities of different types of printers and other information you can use to improve the print quality of your documents.

Chapter 10: Using Frames
Chapter 10 describes how to use frames to liven up your documents, including how to import graphics and text into frames and change text layout using multiple frames.

Chapter 11: Working with Graphics
Chapter 11 gives helpful hints for importing and altering graphics in your word processed documents.

Chapter 12: Grammar Checking and Electronic Mail

Chapter 12 demonstrates how to use the program's grammar-checking feature and how to transmit messages to other users operating on a Novell/Action Technologies Message Handling Service.

Chapter 13: Creating Different Types of Documents

Chapter 13 provides tips for creating documents such as business cards, greeting cards, letterhead, and newsletters.

Appendix A: Installing Professional Write Plus

Appendix A provides useful tips for installing Professional Write Plus on your computer.

Appendix B: Customizing Professional Write Plus

Appendix B demonstrates how to change default settings to customize Professional Write Plus for your particular needs.

Appendix C: Customizing for a New Printer

Appendix C provides detailed instructions for setting up Professional Write Plus to work with various types of printers.

Appendix D: Troubleshooting

Appendix D provides the answers to some of the major problems that can occur when using Professional Write Plus.

Introducing Professional Write Plus

In the last couple of years, a new generation of programs has radically changed the way in which people interact with personal computers. These programs are written to run under the operating system called Microsoft Windows. The basic attitude built into this software is that computers should be as easy as possible to use, and that learning how to use a new program should be simple and pleasurable.

This user-friendly approach is clearly inherent in the design of Professional Write Plus—one of the first word processors to take advantage of the Windows environment. Professional Write Plus is an unusual product: Not only is it easy to use, but it also contains a wide assortment of sophisticated features.

If you have been using a traditional word processsor on an IBM PC-type computer, you'll be amazed at the difference when you begin working with Professional Write Plus. Like all other Windows-based programs, it presents you with graphics-based screens, which are as far from the traditional character-based screens as the Moon is from the Earth. Graphics screens are designed the way an artist composes a picture, and in fact many screens are designed by graphic artists. The screens you see when using Professional

Write Plus have been extremely well thought out, making the program a pleasure to use.

Learning how to use Professional Write Plus is not difficult. You can quickly become familiar with the basic features and begin to do useful word processing. For instance, the File menu contains all the tools needed for storing and retrieving document files. (If you're a seasoned Windows user, this is probably old news.) Similarly, the basic text editing tools can be found in the Text menu. This logical division of features into the various menus completely eliminates the need to memorize complicated and irrational keyboard commands. (Who wants to remember that Shift-F10 is the keystroke for opening a file?)

For the experienced user, Professional Write Plus offers a wide range of speed keys and screen icons as shortcuts for the more common operations. For example, instead of using the File menu to open an existing document file, you can either press the speed key Ctrl-O or click on the screen icon that looks like a floppy disk. You can learn about these shortcuts at your leisure, using the menus in the meantime.

Professional Write Plus offers all the standard advantages of running under Microsoft Windows. For instance, you can use any printer on your system that's set up to run under Windows. Generally, this means you don't need to worry about setting up Professional Write Plus for your current printer. And if various soft fonts for your printer have been installed under Windows, Professional Write Plus automatically knows about them as well.

Because Windows is a multiprogram environment, you can run several copies of Professional Write Plus at the same time, which means that you can edit several documents simultaneously, switching back and forth between them with a click of the mouse.

Just because Professional Write Plus is extremely easy to use doesn't mean that it's a slouch in the features department. On the contrary, the program contains tools usually found only in high-priced desktop publishing software. The most outstanding of these features are style sheets and frames. Style sheets allow you to easily customize specific paragraphs, such as headings and bulleted text. This formatting includes the specification of typeface, type size, line spacing, indentation, and many other characteristics.

Using frames, you can import graphic images in any of the standard graphic file formats, such as PCX, TIFF, and many others. After you have imported a picture, you can customize its appearance using a variety of easy-to-use tools, including cropping, sizing, and repositioning.

Professional Write Plus is a WYSIWYG (what you see is what you get) program. In other words, everything you see on the screen appears just about the way it will when it's printed. Larger letters will be larger on the screen, bold text will look bold, and so on. Moreover, any graphics you use will appear on the screen the way they will be when printed. The end result is that you can easily create interesting page layouts because the screen shows you the true composition at each step.

What Professional Write Plus Offers You

Professional Write Plus offers a spectrum of uses, ranging from casual day-to-day memos and notes up to professional-quality desktop published documents.

On the most basic level, the program is ideal for the occasional user because of its simplicity of design. You can create occasional letters, notes, memos, and so on without worrying about forgetting which commands to use since all the basic word processing operations are contained in three menus.

If you use the program regularly, you can set up various features to create customized documents. For example, you can create templates that allow you to easily generate your own letterhead. And for longer documents, you can include frills like custom headings, multiple columns, and horizontal and vertical ruling lines.

You can also take advantage of the program's desktop publishing features to create newsletters and other documents with a truly professional look. And, the lack of a laser printer is no hindrance to getting high-quality printout: You can easily output your documents to a floppy disk, which can later be used with a laser printer at a print shop.

CHAPTER 1

Introducing Professional Write Plus

What You Need to Run Professional Write Plus

Starting Up Professional Write Plus

The Keyboard

The Main Editing Screen

Using a Mouse

Using the Menus

Using Dialog Boxes

Scrolling Through Text

Using the Side Bar Icons

Getting Help

What You Need to Run Professional Write Plus 1

PROFESSIONAL WRITE PLUS IS ONE OF THE NEWEST WORD PROCESSORS to become available to the microcomputer world. It's also one of the easiest to learn. The program is very well designed, so you should be able to find your way around the various features quite easily. Since the screen menus are well laid out, with a little practice you'll be able to find just about any feature you want.

Before beginning to work with Professional Write Plus, you need to become acquainted with some of its basic features, such as menus and dialog boxes, its use of the mouse and keyboard, and the first-rate help facility it offers. This chapter is devoted to these introductory topics.

What You Need to Run Professional Write Plus

Professional Write Plus is a large and sophisticated program, and to run it you'll need more than a minimum system. This means your computer must have a hard disk, a reasonably fast CPU, and other peripheral hardware. Here's a summary of the minimum hardware and software required to run the program:

Computer At least a 286 or 386 machine. This includes computers compatible with the IBM AT or IBM PS/2.

Monitor Just about any type of monitor (and corresponding controller card) will work, including CGA, EGA, and VGA color monitors, and a monochrome monitor with a Hercules-compatible controller card.

Random Access Memory Your computer must have an absolute minimum of 1 megabyte (Mb) of random access memory (RAM). If you're using the grammar checker, you'll need at least 2Mb. Depending on the version of Microsoft Windows you're running (see "Software," below), you will probably benefit from having even more memory. If you're using a 386-based machine, Windows will really fly if you have 4Mb or more of RAM installed.

Disk Drives In order to run Professional Write Plus, your computer must have a hard disk drive. The program itself occupies approximately 4Mb of hard disk space. In addition, Microsoft Windows occupies about 6 to 8 additional megabytes. Theoretically then, you could get by with a 20Mb hard disk (the smallest available), but you'll probably need additional space if you run programs other than Professional Write Plus, or if you plan to use graphics files with the program. The Professional Write Plus programs are shipped either on 1.2Mb 5$1/4$-inch disks or 720k 3$1/2$-inch disks, so you'll need at least one floppy-disk drive of either type.

Mouse You can use any type of mouse that runs under Windows. Actually, you can run Professional Write Plus without a mouse, but you'll be asking for a lot of frustration. The program is graphically oriented, and many tasks just can't be performed conveniently without a mouse. A good quality mouse costs about $100, but over the long run you'll find that it's money well spent.

You can use a trackball instead of a mouse. If you haven't yet purchased a mouse, try out a trackball at a local computer store. Some of these are wonderfully designed. You may find them easier to manipulate than a mouse, and they take up much less desk space.

Software To use Professional Write Plus, your computer needs to be running under Microsoft Windows 3.0 or later. In addition, you must be running DOS 3.0 or later.

Starting Up Professional Write Plus

You can start up the program either from DOS or from within Windows:

- To start up Professional Write Plus from the DOS prompt, first move to the directory containing the Professional Write Plus program files. Next, enter the command to start up Windows, including the name PWPLUS as a parameter. For example, if the Windows files are in the directory C:\WINDOWS, enter the command **C:\WINDOWS\WIN PWPLUS.**

- To start up Professional Write Plus from within Windows, display the program group containing the Professional Write Plus icon and then double-click on that icon. Or, with the Program Manager displayed, select File/Run, then enter **\PWPLUS\PWPLUS.EXE** (assuming the program is stored in the directory \PWPLUS\).

The Keyboard

It goes without saying that the keyboard will be one of your most important tools when using Professional Write Plus. In addition to entering text, you can use the keyboard to give various instructions to the program. If you know how to type, then you already know a lot about a computer keyboard. There are various types of keyboards, and Figure 1.1 shows the more common layouts. All keyboards, regardless of type, have the same basic sections.

Keyboard Basics

The computer keyboard is divided into several areas.

The Keyboard

- The main section
- The function keys
- The numeric keypad
- The cursor pad

The *main section* of the keyboard contains the letters and numbers, which are arranged in the same order as on a standard typewriter. In addition, various punctuation keys, such as the parentheses and the comma, are included in this part of the keyboard.

Figure 1.1
The most common keyboard layouts

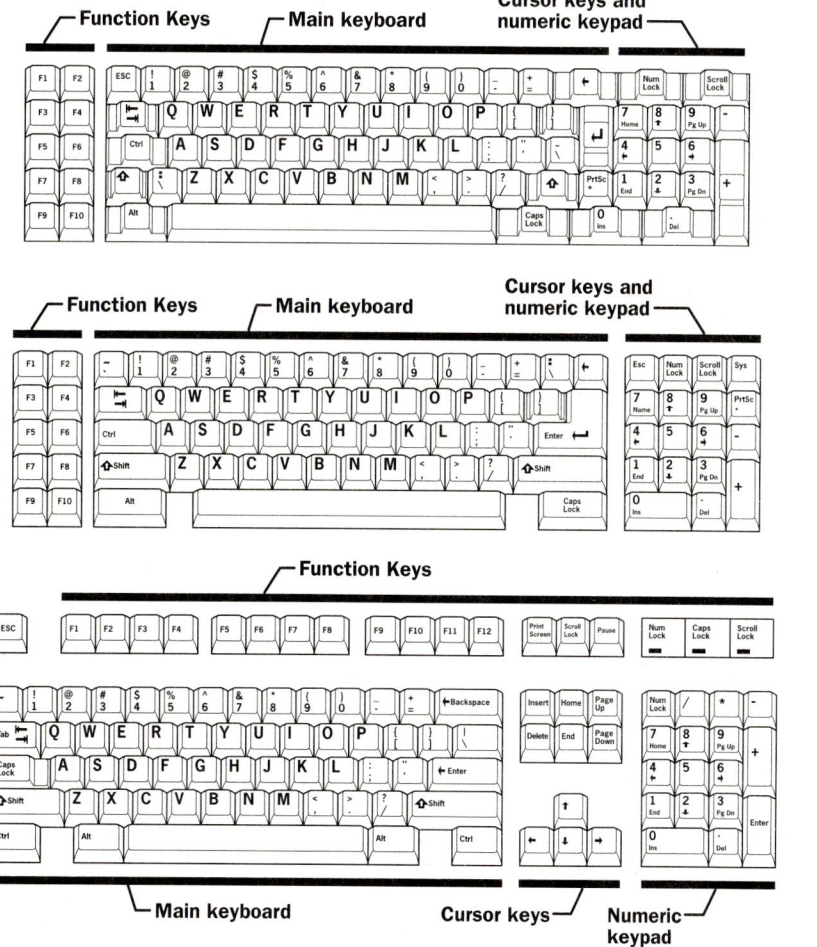

The *function keys* are numbered F1 through F10 (or through F12 on some keyboards). On older-style keyboards, these keys are arranged on the leftmost part of the keyboard; on newer keyboards, they are placed above the main keyboard section. These keys have special purposes within Professional Write Plus that will be explained throughout this book.

The *numeric keypad* is a group of 11 keys placed at the right side of the keyboard, containing the digits 0 through 9 and the decimal point. On some keyboards, the main purpose of these keys is to control the cursor (as indicated by the arrows), but they can also be used for entering numbers.

Some keyboards contain a special group of keys, called the *cursor pad*, used exclusively for moving the cursor. These keys are located just to the left of the numeric keypad.

Special Keys

In addition to the keys just described, you will find other keys that perform certain actions:

- Shift keys
- Caps Lock
- Num Lock
- Enter
- Ctrl and Alt
- Del
- Esc
- Arrow keys
- PgUp and PgDn
- Backspace
- Home and End
- Ins

The *Shift keys* work just as they do on an ordinary typewriter. To enter an uppercase letter, press a Shift key and the letter. In addition, the Shift key is used for entering various special characters, such as ?, +, and others.

Press the *Caps Lock key* once to lock the letters into uppercase. Press it again to return to lowercase letters. Only the letter keys are affected by this key.

The *Num Lock key*, like Caps Lock, is a *toggle:* Press it once to turn it on, and press it again to turn it off. When it is off, the keys on the numeric keypad are used for cursor control. When Num Lock is on, the numeric keypad is used for entering digits. On some keyboards, a light indicates when Num Lock is on.

The *Enter key* is normally labeled Enter, ↵, or both. On some older keyboards, this key is labeled Return. The Enter key has a variety of uses in Professional Write Plus. For instance, you press this key to start a new paragraph. You can also use it to make certain types of menu selections.

The *Ctrl* and *Alt keys* are used in combination with other keys. To use either key, hold it down and then press another key. Professional Write Plus combines Ctrl and Alt with other keys for many different purposes.

Press the *Del key* to delete the character to the right of the cursor.

The *Backspace key* appears at the upper-right corner of the central part of the keyboard. Press this key to delete the character to the left of the cursor.

Esc is the Escape key. You normally use it to back out of whatever you're doing at the moment. For instance, you can press Esc to exit from a menu or dialog box without causing the program to take any action.

The *Up Arrow*, *Down Arrow*, *Left Arrow*, and *Right Arrow* keys are used for moving the cursor up, down, left, and right, whether within text, in a menu, or within a dialog box. On some keyboards, these keys have the numeric labels 8, 2, 4, and 6 because they are part of the numeric keypad.

The *PgUp* and *PgDn* keys are used for scrolling up and down through your text.

The *Home* and *End* keys are also used to move around your text—either by themselves or in combination with other keys.

Ins is the "insert" key; it is used to toggle between inserting and overwriting text in the editing process. (This is explained more fully in Chapter 2.)

The Main Editing Screen

Figure 1.2 shows the screen you'll see when starting up Professional Write Plus for the first time. This is the main *edit screen*, which you'll be using most of the time. It contains a number of important elements:

- Mouse cursor
- Text cursor
- Title bar
- Menu bar
- Side bar icons
- Vertical and horizontal scroll bars
- Status bar
- Page arrows

INTRODUCING PROFESSIONAL WRITE PLUS

- Page Status box
- Windows icons

Figure 1.2
The main edit screen

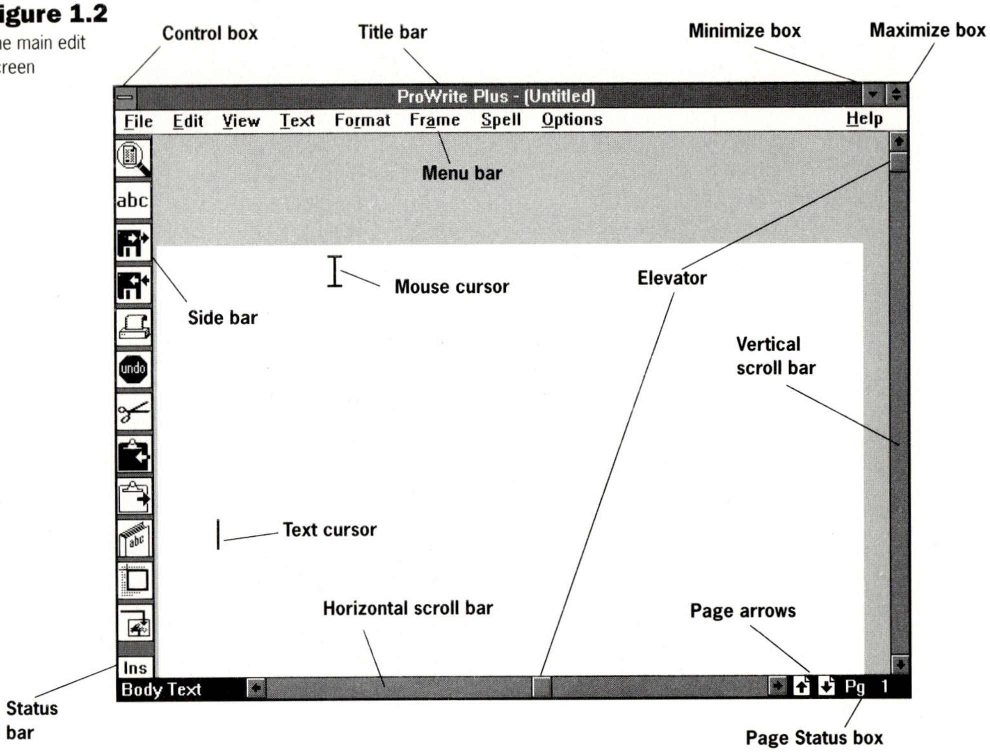

[Screenshot of the ProWrite Plus - (Untitled) main edit screen with labels: Control box, Title bar, Minimize box, Maximize box, Menu bar, Mouse cursor, Elevator, Side bar, Vertical scroll bar, Text cursor, Horizontal scroll bar, Page arrows, Status bar, Page Status box]

The *mouse cursor* is the little vertical bar shaped like a capital "I." You can use the mouse to drag this cursor anywhere on the screen. In some situations the mouse cursor changes, taking the form of an arrow or other shape. Later on, you'll see how to use the mouse and its cursor for different operations.

The *text cursor* is the blinking vertical line on the screen. You always position this cursor exactly where you want to enter or delete text. You can use either the mouse or the cursor keys on the keyboard to drag this cursor to any part of the existing text in a document.

The Main Editing Screen 7

The *title bar* is part of the top line on the screen. It contains the name of the document you're currently working with. If you're creating a new document, the word "Untitled" appears.

The *menu bar* is the second line from the top of the screen. It lists the names of the various pull-down menus, each of which contains various choices you can make. The menu names are designed to help you remember where to look for things. For example, if you want to read or write to a file, you'd use the File menu. You can use either the mouse or the keyboard to select a menu.

Note. You can customize Professional Write Plus by selecting which icons you want to appear in the side bar. See Appendix B for details.

The symbols that appear on the left side of the screen are called *side bar icons*. They represent different tasks you can perform quickly, without having to use the menus. For example, if you wanted to change the page view (the way the page appears), you'd select the top icon on the bar (the magnifying glass). Professional Write Plus offers a fairly large selection of icons for various tasks.

The *vertical and horizontal scroll bars* are the long bars extending down the right edge and across the bottom of the screen. To scroll through a document, you use the vertical scroll bar, and to scan across a page, you use the horizontal scroll bar. The little square box in each scroll bar is the *elevator*, which shows your current position and helps you to scroll around.

The *status bar* is the tiny box below the side bar icons. It indicates which edit mode is being used—either Insert or Overwrite. It can also be expanded to display the column number, line number, and the current directory.

The two vertical arrows immediately to the right of the horizontal scroll bar are the *page arrows*. You can use them to jump to the next or the preceding page.

Just to the right of the page arrows, the *Page Status box* indicates the current page number.

The very top line of the screen contains three icons for performing Windows-related operations:

- Selecting the *Control box icon* (in the upper-left corner) causes the Control menu to appear. With this menu, you can use the keyboard to resize the Professional Write Plus window, switch to other Windows applications, pop up the Windows Control Panel, work with the Windows print spooler, or end your Professional Write Plus session.

- Selecting the *Minimize box icon* reduces the Professional Write Plus session to an icon at the bottom of the screen. You would do this, for example, if you wanted to switch to another application running under Windows without closing your word processing session.

- Use the *Maximize box icon* to change the size of the Professional Write Plus window. Select it once to reduce the size of the window, then select it again to fill the entire screen with the window.

INTRODUCING PROFESSIONAL WRITE PLUS

Using a Mouse

If you're using a mouse for the first time, you'll probably need some practice to gain hand-eye coordination. Spend a bit of time practicing slowly, until your movements begin to become automatic. After a few days, your reflexes will develop, and eventually you won't have to think at all about your hand motion.

Mice can be a bit fussy. If you try to use one on a very smooth surface, you may find that your control is uneven. Either use a textured surface for the mouse or purchase a mouse pad, which is designed to make the mouse work as smoothly as possible.

Later sections of this chapter will describe how to use both the mouse and the keyboard for the various types of operations. As you work with Professional Write Plus, you'll find that the mouse works best for some operations, while the keyboard is faster for others. If you're a speed typist, you may prefer to use the mouse as little as possible, but if you're used to using a mouse, you may give it preference.

Mouse Operations

The mouse controls the mouse cursor on the screen. This cursor, in turn, is used for various types of control operations.

Pointing and Clicking

One of the mouse's main functions is to make various selections on the screen. The operation you perform to make a selection is called *pointing and clicking*. To get some practice with your mouse, follow these steps:

1. Move the mouse so that the mouse cursor points to "View" on the menu bar, as shown below. Notice that the cursor changes shape to an arrow.

2. *Pull down* (select) the View menu by clicking the left mouse button while the arrow is pointing at "View." The View menu will appear, like this:

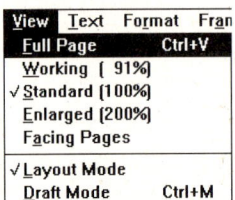

 **Using a Mouse**

3. Now move the mouse cursor off of the menu.

4. Click the left button again and the menu will disappear.

Dragging with the Mouse

Try moving the mouse around on your desk. As you do so, watch the mouse cursor make corresponding movements. This operation is known as *dragging the mouse cursor*. Notice that as you drag the cursor to any edge of the screen, its shape changes to that of an arrow. This indicates that you can select something with the cursor.

In some operations, you use the mouse cursor to drag other objects around the screen. For example, using Professional Write Plus's graphics tools, you can create a picture on the page and then use the mouse to reposition (that is, drag) it from one place to another. (Working with graphic objects is covered in Chapter 11.) To drag an object with the mouse you would follow these steps:

1. Point the mouse cursor at the object.

2. Press the left mouse button and hold it down.

3. Move the mouse, and the object will be dragged in the corresponding direction.

4. When the object is where you want it, release the mouse button.

Mouse Terminology

This book will use the following terminology and conventions throughout:

- Moving the mouse cursor to a particular location on the screen is referred to as *dragging* or *moving* the mouse cursor.

- Instructions to *press* or *click* the mouse button always refer to the *left* button, unless the right button (which is used on rare occasions for special purposes) is specifically referred to.

- To *point* the mouse cursor at an object means to position the cursor so that it is pointing directly at the object. Usually the cursor will change shape to an arrow.

Tip. Double-clicking on an item in a list box often saves you the trouble of selecting the item and then clicking on OK.

- A reference to *click on* an object on the screen means that you first point the mouse cursor at that object, and then you click the mouse button.

- Instructions to *double-click* on an object simply mean to point at that object and then quickly click the mouse button twice.

INTRODUCING PROFESSIONAL WRITE PLUS

Mouse Maintenance

Most mice need occasional cleaning; your mouse manual should have instructions on how to do this. If the mouse begins to function erratically, it's probably time to give it a scrubbing.

Track balls require just about as much care as mice. You'll occasionally need to remove the ball and clean out the interior. If the ball feels sluggish or otherwise doesn't move smoothly, it's overdue for a cleanup.

Using the Menus

The menu bar at the top of the screen lists Professional Write Plus's menus. To make a selection from one of them, you first pull down that menu with either the mouse or the keyboard. You can then select whichever menu option you want.

Menu selections in this book are indicated as follows: "Select Text/Bold" means to select the Text menu, then select the option called Bold. The first word is always the menu; the word following the slash is the option you select. Whether you use the mouse or the keyboard is up to you.

Using the Mouse to Select Menu Items

To select a menu option with the mouse, you first point and click on the menu you want to pull down, and then you select the desired option. For example, to tell the program to begin using boldfacing for text you enter, you would select *Text/Bold*. That is, pull down the Text menu and then click on the Bold option on that menu.

To get some practice with menus, follow these steps to boldface any text you subsequently enter:

1. Drag the mouse cursor so that it points to the Text menu, as shown here:

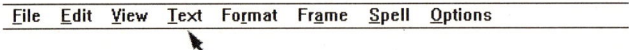

2. Pull down the menu by clicking the mouse button (remember, the *left* button).

3. Drag the mouse cursor down until it points to the option labeled Bold, as shown in Figure 1.3.

4. Click the mouse button. The menu disappears, and you're ready to enter text in boldface. (The next time you select this menu, the item Bold will appear with a checkmark, indicating that it's been selected.)

Using the Menus

Figure 1.3
The Text menu

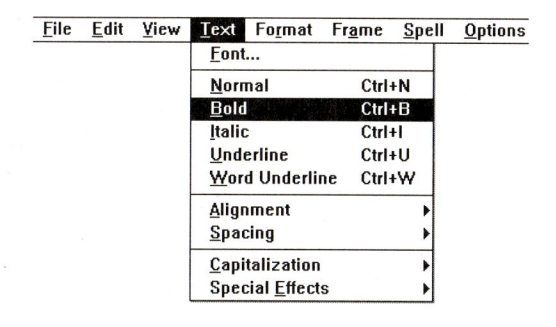

| <u>F</u>ile | <u>E</u>dit | <u>V</u>iew | <u>T</u>ext | F<u>o</u>rmat | F<u>r</u>ame | <u>S</u>pell | <u>O</u>ptions |

<u>F</u>ont...

<u>N</u>ormal	Ctrl+N
<u>B</u>old	**Ctrl+B**
<u>I</u>talic	Ctrl+I
<u>U</u>nderline	Ctrl+U
<u>W</u>ord Underline	Ctrl+W

<u>A</u>lignment ▶
<u>S</u>pacing ▶

<u>C</u>apitalization ▶
Special <u>E</u>ffects ▶

If you like, try typing a few characters to see whether they really look bold. To stop the boldfacing, repeat the preceding steps, this time selecting either the *Normal* or *Bold* option from the Text menu. This causes any text you enter later on to appear as normal text rather than boldfaced.

When you select some menu options, the menu disappears and Professional Write Plus simply carries out the instruction you selected. For other menu options, a submenu or dialog box will appear, as you'll see later.

Using the Keyboard to Select Menu Items

If you like, you can use the keyboard instead of the mouse to make your menu selections. Notice that each item listed on the menu bar has one underlined letter. You can use this letter, along with the Alt key, to select a menu. Similarly, one letter of each option in the pull-down menus is also underlined, indicating which key you can use for its selection.

To get some practice using the keyboard, follow these steps to select the Bold option from the Text menu:

1. Hold down the Alt key and press T. The Text menu will appear (see Figure 1.3).

2. Press the letter B (in the option labeled "Bold," the B is underlined).

Caution. Don't press the Alt key when selecting an item from a pulled-down menu. If you do press Alt, the menu will disappear.

You have now selected boldfacing—any text you type now will be boldfaced. Try this if you like. Before going on, however, repeat the preceding steps and select the Normal option from the Text menu so that any text you enter later on won't be boldfaced.

Keyboard Shortcuts

The preceding example used the keystroke Alt-T. This type of key combination is called a *keyboard shortcut* because it's usually as fast as (or faster than) performing the equivalent operation with the mouse. This book uses a hyphen to link the keystrokes (Alt-T), whereas Professional Write Plus uses a plus sign (Alt+T). Both systems of notation mean to hold down the first key while you press the second.

Other examples of speed keys are shown in the Text menu (Figure 1.3). For instance, notice that "Ctrl+B" appears next to the Bold option. This indicates that instead of selecting Text/Bold to boldface something, you can simply press the speed key Ctrl-B. Professional Write Plus supplies keyboard shortcuts for many different purposes, and they'll be pointed out throughout this book.

From now on, whenever instructions ask you to select an item from a menu, you can use either the mouse or the keyboard, using the steps described in the preceding sections.

Submenus

When you click on some menu options, another menu—called a *submenu*—appears. You can then make a selection from this submenu. For example, if you select the Spacing option from the Text menu, a submenu will appear that lists your various options for spacing, as shown in Figure 1.4.

Figure 1.4
The Spacing submenu

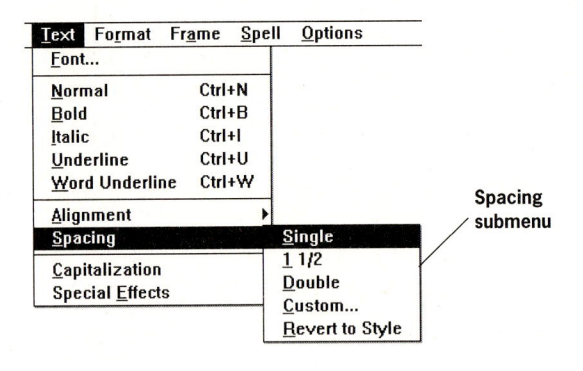

Whenever a menu option has a submenu associated with it, an arrowhead is shown to the right of the menu item. For example, each of the last four options in the Text menu has an associated submenu (see Figure 1.3).

As with menu sections, when you need to select an option from a submenu, we'll instruct you to "select *Menu/Menu-Option/Submenu-Option.*" For example, Text/Spacing/Double means select the Text menu, then select the Spacing option, and finally select Double from the Spacing submenu.

Using Dialog Boxes

Dialog boxes are where you will make many of your selections. You'll encounter a variety of dialog boxes as you use Professional Write Plus. Some of these boxes are tiny, while others take up the entire screen.

Dialog boxes appear when you select certain menu options. Each of these options ends with three dots (...), to indicate that when you select it a dialog box will be displayed on the screen. To see how to use a dialog box, follow these steps to display the one shown in Figure 1.5 (this dialog box is used to retrieve a document file into Professional Write Plus):

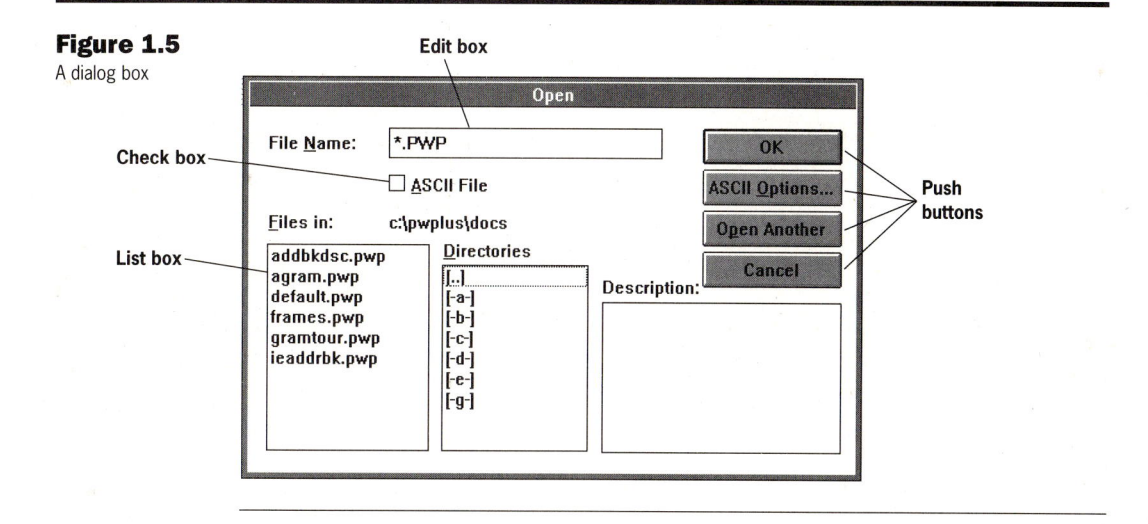

Figure 1.5
A dialog box

1. Pull down the File menu: Either press Alt-F or point the mouse cursor at the File option on the menu bar and then click the mouse button.

2. Select the *Open* option. The dialog box will then appear.

This dialog box contains most of the elements common to all the dialog boxes used by Professional Write Plus:

- A list box
- An edit box
- Push buttons
- A check box

The *list box* contains a list of items. In Figure 1.5, it happens to be a list of file names, but other types of lists will appear in other dialog boxes. To select an item from this list, drag the mouse cursor until it points to the item you want, and then click the mouse button.

You use an *edit box* to enter the name of something. This might be the name of a file, or it might be something else. As you enter text into an edit box, you can use the Del and Backspace keys to erase mistakes.

You select a *push button* to tell Professional Write Plus to do something. Selecting this type of button usually causes the dialog box to disappear and the edit screen to reappear. For example, selecting Cancel in the dialog box in Figure 1.5 would terminate whatever you were doing in the dialog box, and no action would be taken. However, if you selected OK, whatever you had selected in the dialog box would be acted on.

You select a *check box* to indicate a preference. When you make this type of selection, an X appears in the box, but the dialog box doesn't disappear (unlike when you select a push button). A check box is a toggle; select it once to turn on the option, and select it again to turn off the option (if you change your mind, for example).

Using the Mouse in the Dialog Box

Even if you're a keyboard whiz, you'll find that using the mouse inside a dialog box is much faster than using the keyboard. To make a selection with the mouse, you simply point and click on the option you want. Following are some exercises to give you practice working with the dialog box on your screen.

Selecting a Check Box

Follow these steps to select and deselect the option labeled ASCII File:

1. Drag the mouse cursor so that it points to that option—either any part of the text "ASCII File" or the corresponding check box itself.
2. Click the mouse button. An X will then appear in the box, indicating that the option has been selected.
3. To deselect the ASCII File option, click in the same place again.

The Edit Box

Here are the steps for entering text into the edit box (the File Name box in Figure 1.5):

1. Drag the cursor so that it points to the right-hand end of the text in the box (if any text appears there), then click the mouse button.

Using Dialog Boxes

2. Press the Backspace key to delete the existing text.

3. Enter the text you want. (Just make up something for now.)

Notice that when the dialog box shown in Figure 1.5 first appears, the text in the edit box is shaded. If you wish, instead of following the preceding steps, you can immediately enter new text into the box. As soon as you start, the original text will disappear. As you enter text, you can edit it using any of the keys shown in Table 1.1. Also, you can use these same keystrokes to edit the original text that appears in the box.

Table 1.1   Keystrokes for Editing Text Boxes

Keystroke	Action
Left Arrow or Right Arrow	Moves the text cursor left or right
Home	Moves the cursor to the first character in the box
End	Moves the cursor to the last character in the box
Del	Deletes the character to the right of the cursor
Backspace	Deletes the character to the left of the cursor

That's all there is to it. When you eventually select the button labeled OK (but don't select it now) Professional Write Plus will use the text you entered. In the example just given, Professional Write Plus would retrieve the file whose name you entered in the edit box.

The List Box

To use the mouse cursor to select an item from the list box labeled Files In, follow these steps:

1. Drag the mouse cursor to an item in the list box.

2. Click the mouse button to select that item.

Note. The list box that appears on your screen will probably be quite different from the one shown in Figure 1.6. The contents of your list box will depend on what's stored on your hard disk.

Notice that when you select an item in this way, the item also appears in the edit box at the top of the screen, as shown in Figure 1.6. This is typical of many of the dialog boxes: You can select an item either by entering it into an edit box or by selecting it from the corresponding list box.

Figure 1.6
Selecting an item from the list box

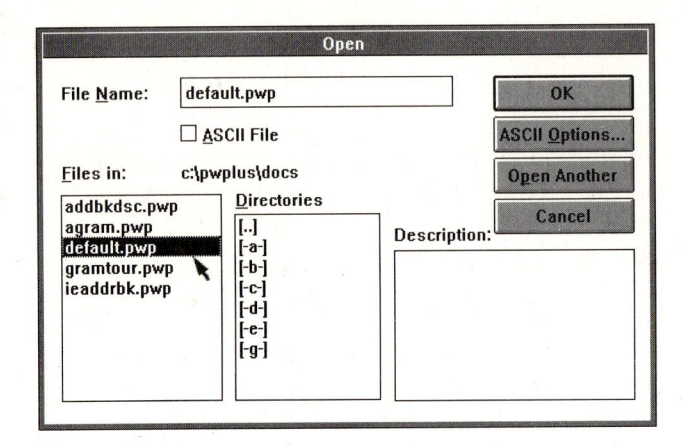

[Dialog box: Open
File Name: default.pwp
☐ ASCII File
Files in: c:\pwplus\docs
addbkdsc.pwp
agram.pwp
default.pwp
gramtour.pwp
ieaddrbk.pwp
Directories
[..]
[-a-]
[-b-]
[-c-]
[-d-]
[-e-]
[-g-]
Description:
OK
ASCII Options...
Open Another
Cancel]

To exit from the dialog box, click on one of the push buttons. In this case, choose the Cancel button. This choice will both exit you from the dialog box and cancel any selections or options you chose.

Using the Keyboard to Make Selections

If you prefer not to use a mouse, it is possible to work your way around a dialog box with the keyboard. Instead of using the mouse cursor, you manipulate a *selection box*—a little dotted rectangle that appears as soon as you begin using the keyboard. Table 1.2 lists the various keystrokes you can use to work with dialog boxes.

To practice using the keyboard to work with dialog boxes, follow these steps:

1. To display the dialog box shown in Figure 1.5, press Alt-F to pull down the File menu, and then press O (for Open). Or, you can press the speed key Ctrl-O instead.

2. Press the Tab key several times. As you do, notice how the selection box jumps from one part of the dialog box to another.

3. Now enter some new text into the edit box. Press Tab until the existing text in the box is highlighted (if there's no text, only the text cursor will appear), and then enter the new text.

4. Next, to make a selection from the list box, press Tab until the selection box appears in the list box (or until one of the items there becomes shaded), and then use the Up Arrow and Down Arrow keys to move the selection box up and down to the item you want to select.

Table 1.2 **Keystrokes for Working with Dialog Boxes**

Keystroke	Action
Tab	Moves the selection box in a clockwise direction to the next group of items, such as items in a list box or a group of check boxes
Shift-Tab	Moves the selection box to the previous group of items (counter-clockwise)
Up Arrow, Down Arrow	Moves the selection box within a group of items
Home	Selects the top item in the currently selected list box
End	Selects the last item in the currently selected list box
Spacebar	Selects, or activates, the item currently indicated by the selection box
Esc	Exits from the dialog box, canceling any selections
Enter	Performs the action of the currently selected push button

5. Now, to select the ASCII File option, press Tab until the selection box appears around that option, and then press the Spacebar. An X will appear in the box.

6. To deselect that option, press the Spacebar again while the selection box still surrounds the option.

7. To cancel the dialog box, press Tab until the selection bar appears within the push button labeled Cancel, and then press Enter.

In most dialog boxes, the OK button is highlighted unless you've specifically moved the selection box to another adjacent button (Cancel, in this example). This means that most of the time (except when the selection box is within another button), you just press the Enter key to exit from the dialog box—whatever instructions you've made will be carried out. One of the push buttons is always selected, whether the selection box appears or not. The one that's selected has a slightly darker outer border—press Enter to use that option and exit.

If you've followed the steps in the preceding sections for both the mouse and the keyboard, you'll probably agree that using the mouse is quicker, simpler, and far less confusing. (If you don't agree, feel free to continue using the keyboard!)

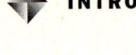

Scrolling Through Text

The horizontal and vertical scroll bars can help you to move around a document. You use the vertical scroll bar, at the right-hand side of the screen, to move up and down in your document. Similarly, if the entire width of your document won't display on the screen, you can use the horizontal scroll bar at the bottom of the screen.

Although you can't use the scroll bars with the keyboard, you can use the PgUp and PgDn keys to scroll vertically through a document one screen at a time. To scroll one page at a time, use Ctrl-PgUp and Ctrl-PgDn. To scroll horizontally with the keyboard, use the Right Arrow and Left Arrow keys.

Scrolling Vertically

As you work with Professional Write Plus, you'll find that the vertical scroll bar, shown at left, is one of your most useful tools because it allows you to view any part of a document quickly. There are three ways you can use this scroll bar to move up and down within your text:

- To scroll the document up or down by approximately one line, click on the arrow at the top or bottom of the scroll bar.

- To scroll down one screen, click on the area below the *elevator* (the little box inside the scroll bar). Click on the area above the elevator to scroll up one screen.

- To scroll to any particular location within your document, use the mouse cursor to drag the elevator up or down. As you do, remember that the length of the scroll bar represents the current total length of your document. For example, if you want to see the middle of your document, drag the elevator to the middle of the scroll bar. However, there's a one-page minimum. If your document is less than one page long, the length of the scroll bar represents an entire page.

To practice using these techniques, follow these steps:

1. Type in a few lines of text. Just enter anything at all, and don't worry about spelling or anything else at this point. Also, don't be concerned if you're not quite sure what's happening, as long as there's a bit of text on the screen.

2. Drag the mouse cursor to the bottom of the scroll bar, point it at the bottom arrow, and then click the mouse button. (From now on, this will be referred to as *clicking on the lower arrow.*) Notice that each time you click the button, the text scrolls up by approximately one line.

3. Next, click on the arrow at the top of the scroll bar, and watch the text scroll down by one line for each click.

4. Now drag the elevator down approximately ½ inch: Move the cursor so it points to the elevator, click and hold down the mouse button, and drag the elevator down. When it has moved down a bit, release the mouse button, and the text will scroll up by 2 or 3 lines.

5. Position the mouse cursor below the elevator, and then click the mouse button. The text will scroll up and move up off the screen.

6. To scroll back down, position the cursor above the elevator, and then click the mouse button once or twice, until the text reappears.

In addition to the vertical scroll bar, you can also use the up and down page arrows, which are positioned next to the horizontal scroll bar in the lower-right corner of the screen. To scroll down one page, click on the down arrow. To scroll up one page, click on the up arrow.

Scrolling Horizontally

In some circumstances, the entire width of your text lines won't be visible on the screen. For example, if you're displaying an enlarged view of your document, only part of each line will fit on the screen. In this situation, you can use the horizontal scroll bar to display various sections of the page.

You use the horizontal scroll bar the same way that you do the vertical one: Click on the arrow at either end of the bar, drag the elevator to the left or right, or click on either side of the elevator.

Using the Side Bar Icons

The *side bar* is the group of icons on the left side of the screen (see Figure 1.2). Each of these icons represents some type of action you can perform with the program. You could perform the same tasks by making various menu selections, but by clicking on the appropriate icon you can save yourself a few keystrokes. Especially for those tasks you do over and over, using the icons can be a timesaving shortcut. As you explore the various features of Professional Write Plus with this book, we'll indicate when a side bar icon can be used as a shortcut.

To use a side bar feature, you simply drag the mouse cursor to the corresponding icon and then click the mouse button. Whatever action that icon represents will be performed immediately. For example, if you click on the top icon (the magnifying glass), the display mode will change (try it and see). As the mode changes, so does the top icon. To restore the original display,

Note. You can't use the side bar with the keyboard.

click on the icon that appears in the same place as the first one. (For a discussion of display modes, refer to Chapter 2.)

Many icon shortcuts are available for your use, and you can select which of these icons appear in the side bar (only a limited number can appear on the screen at one time). On the other hand, you can, if you prefer, remove this side bar from the screen entirely, to free up more space for displaying your work. Of course, in this case the icons aren't available to you. (For details on customizing the side bar, see Appendix B.)

Getting Help

Professional Write Plus is equipped with a very nice help system, which you can use in several different ways. You can display the Help Index, which is a list of topics for which help is available, arranged in pull-down menu order. You can also use context sensitive help, in which on-screen help is available about whatever you're doing at the moment. Finally, you can point and click at any menu option to display help messages about that option.

Using the Help Index

To display the Help Index, select Help/Indexed Help. (Remember, this means to select the Help menu from the menu bar, then select the option called Indexed Help.) The first part of the Help Index will appear on the screen, as shown in Figure 1.7. You can then browse through the list of topics in the Index. When you find a topic that interests you, the help system can provide additional detailed information.

Figure 1.7
The top of the Help Index

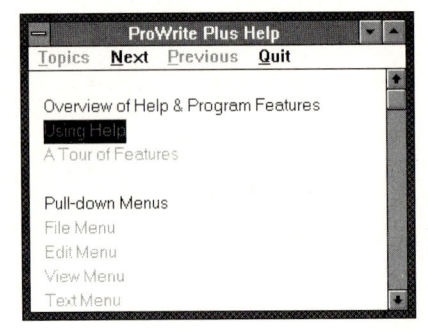

Getting Help

To scroll down through the index, click on the vertical scroll bar located on the right side of the help display. Make sure you click *below* the elevator. To scroll back up, click on the scroll bar above the elevator. (For information about using scroll bars, see "Scrolling through Text," earlier in this chapter.)

To get some experience using indexed help, follow these steps:

1. Find the topic labeled Format Menu by scrolling up or down.

2. To select this topic, move the mouse cursor so that it points to it, and then double-click the mouse button. The help display will change, displaying information about the Format menu, as shown in Figure 1.8.

Figure 1.8
Help information about the Format menu

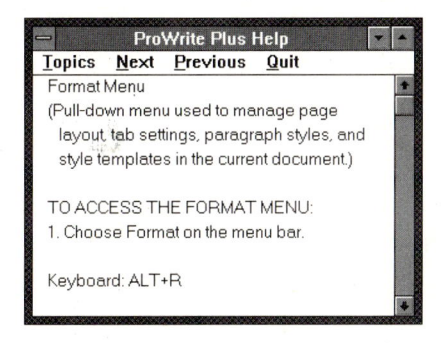

```
─                ProWrite Plus Help           ▼ ▲
Topics  Next  Previous  Quit
Format Menu                                      ↑
(Pull-down menu used to manage page
  layout, tab settings, paragraph styles, and
  style templates in the current document.)

TO ACCESS THE FORMAT MENU:
1. Choose Format on the menu bar.

Keyboard: ALT+R
                                                 ↓
```

3. Browse through this information, using the vertical scroll bar, until you see the topic labeled Page Layout.

4. To get more information about page layout, point the mouse pointer at this topic, and then double-click the mouse button. Again, the display will change, and you'll see additional related information.

5. Read about page layout by scrolling through the display.

6. To return to the top part of the index, select the option Topics from the menu bar at the top of the help display. You can either click on this item with the mouse or press Alt-T.

If you like, you can explore the index further by using the techniques just described.

Browsing Through Help

As you work with the help display, you have various ways to browse through the information:

- Use the vertical scroll bar to browse through the current display.

- To return to the top of the index, select the option Topics from the Help menu bar.

- To explore information about any topic that appears either in red or bold-faced, double-click on that topic. Or, highlight that topic and then click on Next on the Help menu.

- To return to a previous help screen, select Previous from the Help menu bar.

- To exit from Help, select Quit from the Help menu bar.

Exiting from Help

When you're done looking through the index, you can exit in any of the following ways:

- Select the option Quit from the menu bar at the top of the help display.

- Double-click on the control box at the upper-left corner of the help display.

- Click on the Minimize button in the top right corner of the Help window.

- Move the mouse cursor outside the help display, and then click the mouse button.

If you use either of the first two methods, Help is closed. This means that the next time you call up Help by selecting Help menu, the top of the index will be displayed (Figure 1.7). However, if you use either of the last two methods to exit from Help, it remains as an active Windows task, and the next time you call up Help it will be positioned wherever it was before.

Using Context-Sensitive Help

You can also use the help system to find out about whatever you're doing at the moment. Just press F1, and a help display will appear, containing relevant information about what you're working on. (Note that selecting Help from the menu bar won't give you context-sensitive help.) This feature can be used to display an explanation of any error message appearing on the screen.

To see this in action, follow these steps:

1. Select the File menu, using either the mouse or the keyboard.

2. Select the Open option.

3. Press the Help key (F1). You'll see the help display appear for the Open command, as shown in Figure 1.9.

Figure 1.9
A help screen showing information about opening a file

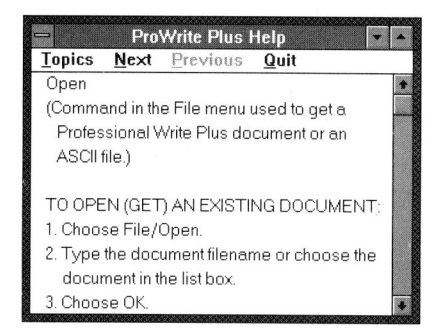

```
┌─────────── ProWrite Plus Help ──────────┐
│ Topics  Next  Previous  Quit            │
│ Open                                    │
│ (Command in the File menu used to get a │
│    Professional Write Plus document or an│
│    ASCII file.)                         │
│                                         │
│ TO OPEN (GET) AN EXISTING DOCUMENT:     │
│ 1. Choose File/Open.                    │
│ 2. Type the document filename or choose the│
│    document in the list box.            │
│ 3. Choose OK.                           │
└─────────────────────────────────────────┘
```

4. Browse through this help display using the scroll bar. In particular, note the related topics at the bottom.

5. You can select any related topic (appearing either in red or boldfaced) by double-clicking on it.

6. When you're finished with the help display, exit by using any of the methods described above.

Using Point-and-Click Help

There's one other clever way to use Professional Write Plus's help feature. With the mouse cursor, you can point-and-click on the feature you want, and the corresponding help information will appear.

As an example, here is how to use this feature to get help about the Bold option on the Text menu:

1. Make sure that the main edit screen is displayed, with no menu or dialog box showing.

Note. You can't use the keyboard to move the question-mark cursor.

2. Press Shift-F1. You'll see the mouse cursor turn into a question mark.

3. Select the Text menu, either with the mouse or the keyboard.

4. When the Text menu appears, select the Bold option, again using either the mouse or the keyboard. A help screen containing information about boldfacing will then appear.

5. Browse through this help screen using the methods described earlier in this chapter.

6. Exit from the help screen using any of the methods previously described.

Summary

The various tools described in this chapter are the ones you'll be using over and over as you work with Professional Write Plus. Before going on, make sure that you're reasonably familiar with them. In due course, they should become second nature to you, and you can then concentrate on the other aspects of the program.

The following chapter will begin to explore some of the basic word processing features, which you'll be able to use immediately to create simple documents.

CHAPTER 2

Word Processing Basics

- Starting a New Document
- Basic Text Editing
- Saving a Copy of Your Document
- Printing Your Document
- Starting Over
- Working with a Previously Saved Document
- Using Different Display Modes
- Working with Blocks of Text
- Changing the Text Appearance
- Using Different Fonts
- Changing the Page Appearance
- Ending a Professional Write Plus Session

Basic Text Editing

27

THE PREVIOUS CHAPTER DESCRIBED SOME OF THE BASIC TOOLS YOU'LL be using with Professional Write Plus. Now it's time to put these tools to work, as you begin to explore the basic word processing elements. If you practice using the various features presented in this chapter, you should be able to create reasonably attractive documents.

Starting a New Document

Each time you begin a session with Professional Write Plus, you must go through the steps for starting up the program, as described in Chapter 1. In each session, you can create as many new documents as you wish, as well as work with those you created previously.

The term *document* will be used in this book to refer to any combination of text and graphics you create with Professional Write Plus: a report, a simple letter, a memo, a full-length novel, or a multipage newsletter with illustrations. When you create a document, you usually go through the following steps:

1. Start up Professional Write Plus (unless it's already running).
2. Enter the basic text on your keyboard.
3. Make whatever changes are necessary, using the program's various word processing features.
4. At regular intervals, save a copy of your work to a disk file. Taking this step prevents catastrophic loss of work.
5. Periodically print out a rough draft of your work. (This step is optional. Use it if you prefer to check your work from a hard copy rather than from the screen.)
6. When you're finished, save a copy of the document to a disk file.
7. Print a final copy of the document.

Basic Text Editing

The term *text editing* refers to the process of entering text, correcting errors, adding and deleting text, moving text from one place to another, and taking any other steps involved with generating text.

Entering Text

To begin creating a new document, all you need to do is start typing. If there's already some text on the screen, you can easily delete it first (see the section "Starting Over," later in this chapter). For now, you can ignore any text on the screen and read on. As you start entering text, try to keep these basic points in mind:

- The text you enter always appears on the screen at the position of the text cursor (the blinking vertical line). As you enter each character, the cursor moves along in preparation for the next one.

- When you reach the end of a line, *don't* press the Enter key (as you would press the Return key on a typewriter). The program recognizes the end-of-line situation and automatically moves the text cursor to the beginning of the next line. This feature, common to all word processors, is called *reformatting* or *automatic word-wrap*. Just keep typing, and let Professional Write Plus do the formatting work.

- If you notice a typing error at the instant it happens, you can use the Backspace key to delete the offending characters, and then carry on.

- If you prefer, you can ignore your errors as they occur and later proofread your document, making whatever corrections are needed. (Some people feel it's faster to do all their edits at the same time.)

- When you want to end a paragraph and start a new one, press the Enter key. This places a *hard return* at the end of the paragraph, which forces a new line to begin. To double-space between paragraphs, press Enter twice.

- To create a tab, just press the Tab key as you would on a typewriter.

Note. When you first use Professional Write Plus, you won't be able to see the hard return created when you press Enter. Appendix B describes how you can customize the program to display the hard return character.

As a simple exercise, and keeping in mind the points just mentioned, enter the following text:

**Dear Sam:
I just found out that our annual picnic will be held next Monday at Tilden Park, instead of at the Fishermen's Roost. I'll bring the chicken if you'll bring the soup!**

When you've finished, your screen should look something like the one in Figure 2.1. If you made any typing errors, ignore them for now. You'll learn how to fix them shortly.

Once you have entered a bit of text, you'll undoubtedly want to make some changes. For example, you might want to fix spelling mistakes, delete some words or add others, or you might want to do some *cutting and pasting*—the process of moving groups of words from one location to another. (See the section "Working with Blocks of Text" later in this chapter.)

To make any of these types of changes, you'll need to move the text cursor from one place to another on the screen since you can make changes only at the cursor position. You can move the cursor with either the mouse or the

Basic Text Editing

keyboard; each method has its advantages and disadvantages. In some cases the mouse is faster, and in other cases the keyboard is. You'll probably use both as you develop your editing skills.

Figure 2.1
A very simple document

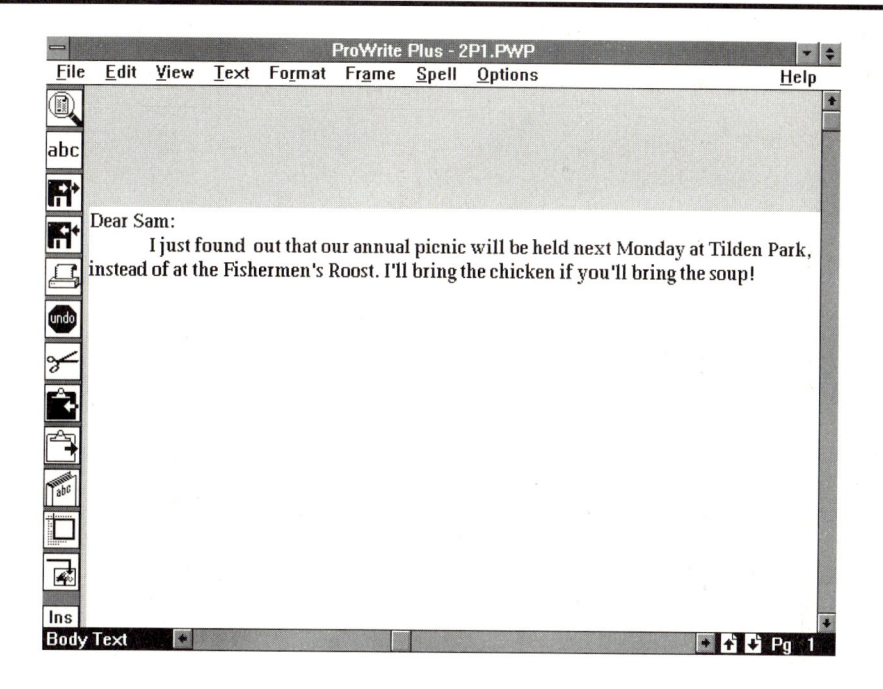

```
ProWrite Plus - 2P1.PWP
File  Edit  View  Text  Format  Frame  Spell  Options              Help

Dear Sam:
        I just found out that our annual picnic will be held next Monday at Tilden Park,
instead of at the Fishermen's Roost. I'll bring the chicken if you'll bring the soup!

Ins
Body Text                                                          Pg 1
```

Moving the Text Cursor with the Mouse

Using the mouse to move the text cursor is quite easy. You simply drag the mouse cursor to where you want the text cursor to be (anywhere within the existing text) and then click the mouse button. Using the mouse is the fastest way to move the text cursor around the page or from one end of the screen to the other. However, many people use the mouse for just about every text cursor movement. To get a little practice in using the mouse, follow these steps to move the text cursor to the beginning of the word "Tilden" on the screen:

1. Drag the mouse cursor until it's positioned just to the *left* of "Tilden".
2. Click the mouse button.

That's it! As soon as you click the button, the text cursor jumps to the mouse cursor position. You can then make whatever changes you want at that position.

You can also use the mouse to move the text cursor quickly to some other part of the current page or to a different page. Table 2.1 summarizes these operations.

Table 2.1 **Text Cursor Movements Using the Mouse**

Text Cursor Movement	Operation
To the next screen up	Click above the elevator on the vertical scroll bar
To the next screen down	Click below the elevator on the vertical scroll bar
To the next page up or down	Click on the page up or page down arrow near the bottom right-hand corner of the screen
To any part of the document	Drag the elevator to the corresponding part of the vertical scroll bar

Moving the Text Cursor with the Keyboard

You can use many different keys to move the text cursor on the screen. The basic cursor keys, labeled →, ←, ↑, and ↓, are used for moving the cursor one character or line at a time. To practice using these keys, follow these steps:

1. Press the Down Arrow key until the text cursor is on the last text line.

2. Press the Left Arrow key several times, and watch how the text cursor moves on the screen.

3. Continue pressing the Left Arrow until the text cursor is at the beginning of a line.

4. Now press the Left Arrow once more, and you'll see the text cursor jump to the end of the previous line.

Try using the other three cursor keys as well, and watch the cursor movement on the screen.

There are several other keys you can use for moving the text cursor (listed in Table 2.2). The list is quite formidable—you may wonder why you should bother learning all these movements when you can use the simple mouse control for any text cursor movement. The reason is that in many circumstances, using keystrokes for cursor movement is faster than using the mouse. Try practicing the first 12 entries in Table 2.2, but forget about the last 4 for the time being. Instead, use the mouse for these other cursor movements.

Table 2.2 **Keystrokes for Cursor Movement**

Cursor Movement	Keypress
Left or right one letter	Left Arrow or Right Arrow
Up or down one line	Up Arrow or Down Arrow
Right one word	Ctrl-Right Arrow
Left one word	Ctrl-Left Arrow
To the beginning of the current line	Home
To the end of the current line	End
To the next screen up	PgUp
To the next screen down	PgDn
To the top of the previous page	Ctrl-PgUp
To the top of the next page	Ctrl-PgDn
To the beginning of the document	Ctrl-Home
To the end of the document	Ctrl-End
To the beginning of the current sentence	Ctrl-, (comma)
To the beginning of the next sentence	Ctrl-. (period)
To the beginning of the current paragraph	Ctrl-Up Arrow
To the end of the current paragraph	Ctrl-Down Arrow

Adding and Deleting Text

Before going on, make sure that the letters INS appear in the box at the lower-left corner of your screen. If they don't, but the letters TYP appear instead, press the Ins key once; INS should then appear. This puts Professional Write Plus into the insert editing mode, described in the next section.

To add or delete text at a particular location, you must first move the cursor to that spot in the text. Then,

- To add text, just type it in. Text to the right will automatically be pushed over to make room.

- To delete the character to the left of the cursor, press the Backspace key.
- To delete the character to the right of the cursor, press the Del key.

If you'd like to get some practice using these features, follow these steps:

1. Using the sample text from the earlier example (the text that appears in Figure 2.1), move the cursor to the beginning of the word "Monday" and remove the entire word, using the Del key. Note that the remaining text on the line moves over to fill in the gap created by the deleted text.

2. After you've deleted "Monday", type **Friday**, making sure there's a space after the word. Notice how the text moves over to make room for the new word.

Tip. When using the Del key, you can either press it once for each character to be deleted, or you can hold it down, in which case characters will be rapidly deleted as long as the key is held down.

Using the Insert and Typeover Edit Modes

When editing text, you can use either of two modes: *insert* or *typeover*. Insert mode is set as the default when you begin running Professional Write Plus. It's usually the more convenient mode to use for text editing, although you'll find that typeover mode is occasionally useful.

To toggle (switch back and forth) between the two modes, press the Ins key. The little box at the lower-left corner of the screen indicates which mode is running—it shows INS for insert or TYP for typeover. When you enter text in insert mode, any text beyond the cursor is pushed over and down, to make room for the new text. Professional Write Plus automatically reformats paragraphs as needed, so you don't need to worry about lines being too long or too short.

In typeover mode, text that you enter overwrites whatever is at the cursor position. That is, existing text is pushed neither over nor down—it is simply typed over. This method of editing is useful if the text you want to enter is exactly the same length as the text you want to replace.

Saving a Copy of Your Document

As you work with a document, it's stored temporarily in your computer's main memory. If your computer loses power for any reason, or if you make a disastrous mistake at the keyboard, everything in the main memory will be lost. To avoid having to start over, you should periodically save a copy of your work to a disk file—perhaps every 15 or 20 minutes. Then, if your computer's main memory is wiped out, you can start up again from the last-saved version of the document.

You'll also want to save a copy of your current document whenever you end your current word processing session. This procedure allows you to stop

Saving a Copy of Your Document

Note. Professional Write Plus contains an advanced feature that can automatically save a copy of your work at regular intervals. This handy backup feature is described in Chapter 5.

in the middle of whatever you're writing, turn off the computer, and then come back later and start up where you left off.

You can save your work either to a floppy disk or to your computer's hard disk. To be extra safe, especially with long documents, you can save copies to both your hard disk and a floppy. That way, if your hard disk crashes (and they all do sooner or later), you'll still have a backup copy on the floppy disk.

If you're saving to the hard disk, your work is automatically written to the *default directory*, which is initially the \DOCS directory, whose parent directory is the one containing the Professional Write Plus program files. For example, if the Professional Write Plus programs are on the \PWPLUS directory, then the default directory is \PWPLUS\DOCS.

You can alternatively select another directory on your hard disk for saving your work. For details, see Chapter 5 and Appendix B.

When you save a copy of your work to a disk file, the contents of the computer's main memory are undisturbed, so you can continue editing as soon as the copying process has finished.

Saving for the First Time

The first time you write a copy of your document to a disk file, you have to give the new file a name. A file name can contain up to eight characters, including letters, digits, and various special characters (& and #, for example). Here are the steps for saving your document (if you're saving to a hard disk, skip step 1):

1. If you're saving to a floppy, insert the disk you want to use into either drive A or drive B of your computer (make sure that the floppy has been formatted first).

2. Select the Save As option on the File menu. You'll see the dialog box shown in Figure 2.2.

3. Enter the full name of the file to be created—the text cursor is initially positioned in the File Name edit box at the top of the dialog box, so you can just begin typing. (See the next section for additional information about file names.)

4. Click on the OK button or press the Enter key. After a few seconds, the edit screen will reappear, and you're ready to continue editing.

Specifying the File Name

In step 3 above, you entered the name of the file you're creating. Professional Write Plus automatically adds the extension .PWP to each document file name. For example, if you specify the file name **MYFILE**, Professional Write Plus actually names the file MYFILE.PWP.

Figure 2.2
The dialog box for saving a document to a disk file

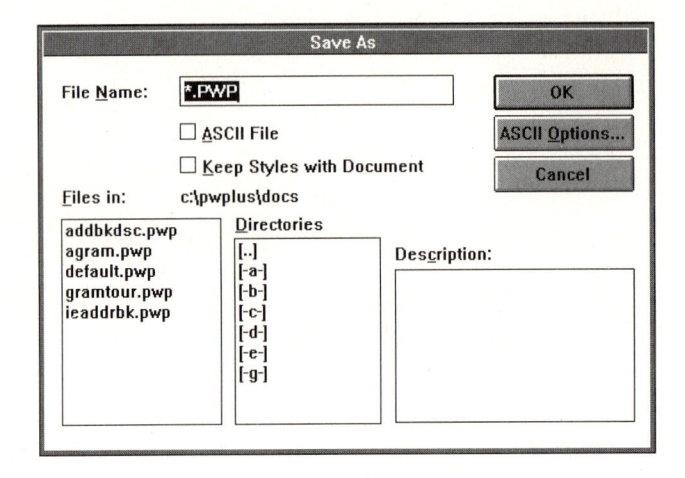

```
                          Save As
File Name:    [*.PWP        ]           [   OK   ]
              ☐ ASCII File              [ASCII Options...]
              ☐ Keep Styles with Document  [ Cancel ]
Files in:     c:\pwplus\docs
addbkdsc.pwp   Directories
agram.pwp      [..]          Description:
default.pwp    [-a-]
gramtour.pwp   [-b-]
ieaddrbk.pwp   [-c-]
               [-d-]
               [-e-]
               [-g-]
```

If you're writing to a floppy disk, include the name of the disk drive as part of the file name. For example, if you wanted to create a file named MYFIRST on drive A, you would enter **A:MYFIRST**.

If you're writing to the hard disk, you can simply enter the name of the file you want to create. The file will then be created on the default directory, which is where Professional Write Plus's files are stored. (You can also set up another directory as the default. See Appendix B for details.) If you want to write the file to another directory, include the complete *path name* (directory and file name) as the file name. For example, if you want to create a file named MYFIRST in the directory \WORK, enter **\WORK\MYFIRST**.

If the directory you want to specify is on a hard-disk drive other than the default one, include the name of that drive as well. For example, if the default disk drive is C, but the directory \WORK is on drive D, you would enter **D:\WORK\MYFIRST** for the file name.

Saving Again

After you've saved a document for the first time, or after you've retrieved it from a disk file, you'll eventually want to save it again, after you've made additional editing changes. In this case, the procedure for saving the document is somewhat different from that just described. When you want to save a document that's already on a disk file, you have two choices:

- You can save the document back to the same file, in which case the previous version on disk is overwritten.

Saving a Copy of Your Document

- You can save the document to a new file so that the older version of the document is also preserved.

Generally, it's much more convenient to save to the same file. You don't need to save to a new file each time because you can set up Professional Write Plus to create a backup file automatically for each document you work with. This means that you'll always have the previous version to fall back on in case you accidentally make a mess of the file. For details about setting up Professional Write Plus to create backups, see Chapter 5.

Saving to the Same File

To save your document to the original file, you can do any of the following:

- Select Save from the File menu.

- Press the speed key Ctrl-S.

- Click on the Save side bar icon, shown here:

A copy of your document is then automatically written to the file containing the earlier version of the document. The earlier version is either lost or, if you've set up Professional Write Plus to create backups, copied to the backup file.

If you happen to be working with a new, untitled document—that is, one for which there is no previous version—Professional Write Plus will realize your error and display the Save As dialog box (Figure 2.2) when you try to use one of these options.

Saving to a Different File

To save a copy of your work to a file that is different from the original one, follow these steps:

1. Select the Save As option from the File menu. The dialog box shown in Figure 2.2 will appear. Notice that the name of the original file appears in the File Name edit box and that it's highlighted.

2. Type in the new file name you want to use. You don't have to erase the old name in the box; as soon as you begin typing, it will disappear.

3. Click on the OK button, and the document will be saved in the file you named.

Should I Save to the Hard Disk or a Floppy?

As already mentioned, you have the option of saving your documents to either your hard disk or a floppy. In deciding which to use, you may find the following considerations useful:

- Writing a file to a hard disk is much faster than writing to a floppy. The same is also true for reading disk files.

- Every hard disk eventually crashes. When this happens, *everything* on the disk is usually wiped out.

- Floppy disks are not invulnerable. They can be misplaced or easily ruined—even by a greasy finger.

Here's a general rule that's often followed: Use the hard disk for your daily work. However, every so often—perhaps once or twice a day—save your work to a floppy disk as well. This way, even if you lose one or more files on the hard disk, you can recover without too much effort by using the files on your floppies.

Other Types of Files

When you save a document using the procedures just outlined, it's written in Professional Write Plus's own special file format. In addition, the file extension is set to .PWP to make sure that the file can be easily identified as a Professional Write Plus document. You can also save your document in other formats so that they can be recognized by different word processors. This topic is covered in detail in Chapter 5.

Printing Your Document

You can print a copy of your current document anytime you wish. There are a great many options you can select as part of the print process (number of copies, collating order, and so on), but the defaults used by Professional Write Plus will probably be adequate for most of your printing.

Before attempting to print anything, make sure that the printer is properly installed for Windows and that the printer's On Line or Select light is on. If the printer isn't yet installed for Windows, see Appendix C for details about printer installation. Here are the steps for printing the document you're currently working with:

1. Select Print from the File menu.

2. When the Print dialog box appears (as shown in Figure 2.3), click on the OK button, and the document will be printed.

Figure 2.3
The dialog box for starting to print a document

If you want to use options other than the defaults, click on Options and then make your selections in the dialog box that appears. (For more information about these options, refer to Chapter 9.)

Instead of step 1 above, you can either press the speed key Ctrl-P or click on the Print side bar icon, shown here:

Starting Over

If you have finished working on your current document, you can save it and then begin a new one. However, if you've made a mess of your current work you can instead abandon it and begin again. In the latter case, the program will give you a further chance to save your work before erasing it from the screen (and from memory).

Caution. If you erase your current work without saving it, it's gone forever (or until you re-enter the text).

If you want to erase your current work and begin over, follow these steps:

1. Select New from the File menu.

2. If you've made any changes since the last time you saved your work, the program will now ask you if you want to save these changes. To erase your work without saving it, click on No.

If you instead wanted to save your changes, you would click on Yes. If your current work hadn't previously been saved to a disk file, the Save As dialog box would appear (Figure 2.2). You would then enter the new file name and then click on OK to save the document.

Alternatively, if you decided that you wanted neither to save nor to erase the document at this point, you could click on Cancel when asked about saving your changes.

Working with a Previously Saved Document

To work with any Professional Write Plus document that you previously saved, it must first be read from the disk file into the computer's memory. When you do this (a process called *opening a document*), the document you're currently working with (if any) is erased from the computer's memory (after Professional Write Plus gives you the opportunity to save it). To open a document, you must specify the name of the file in which the document is stored. Here are the steps to follow:

Tip. You can also either press the speed key Ctrl-O, or click on the Open side bar icon (the floppy-disk icon) to begin opening a file.

1. Select Open from the File menu. The dialog box shown in Figure 2.4 will appear.

Figure 2.4
The dialog box for opening a document

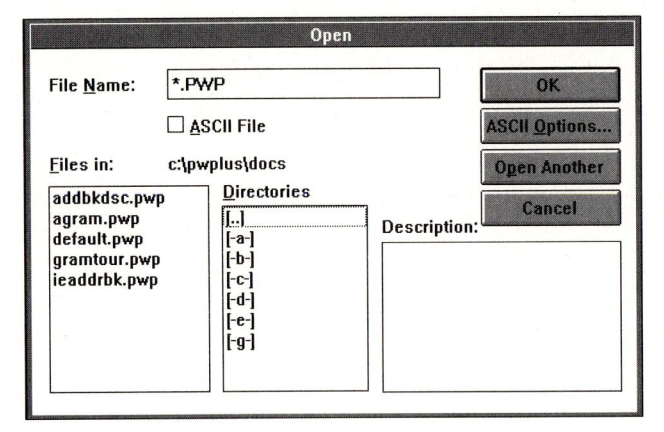

Note. Instead of steps 2 and 3, you can double-click on the name of the file in the list box labeled "Files In".

2. In the File Name edit box (the one at the top), enter the complete name of the file containing your document. You can just start typing; any name highlighted in the edit box will automatically be erased. (For details about entering the file name, see the next section.)

3. Click on OK.

4. If there's already a document in the computer memory, and it has been previously saved, Professional Write Plus will ask you if you want to save the most recent changes, as shown here:

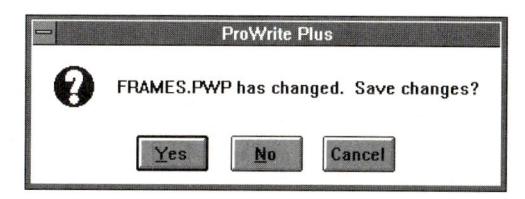

> **ProWrite Plus**
>
> ? FRAMES.PWP has changed. Save changes?
>
> [Yes] [No] [Cancel]

- If you don't want to save the changes, click on No.
- If you do want to save these changes, simply click on Yes.

5. If your current work hasn't been previously saved to a disk file, the dialog box shown here will appear:

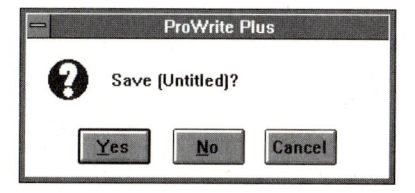

> **ProWrite Plus**
>
> ? Save (Untitled)?
>
> [Yes] [No] [Cancel]

Enter the new file name and then select OK. Your work will be saved, and the screen will then be erased.

Specifying the File You Want to Open

In step 2 of the preceding example, you must enter the name of the file you want to open. If you're opening a file from a floppy, place that disk in an available disk drive. Then include the name of that drive as part of the file name. For example, to open MYWORK on a disk in drive B, you would enter **B:MYWORK**.

If your file is in a directory on a hard disk, enter the complete path name as part of the file name. For example, if the file MYDOC is in the directory \WORK, you would enter **\WORK\MYDOC**. Finally, if this directory were on a hard disk other than the one containing the Professional Write Plus programs, you would include that disk drive as part of the file name, by entering something like **D:\WORK\MYDOC**.

Using Different Display Modes

When working with a document, there are several different ways in which you can display the text on the page. First of all, you can use either of two different *display modes:*

- In *draft mode*, the text always appears in a uniform size, and none of the page formatting (margins, headers, and so on) is displayed. Also, each hard return (the end of a paragraph) is shown on the screen as a ¶, and each tab is shown as a ---->.

- In *layout mode,* the text appears more or less as it will on the printed page. All the page formatting is displayed, and text attributes such as boldface and italics are shown. When Professional Write Plus is first installed, layout mode is the default.

Layout mode has several advantages. Most important is the fact that you can see how your page will appear when it is printed. Also, many of the program's features can be accessed only in layout mode. If you have a high-quality monitor, you'll probably find that text is more attractive in this mode. The disadvantage of layout mode is that the screen may behave sluggishly as you enter or edit text, or when you scroll up or down. However, with a 386 machine, this effect is hardly noticeable.

You may find that you have a strong preference for one mode. Or, you may find that you prefer one mode over the other for certain operations, but not for others. Switching from one mode to the other is easy, and you have several choices:

- Select either Layout Mode or Draft Mode from the View Menu.

- Use the speed key Ctrl-M.

- Click on the Draft/Layout Mode icon on the sidebar (the top one), shown here:

  [abcd]

Using Different Layout Views

In layout mode, you can select from five different *views*, each of which displays a different fraction of a full page on the screen:

- Full page
- Working
- Standard

Working with Blocks of Text 41

- Enlarged
- Facing pages

In addition, you can customize the magnification in the Working view. (See Appendix B for details.)

To select the view you want, first make sure that you're in layout mode, then select the View menu and make your choice. The options are as follows:

Tip. Experiment with the different views to see which one you prefer for editing.

- Selecting Full Page view causes the screen to display an entire page, showing the complete page layout. This is very useful for the final design work on a document, especially when you're using various graphics elements to add life to your work. For normal text editing, this view may not be useful unless you have a superlative monitor, because not all the text may be readable. However, if you can read the text in this view, you may be able to perform cut-and-paste operations very quickly, simply because you can see so much of your work at once.

- Working view may be the most convenient for text entry and editing, because with standard 1-inch left and right margins, both ends of every line are visible at the same time. When Professional Write Plus is first installed, Working view is the default, with the size set to 91 percent of the standard view.

- Standard view corresponds more or less to the size of text displayed in various other applications running under Microsoft Windows. Depending on your monitor and printer, this view may offer the best-quality screen display for standard text sizes.

- Selecting Enlarged view causes only a small part of the page to be visible on the screen. This view, which is twice the magnification of Standard, is useful for reading very small text and for doing fine layout work, such as lining up text and graphic page elements.

- The Facing Pages view displays two adjacent pages at once. You can't do any editing in this view, but it's useful for checking how your final page layout will look when printed.

Working with Blocks of Text

A *block* is a group of consecutive characters, such as a word or two, a sentence, or one or more paragraphs. The key word here is *consecutive*; you can't make a single block out of random words here and there. The screen in Figure 2.5 shows an example of a typical block.

Figure 2.5
A block of text

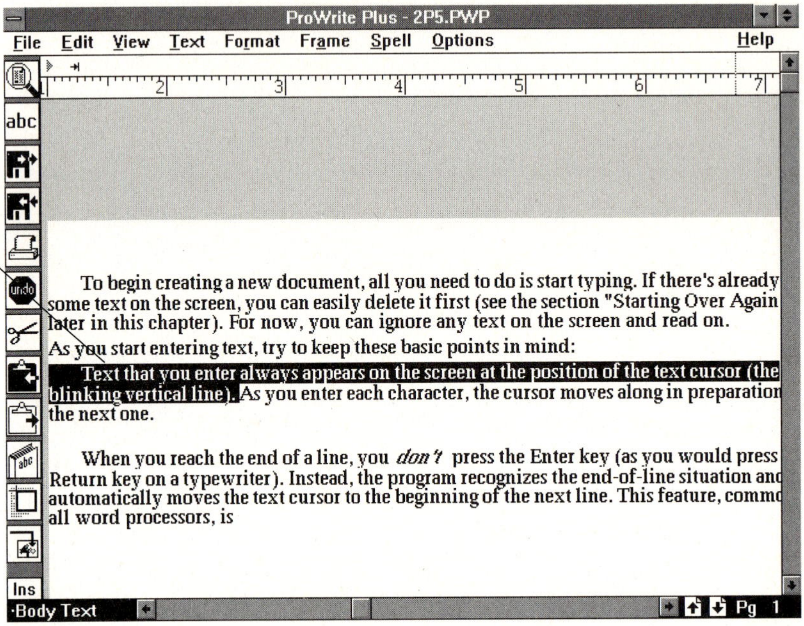

Text block

screenshot of ProWrite Plus - 2P5.PWP window showing document text with a highlighted text block:

> To begin creating a new document, all you need to do is start typing. If there's already some text on the screen, you can easily delete it first (see the section "Starting Over Again" later in this chapter). For now, you can ignore any text on the screen and read on.
>
> As you start entering text, try to keep these basic points in mind:
>
> **Text that you enter always appears on the screen at the position of the text cursor (the blinking vertical line).** As you enter each character, the cursor moves along in preparation the next one.
>
> When you reach the end of a line, you *don't* press the Enter key (as you would press Return key on a typewriter). Instead, the program recognizes the end-of-line situation and automatically moves the text cursor to the beginning of the next line. This feature, common all word processors, is

To work with a block, you first select it either with the mouse or keyboard, and then you do something with it. Here are some typical operations you can perform with a block you've selected:

- Delete it from your document
- Move or copy it to a different part of your document
- Change the size and shape of the characters in the block
- Change the spacing of the lines in the block
- Horizontally center each line of text in the block

These aren't the only things you can do with blocks. As you explore Professional Write Plus's various features throughout this book, you'll be shown how to perform other block operations.

The Clipboard

For many block operations, Professional Write Plus makes use of the *Windows clipboard*, which is a special area in the computer memory set aside for holding text blocks, graphics, or other items of information. You never actually see this clipboard, but you might find it easy to think of it as an actual clipboard where you temporarily place text, like this one:

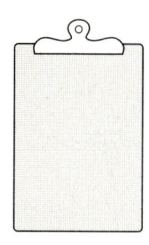

The clipboard can hold up to 64K of text, which is approximately 20 full printed pages, and probably more than you're likely to ever need. If you do want to work with a block larger than this, you can work with pieces of it, one at a time.

There are various ways you'll be using the clipboard to hold text blocks, as described shortly. Once a text block is placed on the clipboard, it remains there until you replace it with something else. The clipboard can hold only one block or other data item at a time.

Selecting a Block

You can use either the mouse or the keyboard, or a combination of the two, to select a block, although the mouse is generally much faster.

Using the Mouse

To select a block with a mouse, move the mouse cursor to one end of the block, press and hold the mouse button down, drag the mouse cursor to the other end, and then release the button. To practice using this technique, follow these steps:

1. Position the mouse cursor so that it's at one end or the other of the block you want to define—either just to the left of the first character or just to the right of the last one.

2. Press the mouse button and hold it down.

3. Drag the mouse cursor until it's positioned at the other end of the block you want. You'll notice that as you drag the cursor, the selected text becomes shaded.

4. Release the mouse button. The block is now selected, and you can perform various operations with it.

If you want to deselect the block, just click the mouse button once, anywhere on the screen. If you want to extend the block beyond the point where you released the mouse button, hold down a Shift key, move the mouse cursor to the new block end, and then click the mouse button.

Using the Keyboard

If you're a real keyboard whiz, you may be able to use keypresses to select text as quickly as you can with the mouse. To select a block, follow these steps:

1. Move the text cursor to one end or the other of the block you want to define.

2. Press a Shift key and hold it down.

3. Using any convenient keystrokes (such as Up Arrow, Down Arrow, and so on), move the text cursor to the other end of the block. As you do, the block becomes shaded.

Recall that Table 2.2 lists the various keystrokes you can use for moving the text cursor. Any of those keystrokes can also be used to help define a block. For example, here's a quick way to define an entire line as a block:

1. Move the text cursor to the beginning of the line.

2. Hold down a Shift key, and then press End.

Using Mouse/Keyboard Combinations

There are a few handy combinations of keys and mouse movements that you can use to select specific text groupings quickly:

- To select a sentence, hold down the Ctrl key, and then point and click the mouse cursor anywhere on that sentence.

- To select a paragraph, hold down the Ctrl key, point the mouse cursor anywhere on the paragraph, and then double-click the mouse button.

Selecting Long Blocks

You can also select a block that extends beyond the text that's visible on the screen. For example, to extend a block down using the mouse, click on the beginning of the block, drag the mouse cursor down to the very bottom of the screen, and then *continue* to hold the mouse button down. The text will then scroll down line by line, extending the block. If you're in layout mode, the scrolling will stop at the bottom of the page. However, in draft mode you can continue scrolling to the end of the document.

To extend a block beyond the current page, you can use either of two methods. The first is to switch to draft mode, where page boundaries don't

Working with Blocks of Text

exist. You can then use the mouse to extend a block down as far as you wish. Alternatively, you can use the keyboard in layout mode to create a long block. Move the text cursor to the beginning of the block, and then use any keys you wish to extend the block down—holding down the Shift key as you do. Here are a couple of examples:

- To extend the block to the beginning of the next page, hold down the Shift key and then press Ctrl-PgDn.

- To define an entire document as a block, move the cursor to the beginning of the document, hold down the Shift and Ctrl keys, and then press End.

Moving a Block

The ability to move blocks of text from one place to another within a document is one of the most useful features a word processor offers. For example, suppose you'd like to move a group of consecutive characters from one part of your document to another. The easiest way to accomplish this is by using block operations. For these operations, you can use either the Edit menu (see Figure 2.6), various speed keys, or the icons on the side bar.

Figure 2.6
The Edit menu

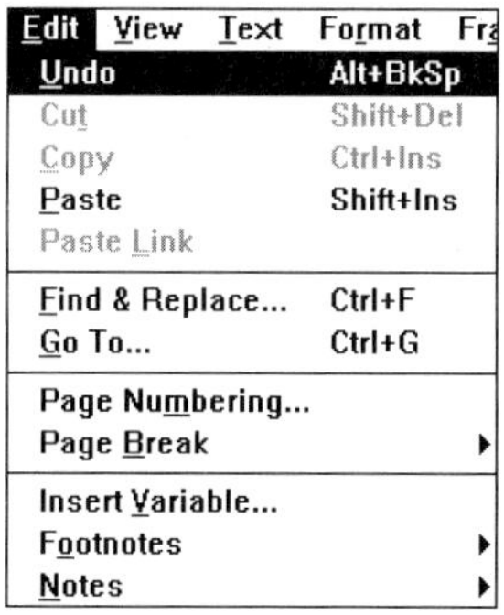

First, you must select the text to move as a block, as described earlier in this chapter. Then, you cut the block out of the document. When you do so, it's automatically copied to the Windows clipboard. Next, you position the text cursor where you want the block of text to be placed. And finally, you paste (that is, copy) the block from the clipboard to the cursor position.

The text shown in Figure 2.7 will be used to illustrate this technique. Here are the steps for moving the second sentence (beginning "Its purpose") to the beginning of the second paragraph:

1. Enter the text shown in Figure 2.7.

2. Select the entire second sentence as a block.

3. Move the block to the clipboard: Select Cut from the Edit menu.

4. Position the text cursor at the beginning of the second paragraph just to the left of the word "This".

5. Paste the block from the clipboard back into the document: Select Paste from the Edit menu. The screen will now appear as shown in Figure 2.8.

Figure 2.7
A small document

This is a small sample of text. Its purpose is to illustrate the basic block operations that are essential to all text editing. You must master block operations before you can get your word processing license.

This is the second paragraph. It's not much different from the first one. Block operations are an essential part of word processing. Without them, you'll always be a WPN (word processing novice).

Figure 2.8
The document in Figure 2.7 after moving a block

This is a small sample of text. You must master block operations before you can get your word processing license.

Its purpose is to illustrate the basic block operations that are essential to all text editing. This is the second paragraph. It's not much different from the first one. Block operations are an essential part of word processing. Without them, you'll always be a WPN (word processing novice).

Copying a Block

To copy a block from one place in a document to another, you follow almost the same steps as for moving a block, except that with a block *copy*, the original text remains in place, whereas a block *cut* deletes the original text. Here are the steps for copying a block:

1. Select the block, using either the mouse or keyboard.

2. Copy the block to the clipboard: Select Copy from the Edit menu. When you copy the block, the original text remains untouched.

3. Position the text cursor where you want the text to be placed.

4. Paste the block from the clipboard: Select the Paste option from the Edit menu.

Deleting a Block

If you want to delete a group of adjacent characters, no matter how large, select the characters as a block and then delete the block. When you delete a block, it's automatically saved by the program, so you can easily recover from an accidental deletion. After you've selected a block, there are several ways to delete it:

- Press Del
- Start typing immediately
- Select the Cut option from the Edit menu
- Press Shift-Del

Note. As a general precaution, use Shift-Del or the Cut option on the Edit menu to delete large blocks, just in case you change your mind.

Although you can use any of the preceding options to delete a block, some are safer than others, with respect to restoring a block you accidentally delete. (I always try to prepare for the worst!) If you use either of the last two options (Cut or Shift-Del), you can restore an accidentally deleted block by using the Paste option on the Edit menu—provided you haven't copied something else to the clipboard. On the other hand, if you use either of the first two options to delete a block, you'll have to use the Undo feature to restore the block, which has its own limitations, as described below.

Undoing a Block Deletion

Suppose that as soon as you've deleted a block, you realize that you made a horrible mistake (it happens to everybody). Fortunately, you can easily recover the block. To perform this small miracle, simply select Undo from the Edit menu, and the deleted block will be restored—in its original location. You can use the Undo feature regardless of how you deleted the block (that is, using any of the four options described earlier).

In order to guarantee a block's recovery, you must make this selection as soon as possible after you make the deletion—preferably immediately. When you select Undo from the Edit menu, the *last change* you made is reversed. Unfortunately, this includes just about any type of change, so you have to act quickly to use this method to recover a block you've deleted. (You can, however, set the Undo feature to remember up to the last four changes. For details, see Appendix B.)

If you deleted a block using either the Cut option from the Edit menu, or by pressing Shift-Del, you have a better chance of undoing the deletion, because the block is copied to the clipboard. You can then later recover the block from there by using the Paste option from the Edit menu (Figure 2.6), provided that you haven't in the meantime copied something else to the clipboard.

To help clarify the preceding discussion, here's a summary of your options for restoring a deleted block:

- If you used the Cut option or pressed Shift-Del to delete the block, you can restore it either by using the Paste option (in which case the block reappears wherever the text cursor is positioned), or by using the Undo option (in which case the block reappears at its original position).

- If you used the Del key, or if you deleted the selected block typing something else, you can use only the Undo option to restore the block.

Block Operations Using Side Bar Icons and Speed Keys

You can speed up block operations by using either the side bar icons or the corresponding speed keys. Either of these methods is faster than using the Edit menu, and you can use whichever appeals to you most.

For example, to cut text from a document, first select the text as a block, then either click on the Cut icon on the side bar or press the speed key Shift-Del. Table 2.3 lists the block operations and their corresponding speed keys and side bar icons. All of these icons are included in the side bar when Professional Write Plus is initially installed.

Table 2.3 Alternatives for Copying and Moving Blocks

Action	Keystroke	Side Bar Icon
Cut block	Shift-Del	✂
Copy block to clipboard	Ctrl-Ins	📋
Paste block from clipboard	Shift-Ins	📋
Undo	Alt-Backspace	undo

Changing the Text Appearance

There are several ways in which you can change the way your text appears on the printed page. You can assign different text attributes, such as boldfacing. You can also change the size and appearance of selected text by using different character sizes and shapes. To change the appearance of all the text in a document, you'll need to work with paragraph styles and templates, which are discussed in Chapters 6 and 7.

Using Special Text Attributes

A *text attribute* is an option that affects the appearance of the text. The most frequently used attributes are boldfacing, italics, and underlining. The following attributes are available for modifying text appearance:

- **Bold**
- *Italics*
- Underline—single or double
- Word underline
- Initial Caps
- SMALL CAPS
- Super^{script} or sub$_{script}$
- Strikethrough
- Overstrike

The difference between the Underline and Word Underline options is that the latter doesn't underline spaces between words. When you select Strikethrough, the text is overwritten with dashes, whereas with Overstrike you select the character that overwrites the selected text.

In layout mode, the various attributes will be displayed on the screen more or less as they will when printed (depending on your monitor). Boldfaced text will appear bold, italicized text as italics, and so on. In draft mode, however, these attributes don't display directly. But, if you have a color monitor you can assign different colors to the different attributes, and these colors will display in draft mode. (For details about assigning these colors, see Appendix B.)

Although you can probably select any of the available attributes and display them on your screen in layout mode, your printer's limitations will determine which of them can be printed. The easiest way to determine your printer's capabilities is to try out the various attributes and see if they actually print. If they don't, and the program has been properly set up for the printer (see Appendix C), then you're out of luck.

To apply an attribute to text, you first select that text as a block and then use the Text menu (see Figure 2.9) to select that attribute.

Figure 2.9
The Text menu

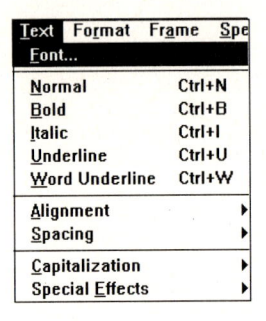

```
Text  Format  Frame  Spe
Font...
Normal          Ctrl+N
Bold            Ctrl+B
Italic          Ctrl+I
Underline       Ctrl+U
Word Underline  Ctrl+W
Alignment              ▶
Spacing                ▶
Capitalization         ▶
Special Effects        ▶
```

To illustrate how this works, here's how to boldface a block of text:

1. Select the text as a block, using either the mouse or keyboard.
2. Select the Text menu, and then select Bold.

To use some of the other attributes, such as overstrike, you must first select the Special Effects or Capitalization option from the Text menu, and then make your selection from the submenu that appears. For example, here's how to create a superscript:

1. Select the character(s) you want to superscript.
2. Select Special Effects from the Text menu, and this submenu will appear:

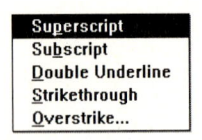

```
Superscript
Subscript
Double Underline
Strikethrough
Overstrike...
```

3. Select the option labeled Superscript—the easiest way is to point and click with the mouse.

When you select an attribute, a check mark will appear on the Text menu next to that option. This is a handy way to see which options have been applied to particular text: click on that text, then pull down the Text menu. Any selected options will be checked.

Working with Upper- and Lowercase

Various options available on the Text menu (Figure 2.9) can help you adjust the case of selected characters. To view these options, select the Capitalization option on the Text menu, and the corresponding submenu will appear:

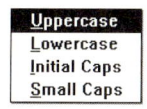

```
Uppercase
Lowercase
Initial Caps
Small Caps
```

If you've selected a block of text, these options have the following effect:

- Uppercase changes the selected text to all capitals.

- Lowercase changes the selected text to all lowercase.

- Initial caps changes the first character of each selected word to uppercase.

- Small caps changes the selected text to all uppercase, but using a smaller character size. Any letter originally entered in uppercase will maintain its original (larger) size.

Assigning Multiple Attributes

You can assign more than one attribute to a group of characters. For example, you might want to boldface and italicize a word or two (perhaps a heading) for emphasis. Most combinations of attributes will work, with some obvious exceptions. For instance, you can't assign both subscript and superscript to the same text (try it and see what happens). Here are a few examples of multiple attributes:

- ***Bold Italic***

- **<u>Bold Underline</u>**

- **<u>Bold Double-Underline</u>**

- *Italic* ^{*Superscript*}

Your printer may have limitations with respect to printing combinations of attributes. Again, a bit of experimentation will show you your printer's restrictions.

Undoing an Attribute

You can remove any attribute from text, returning it to normal. (*Normal attribute* implies the absence of any other attribute.) For example, you might decide that you really don't want a particular block of text to be boldfaced. Here's how to return any block of text to normal.

1. Select the block that has the attribute you want to remove.
2. Select Normal from the Text menu, or click on the attribute you want to undo.

If you're selecting Normal, you can be a little sloppy about selecting the text block, because there's no harm in assigning the normal attribute to text that's already normal.

CAUTION! *When you assign a particular attribute to a block of text, Professional Write Plus remembers that assignment. This can occasionally be a headache if you forget you assigned that particular attribute. For example, suppose some of your text includes the phrase "... my own True Love, who will..." and you assign this block to lowercase by selecting Caps from the Text menu and then selecting Lowercase. The words "True Love" will then be changed to all lowercase. The problem is that you can't then capitalize any part of these words. For instance, if you later try to replace "true" with "True", Professional Write Plus will keep changing it back to lowercase. To capitalize "true", you'll have to select it as a block again, and then select Normal from the Text menu or deselect Lowercase.*

Using Icons and Speed Keys to Assign Attributes

To speed up your work, you can assign many of the text attributes by clicking on the corresponding side bar icons or by using speed keys. For example, to boldface a text block, you can either click on the Boldface icon or use the speed key Ctrl-B.

Table 2.4 lists the text attributes and their corresponding speed keys (when available) and side bar icons.

When Professional Write Plus is first installed, none of these icons appears on the side bar. However, you can customize the program so that the side bar includes the icons you use most frequently. For details on customizing the side bar, see Appendix B.

Using Different Fonts

You can make significant changes to the appearance of your text by assigning different sizes and styles of type to particular text blocks. For example, you might want to use a slightly larger size for headings in a document.

A *font* is a particular typeface and size of text, where the *typeface* determines the overall design characteristics. For instance, the font named Times Roman 12 point means the following:

- The name of the typeface is Times Roman, which is one of the most commonly used ones. (The text you're reading now is a variation of Times Roman.)

Changing the Text Appearance

Table 2.4 **Alternatives for Assigning Text Attributes**

Text Attribute	Speed Key	Side Bar Icon
Boldface	Ctrl-B	**a**
Italics	Ctrl-I	*a*
Underline	Ctrl-U	se h
Word underline	Ctrl-W	se h
Double underline		se h
Superscript		x^a
Subscript		x_a

- The size of the font is 12 point (there are 72 points in 1 inch).

To assign a particular font to a group of characters, first select it as a block, then select the Font option from the Text menu (Figure 2.9), and finally select the typeface and size you want from the dialog box that appears. As an example, here are the steps for assigning a larger font to a block:

1. Select the block of text, perhaps a heading or title.

2. Select the Font option from the Text menu. A Fonts dialog box will appear, similar to the one shown in Figure 2.10. The Fonts dialog box on your system will probably differ from the one shown in this figure, depending on which fonts are included in your Windows installation and on the printer you're using.

3. Click on 18 in the Size list box. If the number 18 does not appear on your list, just select another size in the list.

4. Click on OK.

If you're using layout mode, the block you selected will appear in the new size on the screen. However, in draft mode, you can't tell one font from another. To see how the new font looks, just select Layout Mode from the View menu, or press the speed key Ctrl-M. (For more information about using fonts, refer to Chapter 9.)

Figure 2.10
The dialog box for selecting a different font

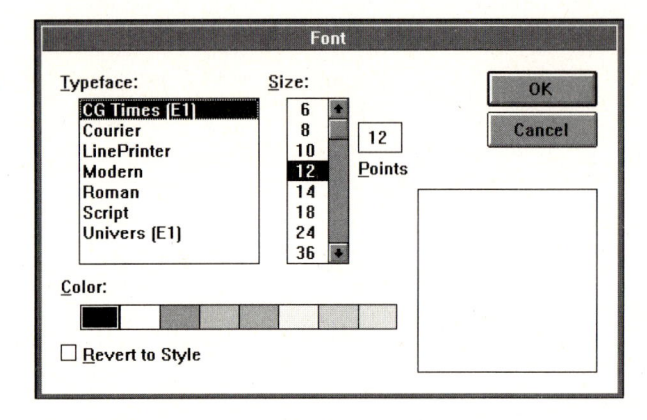

Changing the Page Appearance

There are many ways in which you can control the overall appearance of the pages in a document. You can change the line spacing and adjust the alignment of selected lines. You can also force page breaks at particular places in the text. As usual, when you use these features, they'll display on your screen only if you're in layout mode. In draft mode, the text is just laid out one line after the next, and none of these features is visible, except that a page break is indicated by the symbol <PAGE BREAK>.

Setting the Line Spacing

By default, text is printed single spaced. However, you can set the spacing of selected lines to single, $1^1/_2$, or double spacing, or to any custom spacing you wish. (To set the spacing of the entire document, you'll need to work with styles, which are covered in Chapters 6 and 7.) Here are the steps for setting the spacing of a particular group of lines:

1. Select those lines as a block.

2. Select Spacing from the Text menu, and the Line Spacing submenu will appear.

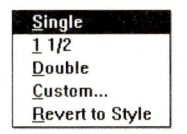

◆ Changing the Page Appearance   55

```
Single
1 1/2
Double
Custom...
Revert to Style
```

3. To select either single, double, or 1½ line spacing, click on the corresponding option.

4. To select any other spacing, select Custom and then in the dialog box that appears enter the number you want, as shown here:

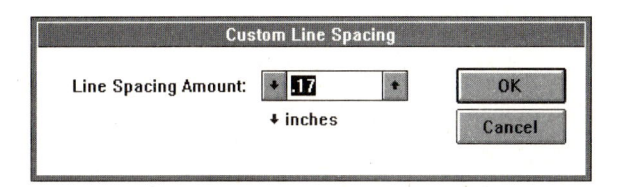

```
Custom Line Spacing
Line Spacing Amount: [ .17 ]     OK
                     inches      Cancel
```

Note. You must enter a valid number in the Custom Line Spacing dialog box, or the program won't let you proceed.

5. Click on OK, and the spacing of the lines you selected will be changed.

There are a few things to remember when you are changing line spacing:

- You don't need to select an entire line to change its spacing. Selecting any part of the line is enough.

- Selecting a new spacing for a line affects the space both above and below that line.

- To change the spacing of an entire paragraph, select it as a block: Point the mouse cursor anywhere in the paragraph, hold down the Ctrl key, and then double-click the mouse button.

Note. There are 6 picas in an inch, and 12 points in a pica.

When you enter a custom line spacing, the default unit of measure is inches. However, you can also enter values either in centimeters, picas, or points. In the Custom Line Spacing dialog box, click on the Inches option, and the units will change to centimeters, then picas, then points. As you switch units, the number in the edit box will automatically change as well.

Aligning Text Horizontally

You can *align* (that is, adjust the horizontal position of) one or more lines so they are placed at the far left of the page (*left-justified*), centered, placed at the far right (*right-justified*), or *fully justified* (meaning that the text abuts against both the left and right margins). (To set the alignment of an entire document, see Chapter 6 for a discussion of paragraph styles.) Figure 2.11 illustrates the different types of alignment.

Figure 2.11
Samples of different text alignments

These lines are left-justified
Another line
Third line
And so on

        This line is centered between the left and right margins
                      So is this one
                            Me too

                                      This line is right-justified
                                              So is this one
                                                    And me

These last few lines are examples of full-justification. To turn this on, select the Justify option on the Text menu. Notice how the text runs up against both the left and right margins? This is sometimes a nice effect, because the right edge of the text is even, rather than being ragged (which it is when text is only left-justified).

    To align a group of lines, first select those lines as a block. Then, select the Alignment option from the Text menu and choose the type of alignment you want. If you'd like to try out this procedure, follow these steps for centering one or more lines of text:

1. Select the lines as a block (for a single line, you can simply place the text cursor anywhere on the line).

2. Select the Alignment option from the Text menu, and the Alignment submenu will appear:

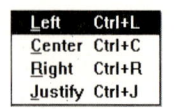

```
Left     Ctrl+L
Center   Ctrl+C
Right    Ctrl+R
Justify  Ctrl+J
```

3. Click on Center.

    Instead of following steps 2 and 3, you can use one of the keyboard shortcuts indicated in the Alignment submenu. For example, to center a group of lines, select those lines and then press Ctrl-C.

Ending a Professional Write Plus Session

When you're ready to end your current word processing session, make sure that you've saved your work to a file (as described earlier in this chapter). To be extra secure, especially for long or complex documents, you might want to save your work to two different files—one on the hard disk and another to a floppy that you can store away safely.

To exit from Professional Write Plus, you can either select the Exit option from the File menu, or press the speed key Alt-F4. If you haven't yet saved your most recent changes, you'll see a query on the screen asking if you want to do so. If you select Yes, your work will be saved to the file you used most recently, and you will then exit back to Windows. If you select No, you will exit to Windows without saving your changes. If you select Cancel, you'll be returned to the edit screen. If you try to exit before you have saved your current work at all, the program will give you an opportunity to save the work to a file. If you don't save the work before exiting, it will be lost forever.

CAUTION! *If you exit without saving your work, any changes made since your last save will be lost.*

Summary

Using the techniques described in this chapter and the preceding one, you should be able to create documents to serve many different purposes. However, this is by no means all there is to Professional Write Plus. The next chapter will explore the different ways in which you can further tailor the printed word to suit your particular needs.

CHAPTER 3

Controlling the Page Appearance

The Elements of a Page Layout

Setting Page Size and Orientation

Setting the Margins for a Document

Working with Tabs

Numbering Your Pages

Selecting the Number of Columns on the Page

Drawing Lines Around Pages

The Elements of a Page Layout

CHAPTERS 1 AND 2 LAID THE GROUNDWORK FOR USING PROFESSIONAL Write Plus to create simple documents. Now that you have some familiarity with the basics of word processing, you can do some further exploration. This chapter examines some of the ways in which you can control the basic characteristics that affect overall page appearance.

The Elements of a Page Layout

Various factors (illustrated in Figure 3.1) contribute to the overall appearance, or *layout*, of pages. They include

- Page size and orientation
- Margin settings
- Page numbering
- Headers and footers
- Tab settings
- Number of columns on each page
- Ruling lines

Initially, Professional Write Plus assigns default values to each of these features, and stores them in the *Page Layout*, which is stored as part of each document. You can make changes to any of these layout features either before you start entering text into a new document, or at any time while you're working with the document. In either case, your changes affect the entire document, and they are stored in the Page Layout for that document.

Whenever you want to make any changes to the Page Layout, you begin by displaying the Page Layout dialog box, shown in Figure 3.2. To display this box, select Format/Page Layout. Then you can make whatever layout changes you want.

Setting Page Size and Orientation

Initially, the default page size is set to 8 $\frac{1}{2}$ by 11 inches, which is standard for most documents. However, you can also choose from among a group of other preset sizes, or you can specify a custom page dimensions that are up to 22 inches on a side.

If the paper in your printer is larger than the size you specify, the pages will be printed in the upper-left part of the paper. If the printer paper is smaller than the size you specify, some of the text may print, or the program may insist that you change to the specified paper size first.

Figure 3.1

Various features of the Page Layout

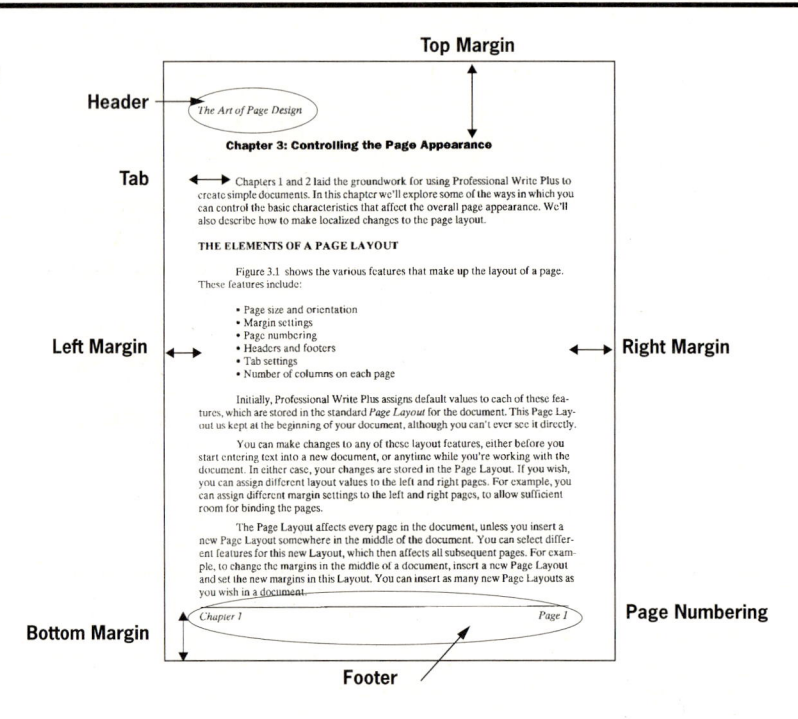

- Top Margin
- Header — *The Art of Page Design*
- Chapter 3: Controlling the Page Appearance
- Tab — Chapters 1 and 2 laid the groundwork for using Professional Write Plus to create simple documents. In this chapter we'll explore some of the ways in which you can control the basic characteristics that affect the overall page appearance. We'll also describe how to make localized changes to the page layout.

THE ELEMENTS OF A PAGE LAYOUT

Figure 3.1 shows the various features that make up the layout of a page. These features include:

- Page size and orientation
- Margin settings
- Page numbering
- Headers and footers
- Tab settings
- Number of columns on each page

Initially, Professional Write Plus assigns default values to each of these features, which are stored in the standard *Page Layout* for the document. This Page Layout is kept at the beginning of your document, although you can't ever see it directly.

You can make changes to any of these layout features, either before you start entering text into a new document, or anytime while you're working with the document. In either case, your changes are stored in the Page Layout. If you wish, you can assign different layout values to the left and right pages. For example, you can assign different margin settings to the left and right pages, to allow sufficient room for binding the pages.

The Page Layout affects every page in the document, unless you insert a new Page Layout somewhere in the middle of the document. You can select different features for this new Layout, which then affects all subsequent pages. For example, to change the margins in the middle of a document, insert a new Page Layout and set the new margins in this Layout. You can insert as many new Page Layouts as you wish in a document.

- Left Margin / Right Margin
- Bottom Margin
- *Chapter 1* / *Page 1* — Page Numbering
- Footer

The *Page orientation* refers to the way in which you hold a page to read it. The normal page orientation, in which the long edge is vertical, is called *portrait*. When the page is read with the long edge horizontal, the orientation is *landscape*. (See Figure 3.3.) You can create documents in either orientation, provided your printer is able to output them.

To select a different page size or orientation, follow these steps:

1. Select Format/Page Layout to display the Page Layout dialog box (Figure 3.2).

2. Click on the Page Settings button. The dialog box will change, as shown in Figure 3.4.

3. In the box labeled Page Size, you can do either of the following:

■ Click on the button corresponding to the size you want.

◆ **Setting Page Size and Orientation** 61

Figure 3.2
The dialog box for making changes to the Page Layout

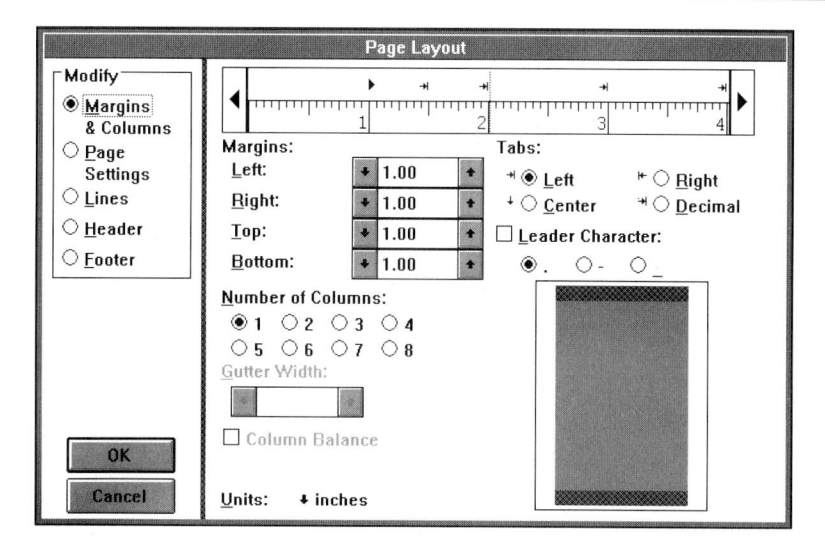

Figure 3.3
Portrait versus landscape orientation

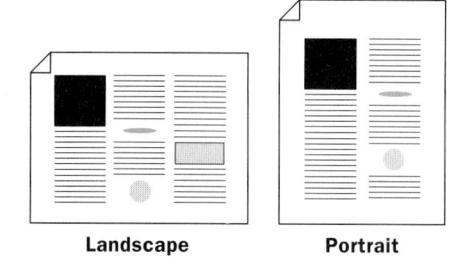

- Specify a custom page size by entering the width in the left-hand edit box (which initially contains the number 8.50) and the length in the right-hand box.

4. Choose the orientation you want by clicking on the appropriate button in the Orientation box.

5. Click on OK (in the lower-left corner of the dialog box) to have your selections take effect, or click on Cancel to nullify your changes.

Figure 3.4
The dialog box for entering the page size and orientation

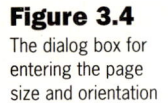

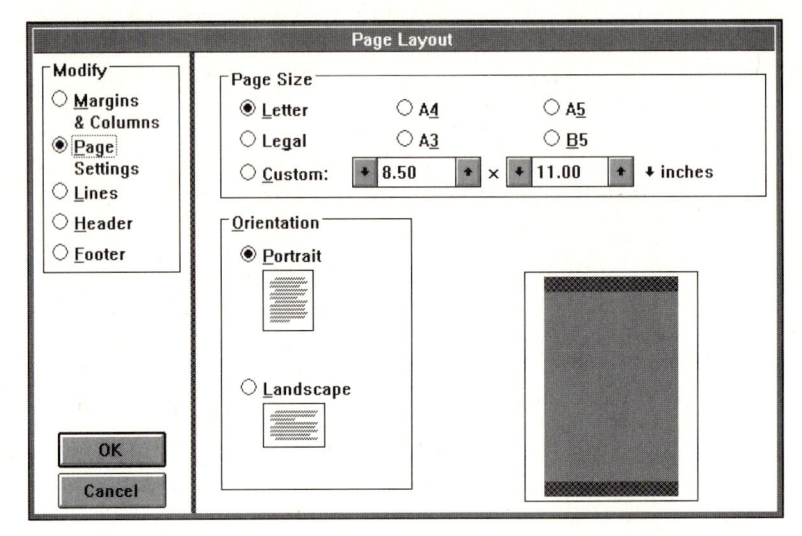

If you click on one of the preset sizes, the corresponding dimensions appear automatically in the left and right edit boxes. You can use these numbers to verify that you've selected the correct sizes.

As you make your selections, the box in the lower-right corner of the dialog box displays a small schematic of your page in the correct proportions. The dark gray areas at the top and bottom represent the top and bottom margins, and the white areas the left and right margins.

Printing in Landscape Orientation

If you select landscape orientation, but your printer can't print in this mode, whatever is printed (if anything) undoubtedly won't be what you want. However, don't be afraid to try out your printer. You can't hurt it, and it may be more flexible than you realize.

If you want to print in landscape orientation, you'll have to reconfigure the printer settings in Windows, which you can do from within Professional Write Plus.

CAUTION! *When you change the printer settings in Windows, the new configuration will apply to all Windows programs, including Professional Write Plus, so be sure to change the printer settings back to portrait orientation when you've finished working with the document.*

Here's how to reconfigure the printer for landscape printing.

Setting Page Size and Orientation

63

1. Select File/Printer Setup, and the Select Printer dialog box will appear, as shown in Figure 3.5. Note that the printer names appearing in this dialog box will be those currently installed for your system.

Figure 3.5
The dialog box for selecting your printer

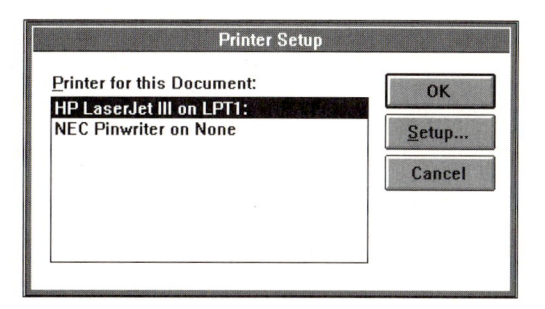

2. Click on the name of your printer, and then click on Setup.

3. When the Setup dialog box appears (see Figure 3.6), click on the Landscape button in the box labeled "Orientation."

Figure 3.6
The dialog box for reconfiguring your printer for landscape orientation

4. Click on OK, then click on OK again, and the edit screen will reappear.

If the name of your printer doesn't appear in the Select Printer dialog box (step 1), the printer probably is not installed for Windows. Before proceeding, you'll have to reconfigure Windows to recognize your printer (see Appendix C for details).

Setting the Margins for a Document

The default margins are set to 1 inch all around, but you can easily change any or all of them to other values. In addition, you can choose to express the margin settings in inches, centimeters, picas, or points. (There are 6 picas to an inch, and 12 points to a pica, therefore 72 points to the inch.)

You can change the margin settings from anywhere in your document, but the new settings apply to the entire document. You can't change the margins for just part of a document (although you can change the effective margins on any page by using frames, which are described in Chapters 9 and 10).

Professional Write Plus offers two methods for changing margins:

- By entering margin values in edit boxes

- Visually, by dragging left and right margin markers in the Page Layout dialog box (left and right margins only)

Either method is fine, but you can control the margins more precisely by using edit boxes.

Using Edit Boxes to Change Margins

To set the margins by entering numbers, follow these steps:

1. Display the Page Layout dialog box (Figure 3.2).

2. To change the units of measurement for the margins (the standard units are inches) to centimeters, picas, or points, click once or more on the word "inches," near the bottom of the dialog box until the unit you want is displayed. Each click changes the unit.

3. To change a margin, use the corresponding edit box, located near the middle of the dialog box. You can do either of the following:

- Click on the box corresponding to the margin you want to change, delete the value there, and then enter the new margin value.

- Click on the arrow at either end of the box to increase or decrease the margin. One click changes the value by 0.05 inches.

4. Click on OK to have your changes take effect, or click on Cancel to erase your changes and return to the edit screen.

As you enter the new margin values, the box in the lower-right corner displays the margins graphically.

Using the Page Layout Tab Ruler to Change Margins

You can also change the margins of your document by using the tab ruler at the top of the Page Layout dialog box. The *tiny* symbols ▶ and ◀ (not the larger symbols with the same appearance) on the top of the ruler represent the current positions of the left and right margins, which are initially set at 1 and 7 1/2 inches. (The right margin symbol is hidden until you scroll the display to the right, as explained below.) You can use these symbols to change the margins, as follows:

1. Click on the symbol for the left margin (when you do, it will become shaded), and hold down the mouse button.

2. Using the mouse, drag the symbol either to the right or to the left (but not past an existing tab marker—see the discussion that follows). As you do, notice that the number in the Left Margin edit box changes.

3. Release the mouse button, and the new left margin is set.

4. Click on the *large* symbol ▶ at the far right end of the tab ruler. As you hold the mouse button down, the ruler will scroll to the right. Continue until the right margin symbol appears, and then release the button.

5. Click on this margin symbol, and then drag it to the new position you want for the right margin.

6. Click on OK to exit from the dialog box.

You can't drag either margin symbol past an existing tab marker (the little symbols that look like is: →|. To move the symbol past the position of a tab marker, you first have to delete that tab: Click on the tab marker and then press the Del key. The marker will disappear, and you can proceed.

Using Temporary Margins to Avoid Horizontal Scrolling

In some circumstances, you may find that both the left and right margins are not visible on the screen at the same time, which means that part of your text may not be visible on the screen. For example, in the Standard view in layout mode, approximately 6 inches of page width is visible, which is less than a full line width of 6.5 inches, assuming 1-inch margins. If this situation exists, you'll probably prefer to avoid having to scroll horizontally.

One of the simplest ways to eliminate this scrolling is to temporarily change the left or right margin of the document. For instance, if you're using the Standard view, you can increase either the left or right margin to 1.5 inches, reducing the maximum line width from 6.5 to 6 inches.

This margin setting is temporary only. When you're ready to do the final layout work for the document, you'll need to change the margins back to the final settings you want. During this latter phase of the document preparation, you'll have to put up with the horizontal scrolling.

Working with Tabs

Whenever you press the Tab key, the text cursor jumps to the next tab setting (or just *tab*) on the current line. The default tab settings are 1.5, 2, 3, 4, and 5 inches, but you can change these tab settings for the entire document, using either of two methods:

- With the tab ruler displayed on the Page Layout dialog box (Figure 3.2).

- By displaying a tab ruler at the top of the edit screen (discussed below) and then changing the tabs directly on that ruler. This is usually the quicker of the two methods.

Initially, both of these tab rulers display the tabs and margin settings for the entire document (two different views of the same items). Later on, you'll see that this isn't always the case.

You can also change the tabs for just part of a document by inserting a new tab ruler wherever you want in the document and then changing the tabs on this ruler. You can insert as many tab rulers as you wish in a document.

Tab Types

You can use four different types of tabs, as illustrated in Figure 3.7.

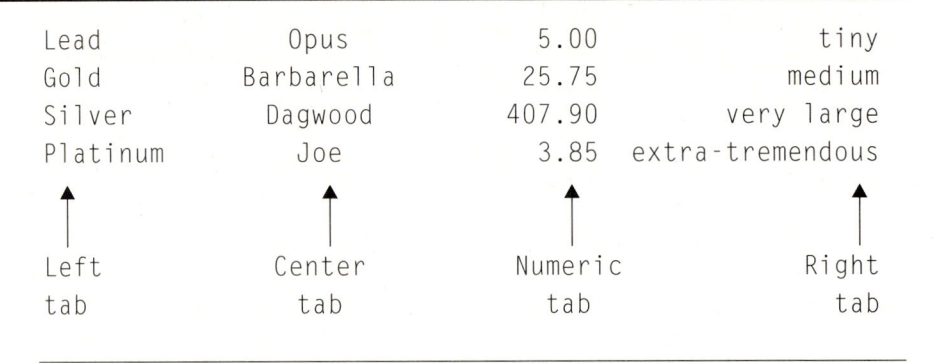

```
Lead           Opus            5.00            tiny
Gold           Barbarella     25.75          medium
Silver         Dagwood       407.90      very large
Platinum       Joe             3.85  extra-tremendous
  ↑              ↑               ↑               ↑
  |              |               |               |
Left          Center          Numeric          Right
tab            tab              tab             tab
```

Figure 3.7
A sample of each type of tab setting

Left Tab The left tab is the most common type; it is like the ones on most typewriters. When you press the Tab key to reposition the text cursor to this type of tab, the next character you enter will appear just to the right of that tab, and subsequent characters will appear farther to the right.

Right Tab When you press Tab to move the cursor to a right tab, characters you enter will appear to the *left* of the tab. When you use this type of tab, characters will continue to move to the left of the tab until they come up against either another tab setting, the left margin, or other text on that line. Subsequent characters will then appear after the tab.

Center Tab   After you press Tab to move the cursor to a center tab, the new text you enter will be centered on that tab. Centering will end when the new text runs up against either a margin or another tab position to the left. Any remaining text will wrap around to the next line.

Numeric Tab   Numeric tabs are handy for lining up columns of numbers on their decimal points. After Tab is pressed, anything you enter will appear to the left of that tab position until you enter a decimal point (that is, a period). Then, new characters will appear to the right of the decimal.

Tab Leaders
An additional type of tab formatting is provided in tab leaders. A *tab leader* is a group of characters inserted into the text between tabs. You can assign a leader to one or more tab settings, and you can use a period, dash, or underscore as the *leader character*. When you assign a leader to a tab, the leader will appear before the text inserted at that tab position. Here's an example of how a tab leader can be used:

    Age.................. 25
    Weight............. 35
    Hair.................. brown

Here, a period is assigned as a tab leader to the *left* tab that begins at the end of the periods.

Using the Edit Screen Tab Ruler

Like the tab ruler in the Page Layout dialog box, the tab ruler at the top of the edit screen displays the current tab settings, the left and right margins, and a horizontal ruler to help you work with the tabs. When you first start using Professional Write Plus, this tab ruler is not shown. Select Options/Show Tab Ruler to display the tab ruler as shown here:

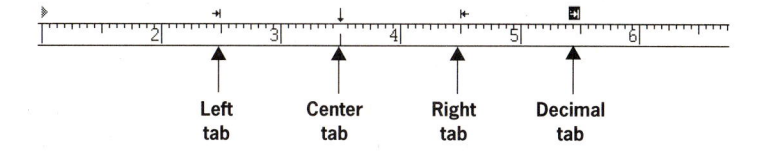

            Left   Center   Right   Decimal
            tab   tab   tab   tab

If you're in draft mode, you must use the View menu to switch to layout mode before you can display the tab ruler.

    With the tab ruler displayed, you can use the mouse to make changes to the current tabs for your document, and you can also insert new tabs.

Although the margin settings appear, you can't use this ruler to change them. (Use the ruler on the Page Layout dialog box for this purpose.)

Remember, when you change or delete one of the current tabs, it will affect the entire document unless you use a different tab ruler for part of the document. (See "Changing Tab Settings," later in this chapter.)

Moving Tabs

One way to create a tab at a new position is to move one or more of the existing tabs on the tab ruler.

To move an existing tab from one location to another, follow these steps:

1. Click on the tab you want to move, and hold the mouse button down.

2. Drag the tab either right or left to the new location, and then release the mouse button. (But you can't drag a tab past either another tab or a margin.)

Tip. You can move the mouse cursor back into the text of the document to help you set the exact position of tab; as you move the mouse left or right, you'll see the vertical line on the ruler move correspondingly.

In addition, you can simultaneously move two or more tabs by exactly the same amount. First, select the tabs you want by holding down the Shift key and clicking on the tabs to be moved. Then, still holding down the Shift key, select any one of these tabs and drag it to either the left or right. As you do, all the selected tabs will move by the same amount. To move all the tabs, click on any one of them, press A (for *All*), hold down the Shift key down, and then drag any of the tabs right or left. They will all adjust by the same amount.

Deleting a Tab

To delete a tab, click on it so that it becomes shaded, and then press Del. To delete two or more tabs at once, hold down the Shift key, click on each tab you want, and then press Del. If you want to delete all the current tab settings, click on any tab, press the letter A (for *All*), and then press Del.

Inserting Tabs

You can use the tab ruler to insert any type of tab. You can also use it to assign the period (.) as a leader character for any tab. (To assign either the dash or underscore as a tab leader, use the Page Layout dialog box, as described later.) Here are the steps for inserting a new tab using the tab ruler:

1. Point the mouse at the position where you want to insert the new tab on the tab ruler line, then click the mouse button.

2. Select the type of tab setting you want by pressing the appropriate key, as follows:

    l   Left tab
    r   Right tab
    c   Center tab
    d   Numeric tab

    L   Left tab with period leader
    R   Right tab with period leader
    C   Center tab with period leader
    D   Numeric tab with period leader

If you assign a leader to a tab, a little dot will appear directly over the tab symbol on the tab ruler.

Using the Page Layout Dialog Box to Change Tabs

Instead of using the tab ruler on the edit screen, you can use the Page Layout dialog box to move, delete, or add tabs. This is convenient if, for example, you happen to be setting up other page layout features and you also want to make some changes to the tab settings. Also, you must use this dialog box if you want to assign either the dash or underscore as a tab leader character.

    To begin, select Format/Page Layout so that the Page Layout dialog box appears. In the upper-right corner is a tab ruler similar to the one displayed at the top of the edit screen:

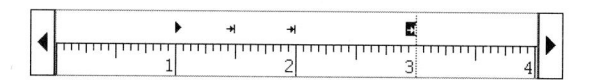

You can manipulate the tabs on this ruler in much the same way as you do the ones on the edit screen rulers.

Moving a Tab

To move a tab, click on that tab, and then use the mouse to drag it either to the left or right. To move two or more tabs, hold down the Shift key, click on the tabs, and then drag them left or right with the mouse. To move all the tabs, click on any one, press A (for *All*), hold down the Shift key, then drag any of the tabs left or right—they will then all move by that amount.

Deleting a Tab

To delete a tab, click on it and then press Del. To delete two or more tabs, hold down the Shift key, click on the tabs to be deleted, and then press Del. To delete all the tabs, click on any one, press A, and then press Del.

Inserting a New Tab

To add a new tab, follow these steps:

    1. Select the type of tab you want (left, center, right, or numeric) by clicking on the appropriate button.

2. If you want to assign a leader character to the new tab, click on the option labeled Leader Character, so that an X appears in the box. Then, click on the leader character you want (select one of the three buttons directly under the Leader Character option).

3. Move the mouse cursor onto the tab ruler and click on the new tab position. A new tab symbol will appear at that position, and if you've assigned a leader character, a small dot will appear over the tab symbol.

4. To have the new tabs take affect, click on OK. To cancel your changes, click on Cancel.

Using Relative Tabs

If you want to change the left margin setting, you may need to reposition some or all of the tabs as well. However, there is a way in which you can reposition both the left margin and all the tabs at the same time, so that the tabs remain in the same relative positions with respect to the margin. The method is very simple:

1. Display the Page Layout dialog box.

2. Select all the tab settings (click on any one, then press A).

3. Holding down the Shift key, click on the left margin symbol.

4. Still holding down the Shift key, drag the margin symbol (or any tab symbol) left or right to its new position.

This method works as well for the right margin as for the left, but usually it makes more sense to keep the tabs relative to the left margin. Also, note that you can't use this method with the tab ruler on the edit screen, because you can't move the margins on that tab ruler.

Changing Tab Settings

The tab ruler that's displayed in the Page Layout dialog box (and initially on the edit screen when you select Options/Show Tab Ruler) is a basic part of the Page Layout. It's actually called the *Page Layout tab ruler*. This ruler displays the default tab settings of the entire document. However, you can change the tabs in the middle of a document by inserting a new tab ruler at that point and changing the tabs on this new ruler.

The tab settings on the new ruler will affect all the text that comes after it. In other words, the new tab ruler takes precedence over the Page Layout tab ruler. You can insert as many different tab rulers as you wish throughout a document, and each one takes precedence over the previous one. When you have added rulers, the tab ruler that appears at the top of the edit screen is always the tab ruler *currently* in effect. However, the Page Layout dialog box *always* displays the Page Layout tab ruler.

You can insert a tab ruler as you're creating a new document, wherever you want to change the tab settings. Or, you can insert any number of tab rulers into an existing document, each with its own tab settings. The text following each new ruler will be reformatted to conform to the tabs on that ruler. In addition, at any place in a document you can restore the default tab settings on the Page Layout tab ruler. These tabs will then remain in effect until you enter yet another tab ruler.

Inserting a New Tab Ruler
Follow these steps to insert a new tab ruler:

1. Position the text cursor where you want the new ruler to take effect. This can be anywhere on a page.

2. Select Format/Tab Ruler/Insert Tab Ruler.

If the new tab ruler isn't displayed at the top of the screen (when you're in layout mode), select Options/Show Tab Ruler. If the Marks Option is turned on, a →| symbol will appear on the line where the new ruler has been inserted. (To turn on the Marks option, select Options/Layout Mode Options/Marks.) Initially, the new ruler will contain the same tabs as the previous ruler, but you can change them by using the steps described earlier. Remember, you can't see the tab ruler in draft mode.

Deleting a Tab Ruler
When you delete a tab ruler, the tabs revert to those of the previous ruler, which could be either another inserted ruler or the Page Layout ruler. Use the following steps to delete a tab ruler:

1. Place the text cursor anywhere in the text that is affected by the ruler (that is, after that ruler and before any following one).

2. Select Format/Tab Ruler/Remove Tab Ruler.

Restoring the Settings of the Page Layout Tab Ruler
At any place in a document you can switch back to the default tab settings (those of the Page Layout tab ruler). When you do this, the tabs of all subsequent text will be determined by the settings of the Page Layout tab ruler, unless you subsequently insert another tab ruler.

The following will restore the settings of the Page Layout tab ruler:

1. Position the text cursor where you want the Page Layout tabs to take effect.

2. Select Format/Tab Ruler/Reset to Page Layout.

CAUTION! *Any tab changes you make in the document beyond the new tab ruler will be to the Page Layout tab ruler itself. Consequently, these changes will affect the tabs of all parts of the document under the control of the Page Layout tab ruler.*

Using Headers and Footers

A *header* is one or more lines of text that appear at the top of each page. Similarly, a *footer* appears at the page bottom. Headers and footers are convenient ways of including document identification as part of each page. For instance, if you're creating a semiannual company report, you could include something like "ABC Corporation 1991 Report" at the top of each page. Headers and footers are also handy places to insert page numbers.

Each document can have only one header and one footer. The text in the header (or footer) is the same on each page, except for page numbers. Figure 3.8 illustrates a footer that contains both descriptive information and the page number.

Figure 3.8
The footer contains the chapter name and the page number

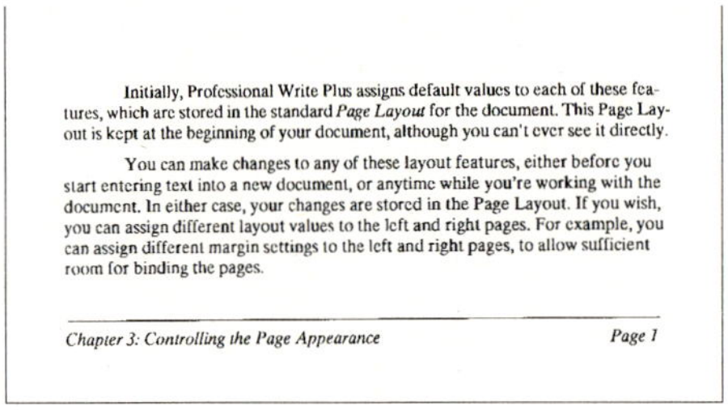
Initially, Professional Write Plus assigns default values to each of these features, which are stored in the standard *Page Layout* for the document. This Page Layout is kept at the beginning of your document, although you can't ever see it directly.

You can make changes to any of these layout features, either before you start entering text into a new document, or anytime while you're working with the document. In either case, your changes are stored in the Page Layout. If you wish, you can assign different layout values to the left and right pages. For example, you can assign different margin settings to the left and right pages, to allow sufficient room for binding the pages.

Chapter 3: Controlling the Page Appearance *Page 1*

You can control the layout of a header or footer using some of the same features available for controlling the overall page layout. For example, you can set the margins and tabs for headers and footers. You can set the font and attributes of header and footer text, and you can also set the alignment and spacing for the lines of text in headers and footers. These features are all set independently from the settings of the main part of the document.

Headers and footers are displayed in the space allocated for the top and bottom page margins. You can assign top, bottom, left, and right margins to a header or footer (see Figure 3.9). The left and right header and footer margins are measured from the left and right page edges, whereas the top and bottom header and footer margins are measured within the *page margin area*, that is, the space between the top or bottom of the page and where the body text begins. For laser printers, the 3/8 inch (approximately, depending on the printer) at the top and bottom of each page isn't used. Therefore, the top margin of a header and the bottom margin of a footer should be set to at least ³/₈ inch for laser printers.

Figure 3.9
Headers and footers

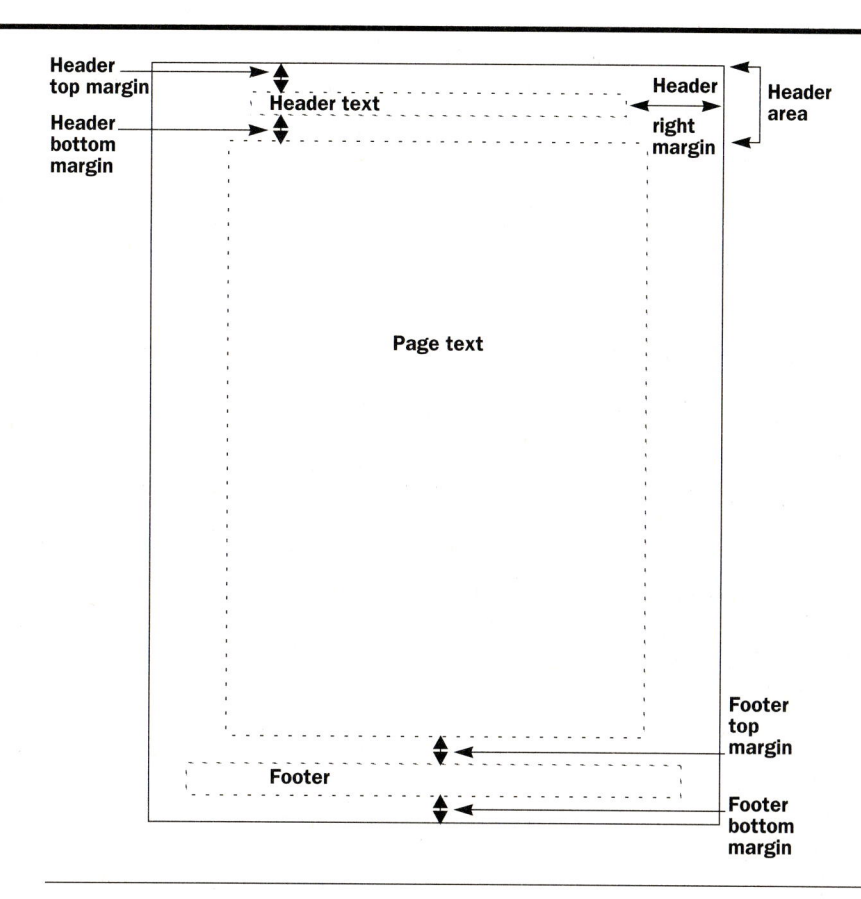

[Diagram showing a page layout with labels: Header top margin, Header text, Header right margin, Header area, Header bottom margin, Page text, Footer top margin, Footer, Footer bottom margin]

Inserting a Header or Footer

To insert a header or footer, you must be in layout mode (headers and footers don't appear on the screen in draft mode). In addition, you can display the program's vertical ruler to help you place the header or footer. To create a header, follow these steps (the steps for creating a footer are almost identical):

1. Make sure that you're in layout mode (if not, switch to that mode using the View menu).

2. Turn on the vertical ruler: Select Options/Layout Mode Options. When the Display Options dialog box appears (Figure 3.10), click on Vertical Ruler, and then click on OK. The vertical ruler will appear on the left side of your screen, as shown in Figure 3.11.

Figure 3.10
The dialog box for turning on the vertical ruler

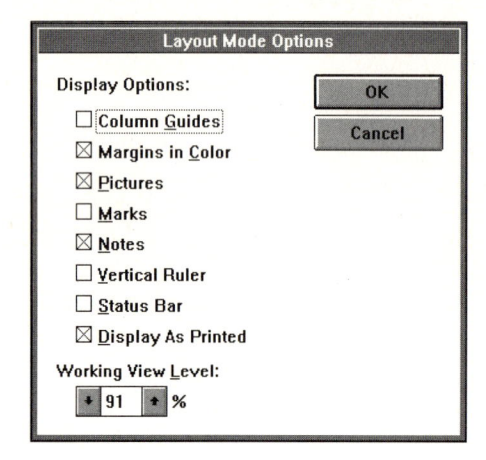

Figure 3.11
The vertical ruler, which helps you adjust different parts of a page

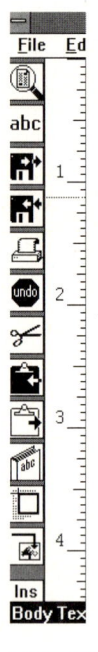

3. Select Format/Page Layout.

4. When the Page Layout dialog box appears, click on Header.

5. In the four Margins boxes, enter values for the left, right, top, and bottom header margins.

6. Set any tabs you want for the header, using the tab ruler in the upper part of the dialog box. (See the preceding section for a discussion of setting tabs; also see the following section for an alternative method.)

7. If you want to assign multiple columns to the header, make your selection in the area near the middle of the dialog box. (See "Selecting the Number of Columns on the Page" later in this chapter.)

8. Click on OK to record your header settings and return to the edit screen. Now you can enter the header text.

9. Using the vertical ruler as a guide, scroll up on *any* page, so that the very top of the text on that page is visible.

10. Drag the mouse cursor into the blank area above the top text line. Then click the mouse button at the very top of that space. Notice how the vertical ruler changes appearance (see Figure 3.12).

Figure 3.12
The space available for the header

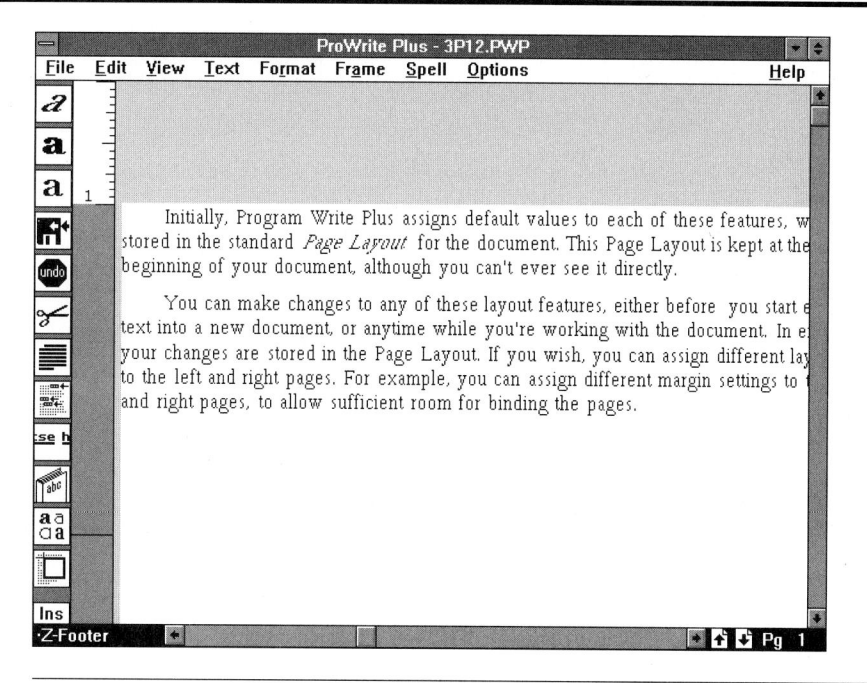

11. Enter the header text. For each new line, press Enter. The total number of lines you can enter will depend on the text size being used in your header and the size of the top margin of the document.

12. When you're finished entering the header or footer text, move the mouse cursor back into the body text, and then click the mouse button. You can then resume normal editing, or you can adjust the layout of the text in the header, as described in the next section.

Remember, you can control the verical position of the header by adjusting the top and bottom header margin.

The vertical ruler (turned on in step 2) is a handy tool for measuring vertical distances on the page. For example, when you click in the margin area (step 10) only the top part of the ruler remains visible, indicating the area that is available for the header.

In step 5, the margins you enter must fall within limits dictated by the size of the top margin. For example, the sum of the top and bottom margins for a header can't be greater than the top margin itself. If you try to enter a margin value that is too large, the program will beep and not let you go on until you correct the error within the edit box.

In step 11, the total number of lines you can enter depends on the size of the top margin and on the font being used. Remember, you can set the font in the header independently of the font in the main body of the document (see the next section).

Another Way to Set Header and Footer Tabs

Instead of using the Page Layout dialog box, you can use the tab ruler on the edit screen to adjust the tabs in a header or footer. Here's how:

1. Click on any part of the header or footer. The tab ruler will then show the current tab settings for the header or footer.

2. Make the desired changes to the tabs. These will affect only the header or footer.

3. When you've finished, click on any part of the main text.

Adjusting the Appearance of a Header or Footer

Regardless of where you are in the document, you can change the margins and tabs for a header or footer. Simply display the Page Layout dialog box, click on Header or Footer, and make your changes. You can also use the tab ruler to change the tabs, as described above.

In addition to assigning layout features such as margins and tabs to a header or footer, you can assign different fonts and text attributes to all or

◆ **Working with Tabs** 77

part of the text in a header or footer. You can also adjust the alignment and spacing of selected text lines.

To adjust any of these elements, first select the text to be adjusted in the header or footer. Then use the same menu selections you would for making the adjustments to text in the main body.

For example, to set the font for all or part of a header or footer, select the desired text as a block, click on Text/Font, and then select the font you want.

You can perform any of these operations on a header or footer from any page in your document: Simply move the mouse cursor into the header or footer area on that page, and then make your changes. The changes will affect the headers or footers on every page.

Example: A Three-Element Footer

You can control the exact placement of the various elements that make up a header or footer. As an example, Figure 3.13 shows a footer consisting of three parts:

- Chapter number, starting at the left margin

- Chapter title, centered on the page

- Page number, right-aligned

Figure 3.13
A three-part footer

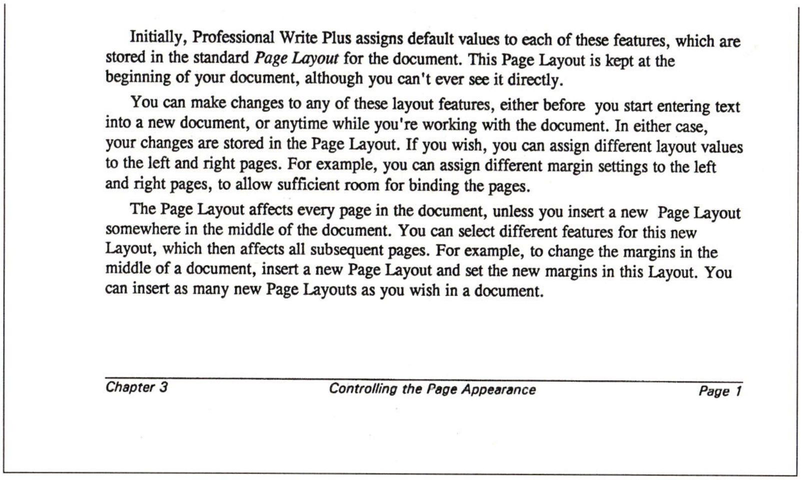

> Initially, Professional Write Plus assigns default values to each of these features, which are stored in the standard *Page Layout* for the document. This Page Layout is kept at the beginning of your document, although you can't ever see it directly.
>
> You can make changes to any of these layout features, either before you start entering text into a new document, or anytime while you're working with the document. In either case, your changes are stored in the Page Layout. If you wish, you can assign different layout values to the left and right pages. For example, you can assign different margin settings to the left and right pages, to allow sufficient room for binding the pages.
>
> The Page Layout affects every page in the document, unless you insert a new Page Layout somewhere in the middle of the document. You can select different features for this new Layout, which then affects all subsequent pages. For example, to change the margins in the middle of a document, insert a new Page Layout and set the new margins in this Layout. You can insert as many new Page Layouts as you wish in a document.

Chapter 3   *Controlling the Page Appearance*   *Page 1*

Here are the steps for creating this footer:

1. To begin, insert two tabs for the footer.

- A *center tab,* centered horizontally on the page. (For example, if the left and right margins are 1 inch each, this tab should be positioned at 4.75 inches.)
- A *right tab,* positioned against the right margin

Now you can insert the text for the footer.

2. Click in the footer area on any page. If you don't want the footer to begin on the first line, press Enter to position the cursor at the beginning of the line you want. Or, you can adjust the vertical position of the footer by changing its top margin.

3. Enter the chapter number, then press Tab.

4. Enter the chapter title, then press Tab again.

5. Enter the page number specification (see the following section).

Editing Headers and Footers

Although headers and footers don't normally appear in draft mode, you can edit them in either layout or draft mode. To edit in draft mode, click on any part of the header or footer, then switch to draft mode. Only the header or footer text will be displayed, and it can then be edited. To edit a header or footer in layout mode, click in the header or footer area and then edit as usual.

Numbering Your Pages

Page numbers can be placed in either the header or footer area. You can include the page numbering as part of any other text in a header or footer, and you can include special preceding text, such as "Page number," as part of the page numbering. You can also select from several different numbering styles, including upper- or lowercase Roman numerals, conventional Arabic numbering, or upper- or lowercase letters. Notice that in this context, letters can be used as "numbers" (A, B, C, . . . instead of 1, 2, 3, . . .).

You can select the page on which to start numbering, and you can also select the starting number for that page. For example, for a report with a cover page you could start printing page numbers on the second page, calling it page 1.

The appearance of page numbers, as well as their alignment, can be controlled. For instance, you can italicize the page numbers, keeping the rest of the header or footer as ordinary text. You can center page numbers, or align them against the left or right margin.

You can also set up more than one page numbering scheme at the same time. For example, you could have numbering in Arabic at the top of each

Numbering Your Pages

page and numbering in Roman numerals at the bottom. (Don't ask why you'd want to do this, but the option is there.) You can't, however, change the numbering scheme in a header or footer in the middle of a document.

Here's how to include page numbering in a document:

1. Make sure that you're in layout mode (page numbers won't display on the screen in draft mode).

2. Move the text cursor to wherever you want page numbers to appear in the header or footer area, using the vertical ruler as a guide. If you plan to justify the page numbers (left, right, or center), position the cursor at the *left end* of the line where the numbers will appear. If you want the numbers to appear at a particular tab, press Tab to move the cursor to that setting. Remember, the tabs for headers and footers are both independent of the tabs for the main body of a document.

3. Select Edit/Page Numbering. The Page Number dialog box, shown in Figure 3.14, will appear. The number appearing in the bottom part of the box indicates the current page number, assuming that numbering starts at 1 on the first page of the document. As you select the various page numbering options, the box at the bottom indicates how the numbers will appear.

Figure 3.14
The dialog box for turning on page numbering

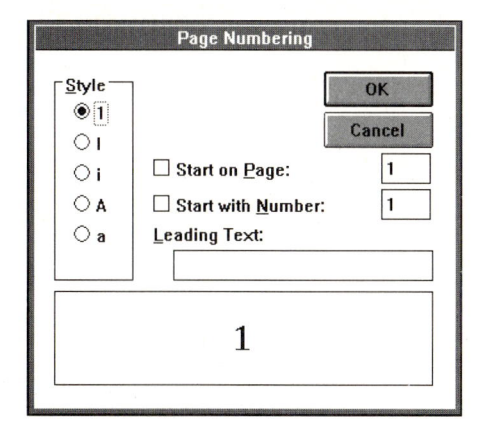

4. Select the numbering style you want from the Style box by clicking on the appropriate button. For example, if you click on the box labeled I, the page numbers will appear as uppercase Roman numerals.

5. If you want numbering to start on a page other than the first, click on the option labeled "Start on Page," and then enter the appropriate number in the edit box to the right.

6. If you want to start numbering with a number other than 1, click on Start with Number, then enter the appropriate number in the edit box to the right.

7. If you want to include any preceding text as part of the page numbers, enter that text in the Leading Text edit box (30 characters maximum).

8. Click on OK.

Formatting the Page Numbers

Note. When you select a page number as a block, any preceding text (assigned in the Page Number dialog box) is automatically included as part of that block.

You can set the font and attributes of page numbers just as you do ordinary text. To make these types of changes, scroll up or down *on any page* until the page number is visible in the header or footer. Then select the page number as a block and make your changes.

To select a different font for page numbers, select the page number as a block, select Font from the Text menu, and then select the desired font. To assign a special attribute such as boldface to the page numbers, select the page number as a block, and then select the attribute you want from the Text menu.

To center the page numbers or place them next to either margin, select the page number as a block, select Alignment from the Text menu, and then select the alignment you want (Left, Center, or Right). Remember, if you plan to align the page numbers, first place the page numbers at the left end—making sure there is no other text (including blanks) on the line—and then assign the alignment.

Editing and Deleting Page Numbers

You can delete any page numbering you've assigned. For example, you might decide to place the numbers somewhere else on the page, or you might decide that you don't want page numbers at all. To delete your page numbering, follow these steps:

1. Scroll up or down *on any page* until the header or footer containing the page number is visible.

2. Select the page number as a block.

3. Delete the block.

If, for some reason, you've included page numbers in more than one place on each page (perhaps once in the header and once in the footer), only the page numbering corresponding to your deletion will be removed from the document.

You can't edit a particular page numbering once you've assigned it. So if you want to change the page numbers in any way, you must delete the original numbering and then create new page numbers.

Selecting the Number of Columns on the Page

The majority of your documents will probably be generated using one column to the page, which is the default set by Professional Write Plus whenever you start a new document. However, you can also create documents with up to eight columns on each page. Combined with the program's graphics features, you can use multiple columns to generate various types of newsletters, brochures, announcements, and so on. Figure 3.15 illustrates a document with a two-column layout.

Figure 3.15
A two-column page layout

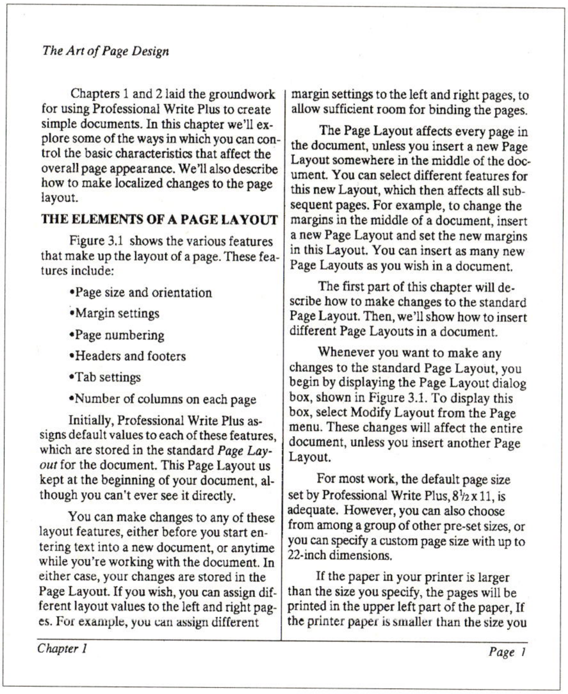

The Art of Page Design

Chapters 1 and 2 laid the groundwork for using Professional Write Plus to create simple documents. In this chapter we'll explore some of the ways in which you can control the basic characteristics that affect the overall page appearance. We'll also describe how to make localized changes to the page layout.

THE ELEMENTS OF A PAGE LAYOUT

Figure 3.1 shows the various features that make up the layout of a page. These features include:

- •Page size and orientation
- •Margin settings
- •Page numbering
- •Headers and footers
- •Tab settings
- •Number of columns on each page

Initially, Professional Write Plus assigns default values to each of these features, which are stored in the standard *Page Layout* for the document. This Page Layout us kept at the beginning of your document, although you can't ever see it directly.

You can make changes to any of these layout features, either before you start entering text into a new document, or anytime while you're working with the document. In either case, your changes are stored in the Page Layout. If you wish, you can assign different layout values to the left and right pages. For example, you can assign different margin settings to the left and right pages, to allow sufficient room for binding the pages.

The Page Layout affects every page in the document, unless you insert a new Page Layout somewhere in the middle of the document. You can select different features for this new Layout, which then affects all subsequent pages. For example, to change the margins in the middle of a document, insert a new Page Layout and set the new margins in this Layout. You can insert as many new Page Layouts as you wish in a document.

The first part of this chapter will describe how to make changes to the standard Page Layout. Then, we'll show how to insert different Page Layouts in a document.

Whenever you want to make any changes to the standard Page Layout, you begin by displaying the Page Layout dialog box, shown in Figure 3.1. To display this box, select Modify Layout from the Page menu. These changes will affect the entire document, unless you insert another Page Layout.

For most work, the default page size set by Professional Write Plus, 8½ x 11, is adequate. However, you can also choose from among a group of other pre-set sizes, or you can specify a custom page size with up to 22-inch dimensions.

If the paper in your printer is larger than the size you specify, the pages will be printed in the upper left part of the paper, If the printer paper is smaller than the size you

Chapter 1 *Page 1*

This feature has limited use, because it requires that all pages have the same number of columns. However, you can obtain more column flexibility by using the program's Frames feature. This is discussed in Chapters 10 and 11.

You can create a layout in which all the columns are the same width, but you can also create a layout with varying column widths, as well as with different amounts of space, called *gutters*, separating the columns.

To create a page layout with more than one column, follow these steps:

1. Display the Page Layout dialog box. As you select the number of columns, gutter width, and other aspects of the column design, the box at the lower-right of this dialog box displays a picture of your page layout.

2. Select the number of columns you want by clicking on the appropriate box (you can select a number from 1 to 8).

3. In the Gutter Width edit box, enter the amount of space (in inches) you want between columns.

4. To adjust the widths of individual columns or change the spacing between the columns, move the corresponding margin markers on the tab ruler at the top of the dialog box (see the discussion that follows).

5. Set any tabs you want in each of the columns, using the tab ruler (see the discussion that follows).

6. To equalize the height of the columns on the last page of the document, click on the Column Balance option.

7. To draw lines between the columns, click on Lines (in the box labeled Modify), then click on Line Between Columns. In the box to the right of this option, click on the line thickness you want drawn. (You'll need to do a bit of experimenting to find the right thickness.) To assign a color to the lines, click on your selection in the line labeled "Color." You'll also need to experiment to determine which colors will print with your printer.

8. Click on OK to return to the edit screen.

When you select multiple columns, all the columns are initially assigned the same width, so that they all fit within the left and right margins. Also, the tab ruler in the Page Layout dialog box will display the following:

- The left and right margin positions for each column
- The tab settings selected by the program

Note. You can't adjust the column margins on the edit screen tab ruler. You must use the ruler on the Page Layout dialog box.

Tabs are automatically assigned only to the first column. You'll have to assign any others yourself.

You can change the width of a particular column (step 4) by manipulating the left or right margin symbol for that column within the Page Layout tab ruler. As usual, you can't drag either margin past a tab setting or another margin. So to widen one column, you must first make another one narrower.

As you change the width of a column, you're also changing the spacing between that column and the adjacent ones. In fact, this is the only way you can adjust the gutters individually.

In step 5, you can add, delete, or move tabs in the columns by using the techniques described earlier in this chapter.

Drawing Lines Around Pages

You can draw lines around any or all of the page edges in your document. These lines can be drawn at the page margins, at the very edges of the page, or at various locations in between. For example, in Figure 3.15, a line is drawn at the bottom margin, separating the footer from the rest of the text on the page.

You can select the thickness of each line, within limits, and if you have a color monitor or printer, you can even display or print the lines in various colors. As with other types of page layout features, lines are displayed on the screen in layout mode but not in draft mode. Here are the steps for drawing lines on each page:

1. Display the Page Layout dialog box.

2. Click on Lines (in the box labeled Modify). The dialog box will change (see Figure 3.16). As you make your selections, the little figure in the lower-right part of the dialog box indicates where the lines will be positioned.

Figure 3.16
The dialog box for selecting the lines to be drawn

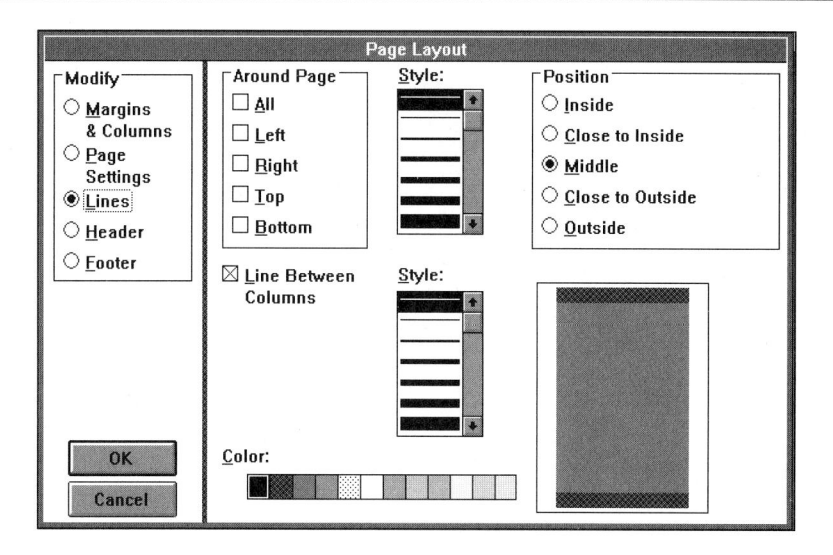

3. In the box labeled "Around Page," select where you want the lines to be drawn. You can select any combination of edges, or all of them.

4. Select the line thickness or pattern you want by clicking on your choice in the Style box to the right of the Around Page box. You may need to do a bit of experimenting when selecting a line thickness because when printed, the lines may look quite different from those that appear on your screen.

5. Select the position of the lines by clicking on your choice in the Position box. You have these choices:

   - Inside—on the page margins
   - Close to Inside—slightly outside the margins
   - Middle—midway between the margins and the page edges
   - Close to Outside—near the outer page edges
   - Outside—at the outer edges of the page

6. If you're using a color monitor or printer, select the color of the lines by clicking on your choice at the bottom of the dialog box. (Note that this color will also be used for lines separating page columns.)

Summary

Using the various features described in this chapter, you can customize the appearance of your documents in many different ways. You should now be equipped to create very attractive documents, but you still haven't begun to tap Professional Write Plus's more advanced features. Before tackling these items, however, in the next chapter you'll learn the techniques for manipulating the various types of files you can use in connection with Professional Write Plus. These include not only the files you create with the program, but also files from other software packages.

CHAPTER 4

Sophisticated Editing Features

Checking Your Spelling

Using the Thesaurus

Finding and Replacing Words

Adding Notes to Your Document

Using a Document Description

Jumping to Different Parts of a Document

Recovering from Accidents

Using Insert Variables

Checking Your Spelling

THE PREVIOUS CHAPTERS HAVE DESCRIBED MANY OF THE BASIC EDITING features you can use when working with documents. In addition to those features, Professional Write Plus contains many other editing aids that can enhance your word processing skills.

Using a built-in dictionary of 130,000 words, the spell checker allows you to check the spelling of part or all of a document, or to verify the spelling of a single word. You can use the built-in thesaurus to check for alternatives to 40,000 key words, and with it you can instantly find synonyms to just about any word you can think of.

The Find & Replace feature allows you to locate each occurrence of a word or phrase within a document and replace it with something else. This extremely useful feature even allows you to search for words whose spelling you're not sure of. You can also use it to insert customized bookmarks anywhere in a document. To complement Find & Replace, the Go To feature allows you to jump to various parts of a document, such as the current tab ruler, the next frame, and so on.

In addition to these powerful features, Professional Write Plus contains two others which help you to record information *about* a document. The first of these allows you to insert notes anywhere in a document; these are the electronic equivalent of the sticky-backed Post-it notes. They don't print along with the rest of a document, but whenever you run across one in the text you can pop it up to display its contents. Another useful aid is the document description, which you can save as part of a file. You can use document descriptions to help locate a particular document. This is a great enhancement to the eight-character limit imposed by the computer's operating system on file names.

One of the program's most useful features is called Undo. It can help you recover from the inevitable accidents that happen when you're working with a powerful word processor. For example, you can quickly restore a block of text you accidentally erase.

Finally, Professional Write Plus maintains a group of memory values, called *insert variables*. They contain a variety of useful values, such as the current date, which you can insert as part of the text anywhere in a document.

Checking Your Spelling

With the built-in spell checker, you can browse through part or all of a document for misspelled words, or you can check the spelling of a single word. The spell checker, which works in conjunction with Professional Write Plus's on-line dictionary, operates much faster in draft mode than in layout mode. Because of this, the program enables you to set a default so that the program will switch automatically to draft mode whenever you spell check an entire

Note. The speller is also capable of using other language dictionaries. However, as of this writing only the American dictionary, which comes with the program, is available.

document and then automatically switch back to the original mode when you're done. (For information on setting defaults, see Appendix B.)

If you frequently use special words that aren't included in the main dictionary, you can include them in a "personal" dictionary. Then, when you check the spelling of a document or a single word, both dictionaries will be used. In addition, you can edit this personal dictionary, much as you would an ordinary document, to add new words or delete unwanted ones.

In addition to the main body of text, a document can contain other text areas (referred to by Professional Write Plus as *associated text*), any of which can be spell checked. These are headers, footers, footnotes, and frames. (A frame is an area within a page that's treated as a separate item. For more information, see Chapters 10 and 11.)

You can spell check the text in any one of these areas separately. For example, to spell check the text in a footer, move the text cursor there and then invoke the spell checker. If the cursor is positioned within the main body text, you can either spell check the text alone, or include in the check all the associated text in the document.

When the spell checker encounters a questionable word, it searches its dictionaries and lists possible alternatives. You can then do one of the following:

- Replace the word with one of the alternatives listed on the screen

- Replace every occurrence of the word in the document with one of the listed alternatives

- Add the word to the personal dictionary

- Leave the word as is

- Leave all occurrences of the word as is

In addition, if a double word (the same word twice in a row) is encountered during a spelling check, you're given the option of deleting one of them.

Spell Checking a Word or Block

Note. To check the spelling of a single word, it's not enough to place the text cursor on it. You must select that word as a block, or the program will assume that you want to spell check all or part of the document.

You can check the spelling of either an individual word or a group of consecutive words. These words can be within the main body of text, or they can be part of the associated text (footer, header, frame, and so on). Here are the steps to spell check a word or a block:

1. To check the spelling of a single word, select it by double-clicking on it with the mouse button. To check the spelling of a group of consecutive words, select them as a block.

2. Select Spell/Spelling.

3. If all the selected words are found in the spelling dictionaries, you'll see the following message:

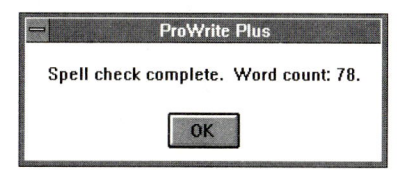

> **ProWrite Plus**
>
> Spell check complete. Word count: 78.
>
> [OK]

You can then click on OK and continue with your editing.

4. If a selected word is not found in a dictionary, or if a double word is found, you'll have to decide what to do about the word. (See the section "Handling Questionable Words" later on in this chapter.)

Spell Checking Larger Portions of a Document

You can spell check either the entire document or that part of it beyond the current text cursor position. The associated text can be included in the check if you wish. You can also confine a spell check to a particular part of the associated text. For example, you might have imported into a frame a block of text from a different file and would like to spell check that text.

To spell check either the main body of text or a particular part of the associated text, follow these steps:

1. Position the text cursor somewhere within the part of the text you want to spell check. If you want to spell check only that part of the text beyond the cursor, position the cursor immediately to the left of the first word you want to include in the check.

2. Select Spell/Spelling, and the Spelling dialog box will appear:

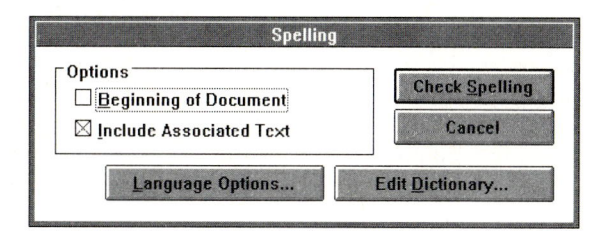

> **Spelling**
>
> Options
> ☐ Beginning of Document
> ☒ Include Associated Text
>
> [Check Spelling]
> [Cancel]
>
> [Language Options...]   [Edit Dictionary...]

3. To spell check an entire document, click on Beginning of Document. Otherwise, spell checking will include text from the current position of the text cursor to the end of the document.

4. To spell check the associated text along with the main body text, click on Include Associated Text.

5. To begin the spell check, click on Check Spelling.

Handling Questionable Words

Regardless of which part of your document you are spell checking, you'll eventually come up with a questionable word—one that can't be found in either of the dictionaries or a double word encountered in the text. Whenever a questionable word is encountered during spell checking, the word is flagged, the spell checker pauses, and you must decide what to do about the word.

Possible Misspellings

If the spell checker comes across a word that's not in either dictionary, the word is flagged and the dialog box shown in Figure 4.1 is displayed. This box includes a list of possible alternatives to the word in question.

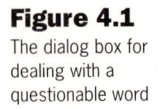

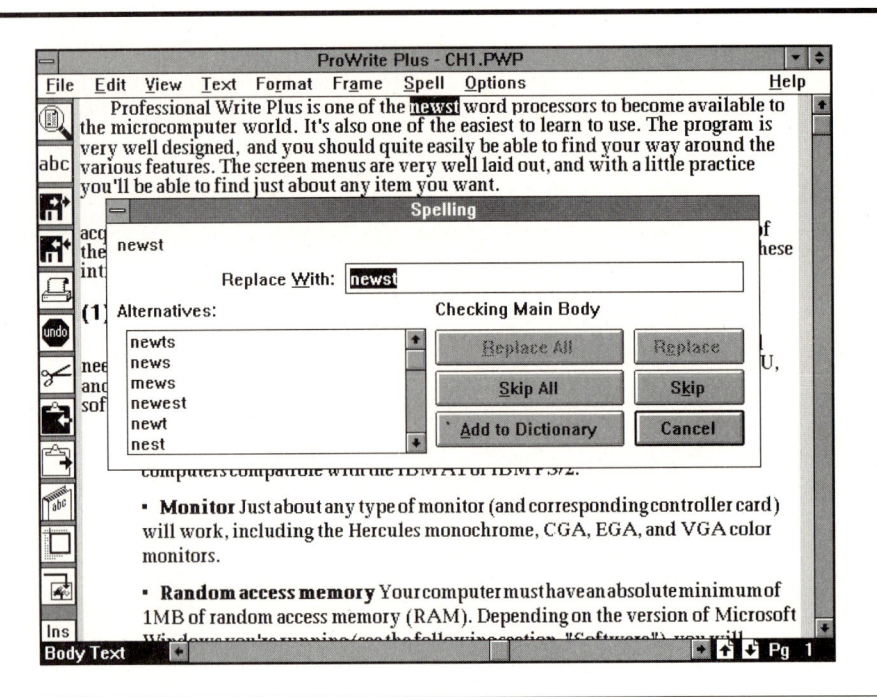

Figure 4.1
The dialog box for dealing with a questionable word

You then have the following options.

- Replace the flagged word with one in the displayed list: Double-click on that word in the list, or click once on that word and then click on Replace.

- Replace every occurrence of the flagged word in the remaining text with a word in the displayed list: Click on the word you want, and then click on Replace All.

- Replace the flagged word with another of your choice: Enter the new word in the Replace With edit box, and then click on either Replace or Replace All, depending on whether you want to replace just the flagged word or every occurrence of that word. If you enter a word that is itself questionable, both the Replace and Replace All options are "grayed out" or dimmed—that is, they are not available.

- Leave the flagged word as it is: Click on Skip.

- Leave untouched every occurrence of the word in the remaining text: Click on Skip All. Note that this feature is *case-sensitive*—only occurrences capitalized exactly like the word you entered will be skipped.

- Leave the word as it is and add it to the personal dictionary: Select Add to Dictionary.

- Abort the spell checking: Click on Cancel.

After you decide what to do about a flagged word, the spell checking goes on until all the selected text has been scanned. A final word count is then displayed for your inspection. You can then click on OK and carry on with your editing.

Double Words

If the spell checker encounters a double word, the second word of the pair is highlighted, and an informative message is displayed:

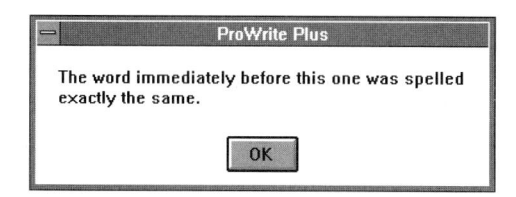

```
┌─────────────────────────────────────┐
│           ProWrite Plus             │
├─────────────────────────────────────┤
│ The word immediately before this one was spelled │
│ exactly the same.                   │
│                                     │
│              ┌────┐                 │
│              │ OK │                 │
│              └────┘                 │
└─────────────────────────────────────┘
```

Click on OK, and you'll see a dialog box similar to that shown in Figure 4.1. You can then do one of the following:

- Leave the double word as is: Click on Skip (or Skip All for all occurrences).

- Delete the flagged word from the text: Delete the word from the Replace With edit box (press Del), and then click on Replace.

- Replace the flagged word with an alternative: Enter the new word in the Replace With edit box, and then click on Replace.

Checking for Capitalization

In spell checking, each word in the text is compared with both the main dictionary and the personal dictionary. Also, both the spelling and the capitalization are checked against that in the dictionaries. Most words in the main dictionary are in lowercase, but a few special words are capitalized, such as proper names. For instance, the dictionary contains an entry for *America* but not for *america*.

If a spelling match is found, and if that dictionary entry is *all lowercase*, the text word is considered to be correctly spelled provided that either of the following is true:

- The text word is either all uppercase or all lowercase.
- The first letter of the text word is capitalized.

If the text word is capitalized in any other way, it will be flagged as questionable.

If a spelling match is found, but the dictionary entry is capitalized in any way, the text word is considered to be correctly spelled only if either of the following is true:

- The text word matches the capitalization of the dictionary entry.
- The entire text word is capitalized.

There's one exception to the preceding rules: If a dictionary entry is completely capitalized, a text word will be accepted as correct if it's spelled in either all uppercase or all lowercase. Table 4.1 illustrates these points with a few examples.

Editing the Personal Dictionary

The personal dictionary is kept in a file with the imposing name of VEAM-AB51.LEX. It's stored in the same directory as the other Professional Write Plus files, and initially it's empty. This dictionary can be useful for those words you use frequently, but that aren't included in the main dictionary. For example, you could include the following:

- Proper nouns, such as personal names, streets, and cities
- Technical terms that are too specialized to be in a standard dictionary
- Acronyms
- Slang words

Table 4.1   Spell Check Examples

Main Dictionary Entry	Word in Text	Word Correct?
automobile	automobile	Yes
automobile	Automobile	Yes
automobile	AUTOMOBILE	Yes
automobile	autoMobile	No
America	America	Yes
America	america	No
America	AMERICA	Yes
AMERICA	America	No
AMERICA	america	Yes

You can add new words to this dictionary by clicking on Add to Dictionary when the Spell Check dialog box is displayed, or you can edit this dictionary directly, just as you would an ordinary document, by adding and deleting whatever words you like. Here are the steps for working directly with the personal dictionary:

1. Save your current document.
2. Select Spell/Spelling/Edit Dictionary, and the contents of the personal dictionary will appear on the screen.
3. Add and delete any words you wish.
4. When you're finished editing, select File/Save.

When the contents of the dictionary appear on the screen, capitalized words are listed first, alphabetically, followed by lowercase words, as shown here:

```
Aflatoxinitis
DBMS
Del
Peritonitis
Professional Write Plus
Samna
```

```
WordPerfect
aflatoxin
online
pathname
sulfanilamide
```

When you are adding words, be very careful to follow these rules:

- Add only one entry per line, followed by a hard return. An entry can be a single word or a group of words, such as a proper name.

- Don't add any extra spaces to the word, either before or after.

- Capitalize each word the way it normally appears. For example, the first letter of a proper name is normally capitalized.

You can add words to the dictionary in any order you wish. When you save the file, the words are automatically rearranged as shown above.

Using the Thesaurus

Sometimes when you're creating a new document, you know what you want to say but you don't like the word you've chosen to say it. Like many other word processors, Professional Write Plus has a handy built-in writing aid that can help you: the *thesaurus*. Professional Write Plus's thesaurus has access to approximately 470,000 words, based on 40,000 root words.

To use the thesaurus, simply position the text cursor anywhere on the word in question (you don't need to select the entire word as a block) and then select Spell/Thesaurus. A dialog box like the one shown in Figure 4.2 will appear, including a list of alternative words. You can then either replace the word in question with one of these alternatives or search further into the thesaurus for other possible substitutes.

There are a number of parts to this dialog box:

- Underneath "Word Looked Up," the word you want a synonym for appears. Initially, this is the word you selected in your text.

- The Meaning Variations list box contains words that represent different meanings for the original word.

- Each word in the Synonyms list box is a synonym for the highlighted word in the Meaning Variations box.

- Initially, the word in Replace With edit box is the same word that's highlighted in the Synonyms box. However, you can enter any word you wish in this box.

Figure 4.2
The dialog box for selecting alternate words

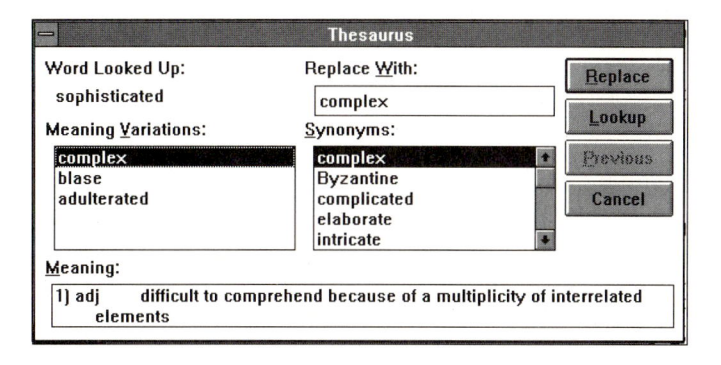

```
┌─ Thesaurus ─────────────────────────────────┐
│ Word Looked Up:      Replace With:          │
│   sophisticated        complex              │  [ Replace ]
│ Meaning Variations:  Synonyms:              │  [ Lookup  ]
│  ┌──────────────┐   ┌──────────────┐        │
│  │ complex      │   │ complex    ↑ │        │  [ Previous ]
│  │ blase        │   │ Byzantine    │        │
│  │ adulterated  │   │ complicated  │        │  [ Cancel  ]
│  │              │   │ elaborate    │        │
│  │              │   │ intricate  ↓ │        │
│  └──────────────┘   └──────────────┘        │
│ Meaning:                                    │
│  ┌──────────────────────────────────────┐   │
│  │ 1) adj   difficult to comprehend because of a multiplicity of interrelated │
│  │          elements                    │   │
│  └──────────────────────────────────────┘   │
└─────────────────────────────────────────────┘
```

- Selecting Replace replaces the original word with the one currently in the Replace With edit box.

- Use the Lookup option to find synonyms for the word currently in the Replace With edit box. When you select this option, another search is made of the thesaurus, and a new set of words appears in the dialog box.

- Selecting the Previous option restores the previous display in the dialog box. This is useful if you've been looking for synonyms of a synonym and want to thread your way back to an earlier word that appealed to you. This option is dimmed until you look up a synonym of a synonym.

- The Meaning box gives a brief description of the word highlighted in the Meaning Variations box. It also lists whether the word is a noun, verb, and so on.

The following is a description of how to proceed when the Thesaurus dialog box appears. (Some of the words that appear in this box may seem pretty far afield from the original word, but then there's no accounting for the mind of a thesaurus.)

1. In the Meaning Variations list box, click on the word that's closest to the intent of the original word. The synonyms for that word will then appear in the Synonyms box.

2. If you see a suitable replacement word (in the Synonyms box) for the original word, click on it and then click on Replace. This word will then replace the original word in the text.

3. If you want to search for other possible synonyms, highlight the word in the Synonyms box that's closest to the meaning you have in mind, and then click on Lookup. The possible meanings for that word will then appear in the

Note. You can continue to edit while the Synonyms edit box is displayed. Just click anywhere in the text (or press Alt-F6) and then carry on with your editing.

Meaning Variations list box, and a new set of synonyms will appear in the Synonyms box. You can carry on with this procedure as long as you wish.

4. To back up to the previous list of synonyms, click on Previous.

If at some point in your search you think of a word that's close to what you have in mind, enter it in the Replace With edit box and then click on Lookup. The possible meanings for that word will appear in the Meaning Variations box, and a list of synonyms will appear in the Synonyms box.

Finding and Replacing Words

The Find & Replace feature is a very useful one to have at your fingertips for performing two different types of operations:

- Searching for each occurrence of a particular *search string*, which can be a whole word, a phrase, a part of a word, or an arbitrary group of characters.

- Replacing each occurrence of a search string with a *replacement string* of your choice. For example, you could replace "the cars" with "the automobiles" everywhere in a document.

You can search for every occurrence of a string either with capitalization matching what you specify or with any capitalization. You can also search for a string that has been assigned one or more text attributes. For example, you might want to locate only those occurrences of "big bad wolf" that are boldfaced, and ignore any other occurrences.

You can also specify that the replacement string be assigned particular text attributes. For example, you could replace each occurrence of "**big bad wolf**" with "*Little Red Riding Hood*".

The capitalization of the replacement word can be the same as that of the original string, or you can specify how you want the replacement string to be capitalized. For instance, you could replace each occurrence of "The Old Testament" with either "The Good Book" or "the good book".

Note. You can also use the Find & Replace feature to locate and replace paragraph styles. This topic is discussed in Chapter 7.

When performing find-and-replace operations, you can have all replacements done automatically, or you can verify or reject each individual replacement. You can begin a find-and-replace operation from the current position of the text cursor or from the beginning of the document, and you can search either forward or backward in the text. You can optionally include in the search associated text (footers, headers, footnotes, and frames). Alternatively, you can confine a search just to a particular part of the associated text, such as the contents of a single frame.

Finding a Word or Group of Words

As already mentioned, you can search for a word, a group of words, or any arbitrary group of characters. Let's first see how to find a word or group of words, since it's the simplest type of search to make. You enter the word or group of words you want to locate, and the program will find the first occurrence of that string, provided it exists. You can then optionally look for additional occurrences of the same string.

In the following simple example, you don't have to specify the exact capitalization of the words you want to locate. The search will locate the word or words regardless of how they are capitalized. Here are the steps for locating a word or group of words:

1. Position the text cursor where you want the search to begin. If you plan to search the entire document, you don't need to move the cursor from wherever it is.

2. Select Edit/Find & Replace, and the dialog box shown in Figure 4.3 will appear.

Figure 4.3
The dialog box for entering the word(s) you want to locate

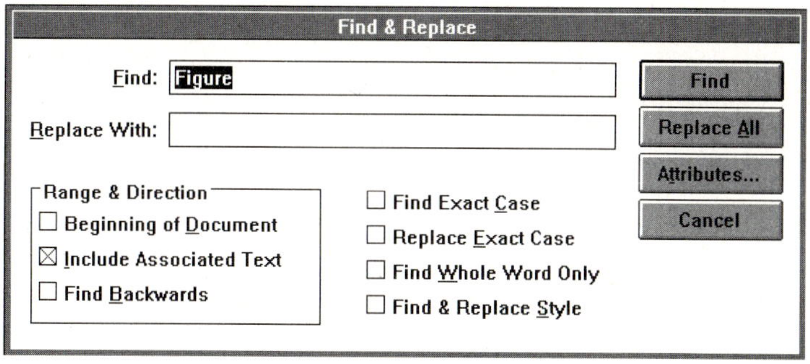

3. In the Find edit box, enter the word or words you want to find.

4. Click on Find Whole Words Only, then click on Find.

5. If the word is found, it will be highlighted. Also, the dialog box shown in Figure 4.4 will appear, and you then can click on either of the following options:

- Click on Find Next to look for the next occurrence of the word.
- Click on Cancel to terminate the search.

Figure 4.4
The dialog box for continuing or canceling the search operation

[Find & Replace dialog: Finding: Figure / Replacing With: / Checking Main Body / Buttons: Replace & Find Next, Find Next, Cancel]

CAUTION! *Don't select Replace & Find Next, or the word that was found will be deleted! If you do accidentally delete a word in this manner, select Edit/ Undo to restore the deleted text.*

Finding a String

You can also search for any group of consecutive characters. This could be part of a word or just a selection of characters that you happen to know exists somewhere in the document. (For a useful application of this technique, refer to "Creating Bookmarks" later in this chapter.) Here are the steps for finding any character string:

Note. You can search for *any* group of consecutive characters, including special characters and blanks.

1. As in the preceding example, position the text cursor and then display the dialog box shown in Figure 4.3.

2. In the Find edit box, enter the character string you want to find.

3. Make sure that the option Find Whole Word Only is *not* selected. If it is, click on it so that the X disappears from the box.

4. Click on Find. The search will now proceed, stopping at the first occurrence of the string you specified.

Specifying Text Attributes and Capitalization

In the preceding examples, capitalization was ignored during the searches, as were text attributes such as boldface and underlining. However, you can optionally specify the capitalization of the string you want to locate. You can also assign one or more text attributes to the search string. In either case, only those strings in the document that exactly conform to your specifications will be considered matches. Any others, even if they're spelled the same, will be ignored during the search.

To specify capitalization as part of a search, follow these steps:

1. Position the text cursor where you want the search to begin, and then display the Find & Replace dialog box (Figure 4.3).

Finding and Replacing Words

2. In the Find edit box, enter the search string you want to locate. Include the exact capitalization as part of the spelling.

3. Click on Find Exact Case.

4. Click on Find. The first occurrence of the string that conforms to your spelling and capitalization will be highlighted.

If you do not select Find Exact Case, then the search will completely ignore capitalization and find all instances of the word.

To help you understand how searches involving capitalization work, Table 4.2 shows the outcomes of various types of searches.

Table 4.2   Searching With and Without Specifying the Find Exact Case Option

Is Find Exact Case Specified?	Specified Word	Word in Text	Does Word Match?
No	Alpha	alpha	Yes
Yes	Alpha	alpha	No
Yes	Alpha	Alpha	Yes
No	alpha	Alpha	Yes
Yes	alpha	Alpha	No

You can also specify text attributes as part of a search. For example, you can search for occurrences of "**cat**", ignoring any occurrences that are not boldfaced. To include text attributes as part of a search, follow these steps:

1. Enter the string you want to search for, as described earlier.

2. Click on Attributes to display the dialog box shown in Figure 4.5.

3. In the Find & Replace Attributes box, click on each attribute you want to specify as part of the search. For example, if you want to find only boldfaced words, click on Bold. If you click on Normal, only words with no assigned attributes will be found.

4. Click on the Find Exact Attributes option.

5. Click on OK, then click on Find when the original dialog box reappears.

Because you select the Find Exact Attributes option, only those strings that have the exact attributes specified in the Find Attributes box will be found. If you do not select Find Exact Attributes, then each string that's found will have the attributes you specify, but may have others as well. For example, suppose you want to find all the boldfaced occurrences of the word "cat." If you click on the bold attribute, but you don't select Find Exact Attributes, any occurrences of "cat" (no boldface) will be ignored. All occurrences of "**cat**" will be found, but so will any occurrences of "*cat*" (boldface and italic). On the other hand, if you do select Find Exact Attributes, then all occurrences of "**cat**" will be found, and any occurrences of "*cat*" will be ignored.

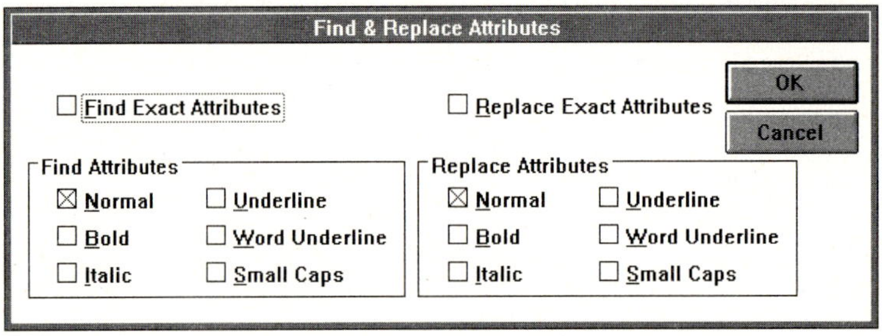

Figure 4.5
The dialog box for including attributes in a search

To help clarify this point, Table 4.3 lists the outcomes of various searches.

Other Search Options

The Find & Replace dialog box, shown in Figure 4.3, contains three additional options, in the Range and Direction box, that can be useful during search operations:

- Select the Beginning of Document option, and the search will begin at the top of your document. Otherwise, the search starts at the current position of the text cursor (which could, of course, be at the beginning of the document).

- The Include Associated Text option allows you to extend the search to footers, headers, footnotes, and frames in the document. This option applies only when your search is in the main text body. For example, if the cursor is located in a footer when you display the Find & Replace dialog box, this option is not available. (You can, however, search *within* a header or footer, frame or footnote. Just position the text cursor there and then perform the search—it will be confined to that area.)

- Select the Find Backwards option to search backward, starting at the current cursor position.

Table 4.3   **Searching With and Without Selecting the Find Exact Attributes Option**

Is Find Exact Attributes Specified?	Specified Word	Word in Text	Does Word Match?
No	**cat**	cat	No
No	**cat**	**cat**	Yes
No	**cat**	*cat*	Yes
Yes	**cat**	cat	No
Yes	**cat**	**cat**	Yes
Yes	**cat**	*cat*	No
No	cat	cat	Yes
No	cat	**cat**	Yes
No	cat	*cat*	Yes
Yes	cat	cat	Yes
Yes	cat	**cat**	No
Yes	cat	*cat*	No

Creating Bookmarks

There are numerous ways in which you can use the Find & Replace feature, not just to find specific words or phrases, but to perform other tasks as well. For example, you can locate a particular section of a long document quickly. Simply specify a word or phrase that you know is there, and the program will find that particular section. If you're not sure where the section is, start the search from the beginning of the document.

    In a variation on this idea, you can create a "bookmark" to help you jump to a particular location in a document. As an example, suppose that you're working on two different parts of a document at the same time (call them sections A and B), and you want to be able to jump back and forth quickly between the two sections. You can create two different bookmarks, consisting of text strings that you're not likely to use anywhere else, then use the Find & Replace feature to locate each of the bookmarks. Here are the details.

1. Position the text cursor somewhere within section A, and then enter an unusual character string, such as "AAAA". This is your first bookmark.

2. Now move the cursor to section B, and then insert another unusual string, say "BBBB". This is the second bookmark.

3. To jump from section B to section A (assuming that A comes before B in the text), display the Find & Replace dialog box (Figure 4.3), type **AAAA** in the Find edit box, select Find Backwards, and then start the search. In a flash, the document will be repositioned at "AAAA" in section A.

4. To jump from section A to section B, repeat the process, but this time enter **BBBB** instead of AAAA, and do a forward search instead of a backward one.

Replacing One String with Another

The previous sections describe how to simply *find* each occurrence of a particular string. By contrast, in a search-and-replace operation you can replace each occurrence of the search string with a *replacement string*. For instance, you could replace each occurrence of "dog" with "cat".

You can have the program automatically replace each occurrence of the search string that's found, or you can specify which occurrences are to be replaced. The capitalization and attributes of each particular replacement can be the same as the string it's replacing, or you can specify a particular capitalization and set of attributes for all replacements.

To replace one string with another, you specify both the search string and the replacement string. You also need to specify any special options that apply to either string. Here are the steps to replace each occurrence of one string with another:

1. Position the text cursor where you want the search-and-replace operation to begin.

2. Select Edit/Find & Replace.

3. In the Find edit box, enter the search string.

4. In the Replace With edit box, enter the replacement string.

5. Enter any special conditions (see the following section).

6. To automatically replace all occurrences of the search string with the replacement string, click on Replace All. When the search-and-replace operation has finished, a message to that effect will appear on the screen.

CAUTION! *You can't use the Undo feature to reverse a Replace All operation.*

Alternatively, to have the program pause as each occurrence of the search string is found, click on Find. As each match is found, it's highlighted, and the dialog box shown in Figure 4.4 appears. You then have the following options:

- Select Replace & Find Next to replace the current match with the replacement string. Then continue the search.

- Select Find Next, in which case the current match is not replaced, but the search continues for the next match.

- Select Cancel to terminate the search.

Find-and-Replace Options

You can specify two types of options in a find-and-replace operation: those that apply to the search string and those that apply to the replacement string. You specify the options for the search string just as described earlier. You can specify the exact case of the search string, or you can perform a case-insensitive search. You can assign particular text attributes to the search string, or you can search independent of any attributes. (For details about either type of option, refer to the previous sections.)

By default, each replacement string will have the same capitalization and attributes as the original string. For example, suppose you begin replacing each occurrence of "cat" with "dog". If one of the occurrences of "cat" is boldfaced, the replacement will be as well. Similarly, if one of the occurrences is spelled "Cat", the replacement will be spelled "Dog".

You can override these defaults by specifying a particular capitalization or attribute for each replacement string. For example, you can have all occurrences of "*cat*" replaced with "**dog**", regardless of the attributes of the original strings. Or, you could replace every occurrence of "*pollution control*" with "*Environmental Control*", regardless of the capitalization of the original strings.

Specifying the Exact Replacement Capitalization

To specify the same capitalization for each use of the replacement string, follow these steps:

1. Enter the search string.

2. Enter the replacement string, using the exact capitalization you want.

3. Click on Replace Exact Case.

4. Click on either Replace All or Find, depending on whether you want all replacements to be made automatically.

If you do not select the Replace Exact Case option in step 3, the capitalization you enter in step 2 will be ignored. In that case, for each replacement, the capitalization will be the same as that of the string that was replaced.

Remember that only those occurrences that are found will be replaced. For example, if you specify "pollution" as the string to search for, and you also click on Find Exact Case, any occurrences of this string that are capitalized will be ignored during the search-and-replace operation. Alternatively, suppose that somewhere in your text a word was entered in all lowercase, but you later assigned it the text attribute Uppercase. During a find-and-replace operation, this word will still be recognized as lowercase, even though it appears on the screen as uppercase!

Specifying the Exact Replacement Attributes

To specify the attributes for the replacement string, follow these steps:

1. Enter both the string to be replaced and the replacement string. Be sure to include the search string's attributes as you did above in the section "Specifying Text Attributes and Capitalization."

2. Click on Attributes to display the dialog box shown in Figure 4.5.

3. Click on Replace Exact Attributes.

4. In the box labeled Replace Attributes, click on the ones you want for the replacement string.

5. Click on OK, then on Replace All.

If you do not select Replace Exact Attributes in step 3, whatever attributes you select in step 4 will be ignored. In that case, for each replacement, the attributes will be the same as those of the string that's replaced.

Attributes are not additive. That is, you can't simultaneously specify the exact attributes for a replacement string and also keep the attributes of each original string. For instance, if you specify Bold for the replacement attribute, but one of the original strings that's replaced was italicized, the replacement string will be boldfaced but not italicized (unless you select both Bold and Italic for the replacement string).

Using Wildcards to Locate and Replace Text

You can use two different *wildcard characters,* the asterisk (*) and the question mark (?), to help you perform a find or a search-and-replace operation. When used as a wildcard, the asterisk stands for any group of characters, and the question mark for any single character.

Either the * or ? wildcard can be placed anywhere in a search string. However, placing the * wildcard at the beginning of a word leads to unpredictable results.

To see how to use wildcard characters, suppose that you want to replace all forms of the verb *stack* with the equivalent forms of *quack* everywhere in a document. You could do this the long way, by searching for each occurrence of the string "stack" and then manually replacing the word with the correct alternate ("quacking" for "stacking"). It is much easier to use the * wildcard, however, as follows:

1. For the search string, enter **stack***.

2. For the replacement string, enter **quack***.

3. Click on Find (*don't* click on Replace All).

Clicking on Find gives you the opportunity to verify each replacement so you can avoid changing any exceptions. (For example, you probably wouldn't want to change the proper name Howard Stackpole to Howard Quackpole.)

The ? wildcard can also be used for various types of searches, such as when you're in doubt as to the exact spelling of a word. For instance, suppose that you want to find every occurrence of the word *receive*, but you're not sure how you spelled it in the text (*i* before *e*, or vice versa). To locate the words, regardless of which spelling you used, you would enter **rec??ve**. To include variations such as *receives* in the search, enter the search string **rec??ve***.

When using wildcards in find-and-replace operations, you must match wildcards in the search string and replacement string. That is, each occurrence of an asterisk or question mark in a search string must be matched by an equivalent asterisk or question mark in the replacement string. Otherwise, the program will display an error message, and you'll have to change one string or the other before you can go on. For example, the program would not allow you to replace "chard*" with "shard?". Table 4.4 illustrates several examples of using wildcard characters.

Searching for Special Characters

In addition to text strings, a search can include various special characters. For example, you may occasionally need to search for a real question mark or asterisk, not as a wildcard character but as itself, such as in the string "Now?"—where the question mark is really a question mark. You can also search for hard returns (which end each paragraph) and tabs.

Searching for * and ?

Suppose you want to search for the string "how is it?". You can't put the question mark directly into the search string because it will be treated as a wildcard. The trick is to enclose the question mark or asterisk in angle brackets: <>. For example, in this case you would enter the search string as **how is it<?>.**

Table 4.4 Examples of Using the Wildcards ? and *

Search String	Word in Text	Does Word Match?
mate	mate	Yes
mate	inmate	No
*mate	mate	No
*mate	inmate	Yes
*mat	mate	No
mat*	mat	No
mat*	mate	Yes
mat	inmate	Yes
m?te	mate	Yes
m?te	mite	Yes
m?te	moot	No
m?o?	moot	Yes
*mat?	inmate	Yes

If a search string involves two or more successive question marks or asterisks, enclose each one in a separate pair of brackets. For instance, to search for the string "ab**de", enter it as **ab<*><*>de**.

Locating Tabs and Hard Returns

You can search for either a hard return or a tab, either by itself or in connection with other characters. To use a hard return as part of a search string, press Ctrl-Enter. The screen will display ¶. To use a tab character, press Ctrl-Tab. The screen will display ».

For example, to search for each occurrence of the text string "end of line." that occurs at the end of a paragraph, enter the following search string: **end of line**.Ctrl-Enter. This will appear in the Find edit box as "end of line.¶".

You can also use a hard return or tab as part of a replacement string.

Unfortunately, you're somewhat limited in the ways you can use hard returns in search strings, since the hard return must be the last character in the string. For example, this prevents you from searching for all occurrences of a double line (two successive hard returns).

However, by being a little clever you can work around this. The trick is to first replace all hard returns with some other character, and then search and replace. To illustrate this technique, here's how to replace all occurrences of a double hard return with a single one:

1. To begin, replace every occurrence of a hard return with an unusual character (one that you're sure doesn't appear in the text), perhaps something like \Z\.

2. Next replace every occurrence of "\Z\\Z\" with \Z\.

3. Finally, replace every occurrence of \Z\ with a hard return.

Using Wildcards to Change Attributes

You can use the * wildcard to change all occurrences of one attribute to another. To illustrate this technique, here are the steps for changing every instance of boldface within a document to italics:

1. In the Find edit box, enter *. This stands for every word in the document.

2. In the Replace edit box, enter *.

3. For the Find attribute, click on Bold.

4. For the Replace attribute, click on Italic.

5. Click on the Replace Exact Attributes option.

6. Select the Replace All option.

Tips on Find-and-Replace Operations

Before you perform a find-and-replace operation, save your work (press Ctrl-S), especially if the operation might affect a significant portion of your document. It takes only a few seconds to do a save, and it's good insurance. That way, if you make a mess of your document because of an incorrectly formulated search, you can retrieve the unchanged document from disk and try again.

If you're replacing whole words, remember to select Find Whole Words Only, or you could accidentally create a disaster, especially when using the Replace All option. For example, suppose you want to replace each occurrence of "the" with "a." If you neglect to select Find Whole Words Only, a word such as "therefore" would become "arefore", and so on.

By default, the Find Exact Case, Find Exact Attributes, Replace Exact Case, and Replace Exact Attributes options are turned off. When these defaults are in effect, each replacement will conform to the capitalization and attributes of the original text.

Once you select Find Exact Case for a find operation, that option remains in effect until you deselect it, or until you end the current Professional Write Plus session. However, this is not the case with the options Find Exact Attributes and Replace Exact Attributes, which are turned off at the end of each search-and-replace operation.

To specify the exact case for a search string you must include the capitalization as part of the search string, and you must select the Find Exact Case option. Similarly, to specify the exact attributes for a search string, you must select those attributes in the Find Attributes box, and you must select the Find Exact Attributes option.

To specify the exact case for a replacement string, you must include the capitalization when you enter the string, and you must select the Replace Exact Case option. Similarly, to specify the exact attributes for a replacement string, you must select those attributes in the Replace Attributes box, and you must select the Replace Exact Attributes option.

If you use the search-and-replace feature frequently, you can speed up the operations by placing the Find & Replace icon on the sidebar. Then, instead of selecting Find & Replace from the Edit menu, you can simply click on the sidebar icon. For information about adding this icon to the sidebar, refer to Appendix B.

Adding Notes to Your Document

A *note* is a remark, comment, or reminder that you insert into a document. Notes can't be printed—they are only displayed on the screen. You can insert a note just about anywhere within a document: in the main text, in a header or footer, within the text in a frame, or even within a footnote.

A note is like a mini-document. It can be as long as you wish, and you can insert, edit, and delete text using all the normal text-editing keystrokes, including the assignment of text attributes and fonts. You can even transfer text from the main body of a document into a note, or vice versa, using block operations. When a note becomes obsolete, you can delete it from the document.

Note. Note markers are displayed on the screen by default. You can change the program default so that these markers are not displayed. See Appendix B for details on setting defaults.

Avoid entering notes as you're typing in text, because the note may be pushed along as new text is entered, depending on where the note appears. Instead, attach each note to text that's already been entered—even if it's just a word or two back from where you're entering new text.

After you enter a note and resume normal text editing, a marker remains visible at that position in the text, indicating the position of the note. You can then display the note simply by double-clicking on the corresponding note marker.

You can enter any number of notes in a document. You can even enter several notes at the same position in the text. As an added documentation feature, the date and time of creation appear at the top of each note.

Entering a New Note

Here are the steps for adding a new note:

1. If you're in draft mode now, switch to layout mode using the View menu (you can't work with notes in draft mode).

2. Position the text cursor where you want the note to be entered.

3. Select Edit/Notes/Insert Note and the blank note will appear on the screen.

4. Enter the text for the note, using any of the standard editing keystrokes. Figure 4.6 shows a note on the screen.

Figure 4.6
You can enter a descriptive note anywhere in the text

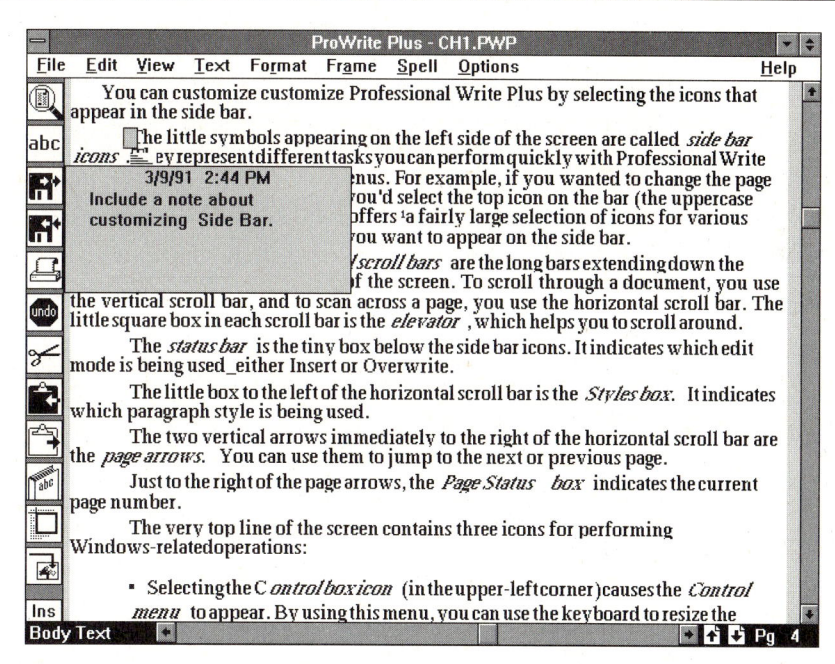

5. When you've finished entering the note, click anywhere outside of the note or press the Esc key. You can then resume normal editing of your document.

Displaying and Editing Notes

Before you can display a note on the screen, you must locate it. There are two ways to accomplish this. First, if you know the approximate location of a particular note, scroll to that section of the document until the little note box indicating the position of the note is shown. Or, if you simply want to browse through any notes you may have written in the dim past, scroll through your document until each note box becomes visible.

The second way is to use the Go To Option to locate the next note. (This method is covered in detail in the next section.) With either method, once you've located the note you want to display, double-click on the note box. You can then scroll through the note, editing it if necessary.

If two or more notes exist at the same position in the document, they'll all be represented by a single note box. However, when you double-click on this box, the notes will appear stacked, as shown in Figure 4.7. To select a particular note, click on one of the edges that peeks out. Each time you click, another note will rise to the surface.

Figure 4.7
Several notes placed in the same location

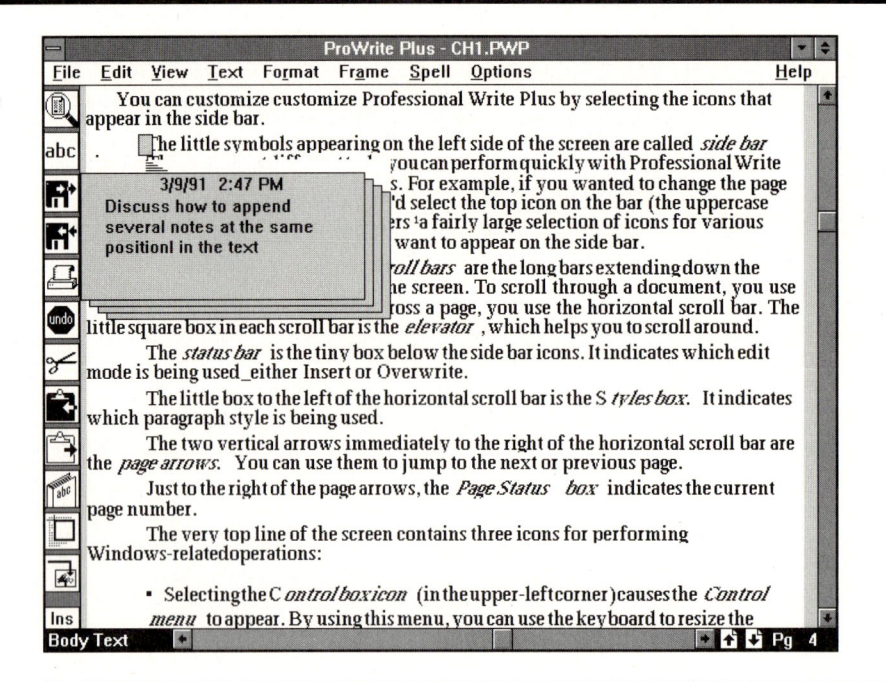

If a note is placed within italicized text, you may have difficulty finding the exact spot on the note box to double-click, since working within italics with the mouse cursor can be tricky and confusing. If this happens, use the following method to find and display the note.

Using the Go To Option

As already mentioned, notes are marked with small boxes. However, in a long document you might spend quite a bit of time scrolling back and forth to locate a particular note or browse through all of the notes.

To avoid this time-consuming process, you can use the Go To feature to jump to the next note in the document. For example, you may know that there's a note somewhere ahead in the text but you don't remember exactly where. Here's how to use the Go To feature:

1. Position the text cursor anywhere before the note you want to find. If you simply want to browse through all of the notes, position the cursor at the beginning of the document.

2. Select Edit/Go To, and the dialog box shown in Figure 4.8 will appear.

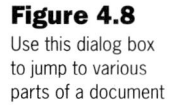

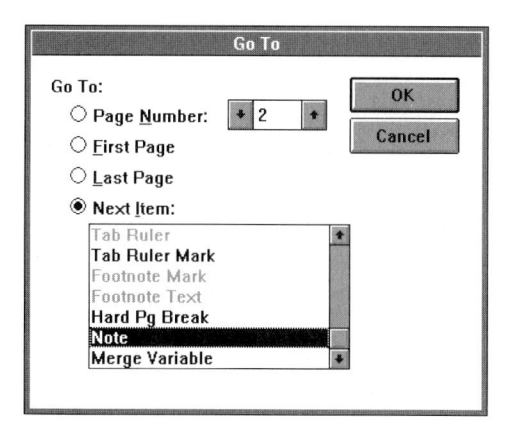

Figure 4.8
Use this dialog box to jump to various parts of a document

3. Scroll down the list box displayed in the dialog box until the item labeled Note becomes visible.

4. Click on Note, and then click on Go To. The text cursor will be positioned on the next note, which will be displayed automatically.

To jump to the next note, you can simply press the speed key Ctrl-H, which effectively repeats steps 2 through 4. Or, you can click on the Go To icon (if it's displayed on the sidebar), which is the equivalent of Ctrl-H.

Deleting an Existing Note

To delete a note, follow these steps:

1. Position the cursor on the note box, or use the Go To feature to display the note.

2. Select Edit/Notes/Remove Note.

Note that the Remove Note option is not accessible unless the text cursor is positioned on a note, or unless a note is open.

If you delete text that includes a note, the note will also be deleted, although a warning message gives you a chance to change your mind about the deletion. If you accidentally delete a note, you can restore it (provided that you haven't made too many other changes to your document) by selecting Undo from the Edit menu. (For more information about the Undo feature, see "Recovering from Accidents" later in this chapter.)

Using a Document Description

Note. You can't include a document description with a file saved in ASCII format.

When saving a document, you can include a short *document description* along with the name of the file. This can be extremely useful when you later try to locate that document, because the eight-character limit on file names is often inadequate to describe the file contents. A document description, on the other hand, can be approximately 120 characters long—more than enough to give a clear identification of the file contents.

You create a document description when you save a file, as follows:

1. Select File/Save As, and the dialog box shown in Figure 4.9 appears.

2. In the box labeled "Description," enter a description of the document.

3. Continue saving the file as usual.

CAUTION! *Don't press the Enter key while entering the document description—that will cause the file to be saved.*

Whenever necessary, you can edit the document description for any particular document. First you must open the file in the usual way. Then, when you save it, using the Save As option on the File menu, just position the cursor in the Description box and make whatever corrections are needed, using the standard editing keys.

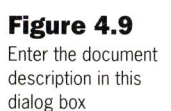

Figure 4.9
Enter the document description in this dialog box

[Save As dialog box showing File Name: *.PWP, ASCII File checkbox, Keep Styles with Document checkbox, Files in: c:\pwplus\docs, file list (addbkdsc.pwp, agram.pwp, default.pwp, frames.pwp, gramtour.pwp, ieaddrbk.pwp), Directories list ([..], [-a-], [-b-], [-c-], [-d-], [-e-], [-g-]), Description: "A memo to the entire staff, regarding paid leaves", buttons OK, ASCII Options..., Cancel]

Locating a Particular Document

Let's suppose that you want to open a particular document, but you can't remember the name of the file in which it's been saved. Here's how the document description can be a lifesaver (provided you can remember in which directory the file was saved):

1. Select File/Open. The dialog box shown in Figure 4.10 will appear.

Figure 4.10
The document description for each file appears in the box labeled "Description"

[Open dialog box showing File Name: *.PWP, ASCII File checkbox, Files in: c:\pwplus\docs, file list (addbkdsc.pwp, agram.pwp, default.pwp, frames.pwp, gramtour.pwp, ieaddrbk.pwp), Directories list ([..], [-a-], [-b-], [-c-], [-d-], [-e-], [-g-]), Description: (empty), buttons OK, ASCII Options..., Open Another, Cancel]

2. Select the directory in which the document was saved. (For details about selecting directories, see Chapter 5.)

3. In the list box labeled "Files in," highlight each file name in turn. As each name is highlighted, the document description, if any, for that file appears in the Description box.

4. When you've located the file you want, select OK to open it.

Jumping to Different Parts of a Document

As mentioned earlier, you can use the Go To feature to jump quickly to various parts of a document. An example of this was given in relation to notes, a few pages back. You can also use the Go To feature to jump to specific pages, the beginning or end of the document, tab rulers, and many other locations.

To access this feature, select Edit/Go To, and the Go To dialog box will appear (Figure 4.8). You can then select from the options listed on the screen. Some of these features operate in both layout and draft mode, whereas others can be used only in layout mode. For example, since headers and footers are visible only in layout mode, you can't use the Go To feature in draft mode to jump to a header.

Here's a list of the options available with the Go To feature:

- To jump to a particular page, click on the Page Number option and then enter the page you want to jump to (layout mode only).

- To jump to either the beginning or the end of your document, click on the First Page or Last Page option (layout mode only).

The following items are selected from the list box labeled "Next Item:"

- Use the Frame option to jump to the next frame on the current page (layout mode only).

- The Header Text and Footer Text options move the cursor to the header or footer on the current page (layout mode only). Note that this is the only way to access these areas without using the mouse.

- The Tab Ruler option moves the cursor to the tab ruler at the top of the page. This option seems somewhat superfluous because you can perform the same action more quickly simply by moving the mouse cursor (layout mode only, and then only when the tab ruler is displayed). Again, this option is the only path to accessing the tab ruler without a mouse.

- Use Tab Ruler Mark to move the cursor to the next tab ruler mark in the document.

- The Footnote Mark option moves the cursor to the next footnote mark in the document.

- The Footnote Text option moves the cursor into the footnote text corresponding to the current position of the text cursor. To use this option, first position the cursor immediately to the left of the corresponding footnote marker in the text (layout mode only).

- Use the Hard Pg Break option to move to the next hard page break in the text.

- The Note option moves you to the next note in the text.

- The Merge Variable option moves you to the next merge variable in a document.

In some circumstances, some of the features just described will appear dimmed. This indicates that the feature is not currently available. For example, if there are no frames on a page, the Frame option will appear dimmed.

Repetitive Jumping

You can use the speed key Ctrl-H to jump to the next occurrence of the item you last jumped to. For example, suppose you select Tab Ruler in the dialog box so that the cursor jumps to the next tab ruler mark in the text. To then jump to the following tab ruler, press Ctrl-H.

Recovering from Accidents

The Undo feature can help you recover from potentially time-consuming mistakes. (You may remember it from Chapter 2, where it was used to restore a deleted block.) As you work with Professional Write Plus, Undo remembers your most recent operations. Using Undo, you can then reverse any of these operations. For example, if you accidentally delete a block of text or a frame, you can restore the deletion with Undo, provided you act quickly enough.

Professional Write Plus can remember the most recent one to four operations, depending on the default value in effect. (For information on setting this default, refer to Appendix B.) Suppose Undo has been set to remember the most recent four operations. When you select Undo, the most recent operation will be undone. If you then immediately select Undo again, the next most recent operation will be undone, and so on, up to the last four operations. You can continue selecting Undo, and it will continue to "play back" the last four changes. Here's a partial list of the operations that can be reversed with Undo:

- Entering any amount of text

Note. If you enter a paragraph of text without performing any other operations during the text entry, and you then select Undo, the entire paragraph will be erased. If you perform some other type of operation in the middle of entering the paragraph, however, when you select Undo, the entire paragraph may *not* be deleted because whatever you did in the middle might be considered a separate operation by Undo.

- Deleting a block of text
- Changing the font or attribute of a text block
- Changing the alignment or spacing of a text block
- Creating, deleting, or resizing a frame

Many operations cannot be undone. These include file manipulation operations (save, delete, and so on), changes to the various default settings within Professional Write Plus, and others.

You can use any of the following methods to activate Undo:

- Select Undo from the Edit menu.
- Press Alt-Backspace.
- Click on the Undo icon in the sidebar (shaped like a stop sign).

When Undo's Memory Is Cleared

Whenever you save your work, or when an automatic timed save occurs, Undo's memory is erased, so that no changes prior to the save can then be undone. For example, if you delete a block and then save your work, you can't then restore that block (except by retyping it). By the way, this is a very weak argument against doing automatic timed backups. You should still do them even though they may occasionally prevent you from undoing an error. (For information about setting up automatic backups, see Chapter 5.)

Whenever you activate Undo, its memory is automatically cleared. To illustrate how this works, suppose that you perform the following steps, where A and B are separate blocks of text:

1. Delete block A.
2. Delete block B.
3. Activate Undo (restores block B).
4. Activate Undo again (restores block A).
5. Do something else, such as enter text or make some type of change to the document.

The moment you perform step 5, blocks A and B are cleared from Undo's memory. The moral of this story is that whenever you activate Undo to correct a particular action you've made, you'd better do it right then, because later on you won't be able to.

Using Insert Variables

Insert variables are special pieces of information kept in Professional Write Plus's memory that you can retrieve into a document. They are called variables because they contain information that may change. Professional Write Plus maintains the following insert variables:

- Today's date
- The system date
- The date of last revision of the current document
- Merge variables, used when creating customized form letters

All but the last type are discussed in this section. Merge variables are described in Chapter 8.

Today's Date

When you copy this variable into a document, the actual *text* of today's date is copied in the format you select. This particular variable is handy because it allows you to record the date on which you made a particular change to a document.

System Date

When you copy this variable into a document, a duplicate of the actual variable itself is copied into your text. This means that whenever you open the document, the current date (in a form such as 5/15/91) will appear wherever you copied the system variable. Note that this is quite different from the Today's Date variable, where the displayed date never changes (see above).

If you have never worked with any type of variable before, you might find the System Date variable a little difficult at first. When you retrieve this variable into a document, you don't actually see the variable itself. Instead, what's displayed on the screen or printed is the *contents* of the variable.

Thus, when you see the date 4/29/91 on the screen, you can't tell by looking whether it's the contents of the System Date variable or whether it's just ordinary text. You *can* tell, however, by trying to move the cursor character by character through the text of the date. If it's ordinary text, the cursor will move through the text in the normal fashion—one character at a time—and the text can be edited. If it's the contents of the System Date variable that is displayed, the cursor will jump from one end of the text to the other.

Date of Last Revision

This variable contains the last date on which the document was revised and saved to a disk file. Like the System Date variable, this value will be updated each time you open and save the document.

Copying an Insert Variable into Your Document

You can copy an insert variable into text located just about anywhere within a document: the main body, text within a frame, headers and footers, and footnotes. You can't, however, copy an insert variable into a note. Here are the steps for placing the contents of an insert variable into your document:

1. Position the text cursor where you want the variable to be copied.
2. Select Edit/Insert Variable. The dialog box box shown in Figure 4.11 will appear.
3. Click on the variable you want to insert.
4. Select the date format you want, using the Date Style list box.
5. Click on OK, and the selected variable will be copied into your text.

Figure 4.11
Selecting the insert variable you want copied into your text

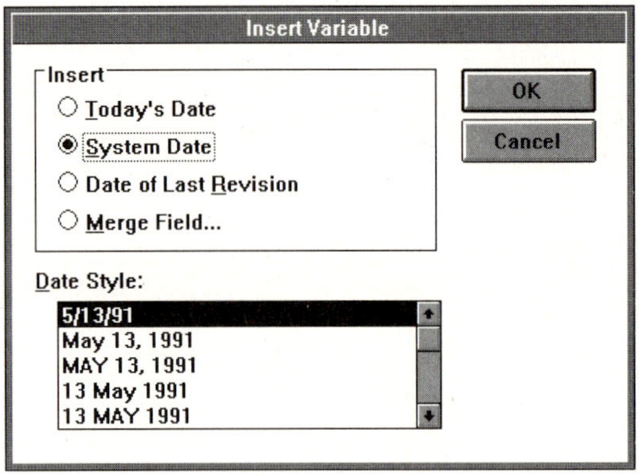

Summary

All the tools presented in this chapter are designed to enhance your word processing capabilities. Some of them you may find indispensable, and others you may seldom use. The spell checker and thesaurus are particularly useful because they directly affect the way your documents appear to the rest of the world. The other features, such as notes and the document description, are for your eyes only. They help you to work with different documents, but the readers of your masterpieces will have no idea of the sophisticated tools you used. Only you will ever be aware of their existence—and their usefulness.

CHAPTER

5

Working with Your Files

Selecting a Different Directory

Making Backups

Working with Several Documents at Once

Importing Text from Other Programs

Exporting Files in Different Formats

Using the File Manager

◆ **Selecting a Different Directory**　　　　　　　　　　　　　　　**121**

L EARNING HOW TO WORK WITH FILES IS AS IMPORTANT AS KNOWING how to work with a word processor. Files are the mainstay of the computing world, and you can't be proficient with the computer unless you are reasonably adept with various types of file operations.

In this chapter we'll explore the various tools available with Professional Write Plus for working with files. Many of these will be invaluable to you, not on the word-processing level, but on the *file* level. That is, these tools manipulate the files themselves, rather than their contents. For example, the program's built-in File Manager is extremely useful for performing the standard types of file operations, such as copying, deleting, moving, and renaming.

Being adept with directories is also a necessity. This is especially true when working in the Windows environment, where you can be handling many different programs and files at the same time. For example, if you're trying to locate a file, but you can't remember exactly where you saved it, you'll be lost unless you know how to search through different directories. If you're familiar with the manipulation of directories under Windows, you're one step ahead. If not, you can use this chapter to learn about Professional Write Plus's directory-searching tools.

Transferring files between different types of programs has become commonplace in today's computer world. For instance, you may sometimes need to import a document file created with another word processor, such as Ami Professional or WordPerfect. Or, you may need to transmit a document to a friend or colleague running a different word processor. Professional Write Plus has features for performing both types of operation. You can import documents from a wide variety of different programs—word processors, database programs, and spreadsheet software. And you can export documents in many different file formats.

Professional Write Plus contains various features that can make your word processing more flexible, convenient, and safe. For example, you can open several documents at the same time, or open the same document in two different windows for easier editing and manipulation. You can also use various built-in backup features to help prevent the accidental loss of valuable information.

Since this chapter applies to many different types of files, the term *file* will be used to refer to any type of file, regardless of its contents. The term *document file* will be used to indicate a file containing a document in Professional Write Plus format.

Selecting a Different Directory

Up to this point in the book, it's been assumed that any documents you store or retrieve are stored in a file on the *default document directory.* When you first install Professional Write Plus, the default document directory is \DOCS,

Note. The techniques described here apply equally well to saving and retrieving files, and also for using Professional Write Plus's File Manager (but not the Windows File Manager).

which is a subdirectory of the directory in which the Professional Write Plus files are stored. For example, if the program is installed in the directory C:\PWPLUS, then the default document directory is C:\PWPLUS\DOCS.

You can change the default document directory so that when you save or retrieve a document, Professional Write Plus looks in that directory. (For details about changing defaults, refer to Appendix B.) However, you don't *need* to change the default directory in order to save and retrieve files from anywhere on your disks. As part of the save or retrieve process, you can indicate which disk drive and directory you want to access.

To illustrate how to access any directory, we'll use the Open dialog box, shown in Figure 5.1. This is the box you use to open a file (by selecting File/Open).

Figure 5.1
Use this dialog box to open a file

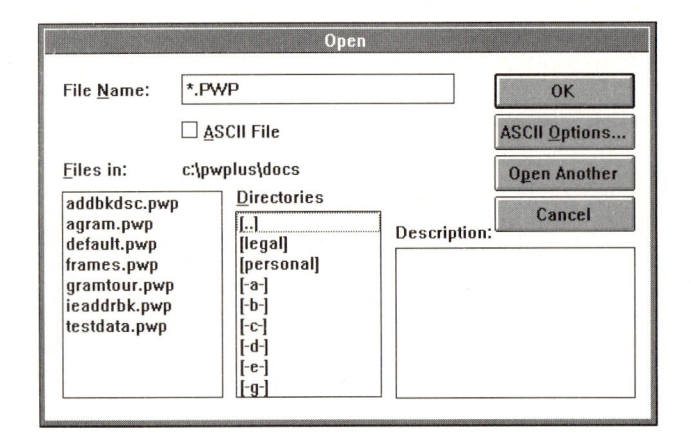

Open
File Name: *.PWP
☐ ASCII File
Files in: c:\pwplus\docs
addbkdsc.pwp Directories
agram.pwp   [..]
default.pwp [legal]
frames.pwp   [personal]
gramtour.pwp [-a-]
ieaddrbk.pwp [-b-]
testdata.pwp [-c-]
[-d-]
[-e-]
[-g-]
OK
ASCII Options...
Open Another
Cancel
Description:

In Figure 5.1, the current disk drive and directory are listed on the line labeled "Files in". This is the directory Professional Write Plus uses for opening and saving files. Initially, the default document directory is shown here, although you'll learn below how to select other directories. In Figure 5.1, C is the current disk drive, and \PWPLUS\DOCS is the current directory.

For the current disk drive and directory, the edit box on the top line (File Name) shows the current *file name specification*. This indicates which group of file names is listed in the box in the lower-left part of the dialog box. For example, in Figure 5.1 the edit box displays *.PWP. Here, the asterisk is the DOS wildcard, which represents any group of characters, so that *.PWP represents any file name ending with the extension .PWP. Therefore, the list box in the lower-left corner shows all files whose names end with this extension.

The specification *.PWP is used by default because you'll normally be concerned with Professional Write Plus document files. (.PWP is the extension attached to each document stored in Professional Write Plus format.) However, you can change this to whatever extension you wish.

The list box labeled "Directories" lists the disk drives and directories currently available to you, as follows:

- [..] is the parent of the current directory. For example, if the current directory is C:\MYWORK\SCHOOL, then the parent directory is C:\MYWORK.

- [-a-], [-b-], and so on represent the disk drives that Professional Write Plus knows about. Usually, these are all the drives on your computer, including all the logical hard disk drives.

- [*directory-name*] is the name of a directory under (a *subdirectory* of) the current one. For example, in Figure 5.1 two directories, \PERSONAL and \LEGAL, are listed under the current one.

Using the Mouse to Switch Directories

To switch to another disk drive or directory, simply double-click on it in the Directories box (or click on it and then click on OK). Here are some examples of switching drives and directories, using the contents of Figure 5.1:

To Switch To	**Click On**
The parent directory of C:\PWPLUS\DOCS	[..]
Disk drive A	[-a-]
Directory \LEGAL under \PWPLUS\DOCS	[legal]

Selecting the Directory by Direct Entry

Instead of using the Directories box to select the disk drive and directory, you can enter the drive and directory name directly in the File Name edit box. For example, to switch to the directory \UTILS on drive C, select the current contents of the edit box (by double-clicking anywhere in the box), enter **C:\UTILS**, and then press Enter.

Selecting the Files You Want Displayed

When you switch to a new disk drive and directory, the program automatically retains the original file name specification in the File Name edit box. For example, in Figure 5.1 the file specification is *.PWP. When you enter a new disk drive and directory, such as C:\UTILS, the drive and directory are changed, but the same specification, *.PWP, is displayed in the edit box. And, the box in the lower-left part of the screen then lists all the files in the new directory that match the file name specification.

However, you're not limited to displaying only the names of Professional Write Plus document files. In fact, you can display the names of any group of files, simply by changing the specification in the File Name edit box. To change the file name specification, delete the current one and enter another. Here are a few examples of specifications you can use:

File Name Specification	File Names Displayed
*.PWP	Professional Write Plus document files
*.ABC	All files with the extension .ABC
.	All files

There are several ways to enter a new file name specification:

- Double-click on any part of the current contents of the box (this highlights the text), and then enter the new specification. The instant you begin typing, the highlighted contents will disappear.

- If the current contents of the edit box are already highlighted, just begin entering the new specification.

- Click anywhere in the edit box, use the Delete and Backspace keys to delete the contents, and then enter the new specification.

Remember to end by pressing Enter. The instant you do, the files conforming to the new specification will appear in the list box in the lower-left part of the display.

Using One Operation to Change the Directory and File Specification

As mentioned earlier, the file name specification remains the same when you select a new directory. However, you can also enter a new file name specification at the same time as you select a new directory. Using Figure 5.1 as an example, suppose you want to switch to the \DOCS directory and display *all* the files there. To accomplish this, enter **C:\PWPLUS\DOCS*.*** in the edit box, then press the Enter key. The specification *.* will appear in the edit box, and all the files in the new directory will be displayed in the lower-left list box.

In some cases you can use a shortcut to minimize your typing. For example, instead of entering C:\PWPLUS\DOCS*.* in the above example, you can simply enter **DOCS*.***. Here's the rule to follow: If you want to switch to a disk drive or directory whose name appears in the Directories list box, just enter that name by itself (or along with a new file specification if you wish). Remember, this shortcut works *only* if the name is listed in the Directories box.

To switch to another directory that's not listed on the screen, enter the full path name of that directory in the File Name edit box. If the directory is on a different disk, include that drive name as part of the directory name. For example, to switch to \TOMS on drive D, enter **D:\TOMS**.

A Note About Switching Directories

The Open dialog box always displays the directory in which the current document is displayed. For example, if you display this dialog box, switch to some other directory to browse around, and then return to the same document on the edit screen (by clicking on Cancel), Professional Write Plus won't remember the directory you switched to. That is, the next time you display the Open dialog box the directory belonging to the current document will again be displayed.

A similar situation exists for the Save As dialog box: It always displays the directory in which the current document is stored. However, if you use the File/Save As option to save the current document in a different directory, then *that* directory will be selected the next time you display either the Open or Save As dialog box.

Making Backups

A backup is a simple device that can save you hours of aggravation and anxiety. When a file is *backed up*, a duplicate of it is made, either to a floppy disk, another hard disk, or to some other part of the same hard disk.

Making backups should be a normal part of your daily word processing. In a sense, you need to have a somewhat pessimistic attitude about using computers, because just about anything that can possibly go wrong will happen eventually, so you always need to be prepared for the worst.

There are endless ways in which you can lose part or all of your work. Some of these, like a power failure or a hard-disk failure, are beyond your control; others may be your own doing. For example, with a couple of keystrokes you can erase an existing file. Or, you could accidentally erase a large block within the current document, and then compound the error by saving this mutilated version back to the same file, erasing the original version in the process.

Professional Write Plus offers a variety of features that help you to create backups of your work:

- Whenever you do a regular save to the same file, the *automatic backup* feature copies the previous version of your document to another file of the same name in a special backup directory.

- The *automatic timed save* feature saves your work at regular intervals. This can help to prevent the loss of large amounts of work, due either to an oversight on your part or to a software or hardware failure. For example, in some circumstances Windows will completely freeze up, causing you to lose your current work. But if the automatic timed save is turned on, you'll lose only the changes since the last save.

- Using the Save As option, you can save your work to a different file in another directory or on a different disk.

Using Automatic Timed Save

The Automatic Timed Save feature automatically saves your work at regular intervals. The first automatic save is to the file from which the document was originally retrieved, and each subsequent save is to the same file. Unless, that is, you have saved your work to a *different* file by using the File/Save As option. In that case, from then on the automatic saves will be to the new file.

When Professional Write Plus is first installed, this feature is turned off, but you can turn it on as follows:

Note. Automatic backups take only a few seconds, and they're worth every second for the peace of mind they buy you!

1. Select Options/Backup Options, and the dialog box shown in Figure 5.2 will appear.

Figure 5.2
Use this dialog box to set the backup options

2. Click on Auto Timed Save, so that an X appears in that box.

3. In the edit box labeled "minutes," enter the time interval between saves—10 to 20 minutes is a reasonable time interval in most circumstances. Then click on OK.

A Caution About Timed Saves

When you change the setting of the automatic timed save option (you either turn it on or off or change the time interval between backups), it will immediately take effect for the *current document.*

If, during the same word processing session, you later open another document in the same window, the new backup setting will apply to that document as well. However, if you open another document in a *different* window (using the Open Another option in the Open dialog box), the new backup setting will not apply there.

If you have several documents open at the same time and you change the backup setting to one of them, this new setting won't apply to the other documents. Furthermore, the last document you save will determine the backup setting to be used for subsequent word processing sessions—that is, when you exit from Windows and later come back.

Using the Automatic Backup Feature

When the Automatic Backup feature is turned on, each time you save your work the *previous* contents of the file are copied to a backup file with the same name, but in a different directory. This feature is turned off when Professional Write Plus is first installed, but you can turn it on as follows:

1. Decide in which disk drive and directory you want your backup files to be saved. You can, if you wish, create a new directory just for this purpose. (For information about creating directories, see the Microsoft Windows *User's Guide*, or refer to any standard text on Microsoft Windows or MS-DOS.)

2. Select Options/Backup Options, and the dialog box shown in Figure 5.2 will appear.

3. Click on Auto Backup.

4. In the edit box labeled "Path", enter the full name of the directory where the backup files are to be written.

When Professional Write Plus is first installed, a special directory named \BACKUP is created under the directory in which the program files are kept (normally C:\PWPLUS). This is the default directory in which all backup files are saved, and the name of this directory appears in the Path edit box the first time you display the Backup Options dialog box. You can continue to use this directory for your backups, or you can select another.

You can use any directory you want for your backups. However, do not use a directory that contains any of your document files, because each backup file is given the same name as the original file. To be safe, use a directory for the backups that's not used for anything else.

In step 2 you must enter the name of an existing directory. Otherwise, an error message to that effect will appear because Professional Write Plus can't create a new directory for you. You must create it yourself (step 1) *outside* of Professional Write Plus.

When you select a new backup directory, it takes effect immediately for the current file and also for any other files you may open in the current word processing session. Note that this is quite different from the Automatic Timed Save feature (above), which may not take effect for other files until the next time you start up Professional Write Plus.

Saving to a Different File

One of the safest ways to ensure against catastrophic loss is to copy your work periodically to a file on a backup floppy disk. For instance, whenever I'm writing I always keep a floppy in one of the computer's drives, and about every half hour (or whenever I remember) I make a copy of the current document to that floppy. That way, I'm just about guaranteed never to lose more than 30 minutes of work, no matter what type of blunder I commit at the computer.

A backup floppy should be clearly labeled, and it should be used only for making backups. That way, your backup files have the best chance of not being lost among your various data disks.

Let's suppose that you're working with a document that's saved in the file C:\MYWORK\CURRENT. Here's how to create a floppy backup of your work:

1. Select File/Save As.

2. When the dialog box appears, enter the full name of the file to hold your work. Include the disk drive as part of the file name. One simple technique is to use the same file name for the floppy as for your regular file. For instance, in this example you could enter **A:CURRENT**.

3. After the disk drive light goes out, save the file to its normal file: Select File/Save As, then enter the full file name, including the disk drive and directory. For instance, in this example you would enter **C:\MY-WORK\CURRENT**.

The reason for step 3 has to do with automatic timed saves. Each automatic save is to the file last used for a save. Thus, in the absence of step 3, this will be to the floppy disk used in step 2. This is to be avoided because saving to a floppy can take a relatively long time, whereas saving to a hard disk requires only a few seconds at most.

Working with Several Documents at Once

You can work with several different documents at the same time—a handy feature that has many applications. For example, you might want to create a new document, while at the same time keeping one or more other documents open for reference. As part of this process, you can easily perform block transfers between the documents.

You can also keep two copies of the same document open at the same time. Each copy can be positioned independently of the other, which can help you to make proper intra-document references. When doing this, however, there is some danger of losing data unless you're careful to follow some strict guidelines.

When you open a second document, Professional Write Plus opens a second copy of itself in another window, sharing the screen with the original document. You can work with up to seven different documents at once, depending on what else you have running under Windows. As the number of other programs running under Windows increases, fewer Professional Write Plus documents can be opened, simply because Windows has a limited capacity for running multiple programs. When Windows can't open any more copies of Professional Write Plus, this error message will appear:

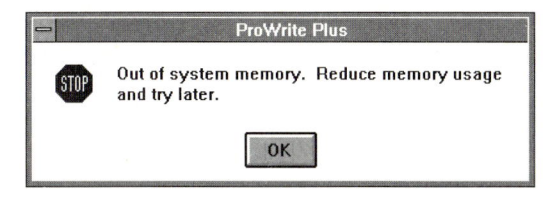

[Dialog box: ProWrite Plus — Out of system memory. Reduce memory usage and try later. OK]

CAUTION! *If this message appears, you should close one or two of the programs running under Windows. This will prevent unpleasant side effects from happening.*

Opening another document requires only a few steps:

1. Select Open/File.

2. When the Open dialog box appears (Figure 5.1), enter the name of the file you want to open.

3. Click on Open Another.

4. The new document will be opened in a window in the bottom portion of the screen, as shown in Figure 5.3.

You can work with either document, simply by clicking in either window. The documents are completely independent because you're using two entirely separate copies of Professional Write Plus. And because each window represents a separate running copy of the program, you can use each to open, close, and work with different documents.

For example, suppose you're editing a document in window A. To help you work with this document, you open another document (perhaps for reference) in window B. When you're through with this reference document, you can close it and then open another one, still in window B. This process will have no effect on the document in window A.

With two or more documents open, the screen is initially divided equally among them. However, you can change the sizes of the different windows in any way you wish, using the standard techniques for managing windows.

Figure 5.3
Two documents sharing the screen

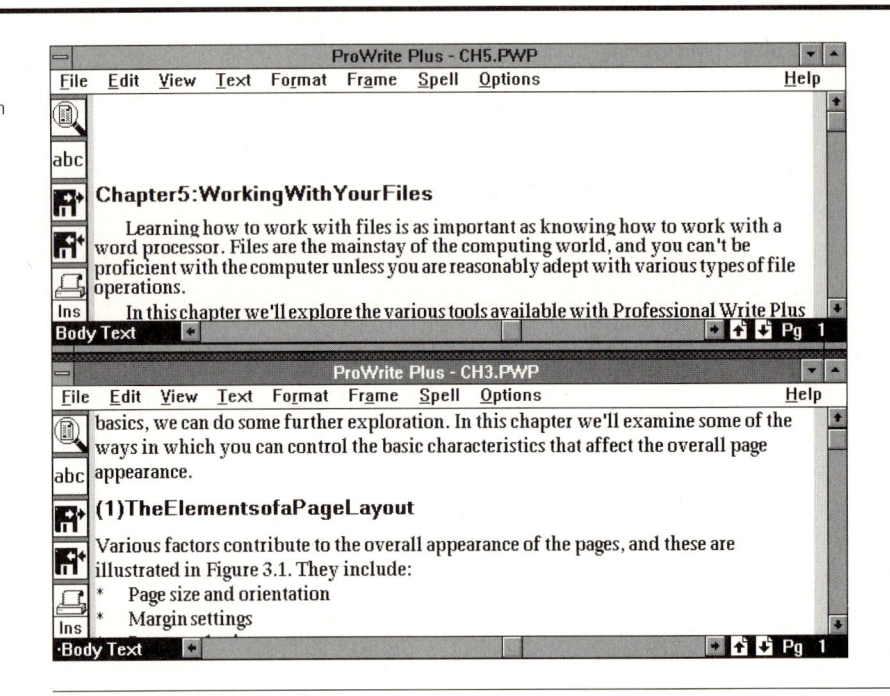

[Screenshot: Two ProWrite Plus document windows stacked — "ProWrite Plus - CH5.PWP" above and "ProWrite Plus - CH3.PWP" below, showing menu bars (File, Edit, View, Text, Format, Frame, Spell, Options, Help) and body text.]

Here are some of your options:

- To enlarge a window to fill the entire screen, click on the maximize button in the upper-right corner of that window (see below). When you do this, any other open windows are still there, but they're hidden beneath the current document. Later, you can restore the window to its original size by clicking on the same button again.

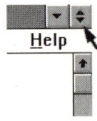

- To resize a window, grab an edge of the window and drag it in or out to reduce or increase the window size.

- To reduce a window to an icon, click on the minimize icon in the upper-right corner of the window (see below). Later, you can restore that window by clicking on the icon.

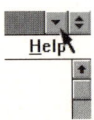

Working with the Same Document in Two Windows

Opening the same document in two different Professional Write Plus windows can be extremely useful, if, for example, you want to refer to one part of the document in another part. However, if you don't exercise a high degree of caution you may lose a good deal of your work.

To illustrate how this can occur, let's suppose that you open the same document in two different windows—call them windows 1 and 2. Let's also suppose that you carry out the following steps in the indicated order:

1. Make a set of corrections, C1, in window 1.

2. Make another set of corrections, C2, in window 2.

3. In window 1, save the document (using Ctrl-S, for example).

4. In window 2, save the document (again using Ctrl-S).

At the end of these steps, the set of corrections C1 will be lost, because the save in step 4 overwrites the copy of the document saved in step 3.

In order to avoid this type of situation, follow these rules:

- Make changes in only one copy of the document.

- Save only from that same copy. *Do not save from more than one open copy.*

- Turn off the Automatic Timed Save feature in all windows except the one in which you're editing the document.

All of these are extremely important. If you don't turn off the Automatic Timed Save feature, the scenario listed above will automatically take place over and over, and your document will turn into a pile of rubbish.

You can also take out extra insurance by creating a backup copy of the document before you open it in two or more windows. Then if you do have a tragedy, you can recover by starting over using the backup.

Transferring Text Between Documents

One way to transfer blocks of text from one document to another is to open both documents, then use standard block operations. This technique is possible because the Windows clipboard and its contents are accessible to any program running under Windows.

To illustrate this, let's suppose that you have opened two documents, A and B, and you want to copy a text block from document A to document B. Here are the steps to follow:

1. Select document A (simply click anywhere in its window).

2. Scroll to the text you want to copy.

3. Select the text as a block, then select Edit/Copy.
4. Select document B (click anywhere in its window).
5. Position the text cursor where you want to place the block.
6. Select Edit/Paste, and the block will be copied.

In step 3 the block is copied to the Windows clipboard, and in step 6 it's copied from the clipboard to document B, as shown in Figure 5.4.

Figure 5.4
Transferring a text block between documents

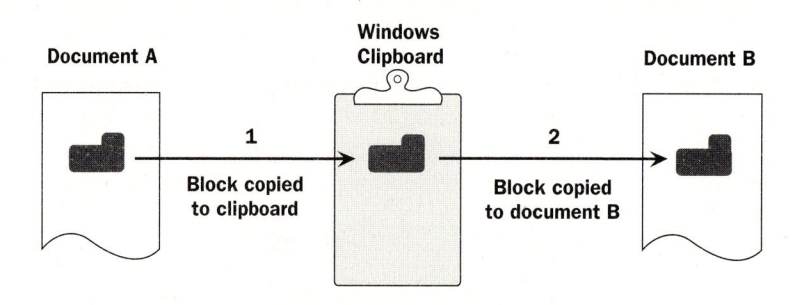

Appending One Document to Another

The ability to open two files simultaneously offers an easy method for attaching (or appending) one Professional Write Plus document to another. The basic idea is to open both documents at the same time, then transfer the entire contents of one into a chosen position in the other. The appended document can be placed anywhere in the target document—at the beginning, the end, or anywhere in between.

Suppose that you want to append document B to a particular spot in document A, as shown in Figure 5.5. Here are the steps to follow:

1. Open both documents in separate windows.
2. Select the entire document B: Position the text cursor at the beginning, hold down the Shift key, and press Ctrl-End. The entire document will be highlighted.
3. Select Edit/Copy, and the document will be copied to the clipboard.
4. Position the text cursor at the position in document A where you want to append document B.
5. Select Edit/Paste, and document B will be appended at the spot you selected.

Figure 5.5
Appending one document to another

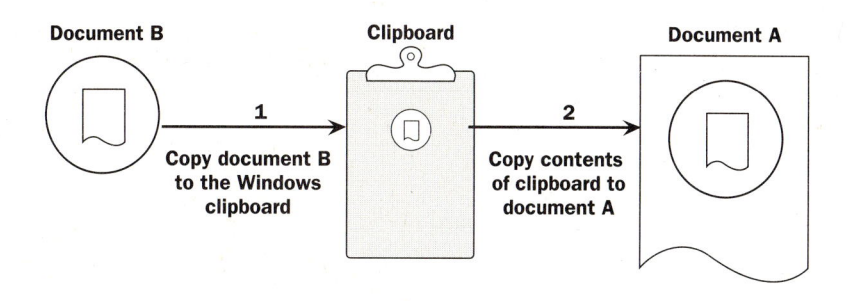

You can append a document of just about any size using this method. The clipboard is able to accommodate text blocks up to 300 pages long—which should be sufficient for most purposes.

Importing Text from Other Programs

The ability to transfer information from one program to another has become an important trend in the microcomputer world. This is more than a passing fancy, and you may occasionally find yourself in a situation in which you need to access information that has been generated somewhere else. Moreover, this information may not be in a Professional Write Plus document format. Instead, it may have been generated by a database, a spreadsheet, or another word processor.

Using Professional Write Plus, you can import text from a variety of different sources. (The term *import* here refers to reading information that's in non-Professional Write Plus format into a Professional Write Plus document.) This information can be merged with an existing document, or it can be the basis of a new one. Table 5.1 lists the different types of file formats Professional Write Plus can import.

ASCII Files

Professional Write Plus can import many different styles of ASCII files, which are the real common denominators in linking diverse types of software (and hardware). Nearly every type of word processor can generate a document file in some type of ASCII format. In addition, most spreadsheet and database programs can output textual information as ASCII files. However, many programs use a term other than *ASCII* for these types of files. For example, WordPerfect refers to them as *DOS text files*, and WordStar calls them *non-document files*.

Table 5.1   **File Formats Professional Write Plus Can Import**

Word Processor Formats

Ami and Ami Professional

Microsoft Windows Write

Microsoft Word (DOS and Windows versions)

Multimate

OfficeWriter

Professional Write (DOS version)

Rich Text Format

SAMNA Word IV

WordPerfect (versions 4.2 and 5.x)

WordStar

WordStar 2000

Specialized Formats

ASCII (various formats, including 7-bit and 8-bit)

DCA/FFT

DCA/RFT

Spreadsheet Formats

DIF

DIF (Navy)

Enable (versions 1.5 to 2.5)

Excel

Lotus 1-2-3 (versions 1A, 2.0, and 2.01)

Lotus Symphony (versions 1.0, 1.01, 1.1)

SuperCalc3 (version 2.1)

SuperCalc4 (version 1.10)

Database Formats

dBASE (II, III, III+, and IV)

If you can't get Professional Write Plus to import information generated by some other program, see if that program can output the text in an ASCII file format. If so, you can almost certainly import that file. Here are the different types of ASCII files you can import:

7-Bit ASCII   This format includes the first 128 characters of the IBM PC ASCII set. This consists of all the upper- and lowercase letters, the digits, and the more common special characters, including all those on most keyboards.

8-Bit ASCII   This includes the complete IBM PC ASCII character set: all the upper- and lowercase letters, the digits, and many special characters, including those on the standard keyboard.

8-Bit ANSI   This type of ASCII file includes the complete ANSI character set. Again, this consists of letters, digits, and a wide variety of special characters.

Single CR or LF Paragraph Endings   These are files in which each hard return or line feed is treated as an end-of-paragraph.

Double CR or LF Paragraph Endings   These are files in which only the following are treated as an end-of-paragraph: two consecutive hard returns or line feeds, or a hard return or line feed followed by a tab character.

Formatting Information

You can reasonably expect that text will never be imported with all of its formatting features intact. If you make this assumption, you'll never be disappointed, but you may occasionally be pleasantly surprised. For example, a document generated in WordPerfect 5.1 format may contain dozens of different types of formatting codes. The more common ones will certainly be translated properly, but many of the others will simply be ignored.

Here are a few other generalities about importing text. These are only generalizations, with many exceptions, because each type of file format is translated differently:

- Text imported into a Professional Write Plus document will conform to the page layout features of that document, but some formatting information may also be imported along with the text, as noted below.

- Text attributes, such as boldface, italics, and so on, will usually be imported.

- Tab information may be imported in some cases (see the following section for more information about tabs and tab rulers).

- Headers and footers may be imported, and they may be appended to existing ones in the document.

- Text alignment may be preserved. For example, if an imported WordPerfect document contains lines that are centered or right-justified, those lines will be adjusted correspondingly in Professional Write Plus.

- Professional Write Plus may attempt to maintain any paragraph style information included with an imported document. These styles may or may not be what you want, so you would be wise to carefully check the text after it has been imported.

- When information from a database or spreadsheet file is imported, field values are separated by tabs, and each record begins a new paragraph. However, none of the original alignment information is kept. For example, cells in a spreadsheet file may be aligned on either the left, right, or center, but this alignment information is lost during translation.

- An ASCII file contains text, but no formatting information, so when you import an ASCII file the text is reformatted to conform to the layout features of the Professional Write Plus document. There is one exception to this rule: Some word processors will attach a paragraph style name to the beginning of each paragraph in a file. If that style name is the same as one associated with your document, the paragraph will be reformatted to match the specifications of your style.

These are just some of the more common formatting issues to be dealt with when importing a document. To find out more about the translation details for particular file types, refer to the *Professional Write Plus User's Manual,* which accompanies the software.

Tab Rulers
When you import a text file, the tabs in your document may be changed. If the imported text contains a code specifying new tabs (this code would have been inserted by the word processor that created the file), and if Professional Write Plus can interpret the code, a tab ruler will be inserted into the imported text near the position of the original code, and the settings on the ruler will correspond to the tab setting codes in the original text. For each new-tabs code in the file, a corresponding tab ruler will be inserted into the document.

A tab ruler will also be inserted in your document at the beginning of the imported text, with the tabs set every half inch. The purpose of this inserted ruler is not clear, and in most circumstances it's more of a nuisance than anything else. However, you can prevent it from being inserted as follows: Before importing the text, insert a new tab ruler of your own at the spot in the document where the text will be placed.

If a new tab ruler is inserted during the import process, it will affect all the text that follows—both the imported text and any original text. If this is not what you want, you can delete the inserted tab ruler. To be absolutely sure about whether or not any new tab rulers have been inserted, select Options/Layout Mode Options, then turn on the Marks option. A visible mark will appear wherever a tab ruler has been inserted. You can also use the Go To option on the Edit menu to search through the imported text for any new tab rulers. Any that you find can be deleted by using the Format/Tab Ruler/Remove Tab Ruler option.

Importing a File

You can import any of the file formats listed in Table 5.1. In all cases, the data is converted to Professional Write Plus format and merged with the current document at the position of the text cursor. The exact nature of the data conversion depends on the type of file format being converted. The possibilities are too numerous to detail here, because so many types of data files can be imported, each of which is treated differently.

CAUTION! *Carefully check any text after it's been imported into your document—some of the original formatting may have been lost during the conversion, and codes in the text may change some of the page layout features.*

Here are the steps for importing any type of text file, regardless of whether it was generated by a word processor, database program, or spreadsheet software:

1. Select File/File Conversions/Import, and the dialog box shown in Figure 5.6 will appear.

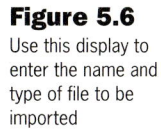

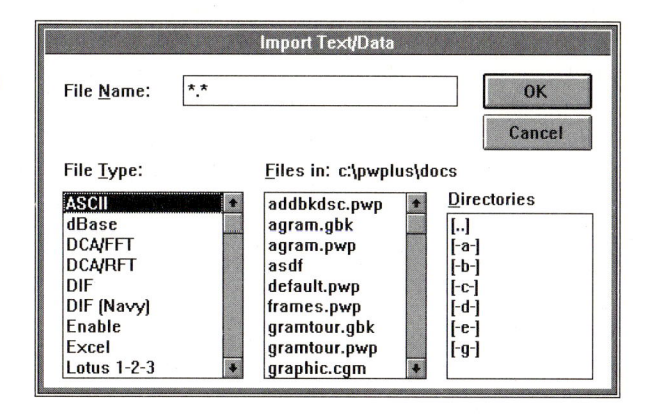

Figure 5.6
Use this display to enter the name and type of file to be imported

2. In the box labeled "File Type", select the format of the file.

3. Enter the complete name of the file, including the disk drive and directory where it's stored. You can enter this name directly in the File Name edit box, or you can use the boxes labeled "Files in" and "Directories" to make your selections.

4. Click on OK.

5. If you're importing any file type other than ASCII, follow any additional instructions on the screen (see below).

If you're importing an ASCII file, the dialog box shown in Figure 5.7 will appear. Select the options you want (see "ASCII Options," below), then click on OK to import the file.

Figure 5.7
Use this display to select the exact type of ASCII file

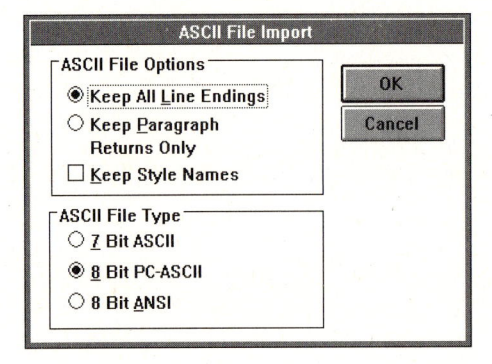

For some types of non-ASCII files, an additional dialog box may appear. For example, if you're importing a dBASE file, the screen shown in Figure 5.8 will appear. You can then select whether you want to import the entire file or just selected fields. (You'll have to know the field names, because they're not displayed on the screen.)

In some cases, you may be asked to supply the location of one or more files associated with the file you're importing. For example, some Microsoft Word files have associated printer files. If you don't know the location of a file requested by Professional Write Plus, select Cancel. The document will be imported anyway, but some formatting information will be lost.

ASCII Options
In step 5 above, you must select the correct options for the ASCII file you're importing. To understand your choices, the following paragraphs list all the options, and then discuss how to select the correct ones.

Figure 5.8
The dialog box for importing a dBASE file

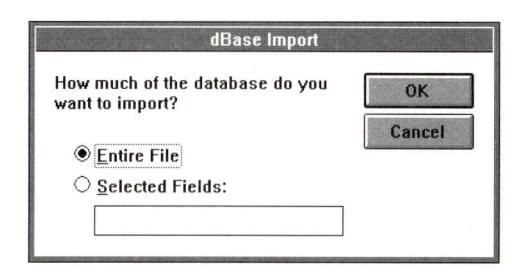

Keep All Line Endings Every hard return or line feed is treated as an end-of-paragraph mark. Use this option for the following types of files:

- ASCII files generated by database or spreadsheet programs
- Program listings

Keep Paragraph Returns Only When this option is selected, only the following are treated as end-of-paragraph indicators:

- Two consecutive hard returns
- Two consecutive line feeds.
- A hard return or line feed followed by a tab character

This is normally (but not always) the option to select when importing text files generated by other word processors.

Keep Style Names As each paragraph is imported, it is scanned for text in the format <*Style-name*> (brackets included). If text in this format is found anywhere in the paragraph, and if *Style-name* matches the name of an existing style, either in the current template or attached to the document, then that paragraph is assigned that style. (Chapters 6 and 7 explain about styles and templates.)

You must choose between Keep Paragraph Returns Only or Keep All Line Endings. If you don't know which is the correct one, make a guess, import the file, and then see if the paragraph breaks look correct. (Don't worry—it's almost always excruciatingly obvious when you've made the wrong choice.) If you make the wrong choice, delete the imported text, and then try again with the other option.

ASCII File Type In the box with this label, select the correct type of ASCII file. If the file contains only the standard characters (letters, digits, and the special characters on your keyboard), it won't matter which option you select. If, however, the file contains other special characters, you'll need to specify the correct file type if you want to retrieve those characters. In the absence of any other information, use trial and error. Just select a file type, import the file, and see if the text contains whatever special characters you expect to be there. If not, try the other file types.

A point to ponder: If you have no idea as to the contents of the file, you may never know if you select the wrong file type!

Opening an ASCII File

You can also *open* an ASCII file, in which case the contents of the new (ASCII) file replaces the current document. Notice that this is quite different from *importing* an ASCII file, where you merge the text *into* the current document. To open an ASCII file:

1. Select File/Open.

2. When the Open dialog box appears (Figure 5.1), click on ASCII File.

3. Select the name of the file to be imported, including the drive and directory.

4. Click on ASCII Options, and then select the correct options in the dialog box that appears. (For details, see the preceding section, "ASCII Options.")

Ami Professional Files

There is one file format that needs no conversion at all—Ami or Ami Professional—because these formats are completely compatible with Professional Write Plus. To open a file in this format, you follow the normal procedure for opening a Professional Write Plus document file, with a couple of extra steps to accommodate the fact that Ami document file names usually include the .SAM extension. Here's how to open an Ami document:

1. Select File/Open.

2. When the Open dialog box appears (Figure 5.1), select the directory you want.

3. In the File Name dialog box, enter ***.SAM**, then press Enter.

4. Select the file you want to open.

The reason for step 3 is that when the Open dialog box appears, the file name specification *.PWP appears in the File Name dialog box because the program assumes that you want to open a Professional Write Plus document. Since Ami document file names usually end with .SAM, you change this specification to *.SAM.

Later, if you want to save the document to a Professional Write Plus file, use the File/Save As option, then enter a new file name. As it's saved, the program automatically attaches the .PWP extension to the file name.

Exporting Files in Different Formats

The last section described how to import text files with various formats. You can also save your documents in wide variety of formats, a process known as *exporting*. For example, to send a copy of a document to a colleague who uses WordPerfect, you would export the text using the WordPerfect format.

When a document is exported to another format, a good deal of the document formatting is retained. For example, headers and footers are usually kept, as are text attributes such as boldface and italics. Some features, such as graphics, are never included with the exported text, and other features may or may not be included, depending on which export format is being used.

Regardless of these limitations, exporting is a powerful feature that can expand your communication abilities with the PC world. If you know others with IBM-compatible computers, chances are very good you can create document files that can be read with their word processors.

The Types of Files You Can Export

Using Professional Write Plus, you can export documents in many different file formats, including those for other word processors, as well as spreadsheet and database programs. You can also export files in various ASCII formats, giving you an enormous range of flexibility. Here are the word processor file formats you can create when exporting a file:

- Ami and Ami Professional
- Multimate
- OfficeWriter
- Professional Write (DOS version)
- Rich Text Format
- SAMNA Word IV
- Microsoft Windows Write
- Microsoft Word and Word for Windows
- WordPerfect (versions 4.2 and 5.x)
- WordStar
- WordStar 2000

In addition to these, you can also export in the following specialized formats: ASCII, DCA/FFT, DCA/RFT, DIF, and Enable.

You can't create files that are in other database or spreadsheet formats, such as dBASE or Lotus 1-2-3. Nevertheless, you can export data files that be *read* by any database or spreadsheet program, simply by creating files in ASCII format. Just about every program in the world can read ASCII files, and although you can't include any formatting information in an ASCII file, it's a lot better than not being able to send any data at all!

Formatting Information

When a document is exported in a different word processor format, most of the vital formatting information is included. However, because every word processor is unique, you can safely assume that something will be lost in the translation. Professional Write Plus may not translate everything with 100-percent accuracy, so the word processor at the other end may not be able to read everything in a file perfectly. (These remarks refer to the document formatting only. It is almost assured that the text itself will be copied correctly.)

Here's a list of the formatting specifications that Professional Write Plus attempts to output, along with the text, to an exported file:

- Footnotes
- Headers and footers
- Text attributes
- Alignments
- Line spacing
- Hard page breaks
- Tabs and tab rulers
- Page numbers
- System dates
- Text in frames

The majority of these features will be exported with little or no change. However, there are many exceptions, so try to make sure that the document is carefully checked when it's used at the other end. Here are the most notable points to be aware of:

- All text attributes (boldface, italics, and so on) are exported, provided the export format can handle them. For example, many word processors don't know about initial caps or overstrike.

Exporting Files in Different Formats

- All text alignments are included (left-justified, centered, and so forth), provided the export format knows about them.

- Footnotes are always included, either as footnotes or as regular text at the end of the document, depending on whether the export format knows about footnotes.

- If the original document doesn't include any inserted tab rulers, the default tabs in the exported document are set to every $1/2$ inch. If the original document does include inserted tab rulers, the tab positions and types are included in the exported text. If the export format can't deal with a particular tab type (such as decimal), it's converted to a left tab.

- Frames themselves are not exported. However, any text within an anchored frame is included as ordinary text, in the same position in which it appears in the original document. Text included in an unanchored frame is included at the end of the exported text.

A Word of Warning

Many other changes, too numerous to detail here, may occur when you create a file in a different format. As a general rule, any document exported to another file type should be handled with great care by whoever uses it.

Worse yet, there is always a chance that a file you export won't work at all when another word processor attempts to input it. If this occurs, there's a nearly foolproof method of transferring text to another word processor: export it as an ordinary ASCII file. This type of file contains nothing but text, and just about every word processor can import it with little if any difficulty. The details of exporting ASCII files are discussed shortly.

Exporting a File

Generally, the steps for exporting a document to a different format are the same, regardless of the type of file you're creating. There is one exception however: ASCII files require one or two extra steps. To export a document to a different file format, follow these steps:

1. Select File/File Conversions/Export, and the dialog box shown in Figure 5.9 will appear.

2. Select the disk drive and directory to which the new file is to be written.

3. In the lower-left selection box, select the type of file format to be created.

4. In the File Name edit box, enter a name for the file that you're creating.

5. Click on OK. If you selected a file type other than ASCII, the file is created and you can skip step 6. If you selected an ASCII file type, go on.

Figure 5.9
Use this display to select the file name and export format

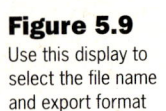

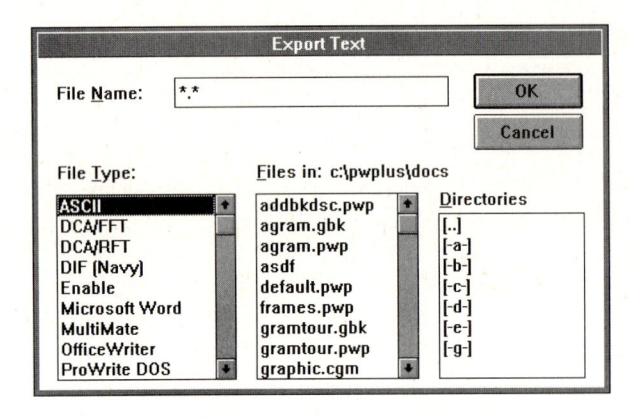

6. When the dialog box shown in Figure 5.10 appears, select the options you want (see below), then click on OK to create the file.

Figure 5.10
Use this display to select the options for the ASCII file being created

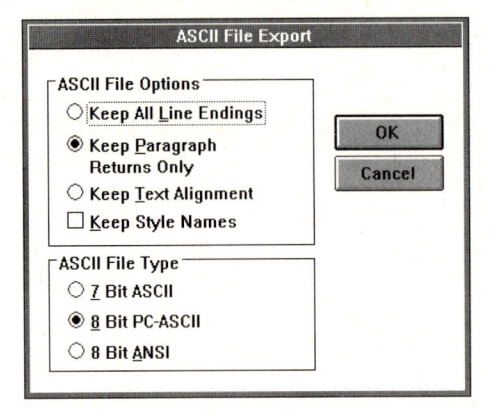

ASCII Options

The options you select in step 6 above determine the exact format of the ASCII file, as follows:

Keep All Line Endings If you select this option, a hard return will be attached to the end of every line appearing on your screen (that is, each soft return will be replaced with a hard return). This is generally *not* what you want for ordinary documents. However, this is usually the correct option for the following types of documents.

- Program listings
- Tables (a document consisting entirely of tables)
- Any other type of document in which you want the exact line endings appearing on your screen to be preserved

Keep Paragraph Returns Only   Use this option for most ordinary documents. When you select this option, soft returns are deleted, and hard returns are inserted only at paragraph endings.

Keep Text Alignment   Select this option only if you want to preserve the exact alignment of each line as displayed on your screen. To do this, the conversion process inserts spaces as needed on each line, as well as a hard return at the end of each line. Normally you do not want to use this option for ordinary documents.

Keep Style Names   If you select this option, each paragraph will begin with the name of the style assigned to that paragraph enclosed in angle brackets, <Body Text>, for example. Select this option only if you plan to read this file with a word processor that can translate the style names properly. If it can't, the names will appear as ordinary text at the beginning of each paragraph (a situation that you definitely do not want).

ASCII File Type   Oddly enough, your choice for the file type may not be very important, because if a document contains only the characters found on most keyboards, *any* choice will be adequate. When in doubt, choose 8 Bit PC-ASCII.

Saving an ASCII File

In addition to the method described earlier, you can also export a document to an ASCII file by using the File/Save As option:

1. When the Save As dialog box appears, click on ASCII File.
2. Click on ASCII Options, then select the options as described in the previous section.

There is no advantage to using this method, compared to the steps described in the previous section. Both methods can generate any type of ASCII file, so use whichever you happen to feel most comfortable with—or flip a coin.

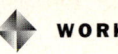

Using the File Manager

The File Manager is a separate module within Professional Write Plus that allows you to perform various types of file manipulations. These are basically the same operations you can perform either from DOS or with the Windows File Manager. However, for simple file operations Professional Write Plus's File Manager is probably the most convenient to use when you're in the middle of working with a document.

Using the File Manager, you can perform any of the following file operations:

- Copy, either to another directory or to the same one
- Delete
- Move from one directory to another
- Rename
- Change the file attributes
- View selected groups of files within any directory

Note. You can manipulate any type of file with the File Manager, not just document files created by Professional Write Plus.

When copying or moving Professional Write Plus documents, use the File Manager instead of either the Windows File Manager or DOS. The reason for this is that many document files are associated with other files containing graphics and style information. Using Professional Write Plus's File Manager, you can easily copy or move these associated files as well.

To access the File Manager, select File/File Manager. The dialog box shown in Figure 5.11 will appear. The box at the top of the screen indicates the currently selected disk drive and directory. The list box at the bottom displays the names of the files in that directory. You can select which directory to access, and you can also select the subset of files to be displayed at the bottom.

Selecting the Directory to Access

When the File Manager dialog box first appears, the default document directory is selected. (For a discussion of this default, see "Selecting a Different Directory," at the beginning of this chapter). You can access a different directory by using any of the following methods:

- Select File/Change Directory, then enter the new directory in the box that appears.
- Click on any part of the box containing the current directory, then enter the new directory name.

Figure 5.11
The File Manager's main dialog box

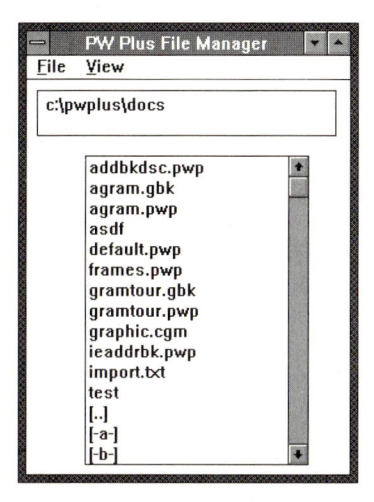

```
┌─────────────────────────────┐
│    PW Plus File Manager     │
│ File  View                  │
│ ┌─────────────────────────┐ │
│ │ c:\pwplus\docs          │ │
│ └─────────────────────────┘ │
│ ┌─────────────────────────┐ │
│ │ addbkdsc.pwp         ▲  │ │
│ │ agram.gbk               │ │
│ │ agram.pwp               │ │
│ │ asdf                    │ │
│ │ default.pwp             │ │
│ │ frames.pwp              │ │
│ │ gramtour.gbk            │ │
│ │ gramtour.pwp            │ │
│ │ graphic.cgm             │ │
│ │ ieaddrbk.pwp            │ │
│ │ import.txt              │ │
│ │ test                    │ │
│ │ [..]                    │ │
│ │ [-a-]                   │ │
│ │ [-b-]                ▼  │ │
│ └─────────────────────────┘ │
└─────────────────────────────┘
```

- Use the entries at the bottom of the list box. For example, to select the parent of the current directory, click on the entry (..). For more details about this procedure, see "Selecting a Different Directory."

- Double-click on a directory name in the box at the top of the display. For example, if the path "C:\PWPLUS\DOCS" appears, you can select the directory C:\:PWPLUS by double-clicking on "PWPLUS".

When you use either of the first two methods, the Change Directory box appears (see below) for you to enter the name of the new directory. If you're selecting a new disk drive, include that as part of the directory name. For example, to switch to the directory \MYSTUFF on drive E, enter **E:\MYSTUFF**.

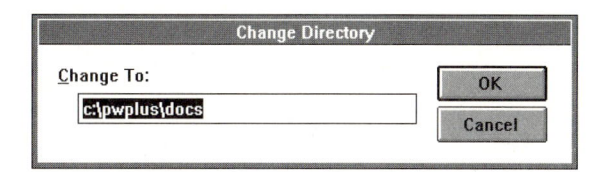

```
┌──────────────── Change Directory ────────────────┐
│ Change To:                                       │
│ ┌──────────────────────────┐   ┌──────────────┐  │
│ │ c:\pwplus\docs           │   │     OK       │  │
│ └──────────────────────────┘   └──────────────┘  │
│                                ┌──────────────┐  │
│                                │   Cancel     │  │
│                                └──────────────┘  │
└──────────────────────────────────────────────────┘
```

Selecting the File Names to Display

After you have selected the directory you want to work with, you can choose which subset of file names within that directory are to be displayed in the list box. You can display all the file names, or any desired subset.

To select the file names to be displayed, begin by selecting the View menu. Then, choose one of the following options:

All Choosing All will display the names of every file in the directory (the default).

***.PWP** Selecting *.PWP will cause only document files in Professional Write Plus format to be displayed.

Partial If you select Partial, another edit box appears (see below), and you can then enter the file name specification of the files you want displayed.

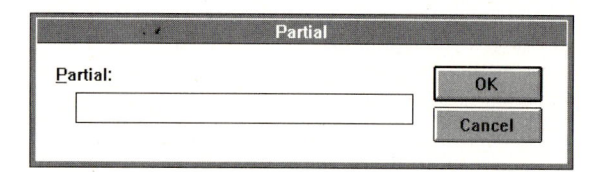

You can use the standard DOS wildcards ? and * to write this specification, where ? stands for any single character and * represents any group of characters. For example, to display all the files ending with the extension .TXT, enter the specification ***.TXT**. Or, to display any files beginning with the name MYFILES, enter **MYFILES*.***.

You can also change to another disk drive and/or directory by using the Partial option. For example, if you want to view all the Professional Write Plus document files in the directory \OLDONES on drive E, enter **E:\OLDONES*.PWP**.

Standard File Operations

Using the File Manager, you can copy, move, rename, and delete files. One of the nice features of this program is that you can perform most of these operations either on a single file or on any group of files you select.

Selecting Files

To perform any file operation, you begin by selecting the files from those displayed in the list box (see Figure 5.11). To select a file, simply click on it. You can select as many files as you wish. Each file will remain highlighted unless you deselect it by clicking on it again. After you have selected the files you want to work with, you can then perform whatever file operations you wish.

Copying and Moving Files

To either copy or move a group of files, follow these steps.

1. Select the files to copied or moved.

2. Choose the Copy or Move option from the File menu.

3. When the next dialog box appears (see below), enter the name of the disk drive and/or directory where the files are to be copied or moved, then click on OK.

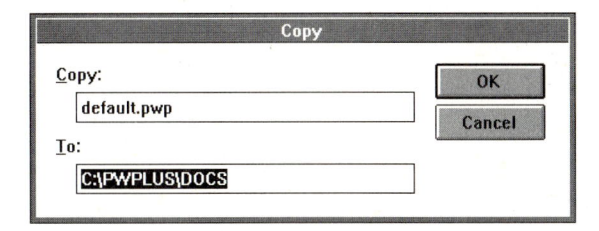

```
┌─────────────────── Copy ───────────────────┐
│  Copy:                          ┌────────┐ │
│  ┌──────────────────────┐       │   OK   │ │
│  │ default.pwp          │       └────────┘ │
│  └──────────────────────┘       ┌────────┐ │
│  To:                            │ Cancel │ │
│  ┌──────────────────────┐       └────────┘ │
│  │ C:\PWPLUS\DOCS       │                  │
│  └──────────────────────┘                  │
└────────────────────────────────────────────┘
```

4. If the files you're copying or moving are Professional Write Plus documents, the dialog box shown in Figure 5.12 will appear.

Figure 5.12
Options for copying and moving files

```
┌──────────────── File Options ────────────────┐
│  Source:                        ┌────────┐   │
│  C:\PWPLUS\DOCS\FRAMES.PWP      │   OK   │   │
│  Destination:                   └────────┘   │
│  C:\PWPLUS\DOCS\FRAMES.PWP      ┌────────┐   │
│  ☐ Take Associated Graphics Files│ Cancel │  │
│  ☒ Take Associated Template     └────────┘   │
│  ☐ Maintain Format,                          │
│    But Do Not Take Associated Template       │
└──────────────────────────────────────────────┘
```

5. Select the appropriate options as explained below, then click on OK.

When you move or copy a file, you must decide whether to copy the associated template and graphics files as well by selecting the appropriate options, as follows:

Take Associated Graphics Files   With this option selected, any graphics files used by the document being copied or moved will also be copied or moved to the specified directory, but *only* if the destination is on a different disk drive. If the destination is on the same drive as the original file, the graphics files will not be copied, but the new copy of the file remembers the original location of the graphics files. This option should definitely be selected if the destination is on a different drive.

Take Associated Template   Using this option, the template file associated with the document being copied or moved will also be copied or moved. Be sure to select this option if the destination is on another disk drive. (For information about styles and templates, see Chapters 6 and 7.)

Maintain Format, But Do Not Take Associated Template   With this option, the styles in the associated template are transferred as local styles to the new copy of the document. If you do not select either this option or Take Associated Template, then the original template will be assigned to the new document (but the template itself is not copied).

Deleting Files

Use the following steps to delete a group of files:

1. Select the files to be deleted.

2. Choose Delete from the File menu.

3. When the next display appears (see below), select OK to verify your choice. Otherwise, click on Cancel.

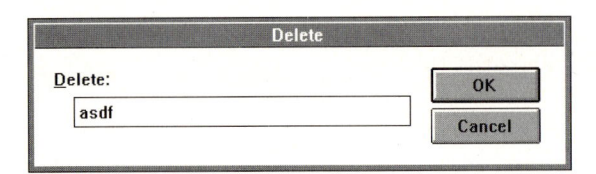

CAUTION! *Deleting files is a dangerous operation within the File Manager because you can wipe out any number of files with a click of the mouse button. Be careful when using this option.*

Renaming Files

To rename a file, first select it, and then choose Rename from the File menu. When the next dialog box appears (see below), enter the new name for the file.

Note. You can select only one file at a time when using the Rename option.

When you enter the new file name, you can actually move the file to a different directory as long as it's on the same disk drive. Just enter the full name, including the directory. For example, if you want to rename the file JACK to JILL and also move it to the directory \HILL, enter the name **\HILL\JILL**.

When you rename a Professional Write Plus document file, you don't have to include the .PWP extension, because it's automatically added to the new file name. If you do *not* want the new file name to have the .PWP extension, include just the period as part of the new name. For example, to rename BEAN.PWP to STALK, enter the new name as **STALK.**.

Changing Read/Write Attributes

Each DOS file has attached to it a *read/write file attribute*. For each file, the normal setting for this attribute is Read-Write, so that the file can be modified as well as read. However, if this attribute is set to Read Only, the file can be read but not modified.

If you want to protect an important file against any kind of modification, you can use the File Manager to set the attribute to Read Only. This will prevent *any* type of change, either with Professional Write Plus or any other software, including Windows or DOS. You can also use the File Manager to change an attribute from Read Only to Read/Write.

You can change the attribute of one or several files at the same time:

1. Select the files whose attributes you want to change.

2. Select Attributes from the File menu.

3. When the Change Attributes dialog box appears (see below), click on either Read Only or Read-Write, then click on OK.

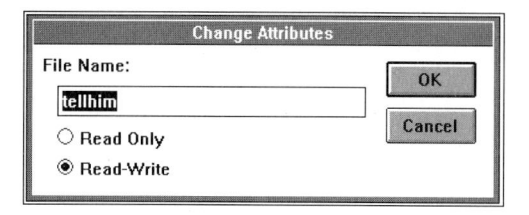

Exiting from the File Manager

With the File Manager dialog box displayed, you can exit back to Professional Write Plus's edit screen in various ways:

- Select Exit from the File menu

- Double-click on the Control box in the upper-left corner of the dialog box.
- Click on the Minimize button in the upper-right corner of the dialog box.

When you use either of the first two methods, the File Manager is closed. However, if you use the last method the File Manager is reduced to a Windows icon, but it's still active. The advantage of this is that when you later display the File Manager (by selecting File/File Manager from the main edit screen), your previous selection for disk drive and directory will still be active.

Summary

File manipulations are an important element of most types of software packages, and using Professional Write Plus is no exception. Take some time to practice using the File Manager. It's a valuable tool that will prove to be useful as you work with your various files, especially since you can use it for any type of file, not just those created with Professional Write Plus.

Some of the most valuable file manipulation techniques are those used to make backups. Developing a regular backup procedure will pay back large dividends (trust me). Make regular backups onto floppy disks, clearly label each disk, and keep them somewhere safe but handy. (You may be surprised how often you need a backup.)

When you import a file, be sure to check the text carefully because the import process is often imperfect and may generate surprises for you. Similarly, if you export a document for use with another word processor or other program, caution the intended user as to the source of the file, so that similar precautions can be taken. But don't let these caveats put you off. Importing and exporting are very useful ways to share information with friends and colleagues. And by taking suitable precautions you'll be in a position to enjoy these powerful features.

CHAPTER 6

Using Styles

Introducing Paragraph Styles

Creating a New Paragraph Style

Modifying Paragraph Styles

Using Different Fonts

Indenting and Aligning Paragraphs

Automatic Hyphenation

Customizing the Line and Text Spacing

Controlling Page Breaks

Creating Bulleted Lists

Creating Numbered Lists

Creating Introductory Text for Paragraphs

Using Ruling Lines

Special Applications for Styles

Using Function Key Shortcuts

THE PRECEDING CHAPTERS HAVE COVERED MOST OF THE BASIC FEAtures needed for day-to-day word processing. If you never learn more about Professional Write Plus than the contents of those chapters, you will probably be able to accomplish the vast majority of your word processing needs.

However, Professional Write Plus contains a set of advanced features that can add a whole new dimension to word processing. These features, which are normally associated with desktop publishing programs, are actually an integral part of the program. Once you learn how to use them, you'll wonder how you managed before.

This chapter covers the first of these desktop publishing features, paragraph styles. First you will create a simple paragraph style and embellish it in various ways. This will give you a feel for how styles work. Later in the chapter, the wide range of options available for customizing paragraph styles will be discussed and demonstrated.

Introducing Paragraph Styles

Note. By definition, a *paragraph* is all the text between two hard returns, or between the beginning of a document and the first hard return.

Simply put, a *paragraph style* (or *style* for short) is a set of formatting specifications that can be applied to any paragraph in a document for the purpose of enhancing the appearance of your documents. If you find yourself repeatedly using the same steps to enhance a paragraph's look, consider creating a paragraph style to do it for you.

You can use Professional Write Plus's built-in paragraph styles, or you can create your own. Throughout this chapter, the different ways to assign various characteristics to a paragraph style will be discussed. In some cases you'll want to make changes to one of the program's existing styles, and sometimes you'll want to create a new style and then customize it.

When you create a new paragraph style, it becomes attached to the document you're working with at the time, and you can then use that style to format any or all of the paragraphs in the document. This type of style is called *local* because it's attached to one particular document. You can attach any number of local paragraph styles to a single document. In Chapter 7, you'll see how to create style templates to make your styles *global*—that is, applicable to any document.

An important point to keep in mind when you use a paragraph style is that it applies to entire paragraphs. For example, if you often italicize entire paragraphs for emphasis, you can create a special paragraph style with that text attribute. Then, for each paragraph you want italicized, you just assign it that particular style. For italicizing single words or phrases, however, you must use the Italics option on the Text menu. The same idea applies to other text characteristics, such as line spacing and alignment. Use paragraph styles to apply special characteristics to entire paragraphs, but use the selections on the Text menu for groups of words or lines.

Even though you assign a particular style to a paragraph, you can to some extent override those established style characteristics for particular parts of the paragraph. For example, suppose you assign a paragraph a style that specifies boldfaced text, and you then assign this style to a paragraph, so that it becomes entirely boldfaced. You could then italicize selected text within the paragraph by blocking that text and selecting the italic option from the Text menu. However, you cannot "unbold" any text within the paragraph because you can't undo an attribute that's part of a style.

Features That Can Be Assigned Using Paragraph Styles

The following is a list of the paragraph features you can customize for the paragraph styles you define. As you read through this list, remember that when you assign a paragraph style to a particular paragraph, each of these features will be assigned to the entire paragraph.

Basic Font The basic font includes the typeface and size to be assigned to the paragraph text. In addition, special attributes such as boldface and italics can be assigned as part of the font.

Text Alignment You can specify paragraph lines to be left-, right-, or fully justified, or you can specify that each line be centered between the left and right margins.

Indentation Both left and right custom indentations (relative to the left or right margin) can be specified for all the lines in a paragraph. In addition, you can specify a special indentation for the first line.

Line Spacing You can specify single, $1^1/_2$, double, or custom spacing. You can also specify extra vertical space to appear before and after each paragraph.

Page Break Control You can determine whether or not to allow a page break in the middle of a paragraph. You can also force a page break before or after a paragraph.

Bulleted Lists You can assign a group of adjacent paragraphs to be bulleted, with a variety of different bullet characters to choose from.

Numbered Lists A group of adjacent paragraphs can be automatically numbered sequentially. This scheme can extend to multiple levels of numbering.

Introducing Paragraph Styles

Other Preceding Text   Each paragraph can be preceded by special text, such as a master phrase. For example, you might want certain paragraphs to begin with "Item:".

Lines   You can specify that a line be drawn either above or below each paragraph, or both. Also, you can control the length, thickness, and position of these lines.

Hyphenation   You can control whether or not hyphenation is used in a paragraph, that is, whether words break at the ends of lines.

Don't be put off by this formidable list of features. When you create a new paragraph style, you don't necessarily have to assign every feature listed. In fact, for many paragraph styles you'll only assign one or two of these features. The remaining ones will be assigned default values by the program. Once you get familiar with the technique, creating a new paragraph style can take just a few minutes—or as long as you like, depending on how fussy you are.

Let's consider a simple example to see how styles work. Suppose you want to create the bulleted list shown in Figure 6.1b. To begin, you enter the text shown in Figure 6.1a. Then, by simply pointing and clicking, you assign the Bullet paragraph style to each line (paragraph) you want bulleted. As each line is assigned the Bullet style, it assumes the form shown in Figure 6.1b.

The Bullet paragraph style, which you would have defined at some previous time (see "Creating Bulleted Lists," later in this chapter) might have the following specifications: "Begin each paragraph with a bullet character, which should be indented 1 inch. Then, insert 0.25 inches between the bullet and the first character on the line."

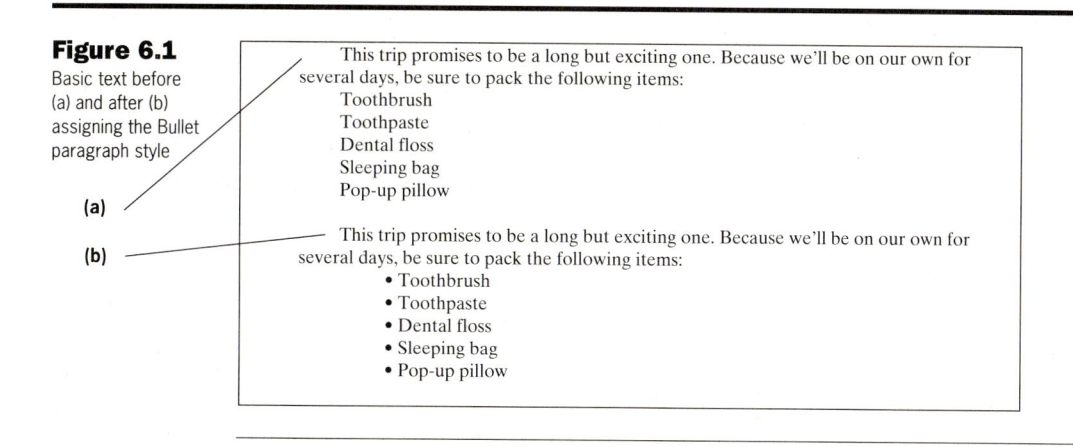

Figure 6.1
Basic text before (a) and after (b) assigning the Bullet paragraph style

(a)

(b)

```
This trip promises to be a long but exciting one. Because we'll be on our own for
several days, be sure to pack the following items:
   Toothbrush
   Toothpaste
   Dental floss
   Sleeping bag
   Pop-up pillow

This trip promises to be a long but exciting one. Because we'll be on our own for
several days, be sure to pack the following items:
   • Toothbrush
   • Toothpaste
   • Dental floss
   • Sleeping bag
   • Pop-up pillow
```

158   ◆   USING STYLES

As a second example, you could use a paragraph style called Indent to format the indented text shown in Figure 6.2b. To begin, you enter the text as shown in Figure 6.2a. Then, by pointing and clicking, you assign the Indent style to the middle paragraph, which is then automatically indented as shown in Figure 6.2b.

Figure 6.2
Basic text before (a) and after (b) assigning the Indent style to the middle paragraph

(a)

One way to avoid high-priced tourism along the Kenya coastline is to do a camping trip. This is not, however, to be confused with camping a l'Americain. For starters, recreational vehicles just do not exist in this part of the world. Most folks go camping in something about the size of a VW beetle (which by the way can easily carry four people plus all required camping apparatus). In fact, here's what one local tourist adviser has to say about touring the coast:

Don't be a tourist; be a traveler. Keep a low profile and you'll have a much better time. One way to do this is to use as small a vehicle as possible. A favorite among those in the know is the "lowly" Volkswagen beetle. It's unbelievably durable (albeit a bit mechanically touchy), it's low on gas consumption, and its drive wheels are where they belong—right under the engine.

Such sage advice from a seasoned veteran should be taken seriously. Do yourself a favor by traveling light, small, and inconspicuously, and you'll have a far better time than if you were to swagger around in a giant Mack truck!

(b)

One way to avoid high-priced tourism along the Kenya coastline is to do a camping trip. This is not, however, to be confused with camping a l'Americain. For starters, recreational vehicles just do not exist in this part of the world. Most folks go camping in something about the size of a VW beetle (which by the way can easily carry four people plus all required camping apparatus). In fact, here's what one local tourist adviser has to say about touring the coast:

    Don't be a tourist; be a traveler. Keep a low profile and you'll have a much better time. One way to do this is to use as small a vehicle as possible. A favorite among those in the know is the "lowly" Volkswagen beetle. It's unbelievably durable (albeit a bit mechanically touchy), it's low on gas consumption, and its drive wheels are where they belong—right under the engine.

Such sage advice from a seasoned veteran should be taken seriously. Do yourself a favor by traveling light, small, and inconspicuously, and you'll have a far better time than if you were to swagger around in a giant Mack truck!

Using the Default Template

To make any type of change to a style, or to assign the style to one or more paragraphs, you must first select it from a *style template* (or *template* for short). Chapter 7 will explain templates in detail; for now, you need only be aware of Professional Write Plus's default template.

Introducing Paragraph Styles

Up to now, without knowing it, you have been using this built-in template, which is called DEFAULT.STY. Like every template, it contains a group of paragraph styles. Also like every other template, DEFAULT.STY is maintained in a separate file. The name of a template is the same as the name of the file in which it's stored. (For that reason, following this book's convention for file names, template names are shown here in capital letters.) When a template is assigned to a document, its formatting information becomes available to that document, as illustrated in Figure 6.3.

Figure 6.3
The DEFAULT.STY template attached to the current document

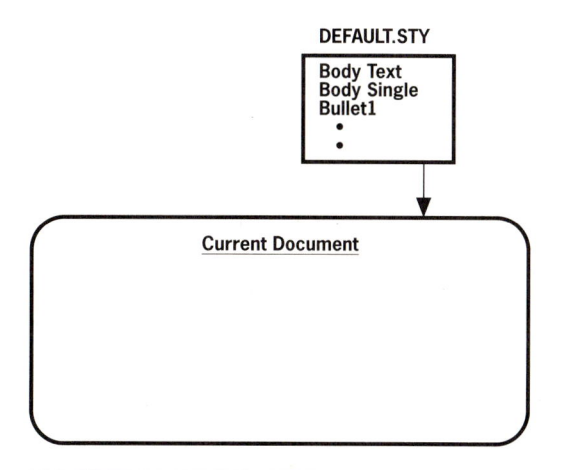

DEFAULT.STY
Body Text
Body Single
Bullet1
•
•

Current Document

The DEFAULT.STY template contains several different predefined paragraph styles, which are designed to help you understand how to use styles. For the time being, this template will be used to illustrate some basic ideas. Later on you'll see how to create your own paragraph styles and templates.

When you open a new document (by selecting Open from the File menu), the DEFAULT.STY template is automatically attached to the document. If this template can't be found, then no template is attached. But this will occur only if you have changed some of the default settings in Professional Write Plus (see Chapter 7 for details).

Using the Styles Box

To help you work with DEFAULT.STY (or any other template), you can display the Styles box, which lists all the styles contained in the template attached to the document. You can display the Styles box by doing one of the following.

- Select Format/Select a Style.
- Double-click on the box in the lower-left corner of the screen (it should contain the words "Body Text").
- Press the speed key Ctrl-X.

The Styles box will appear, as shown in Figure 6.4. It lists the paragraph styles in the template attached to the current document. Notice that the top of this box indicates the name of the current template—in this case, DEFAULT.STY. If, for some reason, there is no template attached, then the word "Styles" appears.

Figure 6.4
The Styles box

```
      default.sty
F2  Body Text
F3  Body Single
F4  Bullet 1
```

The Styles box is a true Windows window, so you can manipulate it in the usual ways, as follows:

- To scroll through the list of styles in the box, use the scroll bar at the right.
- To reposition the box on the screen, click on the bar at the top of the box and hold the mouse button down, drag the box to wherever you want it, and then release the button.
- To resize the box, click on the appropriate corner or edge and hold the button down, drag the mouse cursor in the direction you want the box to expand in, and then release the button.
- To remove the box from the screen, double-click on the Control box in the upper-left corner of the box.

To see how to use paragraph styles, you'll need some text to work with. So before going any further, create a new document consisting of a couple of paragraphs. If you like, use the text shown back in Figure 6.2 (it will be referred to in the following examples), or use any other text you wish.

The Body Text Style
Position the cursor anywhere in the existing text, and then notice the following.

Introducing Paragraph Styles   161

- In the Styles box, the Body Text entry is highlighted.

- In the lower-left corner of the screen, the name "Body Text" appears. The name of the style assigned to the current paragraph always appears in the lower-left corner of the edit screen.

Body Text, one of the paragraph styles contained in DEFAULT.STY, is the default style that's initially assigned to every paragraph in a document. Generally, you'll assign the Body Text style to the majority of the paragraphs in a document, so this style should have the basic features you want to assign to most of your text. (The details of assigning features to Body Text are discussed later in the chapter.)

Assigning a Style to a Paragraph

Tip. If you prefer to work without the Styles box on screen, you can use the following method to select a style. To begin, press the speed key Ctrl-Y to display the Styles box. Scroll through the different style names listed, and then select the one you want. As soon as you select a style, the Styles box disappears.

One of the most basic style operations you'll use is to assign a style to a paragraph. You can assign a style to a paragraph you've already entered or to a new one.

Here are some basic guidelines to keep in mind when you use a paragraph style:

- You can assign an existing style to any paragraph in a document. Simply click anywhere in that paragraph, and then, in the Styles box, click on the name of the style you want to assign.

- You can change the style of a paragraph as many times as you wish. Just click on the paragraph, and then click on the new style name.

The following examples demonstrate how to assign styles.

Assigning a Style to Existing Text

Suppose you want to indent the second paragraph of the text in Figure 6.2a in order to make it stand out. Without paragraph styles, this is almost impossible. If you happen to have a predefined indentation style up your sleeve, however, you can do the job with a couple of mouse clicks.

The DEFAULT.STY template does in fact have such a style, called Indent 1. Any paragraph assigned this style will be indented by 0.75 inches. To assign this style to a paragraph, you first move the text cursor to that paragraph, and then select the style. Here are the steps for assigning the Indent 1 paragraph style to a paragraph:

1. Click the mouse button on any part of the paragraph to be indented.

2. Using the scroll bar in the Style box, scroll down until "Indent 1" is visible.

3. Click on Indent 1.

When you click on the style name, two things happen: The entire paragraph takes on the characteristics of the style you select, and the name of the style assigned to the current paragraph appears in the lower-left corner of the screen.

Assigning a Style to New Text
In the preceding example, you assigned a paragraph style to an existing paragraph. However, you can also assign a style to a paragraph you're about to enter, as follows:

1. Position the text cursor on a blank line where you plan to type the new paragraph.

2. In the Styles box, click on the name of the style you want to assign to the new paragraph.

3. Begin entering the new text. As the text is entered, it will automatically conform to the style you specified.

Once you specify a style for a new paragraph in this way, all paragraphs you enter immediately after the first one will also be assigned the new style, unless you select a different style for the successive paragraphs. For example, suppose you want to enter a new paragraph and have it indented, but you want the paragraphs following it not to be indented. Here are the steps to follow:

1. Click on Indent 1 in the Styles box.

2. Enter the new paragraph to be indented, then press Enter.

3. Click on Body Text in the Styles box.

4. Continue entering additional paragraphs.

Because paragraphs are usually entered as Body Text, you'll need to use these steps only when you want to enter a paragraph with a nonstandard style.

Creating a New Paragraph Style

The preceding section described how to assign an *existing* paragraph style to one or more paragraphs in a document. In many cases, however, you'll have to create a new style to include the characteristics you want to assign to one or more paragraphs. In fact, you'll probably find that as you begin to use paragraph styles and develop a feeling for their power, you'll want to create many different styles for different purposes.

When you create a new paragraph style, it's automatically attached to the current document. You can then assign that style to any paragraph in the document. Optionally, you can add this paragraph style to the template that's attached to the current document. That style is then available to any document that uses the template. (See Chapter 7 for more on templates.)

The remaining examples in this chapter focus on the creation and modification of a sample paragraph style. First, you'll see how to create this new style. Then, successive examples will illustrate how to incorporate different features into this style. As you read through the examples, keep in mind that these features can be used in any paragraph style.

Example: Creating a Style for Headings

Suppose that you want to create a heading for a document, as shown in Figure 6.5. Notice that this heading is different from the body text in three ways: It's in a larger size; it's boldfaced; and it uses a different typeface. You could make these changes to the heading in either of two ways. You could select the text for the heading as a block and then assign a different font to that block. Alternatively, you could create a new style, perhaps called Head (you can use whatever name you like for each style you create), and then assign to this style the larger size, boldfacing, and the different typeface.

Figure 6.5
A new heading created with the help of a paragraph style

> **Along the Kenya Coast**
> One way to avoid high-priced tourism along the Kenya coastline is to do a camping trip. This is not, however, to be confused with camping a l'Americain. For starters, recreational vehicles just do not exist in this part of the world. Most folks go camping in something about the size of a VW beetle (which by the way can easily carry four people plus all required camping apparatus). In fact, here's what one local tourist adviser has to say about touring the coast:
>
> Don't be a tourist; be a traveler. Keep a low profile and you'll have a much better time. One way to do this is to use as small a vehicle as possible. A favorite among those in the know is the "lowly" Volkswagen beetle. It's unbelievably durable (albeit a bit mechanically touchy), it's low on gas consumption, and its drive wheels are where they belong—right under the engine.
>
> Such sage advice from a seasoned veteran should be taken seriously. Do yourself a favor by traveling light, small, and inconspicuously, and you'll have a far better time than if you were to swagger around in a giant Mack truck!

So why go to the trouble to create a new style rather than using the first method? The answer is that you probably wouldn't, for just a single heading. However, if you plan to use the same type of heading many times within the same document, or even in different documents, it's worthwhile to create the new style. Then, for each new heading in the document, you can simply enter the heading text and assign the Head style to it.

To begin creating the new style, select Format/Modify & Create Styles and the dialog box shown in Figure 6.6 will appear. Before going on, let's look in detail at this rather formidable-looking display.

Figure 6.6
The dialog box for creating and modifying paragraph styles

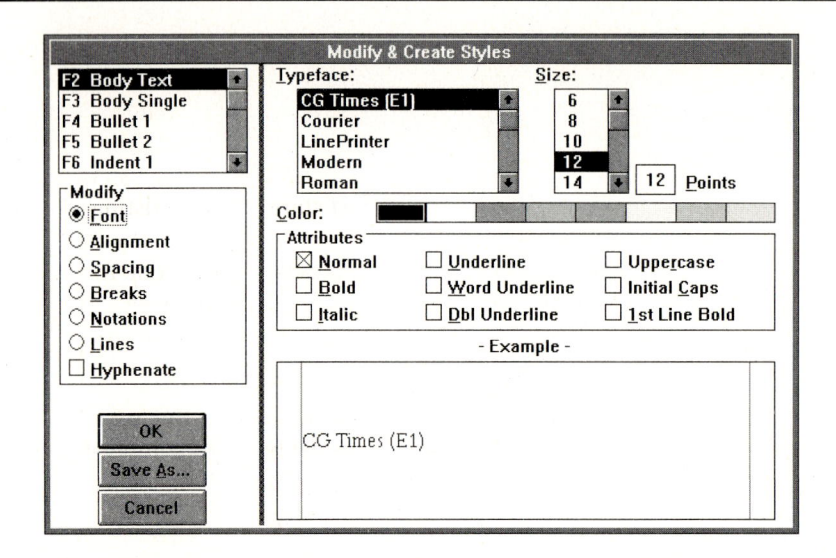

The Modify & Create Styles Dialog Box

You use the Modify & Create Styles dialog box (Figure 6.6) to create new paragraph styles and modify existing ones. Although the display may seem quite complicated at first, you'll find that with a little practice, the various bits and pieces will become familiar and quite easy to work with.

In the upper-left corner of the dialog box is a list box containing the names of all the paragraph styles accessible to the current document.

Below the list of styles is a box labeled "Modify", which displays a list of the different characteristics you can assign to a paragraph style. For each modification you want to make, you select the corresponding option here. For example, to change the font assigned to a style you would click on Font.

When you select an option, the right-hand part of the dialog box changes, displaying the options corresponding to your selection. This part of the dialog box is where you make the actual changes to the paragraph style. The lower-right corner will always display a sample of your current selection, whether it's a typeface, a font size, the line spacing, or any other characteristic of a paragraph style.

Creating the Style and Making the Changes

There are three steps to generating a new paragraph style. First, select a style whose characteristics are similar to what you want your paragraph to look like. Next, you create a new style that's a duplicate of the original one, giving the new one a different name. Then, you make whatever changes you want to the new style.

The logic behind this is that each new paragraph style you create probably resembles one of the existing styles in all but a few characteristics. Therefore, you'll usually save a lot of time by starting off with a duplicate of a known style and then making the few necessary changes, rather than starting completely from scratch and having to define everything about the new style.

In fact, this is the only way in which a new style can be created in Professional Write Plus. That is, you must start with an existing style, copy it, and then modify its characteristics.

In the following example you'll create a new style for headings, using the Body Text style as the basis. After creating a duplicate of the Body Text, and giving it a new name, you'll then make the changes to its specifications. Use these steps:

1. To begin, select the style you want to use as the basis for the new one: Click on the name in the Styles list box in the upper-left corner of the Modify & Create Styles dialog box. (In this example, click on Body Text.)

2. Now create the new style: Click on Save As, and the dialog box shown here will appear:

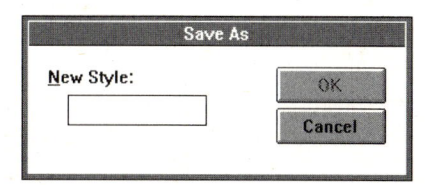

3. Enter the name of the new style, then click on OK. Use a name that describes the type of paragraph you'll be working with. For example, here you could enter the name **Head1**. You can use any combination of letters, digits, and other symbols, including spaces, up to a maximum of 13 characters. Also, capitalization is significant; for instance, you can create two different styles called HEAD and Head.

4. When the original dialog box reappears, the new style name should appear highlighted in the list in the upper-left corner. You can now customize the style by assigning a new font.

5. Click on Font in the Modify box (unless it's already highlighted). The screen should appear like that shown in Figure 6.6.

6. In the list box labeled "Typeface", select the new typeface. Use a sans serif one, such as Helvetica, Helv, or Univers. (Some or all of these may not appear on your screen, however—see below.) Notice that the box in the lower-right corner of the screen displays a sample of your current font selection, including any text attributes you assign.

7. To select the font size, click on 18 (or whatever larger size is available) in the list box labeled "Size".

8. To assign the boldface attribute to the text of this type of paragraph, click on Bold in the Attributes box.

9. Click on OK to return to the edit menu. The new style name should now appear at the bottom of the Styles box on the screen. (You may need to scroll down to see it.)

When you create the new style, all of your changes are recorded as part of that style. In this case, the only changes were to the font. In addition, all the unchanged characteristics of the original style (Body Text) are also saved as part of the new style. This represents a considerable savings in effort on your part, because each style contains numerous features.

The exact fonts displayed in the Typeface box will depend on your particular Windows installation and also on the printer you are using. Consequently, the typefaces listed in step 6 may not be available to you. If that is the case, select an available typeface that's different from the one initially selected. Similarly, if the size 18 (specified in step 7) is not available for the typeface you select, just choose a size that is available (larger than the body text size).

Notice that two different types of paragraph styles are now attached to your document: those that are contained in the attached template, DEFAULT.STY, and the one you just created, which is a local style associated only with this document. Figure 6.7 illustrates this situation. The Styles box on your screen lists both the local paragraph styles and those attached to the current template. If you examine the Styles box, you'll notice that the new style name is preceded by a period (see Figure 6.8). This indicates that the style is local, rather than being attached to the template.

Using the New Style

Now that you've created a new style, let's assign it to the heading, so that your document resembles the one shown in Figure 6.5:

1. Make sure you have entered the title as a single line, ending with a hard return.

2. Click on any part of the title line so that the text cursor is positioned there.

Figure 6.7
Two types of paragraph styles are available to the document

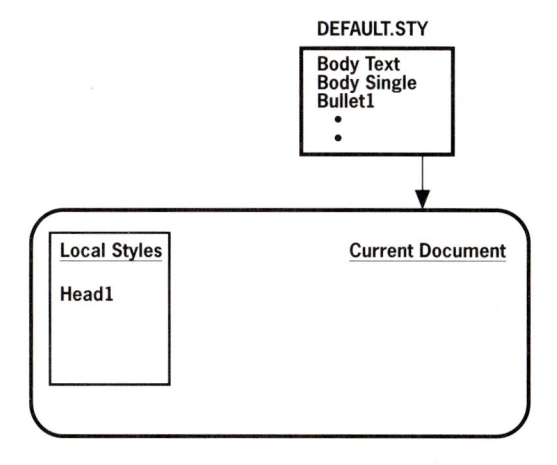

DEFAULT.STY
Body Text
Body Single
Bullet1

Local Styles
Head1

Current Document

Figure 6.8
The period before a style name indicates that the style is attached to the current document

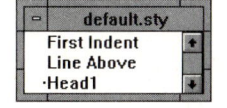

default.sty
First Indent
Line Above
·Head1

3. Click on the name of the new style in the Styles box (in this example, Head1).

The selected line should change immediately into a larger, boldfaced font.

Adding Ruling Lines

A straight line, either above or below a heading, can add emphasis to the beginning of a new section. Without paragraph styles, adding this type of line is so much trouble that it's not worth the effort. With paragraph styles, however, you can easily achieve this type of enhancement. Figure 6.9 illustrates an example of a heading with a ruling line added below it.

To modify a paragraph style, you must first select the style name and then display the Modify & Create Styles dialog box (Figure 6.6), using any of the following methods:

- Double click on the name of the style in the Styles box (in this example it's Head1).

Figure 6.9
A ruling line enhances a heading

> ## Along the Kenya Coast
>
> One way to avoid high-priced tourism along the Kenya coastline is to do a camping trip. This is not, however, to be confused with camping a l'Americain. For starters, recreational vehicles just do not exist in this part of the world. Most folks go camping in something about the size of a VW beetle (which by the way can easily carry four people plus all required camping apparatus). In fact, here's what one local tourist adviser has to say about touring the coast:
>
> Don't be a tourist; be a traveler. Keep a low profile and you'll have a much better time. One way to do this is to use as small a vehicle as possible. A favorite among those in the know is the "lowly" Volkswagen beetle. It's unbelievably durable (albeit a bit mechanically touchy), it's low on gas consumption, and its drive wheels are where they belong—right under the engine.
>
> Such sage advice from a seasoned veteran should be taken seriously. Do yourself a favor by traveling light, small, and inconspicuously, and you'll have a far better time than if you were to swagger around in a giant Mack truck!

- Select Format/Modify & Create Styles, then select the style name from the list box in the Modify & Create Styles dialog box.

- Click on any paragraph that's been assigned that style, then select Format/Modify & Create Styles. For example, if you've assigned the Head1 style to a heading line, click on that line, and then make your selection from the Format menu.

Using any of the above methods, the end result it that the Modify & Create Styles dialog box appears, with the name of the style highlighted in the upper-left corner. If the wrong style is highlighted, simply click on the one you want.

Now you can proceed to assign a ruling line to the style:

1. Click on Lines in the Modify box. The dialog box will change to that shown in Figure 6.10.

2. Click on the Line Below option (in the upper-right part of the dialog box). Note that a sample paragraph appears in the bottom-right part of the screen. You can use this sample to help select your options.

3. Select the line width and style by clicking in the Line Style list box (the one beneath the Line Below option). You might want to scroll through the alternatives before making your selection.

4. Make the line exactly as long as the length of each heading: Click on the option labeled "Text" (just to the right of the Length option).

Figure 6.10
The dialog box for adding a line above or below a heading

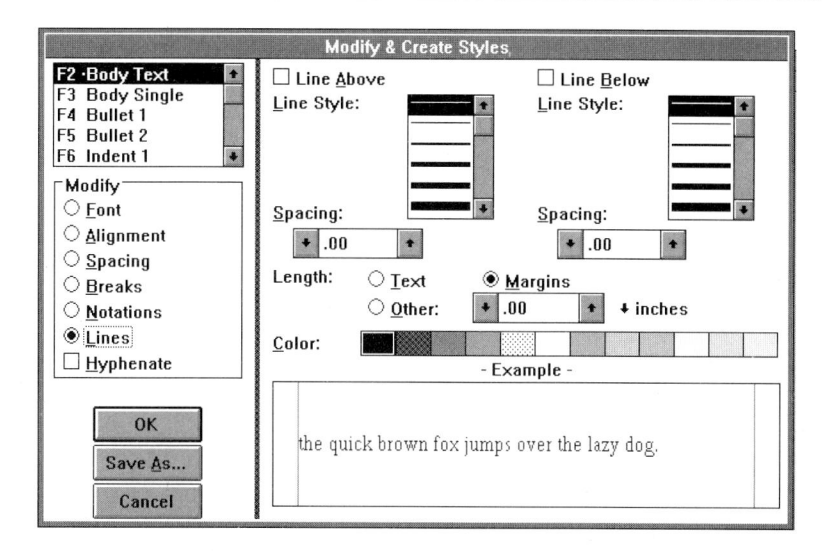

5. In the Spacing edit box (under the Line Below option), select the amount of space between the text and the line. This option is often set to 0, but you can choose any other value. Note that when you select a spacing value, the example in the lower right shows the effect of that spacing.

6. Click on OK to save your choices.

Instead of following step 4, you can make other choices for the length of the ruling line:

- To make the line run the entire distance between the left and right margins, click on Margins.

- To specify an exact line length, click on Other, and then enter the length in the edit box labeled "Inches". If you want to enter the length in picas, points, or centimeters instead of inches, click on "Inches" until the unit you want to use appears. Then enter the number in those units. Note that the units you select also apply to the two Spacing edit boxes.

If you want to draw a ruling line above each heading, select the Line Above option instead of Line Below, and then select the line style and spacing from the corresponding boxes.

For a very unusual effect, you can select a line both above and below each heading. Just click on both Line Above and Line Below, and then fill in the other options for each.

Other Applications for Ruling Lines

The preceding example used a ruling line to enhance a heading. You can, however, assign ruling lines to any type of paragraph style. Just select the style you want to modify, then follow the steps listed above.

Adding Space Below the Heading

In Figure 6.9 the ruling line is definitely an enhancement, but there is not enough space between the line and the following text. Let's assign an extra 0.1 inches to be inserted at the end of each paragraph of this type:

1. Follow the steps given above to select the paragraph style to be modified, in this case Head1, and to display the Modify & Create Styles dialog box.

2. Click on Spacing in the Modify box. The display will change to that shown in Figure 6.11.

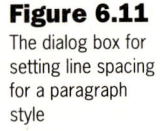

Figure 6.11
The dialog box for setting line spacing for a paragraph style

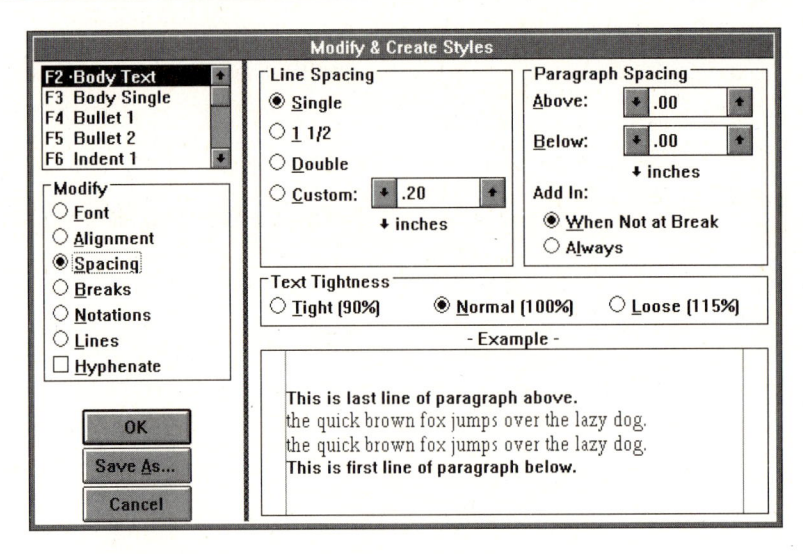

3. The Paragraph Spacing box (in the upper-right corner) contains two edit boxes, where you enter the amount of extra space to be inserted above and below each paragraph of this type. Enter **0.1** in the Below box. You can do this in either of two ways:

- Click on the right arrow until the number you want appears (this is the easiest way).

- Click on the number in the box, delete the value there, and then enter the new value directly.

4. Click on OK to record the changes.

As you change the spacing below the heading, the spacing in the example box at the bottom of the screen also changes. This example indicates how the text will appear on the screen.

Aligning the Heading

In Figure 6.9, notice that the heading is left-justified, which is the default justification used by Professional Write Plus for all text. You can override this default if, for example, you want your headings to be centered or right-justified. (You shouldn't make a heading fully justified—it could cause large amounts of space to appear between the words on the line.) Here's how to modify each heading line so that the text is centered or right-justified:

1. Use the steps described earlier to select the paragraph style to be modified and to display the Modify & Create Styles dialog box.

2. Click on Alignment in the Modify box. The display will change to that shown in Figure 6.12.

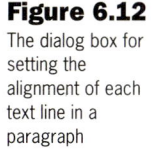

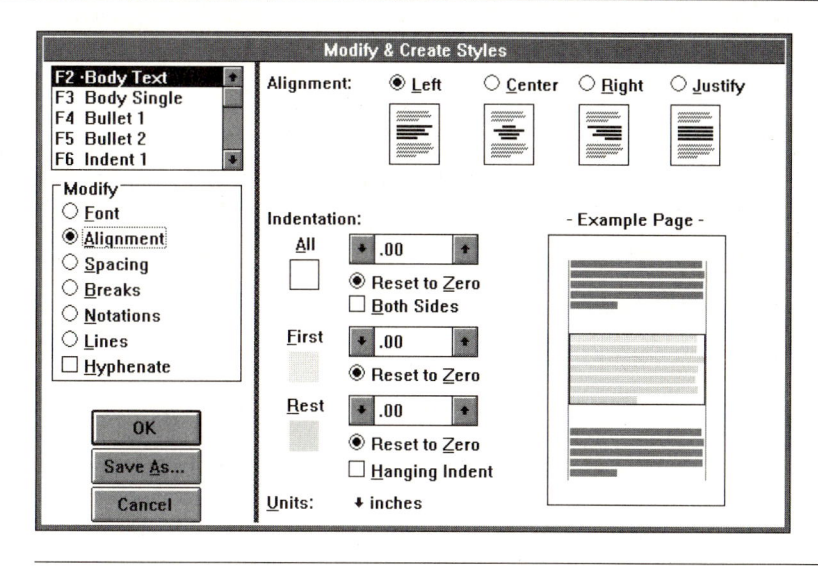

Figure 6.12
The dialog box for setting the alignment of each text line in a paragraph

3. Beneath each alignment option is a sample display. The middle paragraph of those displays shows the different alignments. Select the alignment you want by clicking on the appropriate button (Left, Center, or Right) on the top line of the dialog box.

4. Click on OK to save your selection and return to the edit screen.

If you selected Center, for example, each heading that you assign this style will be centered between the left and right margins.

Modifying Paragraph Styles

The preceding sections have described the basic features of paragraph styles. If you have read that part, you should have a fairly clear understanding of paragraph styles and their purpose. The following sections describe the various ways in which you can customize paragraph styles.

To make any type of change to a paragraph style, you begin by selecting Format/Modify & Create Styles, so that the Modify & Create Styles dialog box appears (Figure 6.6). You can then select from the various options on this screen and the associated ones.

Using Different Fonts

As part of its basic definition, each paragraph style must be assigned a specific typeface and size. Your particular Windows installation determines which typefaces are available. That is, you don't install typefaces specifically for Professional Write Plus. Instead, they are installed under Windows. (These typefaces are then available to *any* program running under Windows.) The typefaces and sizes that are available also depend on your printer. For example, those fonts available with a Hewlett-Packard LaserJet III will be entirely different from those for an Epson 24-pin dot-matrix printer. (For more information about the availability of typefaces and sizes, refer to Chapter 9.)

You can also assign various combinations of text attributes to each style. For example, a style for headings could include both boldface and italic attributes.

Selecting the Typeface, Size, and Text Attributes

To assign a font to a style, you first click on Font in the dialog box (Figure 6.6). The available typefaces are then displayed in the list box labeled "Typeface". If this box is too small to display all the available typefaces, you can use the elevator bar to scroll through the entire list.

Using Different Fonts

Here's how to select the typeface and size for the current paragraph style (the one highlighted in the upper-left corner of Modify Style dialog box):

1. Click on the typeface name in the Typeface box. When you do, the sizes available for that particular typeface will appear in the Size box.

2. To select the type size, do either of the following:

   - Click on the number you want in the Size box.

   - Delete the number in the Points box, then enter whatever number you want.

The second option is available only for scalable typefaces. The most common of these are used for PostScript printers and the Hewlett-Packard LaserJet III and related models. For these, you can enter just about any type size in the Points box.

As you select each typestyle and size, a sample appears in the Example box at the bottom of the screen. What you see in this box is an example of how the text will appear on your screen——it is not necessarily how the text will appear when printed. In fact, it's very unlikely that your printed text will look exactly like that on the screen. (Someday we'll have this technology, but not quite yet.)

You can use the Attributes box to select various types of emphasis for your text. Just click on the attributes you want to become part of the specification for the current paragraph style. For example, you could select Bold or Italic to enhance the text in paragraphs assigned this particular style. To deselect an attribute, click on it so that the X disappears.

Some combinations of attributes are incompatible. For example, you can't select both Uppercase and Initial Caps. But you don't have to remember which pairs of attributes are incompatible because the program monitors your selections. For instance, if you click on Uppercase and then on Initial Caps, Uppercase will be deselected automatically.

If your system includes a color monitor, you can emphasize particular paragraphs by assigning colors. For example, you could assign red or blue to your headings. Unfortunately, these colors won't appear when printed, unless you're lucky enough to have access to a color printer. If you don't, all colors print in black. To select a color, simply click on the one you want in the Color box. The sample at the bottom of the screen will show you how the text will appear. All the paragraphs to which you later assign this style will appear on the screen in that color.

Tips on Selecting Fonts

It's tempting to go wild when presented with so many different choices of typefaces, sizes, and attributes. However, just as too many cooks can spoil the broth, too many fonts can ruin a document.

Be conservative in your selection of fonts. A page full of boldface, italics, and underlining can be distracting to the reader——even though you may think it looks great. Similarly, too many different typefaces can make the page appear "busy."

Body Text

Note. Every template contains the Body Text style, which you cannot delete.

Almost by definition, Body Text is the style most often used on a page, so its characteristics need to be chosen carefully. Of course, you can set up Body Text to have any characteristics you wish. For example, for the style used for ordinary correspondence, you might assign a 10-point font such as Roman or Times Roman to the body text. However, for a style to be used for creating flyers, you might use 24-point Helv or Helvetica for the body text font.

For ordinary documents (correspondence, reports, and so on), a serif typeface is usually the best choice for the Body Text style. *Serifs* are the little wedges at the ends of letters. You can see them on the type you're reading right now. Serifs help the eye move easily from one letter to the next. The most commonly used serif font is Times Roman (along with its many descendants). For the majority of documents, the font size for most of the text lies between 10 and 12 points.

Finally, unless you have a compelling reason to do otherwise, avoid assigning boldface, italic, or any other special attributes to Body Text. However, if you want some paragraphs to be specially emphasized (boldfaced or italicized, for example), you can create a special style that has the same characteristics as Body Text, but includes the boldface or italic attribute. For easy recognition, you could call this style something like Body Ital or Body Bold.

Headings and Other Special Applications

You can create a multitude of different heading styles, using names like Head1, Head2, and so on. For aesthetic reasons, headings are often assigned a *sans serif* font (one without any serifs), such as Helv or Helvetica. Headings are also usually assigned a size that's somewhat larger than that of the body text—but don't get carried away. A heading that is too large looks clumsy on the page, and you might be surprised how well a 12-point boldface Helvetica heading stands out from ordinary 10-point body text.

Indenting and Aligning Paragraphs

The term *alignment* (also called *justification*) refers to the horizontal positioning of each line in a paragraph. A previous section described how to align a single-line heading. Using a paragraph style, you can also assign one of the following alignments to every line in a paragraph.

Left Each line begins at the left margin, but the right margin is left ragged. This is the most common type of alignment.

Right Each line ends exactly at the right margin, producing a ragged left margin.

Justify Each line is spaced so that it just fits between the left and right margins. This type of justification works best when used in conjunction with automatic hyphenation (see "Automatic Hyphenation").

Center Each line is centered between the margins.

These are the same alignment options you can apply to blocks of text using the Text menu. You may remember them from Chapter 2.

Indentation is a type of alignment in which selected lines within a paragraph are moved in by a specified amount from the left or right margin (or both). You have a number of indentation options, as shown in Figure 6.13.

Figure 6.13
(a) First line indent;
(b) Left indent; (c) Left and right indent; (d) Hanging indent

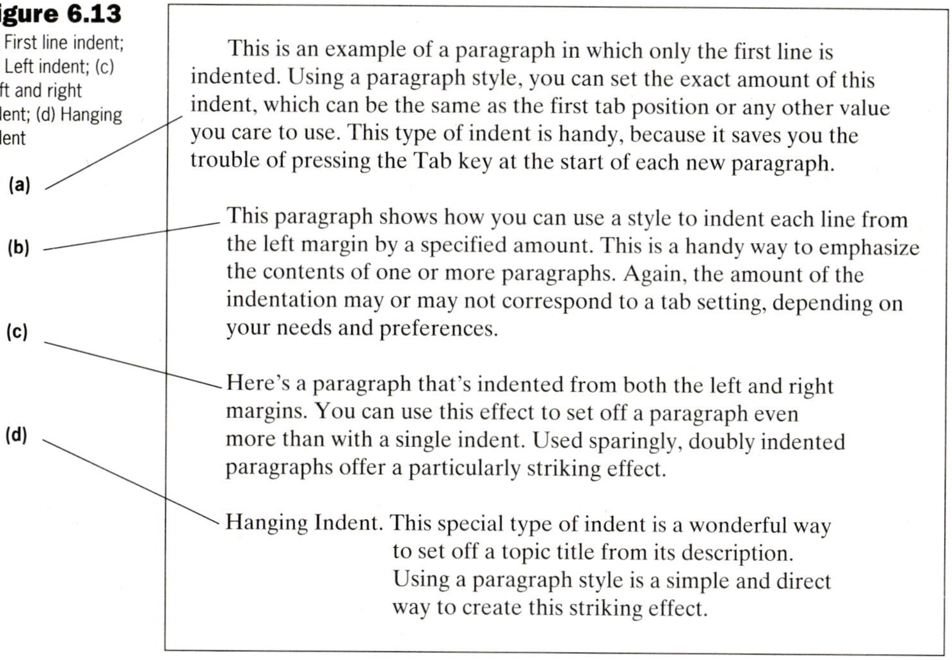

(a)

(b)

(c)

(d)

    This is an example of a paragraph in which only the first line is indented. Using a paragraph style, you can set the exact amount of this indent, which can be the same as the first tab position or any other value you care to use. This type of indent is handy, because it saves you the trouble of pressing the Tab key at the start of each new paragraph.

    This paragraph shows how you can use a style to indent each line from the left margin by a specified amount. This is a handy way to emphasize the contents of one or more paragraphs. Again, the amount of the indentation may or may not correspond to a tab setting, depending on your needs and preferences.

    Here's a paragraph that's indented from both the left and right margins. You can use this effect to set off a paragraph even more than with a single indent. Used sparingly, doubly indented paragraphs offer a particularly striking effect.

    Hanging Indent. This special type of indent is a wonderful way to set off a topic title from its description. Using a paragraph style is a simple and direct way to create this striking effect.

Choosing the Paragraph Alignment

To set the alignment of a paragraph style, begin by clicking on Alignment (in the box labeled "Modify") in the Modify & Create Styles dialog box. When you do, the dialog box changes to the form shown in Figure 6.12.

In the upper-right part of the dialog box are buttons for the four possible alignments (Left, Center, Right, and Justify). Under each button is miniature page, and the middle paragraph in each one shows how that particular alignment will affect the paragraph appearance. To select one of these alignments, just click on the corresponding button.

Setting the Paragraph Indent

To set any type of indent, you work with the options under "Indentation" in the Modify & Create Styles dialog box. In the lower-right corner of the display is a box labeled "Example Page", with three model paragraphs displayed. As you select an indent format, the *middle* paragraph in this display illustrates how a typical paragraph will appear. Before you select any type of indentation, this paragraph has the same appearance as the other two.

Notice that the first line of this middle paragraph is highlighted to set it off from the others. This is because you can indent the first line independently from the rest of the paragraph; the highlighting helps to call attention to this formatting.

Generally, if you want to create a particular type of paragraph indent, you should set Alignment to Left. This is by no means an absolute requirement, and you can obtain a wide variety of special effects by combining Right, Center, and Justify alignments with various types of indents. This section assumes, however, that left-alignment has been selected.

Available Options for Indentation

The options for indentation are all listed to the left of the example page under the heading labeled "Indentation". These are the options:

All   The number in the edit box just to the right of the All option controls the indent of every line in a paragraph. To indent a certain amount from the left margin, enter that number in the edit box. You can enter the number directly, or you can click on the up arrow (each click increases the indent by 0.05 inches).

Reset to Zero   To reset the number in the All edit box back to zero, you can click on this option. Conversely, if you manually set the number back to zero, this button is automatically selected. The other options labeled "Reset to Zero" have a similar function for their respective edit boxes.

Both Sides If you click on this option, the paragraph is indented on both sides by the amount shown in the All edit box.

First The number in the edit box just to the right of this option controls the indentation of the *first line only* in a paragraph. To indent this line a certain amount, enter that number (in inches) in the edit box. This amount is in addition to any amount entered in the All box.

Rest The number in the edit box just to the right of this option controls the indenting of every line in a paragraph *except the first*. To indent these lines a certain amount, enter that number in the edit box. This amount is in addition to any amount entered in the All box.

Hanging Indent This option controls the position of text following a tab on the first line only of a paragraph. When you press Tab, the following text will be indented by an amount equal to the value shown in the Rest edit box.

Notice that the numbers in the edit boxes labeled "First" and "Rest" represent indents *in addition to* the amount of indent shown in the All edit box. For example, if you enter 1.0 in the All edit box, every line in a paragraph will be indented on the left by that amount. If you also enter 0.25 in the First edit box, the first line of the paragraph will be indented an additional 0.25 inches.

Changing the Unit of Measure

Inches are the default unit of measure for the numbers appearing in the All, First, and Rest edit boxes. However, you can switch to centimeters, picas, or points by clicking on the word "inches" to the right of the Units option at the bottom of the screen. Each time you click, a new unit (centimeters and so on) will appear. As you change units, the numbers in the edit boxes will also change correspondingly.

Creating Common Types of Indents

Using the options described above, you can create many different types of indents. Here are the most common ones:

Indent First Line Only Figure 6.13a shows a sample of this type of indent, which is a handy way to automatically indent each paragraph without having to press the Tab key. A first-line indent is often used with the Body Text style. To create this type of indent, just enter the indent amount in the First edit box, and set to zero the values in the All and Rest edit boxes.

Left Indent With this common type of indent (see Figure 6.13b for a sample), every line in the paragraph is indented. To create this type of indent, enter the amount of the indent in the All edit box, and set to zero the value in the Rest edit box. The first line can optionally be indented by an additional amount. Just enter the value in the edit box labeled "First".

Double Indent   Here, the paragraph is indented both from the left and right margins, as shown in Figure 6.13c. To create a double indent, enter the amount of the indent in the All box. Then click on Both Sides. Again, the first line can optionally be indented an extra amount by entering that value in the First edit box.

Hanging Indent   To create this type of indent (illustrated in Figure 6.13d), enter the amount of the indent in the Rest box, and then click on Hanging Indent. Set the values in the All and First edit boxes to zero.

When you enter a paragraph with the Hanging Indent style, all but the first line will be indented by the specified amount. In addition, you can break the first line to create a block effect with the remaining lines, as shown in Figure 6.13d, by using the Tab key. For example, to create the paragraph shown in this figure, you would enter **Hanging Indent**, press Tab, and then continue entering text (starting with "This special..."). Note that in this particular case pressing the Tab key does *not* cause the text cursor to jump to the next tab setting. If you don't want to create this block effect on the first line, you don't need to click on the Hanging Indent option.

You can create many other types of paragraph formats by using combinations of these indent features in conjunction with the Right, Center, and Justify alignment options. It's easy to experiment. Make your selections in the dialog box, and the sample paragraph in the lower-right corner will display the format.

To practice changing indentations, follow these steps:

1. Click on the right arrow in the All edit box. Do it several times, and as you do watch the middle paragraph in the Example Page box become indented.

2. Now click on the Both Sides option. As you do, notice how the right side of the middle paragraph becomes indented as well.

3. Click on Reset to Zero, and watch the middle paragraph revert to its original format.

Automatic Hyphenation

You can assign automatic hyphenation to any paragraph style you wish, but it's most often used with body text. Hyphenation is particularly useful when used in conjunction with paragraphs that are fully justified (i.e., aligned at both left and right margins).

When hyphenation is active, any word longer than four characters that doesn't fit at the end of a line will be hyphenated, with the following exceptions:

- No more than two successive lines will be hyphenated.
- If a word contains any numerals it is not hyphenated.

You can also force hyphenation at a particular place in a word by manually inserting the hyphen (the key just to the right of the zero) where you want it. However, this is a *hard hyphen*, and it will remain in the text even when it's no longer needed. Reserve hard hyphens for words that always require them, such as hyphenated personal names.

Even when hyphenation is active, you can't see the results in draft mode. To view hyphenation, you must select layout mode. Here's how to turn on hyphenation:

1. Select Format/Modify & Create Styles.
2. Click on the name of the paragraph style for which you want hyphenation to be active.
3. Click on Hyphenate, then click on OK.

Customizing the Line and Text Spacing

You can assign specific line spacing to a paragraph style, which is then applied to each paragraph of this type. Single, 1½, and double spacing are available, or you can specify custom line spacing. You can also specify that extra space be inserted before and after each paragraph. This type of fine control can add a really professional touch to your documents. For example, adding as little as 0.05 inch after each normal paragraph sets off paragraph breaks. Similarly, an extra bit of space after headings helps to accentuate them.

A limited amount of control is also available for specifying the *text tightness*, which is a measure of the amount of space between letters and words.

To set these options, begin by selecting Spacing from the Modify & Create Styles dialog box, which will then change to the box shown in Figure 6.11. As you make your selections, the Example box at the bottom of the dialog box illustrates how sample lines of text will appear in typical paragraphs.

Setting the Line Spacing

To set the line spacing within the paragraph, make your selection from the box labeled "Line Spacing". If you click on Single, a spacing is selected that's consistent with the typeface and font size for the paragraph style. For example, if the font size has been set to 12-point Tms Rmn, the line spacing will be set to 0.19 inches. If you select either 1$^{1}/_{2}$, or Double, the spacing chosen is a corresponding multiple of the value for single spacing. Whichever option you select, the value selected by the program appears in the Custom edit box.

Alternatively, you can select any other value for the paragraph line spacing by entering that value in the Custom edit box. You don't need to click on Custom—just enter the value. You can also set the custom spacing by clicking on the up or down arrows at either end of the Custom edit box. Each click on an arrow changes the spacing amount by 0.05 inches.

By default, the values in the edit box are displayed in inches, but you can optionally select centimeters, picas, or points as the displayed units. Click on the word "inches" below the Custom edit box. For each click, another unit of measure will appear, and at the same time the value in the Custom edit box will change to reflect these units. For instance, suppose the edit box displays 1.0 inches. If you click once on "Inches", it will change to centimeters, and the value in the edit box will change to 2.54.

Adding Space Above and Below a Paragraph

To add space above or below each paragraph, enter the amount in the corresponding edit box in the upper-right corner of the screen. For example, a typical value for paragraphs consisting of 12-point body text would be in the range of 0.05 to 0.1 inches. You can also specify space to be placed both above *and* below each paragraph.

The two options at the bottom of the Paragraph Spacing edit box offer control over adding space when a paragraph either begins or ends a page. When you select the When Not at Break option, space will not be added above a paragraph if it begins at the top of a page or below a paragraph that ends at the bottom of a page. If you select the Always option, space will always be added above or below, regardless of where a paragraph appears on the page. Unless you have a compelling reason for doing otherwise, select When Not at Break. It will prevent unnecessary space from being inserted and avoid other potential page layout problems.

Space added above and below paragraphs is additive. For example, suppose that paragraph A is followed by paragraph B. Paragraph A is assigned 0.75 inches of space below, and paragraph B is assigned 0.25 inches of space above. The total amount of space between the paragraphs will be 1.0 inches, as shown by the example in Figure 6.14.

Figure 6.14
How the Above and Below spacing options affect the space between paragraphs

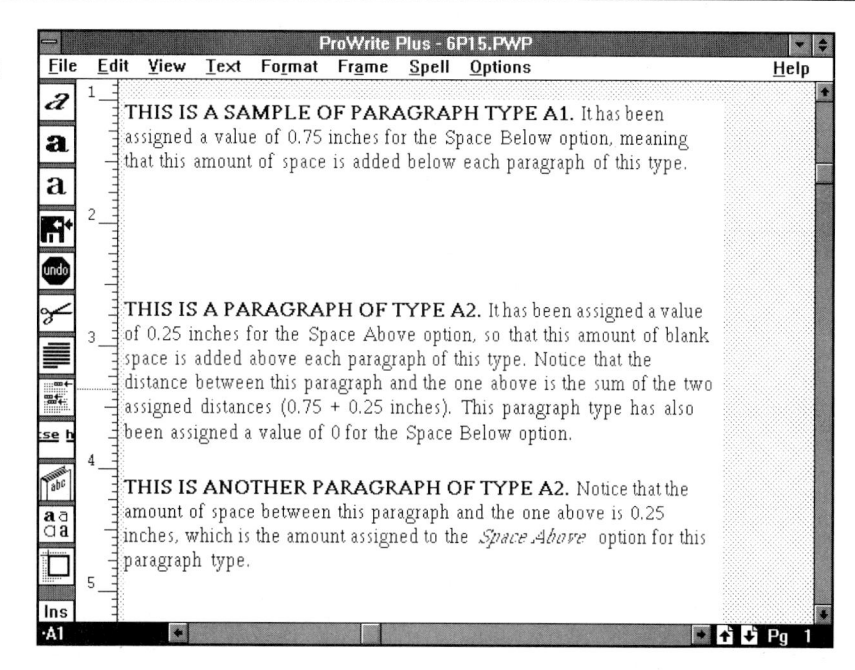

A Note of Caution

The Above and Below options are quite powerful formatting features, offering a sophisticated tool for adding a professional touch to your documents. However, used indiscriminately, this tool can turn into a real headache. For example, suppose that you're using five or six different paragraph styles within a document. Ideally, you would like to be able to control the amount of space between every pair of adjacent paragraphs, regardless of their type. With six different types of paragraphs, there are 36 possible combinations of adjacent paragraph styles. If you assign space before and after each paragraph type without some forethought, you'll find that controlling the space between the 36 different combinations of paragraphs becomes just about impossible.

There are several possible techniques for dealing with this problem, and you may want to work out your own. Here are a couple of alternative starting points for keeping things fairly simple and organized, although none offers a complete solution:

- Only assign space below each paragraph style.

- First assign space above and below the principal paragraph styles, such as Body Text and headings. Then add space above or below each of the other styles, one at a time and very carefully.

- First work on adjusting the spacing between those paragraph combinations that appear together most often (such as two successive body text paragraphs and a heading paragraph followed by a paragraph of body text). Then do the best you can with the remaining combinations as they arise.

Specifying the Text Tightness

The box in the middle of the Modify & Create Styles dialog box shown in Figure 6.11 offers you three options for controlling the amount of space between letters and words. To a limited extent, this allows you to adjust the appearance of the text in a paragraph, and it also gives you a degree of control over how much text can fit on a line or within a specific amount of space. For example, tightening up the text spacing for a long title could help squeeze it onto a single line.

The three options are Tight (90%), Normal (100%), and Loose (115%). The numbers in parentheses approximately indicate the relative amounts of linear space occupied by text. Try selecting each of these options, and then note the appearance of the sample lines in the Example box. In most cases, the Normal option offers the best appearance. Use the other options only when you need to increase or decrease the amount of space occupied by a paragraph or group of paragraphs.

Controlling Page Breaks

For some types of paragraphs, it's convenient to control the relative location of page breaks. For example, a page break is often desirable before each chapter heading. In other cases, you might want to avoid having a page break separate one paragraph from either the one before it or the one after it. For instance, you would probably want to prevent a page break from occurring between a heading and the following text.

By default, the program allows pages to break anywhere. However, by using paragraph styles, you can fine-tune where and how page breaks occur. You can specify that page breaks

- Occur *either* before or after each paragraph
- Occur *both* before and after each paragraph
- Not occur either immediately before or after a paragraph
- Not occur within a paragraph

To select any of these options, begin by clicking on Breaks in the Modify & Create Styles dialog box, which then changes to the screen shown in Figure 6.15. You can then choose one of the following options.

Figure 6.15
The dialog box for controlling paragraph breaks

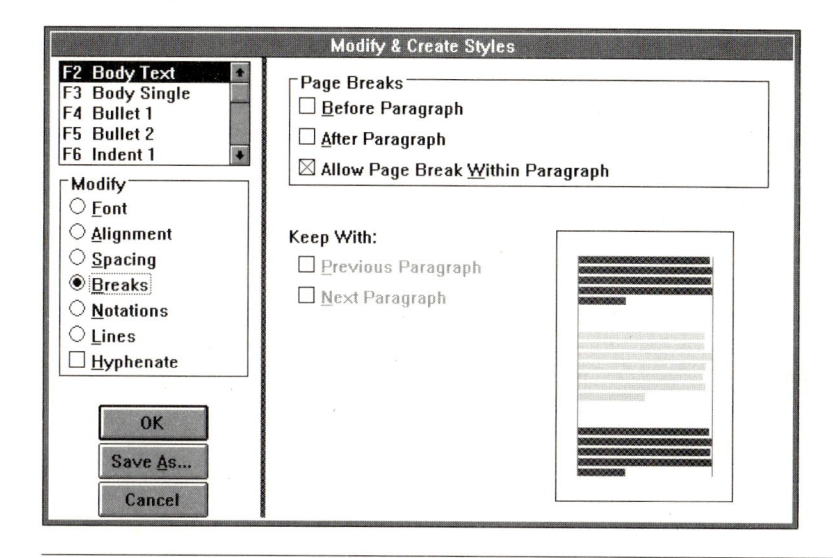

Before Paragraph   If you select this option, each paragraph of this type will be preceded by a page break. This option is used most frequently with headings that must be placed at the top of the page.

After Paragraph   This option specifies that a page break will be inserted after each paragraph of this type.

Allow Page Break Within Paragraph   When this option is *not* selected, Professional Write Plus will do its best to avoid placing a page break within a paragraph. For a paragraph longer than a page, however, this option is irrelevant.

Keep with Previous Paragraph   Select this option to avoid inserting a page break before this type of paragraph.

Keep with Next Paragraph   This option specifies that a page break should not be placed between this paragraph and the next one. You would use this option for just about any type of heading.

The last two options are available only when the "Allow Page Break Within Paragraph" option is *not* selected.

Example: Keeping a Heading with the Following Text

It's important that a page break not intervene between a heading and the following text. In normal word processing, you must arrange this by scrolling through a document after all the edits have been finished, manually inserting either blank lines or page breaks at appropriate places in the text. You can avoid this tedious process by placing the burden on the paragraph style for your headings. Here are the steps:

1. Select the paragraph style to be modified, and then display the Modify Style dialog box.

2. Click on the Breaks option. The dialog box will change to the one shown in Figure 6.15.

3. In the Page Breaks box, make sure that none of the options is selected. (To deselect an option, click on it.)

4. Under the Keep With option, click on Next Paragraph.

5. Click on OK to record the changes.

Creating Bulleted Lists

Paragraph styles offer a convenient way to generate bulleted lists. To create this type of customized list, you enter each item in the list as a separate paragraph. Then you assign the appropriate style (which you have previously defined) to those paragraphs. As you do, they will be reformatted with leading bullets. Figure 6.16 illustrates two of the many types of bulleted lists you can create.

Figure 6.16
Two styles of bulleted lists

☐ This is a sample paragraph that has been assigned a style that includes a bullet. The spacing between the bullet and the text in the first paragraph line has been set to 0.25 inches. Notice that all lines but the first are aligned with the left margin.

☐ This is a second paragraph of the same type. You can use a variety of bullets for different effects in your documents.

☐ This is another type of bulleted paragraph, in which a hanging indent is created. To accomplish this effect, the Rest option in the Modify Style dialog box is set to the same value as the Space For option.

☐ Here's another paragraph of the same type. If it manages to extend to the second line, you'll again see the hanging indent effect.

You must first create a new paragraph style that will be used only for bulleted lists. Normally, you would use the Body Text style as a model for creating the new style, as described earlier in the chapter. Then you make the necessary modifications to the new style to format the paragraphs assigned this style. These changes include selecting the type of bullet you want as well as the spacing between it and the beginning of the text in the paragraph. You can choose from a wide range of bullets, including various sizes of circles and boxes, diamonds, and check marks.

Note that the style template that you're using, DEFAULT.STY, contains two styles for creating bulleted lists. These styles are named BULLET1 and BULLET 2, but we'll ignore these for now and create our own.

Creating a Paragraph Style for Bulleted Lists

To create a special style for bulleted paragraphs, begin by creating a duplicate of a paragraph style with similar font and spacing characteristics. (If there isn't one, just duplicate the Body Text style, then select the font and spacings you want.) Next, select the type of bullet you want, and then assign the amount of space between the bullet and the start of the paragraph text. Here are the steps to follow:

1. Create a new style, as described earlier in this chapter. Name it something like Bullet.

2. With the Modify Style dialog box displayed, click on Notations. The dialog box will then change to that shown in Figure 6.17. The upper section of this box contains the options used for creating this type of paragraph style.

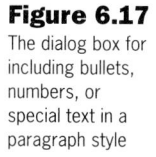

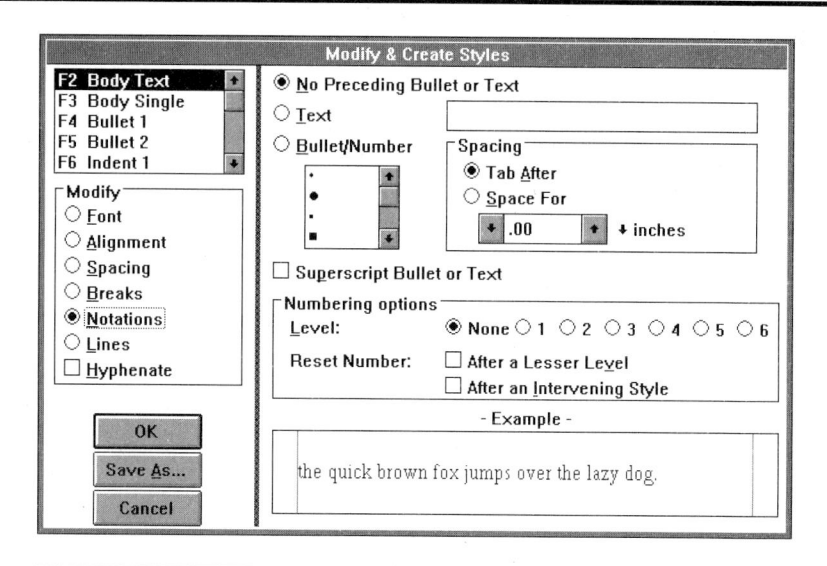

Figure 6.17
The dialog box for including bullets, numbers, or special text in a paragraph style

3. In the list box labeled "Bullet/Number", click on the style of bullet you want to use. You can use the elevator to scroll through the different bullets.

4. If you want the bullet to appear as a superscript (that is, above the center line of the text), click on Superscript Bullet or Text.

5. Select the spacing between the bullet and the paragraph text, using either the Tab After or Space For option.

If you use the Tab After option, the text following the bullet will begin at the first tab setting beyond the bullet. Alternatively, you can specify an absolute spacing by entering the number in the edit box labeled "Space For". This number represents the distance between the *beginning* of the bullet and the beginning of the paragraph text.

By default, any number you enter in the Space For edit box is in inches, but you can optionally use centimeters, picas, or points. To change the units of measure, click on the word "inches". Each time you click, a different unit will appear, and at the same time the current number in the edit box will be adjusted to the new units. You can also click on the up and down arrows to change the spacing. Each click on either arrow changes the spacing by 0.05 inch.

The value in the Space For box is directly linked to the First option in the Alignment section of the Modify & Create Styles dialog box. That is, whatever value you enter for the alignment of the paragraph style's first line automatically appears in the Space For box here, and vice-versa.

Using Indents in Bulleted Lists

The first example in Figure 6.16 illustrates a pair of paragraphs that have been assigned a bulleted paragraph style. For this style, the distance between the bullet (from its left edge) and the beginning text has been set to 0.25 inches. Notice that all lines except the first are aligned at the left margin.

Alternatively, you can create a hanging indent with bulleted paragraphs, as shown in the second example in Figure 6.16. To do this, you need to modify the style for the bulleted paragraphs as follows:

1. Click on Notations in the Modify & Create Styles box.

2. Using the Space For option, set the space between the bullet and the text to whatever value you want (0.25 inches, for example).

3. Click on Alignment in the Modify list box on the left side of the dialog box.

4. In the edit box labeled "Rest", enter the same value as in step 2.

5. Make sure that the value in the All edit box is set to zero.

In addition to creating a hanging indent, you can indent every part of a bulleted list—the bullets as well as the text. To do this, select Alignment, then enter the amount of the indent in the box labeled "All". You can do this with any type of bulleted list, including those shown in Figure 6.16.

Creating Numbered Lists

You can use paragraph styles as a tool for creating numbered lists. To create this type of list, you enter each item as a separate paragraph. Then you assign the appropriate style (previously defined) to those paragraphs. The paragraphs will then be reformatted and numbered sequentially. You can attach a period, dash, or colon to each number, and you can also assign the amount of space between the number and the paragraph text. Figure 6.18 illustrates a few different types of simple numbered lists.

Figure 6.18
Different types of numbered lists

> The following paragraphs have been reformatted using a style that specifies automatic paragraph numbering.
>
> 1. This is the first paragraph in the group.
> 2. Notice that each number ends with a period. This is optional, and it was added to emphasize the fact that a numbered list is being used.
> 3. Notice that in each paragraph every line except the first aligns against the left margin.
> 4. If you insert a new item between existing ones, or if you delete a paragraph, the paragraphs are automatically renumbered.
>
> Here is another example of numbered lists, in which every line of each paragraph is indented by the same amount:
>
> 1. This is the first paragraph for this style of numbered lists.
> 2. Here, each line of each paragraph is indented by the same amount, giving a uniform appearance to each list item.
> 3. You can create this type of hanging indent by assigning the same values to the Space For and Rest options in the Modify Style dialog box.
>
> 1. With this type of numbered list, you can insert ordinary paragraphs within the numbered ones.
> 2. Second item in the numbered list.
>   This is an ordinary paragraph inserted within the numbered list. It could be just about any type of text.
> 3. This is the third item in the numbered list.

You can also create multilevel numbered lists, using up to six levels of numbering. You can assign different number styles to each level, and you can also control when the numbering of any particular level is reset.

There are two main advantages to using styles for creating numbered lists. First, the style does all the formatting work, including entering the numbers and automatically incrementing them for each new paragraph. Second, when you add or delete an item from a list, the remaining items are automatically renumbered.

Note that in order for automatic numbering to be visible, you must be in the layout mode.

Single-Level Numbered Lists

The lists in Figure 6.18 are examples of single-level numbered lists—the simplest type you can create. Before creating this type of numbered list, you must first define a paragraph style that will format paragraphs with automatic numbering.

Creating the Paragraph Style

To begin, you create the style that will be used for automatically numbering paragraphs. Here are the steps to follow:

1. Display the Modify & Create Styles dialog box.
2. Create the new style, naming it something like NumList.
3. Click on Notations. The dialog box will then change to that shown in Figure 6.17.
4. In the box labeled "Bullet/Number", scroll down to near the end of the list, then click on the punctuation to follow each number (you can choose a period, dash, colon, or no punctuation).
5. If you want the numbers to appear as superscripts, click on the option labeled "Superscript Bullet or Text".
6. Select the spacing to appear between each number and the paragraph text. You can use either the Tab After or Space For option. (For details, see the preceding section, "Creating Bulleted Lists.")
7. Click on the option After an Intervening Style, opposite "Reset Number:".
8. Click on OK to have your selections take effect.

The purpose of the After an Intervening Style option in step 7 is to terminate the numbered list. That is, whenever you enter a paragraph with a style that's different from the numbered list style, the list terminates. You can then create another numbered list further on in your document.

Using the Paragraph Style to Create a Numbered List

Let's assume that NumList is the name of the paragraph style you have created with the preceding steps. To use this style to create a numbered list, follow these steps:

1. Enter the first list item, ending it with a hard return.

2. Assign the NumList style to that paragraph. It will be reformatted immediately with a leading number.

3. Enter the rest of the items, ending each with a hard return. The same style, NumList, will be applied automatically to each of them.

4. After you have entered the last item, position the cursor at the beginning of a new paragraph, and then assign it Body Text or some other paragraph style.

Assigning a paragraph another style (as in step 4) ends the numbering sequence. If you later create another numbered list, it will begin again with number 1 (or the equivalent).

You can also create numbered lists with a hanging indent, as shown in the second and third examples in Figure 6.18. For details, refer to "Using Indents in Bulleted Lists" earlier in this chapter.

Inserting Intervening Text

As described above, a numbered list ends when you insert a different style of paragraph. This allows you to insert as many numbered lists as you wish in a single document. However, it prevents you from using a numbered list like the last example shown in Figure 6.18, where one of the items (2) consists of more than one paragraph. To keep the second of these paragraphs from being numbered, it's assigned the Body Text style.

To create this type of list, you must turn off the After an Intervening Style option when creating the paragraph style. This means that the numbering is not reset when you insert a paragraph of a different style. However, this also means that you can't create more than one numbered list using this paragraph style, because you can't ever reset it.

But what if you want to create more than one numbered list similar to the last example in Figure 6.18? The solution is quite simple, although somewhat less than elegant: Create a new paragraph style for each numbered list. For example, let's say you create the style NumList1 for the first numbered list. To create a second list, just create a duplicate of NumList1, giving it a different name (perhaps NumList2).

Multilevel Numbered Lists

You can create numbered lists with up to six levels, using a different numbering style for each level. Figure 6.19 illustrates a numbered list with two levels.

Figure 6.19
A multilevel numbered list

> Here is an example of a two-level numbered list. You can create a numbered list with up to six levels of numbering.
>
> 1. Food products good for you:
>   - 1: Nonfat milk
>   - 2: Turkey white meat
>   - 3: Lots of vegetables
> 2. Food products not so great for you:
>   - 1: Peanuts
>   - 2: Crackerjacks
>   - 3: Popcorn
> 3. Eat these at your own risk:
>   - 1: 15 eggs a day
>   - 2: 1/2 lb. butter a day
>   - 3: Fatty meats

For each level in a multilevel list you must create a separate paragraph style and assign the appropriate indentation for each level. For example, two different styles must be created for the list shown in Figure 6.19—one for the items numbered 1., 2., and so on, and another for the items labeled 1:, 2:, and so on.

Setting the Options

When creating multilevel styles, you must supply values for a number of options.

- For the Level option, select Level 1 for the paragraph style for the main items, Level 2 for the first sublevel style, and so on.

- The Reset Number option controls when the number on a particular level is reset to its initial value. After a Lesser Level is the normal option for multilevel lists. When you select it, numbers at each level are reset whenever the preceding paragraph is at a lower-numbered level. For example, in Figure 6.19 the line containing Peanuts (which is Level 2) begins with 1: because it is preceded by a paragraph that is Level 1.

- Set the indentation. Each level must be indented more than the previous one. To set the indentation, first select the Alignment option. Then use the All option to indent each level. Typically, you might use a value of 0 for the first level, a value of 0.2 inches for the next level, and so on. You can also

Creating Numbered Lists

create hanging indents for each level, as described earlier in "Creating Common Types of Indents."

- The numbering style. Unfortunately, the program doesn't offer you very many options. The only choices are whether to append a period, hyphen, colon, or space after each number.

When working with multilevel lists, the easiest way to set the spacing between numbers and following text is by assigning the number directly in the Space For edit box. (You can try using the Tab After option, but it's more complicated.) For instance, a typical value might be 0.25 inches for each level. Remember, this is the distance between the *beginning* of each number and the start of the paragraph text.

The following are the settings for the list shown in Figure 6.19. For the purposes of this discussion, the paragraph styles for the main and sublevels are named Level1 and Level2.

Here are the Level1 options:

Level	1
Space For	0.25 inches

You might also want to insert additional spacing above and below each paragraph of this type to set it off from adjacent lines, as described earlier in "Adding Space Above and Below a Paragraph."

Here are the Level2 options to be set:

Level	2
Reset Number	After an Intervening Style
Space For	0.25 inches

In addition, for this level you must indent each line (including the leading number) to set it off from the lines at the main level. To do this, click on Alignment (in the Modify box at the left side of the dialog box). Then, enter the amount of the indent in the All edit box. For example, in Figure 6.19 the Level2 lines are indented 0.5 inches from the left margin.

Now, to create the list shown in Figure 6.19, just enter each line of text (without the numbering), and make sure to end each with a hard return. Then assign the appropriate style to each paragraph, and it will be reformatted with the numbers and indents.

Documents with Several Multilevel Numbered Lists

The technique just described works when you want to create only one multilevel list in a document, and frequently this is exactly what is desired. In fact, many types of documents consist of one long multilevel list. Typical examples are outlines for books, plays, and research papers. Also, many legal documents consist of lengthy numbered lists with many levels.

However, you might also want to create a document that contains several multilevel numbered lists, in which case, you can't use the preceding scheme exactly as described. The reason is simply that you can't ever reset the main level in the list. To solve this problem, you'll need to resort to a little sleight of hand, using either of two methods.

Method 1

To illustrate the first technique, suppose you want to create two different lists in the same document, both of which are similar in structure to the one in Figure 6.19. For the style for the first-level paragraphs, assign an outline level of 2 (instead of 1 as described earlier). For the next subitem style, assign an outline level of 3 (instead of 2).

Then create a new style that's a duplicate of the Body Text style in all but two aspects:

- Assign it a level number of 1.
- Assign it the smallest font size you can find in your Modify Style dialog box.

Here's how to use this new style: After you finish entering the first multilevel list in a document, enter a blank line (a line consisting only of a hard return) and assign it this special style. This will cause the first level in the list to be reset. The reason is that the style for each level in this list is assigned the option Reset After a Lesser Level, and the special style you created is at level 1, which will cause the first level in the list (level 2) to be reset.

The reason for assigning a small font to the special style is simply to minimize the amount of vertical space the extra line occupies on the page. Since you would normally want to insert some extra space after a list anyway, the narrow extra line may take care of two problems at once.

This trick reduces the number of available levels in a multilevel list from six to five, but for most documents this should not be a problem. If you happen to need a six-level list, you can use the following alternate method.

Method 2

Using this technique, to begin create the first list exactly as just described. However, before creating the second list, create a new paragraph style that's a duplicate of the first-level style. Then, when you create the new list, simply use this new style for the main level. Because it's being used for the first time, it begins with number 1. If you want to create three different lists in a document, then create still another new style identical to the first-level style.

Inserting Additional Paragraphs

The example in Figure 6.19 shows pure outlines. However, you might want to include additional paragraphs of straight text between outline levels. To accomplish this, you'll need to create still other paragraph styles. As an example, suppose that in Figure 6.19 you want to include paragraphs of text after each heading on the second level. To accomplish this, create a new paragraph style that has the same amount of indent as this level, but don't include any preceding numbers as part of the style options. Then assign this style to each paragraph of straight text that falls within the numbered list.

Creating Introductory Text for Paragraphs

You can create a special style that will automatically begin each paragraph with a particular string of text. For example, you might want to label certain paragraphs with "Item:", as shown in Figure 6.20. If you have read the preceding sections, you'll recognize the technique used to create this particular type of style.

Figure 6.20
Leading text at the beginning of each paragraph

> The group of paragraphs below illustrates the use of a special paragraph style to insert leading text for each paragraph.
>
> Item: This is the first paragraph of this type.
>
> Item: Here's another paragraph of the same type. Notice that each paragraph wraps around to create a hanging indent.
>
> Item: To accomplish the hanging indent, set the Rest option to the same value as the Space After option.
>
> Item: To add a little space after each paragraph, the Paragraph Spacing Below option is assigned a value of 0.1 inches.

Here are the steps for modifying a paragraph style to include special text at the beginning of each paragraph:

1. Click on Notations in the Modify & Create Styles dialog box.

2. In the edit box to the right of the Text option, enter whatever special text you want to have begin each paragraph.

3. If you want this text to appear as a superscript, click on the option Superscript Bullet or Text.

4. Assign the spacing between the special text and the beginning of the ordinary paragraph text, using either the Tab After or Space For option.

194 ◆ USING STYLES

Remember, whatever you enter in the edit box (step 2) will appear at the beginning of each paragraph assigned this paragraph style. This includes letters, numbers, or any other special characters you can find on the keyboard.

Using Ruling Lines

Using a paragraph style, you can insert a horizontal line at the beginning or end of each paragraph, or both. Ruling lines can add a good deal of spark to a document, and they help to focus the reader's attention on certain areas of the page.

Typically, ruling lines are used for headings, but you can use them for any paragraph style. You can make each line exactly as long as the nearest text line in the corresponding paragraph, or you can set the length either to a predetermined value or to the full distance between margins. You can even use a special type of paragraph style just to create a horizontal line on the page. Figure 6.21 presents a few examples of how horizontal ruling lines can be used.

The following steps describe how to modify a paragraph style so that each selected paragraph has a ruling line above or below:

1. Click on Lines in the Modify & Create Styles dialog box. The dialog box will change to that shown in Figure 6.10.

2. Click on the option labeled Line Above (or Line Below).

3. In the corresponding Line Style list box, click on the style of line you want to use. (There are several choices, so scroll through them all before making your selection.)

4. In the corresponding Spacing edit box, enter the amount of space to be inserted between the line and the first (or last) line of text in the paragraph.

5. Select the length of the line. (See the following discussion for details.)

6. If you have a color monitor, you can select the color of the line to appear on the screen. (Selecting a color for the lines will enhance the screen display, but the lines will still print in black unless your printer happens to output in color.)

When selecting a line length, you have the following options:

Text If you select this option, each line will be adjusted to the same length as the first line (or last) in the paragraph.

Margins This option creates a line that extends from the left to the right margin.

Figure 6.21
Using a paragraph style to create horizontal ruling lines

Ruling Line Below

The above heading illustrates how ruling lines can help to set off a particular piece of text. In this example, the ruling line automatically is adjusted to the length of the text. You can set this option in the Modify& Create Styles dialog box.

Ruling Line Above

For some applications, a ruling line above the paragraph is appropriate, as in the above heading. In addition, we have set the ruling line to extend across the entire page, nicely separating one topic from another.

Double Rules

Here's an example of using ruling lines both above and below a heading. For a different effect, we've chosen different types of lines.

Centering a Title

Here's a variation on some of the above themes. We have centered the title, and enclosed it with ruling lines extending from margin to margin. The ruling lines automatically accommodate whatever text size has been set.

Other By selecting this option, you can enter the exact line length in the edit box. The default unit is inches, but you can select centimeters, picas, or points by clicking on the word "inches".

You can also use the preceding steps to attach ruling lines *both* above and below the paragraph. In this case, the line length you select will apply to both lines.

Special Applications for Styles

In some circumstances, you may want to use a specially designed paragraph style for a particular purpose. For example, you can create a style whose only use is to draw a horizontal line on the page. Or, you can create a style for the purpose of adding a small amount of extra vertical space anywhere on a page.

Drawing Horizontal Lines

Here are the steps for creating a special paragraph style whose only purpose is to draw a horizontal line:

1. To begin, create a duplicate of the Body Text style, calling it something like Line.

2. Assign a horizontal line either above or below, following the steps described above in "Using Ruling Lines."

3. Set the line length to be from margin to margin (Margins).

4. Set the line spacing for this style to 0.05 inches. If that's not exactly right, you can modify it later.

To use this style to draw a line, simply enter a blank line (by pressing the Enter key twice) at the desired position in a document, and assign that line the new style.

Customizing the Document Spacing

For very detailed work, you may sometimes want to fine-tune the vertical spacing on a page. For example, suppose you want to add a bit of extra space between two specific paragraphs. You could accomplish this using the Above or Below option for one of the paragraphs, but that would affect the spacing for every paragraph of that type.

Instead, you can use a special paragraph style to insert a tiny bit of vertical space just where you want it. To begin, create the new style, calling it something like Space. Then, set the line spacing for this style to a very small amount, perhaps 0.1 inches. Also, make sure that the Above and Below options are set to zero.

When you want to insert a small amount of vertical space, simply enter a blank line there, and then assign it the Space style. If this amount of space isn't exactly right, you can adjust it: Leave the cursor on that blank line, select Spacing from the Text menu, and then adjust the line spacing; it will affect only that line.

You can even define two or three such styles for adding different amounts of space, perhaps naming them Space1, Space2, and Space3.

Using Function Key Shortcuts

Because assigning styles is such a useful and powerful operation, an additional shortcut has been provided. You can set up any of the function keys (except F1 and F10) as style-assignment keys. For example, you could set up F2 to correspond to the Body Text style. Then, to assign that style to a paragraph, you would click on the paragraph and then press F2.

Function keys are automatically assigned to the first eight styles in a template. If you look at the Style box on the screen, you can see which styles these are because each is preceded by the name of the corresponding function key (see Figure 6.4).

Assigning Function Keys

You can change the function key assignments to suit your particular needs. Normally, the best strategy is to assign the styles you use most often to the function keys that you can most comfortably reach. For example, you might assign F2 to the Body Text style, F4 to the Head1 style, and so on.

Here's how to assign a function key to a particular style:

1. Select Format/Change Template & Active Styles. The dialog box shown in Figure 6.22 will appear.

Figure 6.22
The dialog box for assigning active styles and function key shortcuts

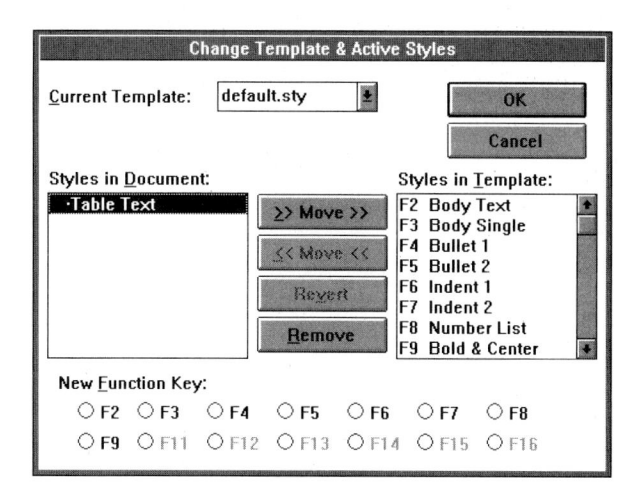

2. Click on the name of the style you want to assign to a function key. This style can be in either the Styles in Document or Styles in Template list box. It doesn't matter whether or not the style is already assigned another function key.

3. Click on the button corresponding to the function key you want to assign (at the bottom of the dialog box).

If the function key you select is already assigned to another style, it's simply reassigned. In addition, if the style you selected was already assigned another function key, the key assignments are switched. For example, suppose that Style1 is assigned to the function key F2 and Style2 is assigned to F4. If you reassign F4 to Style1, then F2 will automatically be reassigned to Style2.

Keeping Your Styles Visible

Here's a handy tip for using the Styles box. As you're assigning styles to various paragraphs, you may find it useful to keep this box displayed on the screen. Because it's an ordinary Windows window, you can adjust the size of this box to display as many styles as you wish. If the box is too large, however, it will hide too much of your document.

You can minimize the box size and still have your most common styles visible by placing them at the top of the list of styles. To accomplish this, simply assign the lowest-number function keys (F2, F3, and so on) to those styles. Then, adjust the size of the box to display just those styles you use most frequently.

Summary

This chapter has presented the basics of paragraph styles. As you have probably gathered, this topic contains many complexities. You may want to use this chapter to refresh your memory from time to time.

You've seen a number of the ways in which you can use paragraph styles to format your documents. But there's a lot more to styles. The following chapter discusses how to manage your style templates effectively.

CHAPTER 7

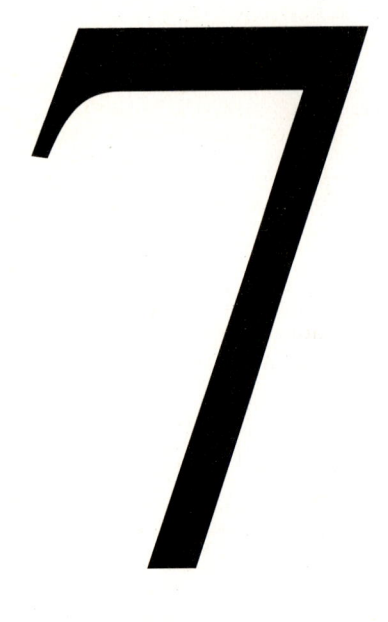

Styles and Templates

Using a Style Template

Creating a New Template

Local and Global Styles

Manipulating Paragraph Styles

Editing Paragraph Styles

Switching Paragraph Style Assignments

Templates and Page Layouts

Deleting a Template

Using Styles and Templates: Hints and Tips

Setting Template Defaults

Including Text as Part of a Template

Generating Rough Drafts

Using the Built-In Templates

Styles and Templates　　　　　　　　　　　　　　　　　　　　　　　　　　**201**

O FTEN, YOU'LL CREATE A PARAGRAPH STYLE THAT COULD BE USEFUL in many different documents. You can make this type of style generally available by adding it to a *style template*, which is a collection of paragraph styles. A style template, or just *template,* is maintained as a separate file. It can contain any number of different paragraph styles, and it can be attached to any document.

As described in Chapter 6, a paragraph style can be either part of a document, or it can be attached to a template. If a style is attached to a document, its effect is limited to that document. On the other hand, if a style belongs to a template, it can be made accessible to any document simply by attaching that template to the document. Whereas Chapter 6 focused on how to work with individual styles, regardless of where they are located, this chapter concentrates on templates.

In addition to containing paragraph styles, each template contains basic page layout settings, such as margins, tab settings, headers, and so on. You can customize these layout settings for each template. Then, when you assign a template to a new document, those page layout features become the default for the document, although you can easily change any of the settings.

Whenever you create a new document, it is assigned a template, either by Professional Write Plus or by you. All the paragraph styles in that template are then accessible to the document, and you can use them to format the various paragraphs. Up to now, each time you have used a document the template named DEFAULT.STY has automatically been assigned. Now you'll find out how to create and use other templates.

You don't have to create a new template for each new document. On the other hand, you wouldn't want to cram into a single template every paragraph style you ever work with. Generally, most people feel comfortable using a few standard templates, each of which contains a small group of styles for a particular type of document.

Over a period of time, you'll probably build up a small repertoire of standard templates. Initially, you might spend a fair amount of time creating them. But eventually you'll find that you spend very little time creating new templates and styles and that your standard templates have become one of your most valuable tools.

Advantages of Style Templates

There are several advantages to using paragraph styles and style templates. The more you use them, the more you'll come to appreciate these advantages. Here are some of their benefits:

Ease of Paragraph Formatting　Using paragraph styles is an extremely quick and easy way to format different paragraphs. You just assign the appropriate style to a paragraph, which is then automatically reformatted. You don't have to assign a style to each paragraph (which would be a real nuisance)—just to the ones that are special. The remaining paragraphs default to the standard Body Text paragraph style.

Automatic Page Layout Setup   You can include standard text and graphics as part of a template. For example, the template you use for your correspondence could contain your return address and logo. If you're using a laser printer, this technique offers you instant access to a variety of custom letterheads. You create a different template for each letterhead, then select the appropriate one for each piece of correspondence.

Time Savings   With the standardization offered by styles and templates, you spend much less time formatting your documents. For example, each time you write a new letter you don't need to make decisions about margin sizes, which fonts to use, and so on. Because these decisions have already been incorporated into the template you use, you can devote your energies to the content of your work, rather than to its form.

Changing Formats Easily   You can change the format of a group of similar paragraphs simply by changing the specifications of the assigned style. For example, to change the font size of all the secondary headings in a document, all you need to do is change the font size assigned to the secondary heading style—all the headings will automatically be resized. (Without styles, you would have to find each heading in the document and manually change its font.)

Increased Quality   Once you've developed a group of paragraph styles, you can use them to create high-quality work. For example, you can create a style called Indent, which you can then assign to each paragraph to be indented. Or you can create a paragraph style called Heading that allows you to make your section headings stand out by boldfacing them and drawing a ruling line above each one. The time you take to develop a few interesting styles will be paid back many times over in the quality of your documents.

Using a Style Template

With few exceptions, whenever you work on a document it's attached to a template, which are referred to as either the *attached template* or *current template*. Each time you open an *existing* document it is automatically attached to the same template it was attached to the last time you saved the document.

Whenever you open a new document by selecting New from the File menu, the current *default template* is assigned to the document. Initially, this default is the built-in template named DEFAULT.STY. Eventually, after you have learned how to create and use your own templates, you can assign any of them to a new document. You can also assign any of them to be the default template. For details about assigning defaults, see "Setting Template Defaults" later in this chapter.

Selecting a Different Template

Note. When you attach a new template to a document, the original one is detached from the document but is left unchanged.

In many cases you will want to assign a different template to a document (one other than the default template originally assigned). For example, if you're creating a newsletter, you'll want a template designed specifically for newsletters. Normally, when you first begin working on a new document you'll select the template you want to use, although you can change templates anytime you wish.

Here's how to attach a different template to the current document:

1. Select Format/Change Template & Active Styles. When the Change Template dialog box appears (see Figure 7.1), the name of the currently attached template is displayed at the top.

Figure 7.1
The dialog box for manipulating paragraph styles

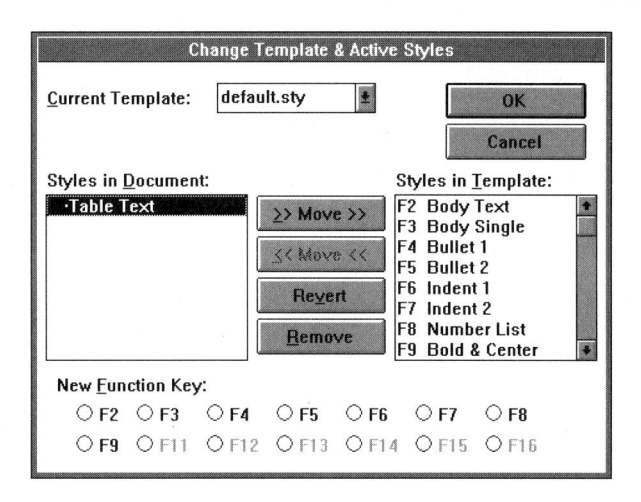

2. Click on the arrow in the edit box labeled "Current Template", and a list of the available templates will appear (see Figure 7.2). These are the templates stored in the current *default template directory*, and these are the only templates accesible to you. Initially, the default template directory is set to C:\PWPLUS\STYLES, but you can change it to any directory you wish.

3. Click on the name of the template you want to attach.

Figure 7.2
Select the name of the template you want to attach to the current document

```
default.sty
default.sty
doc.sty
envel-c.sty
envel-s.sty
fax.sty
legal.sty
```

4. Click on Open Template, then click on OK. The new template will be attached to the document, replacing the old template.

CAUTION! *There may be significant consequences from attaching a new template. For details, see "Switching Templates," later in this chapter.*

You can access only those templates stored in the default template directory (step 2). If you want to access some other template, you have two options:

- Copy the template you want to use into the default template directory.

- Change the default template directory to where the desired template is stored.

For information about the default template directory, see "Setting Template Defaults" later in this chapter.

Creating a New Template

Although Professional Write Plus comes with several built-in templates, such as DEFAULT.STY, you should learn to build your own because it's convenient to have different templates for different purposes. For example, you might want to create one template to hold the styles for all your memos and correspondence, and another template for newsletters.

There's another, secondary, reason for creating new templates. Generally, you should avoid modifying the DEFAULT.STY template (or any of the other templates that come with the software). Because it's one that comes with Professional Write Plus, if you leave it unchanged, you can refer to it to see how a particular style was set up by the Professional Write Plus staff.

When you create a new template (giving it a new name in the process), it initially contains the following:

- All the paragraph styles contained in the template attached to the current document

- Any paragraph styles that are attached to the current document

- All the page layout values in effect for the current document

Note. New templates are automatically saved in the default template directory.

As a result of creating a new template, two things happen. First, the template is created as a separate file (in your default template directory), with the name you assign. As a result, you can attach it to any document you work with. Second, the template is automatically attached to the current document, replacing the template that was previously attached (which remains on disk).

After creating a new template, you can then customize it in various ways. This includes deleting unwanted styles from the new template and adding new ones.

In the following steps, a new template named SAMPLES.STY is created. By default, this template will be stored in the same directory as Professional Write Plus's own templates. (For details on how to choose the directory you want to use for storing your templates, see "Setting Template Defaults.")

1. Select Format/Save As a New Template. The dialog box shown in Figure 7.3 will appear.

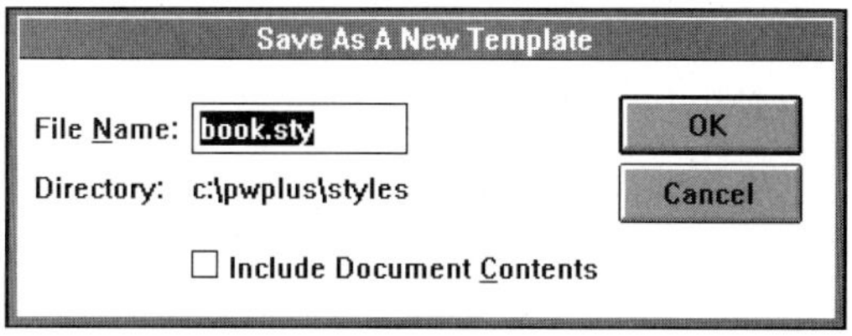

Figure 7.3
The dialog box for naming a new template

2. In the edit box labeled "File Name", enter the name of the new template—**SAMPLES** for this exercise. You can use any combination of up to eight letters and digits. No spaces are allowed. The name you enter will be the name of the file in which the template is saved. Note that the program automatically adds the .STY extension to the file name.

3. Click on OK, and the new template is saved.

In the dialog box shown in Figure 7.3, the line labeled "Directory" shows the default directory in which the new template is stored.

After you have created a new template, you can customize it in various ways, as described in later sections.

Local and Global Styles

You may remember from Chapter 6 that two types of styles can be used by a document: local and global. The global styles are those that are part of the template attached to the document, and thus can be used by any document that attaches that template. On the other hand, local styles are those specifically attached to the document—not to the template—and therefore only can be used by the current document.

You can view the styles attached to a document by selecting Format/Change Template & Active Styles. The dialog box that appears (Figure 7.1) lists all of the attached styles. Those in the left column (Styles in Document) are the local styles, whereas those in the right column (Styles in Template) are global.

If a style name in the right column appears in light gray, it means there's a local style with the same name. (You should be able to find it in the left column.) In this case, the document can "see" only the local style—not the global one, which is why that name appears in light gray, or *dimmed*.

How Styles Become Either Local or Global

It's important for you to understand how a paragraph style becomes part of either a document or the attached template. Here are the general rules:

- When you create a new template, any styles that were local to the document become attached to the new template. Moreover, the local ones are deleted from the document. In other words, *immediately after you create a new template there are no longer any local styles attached to the current document.*

- When you modify an existing style in the current template, the modified style becomes a local one. The original, unmodified style continues to exist in the template, but the document can no longer see it because the local one with the same name takes precedence.

- When you create a new style, it automatically becomes local.

Manipulating Paragraph Styles

You can delete unwanted styles and create new ones—either local or global styles. You can also switch a style from being local to global—and vice versa. With a bit of difficulty, you can even rename a paragraph style.

Deleting Paragraph Styles

You can delete either local or global paragraph styles. Although you use basically the same steps for both style types, the effects can be quite different since a local style influences only the current document, whereas a global style may affect many different documents. If you delete a local style, you'll affect the appearance of any paragraphs in the current document that were assigned that style. However, if you delete a global style, it may affect any document that uses the template.

There are many possible reasons for deleting styles. For instance, when you create a new template, you'll probably want to delete some or all of the styles that were part of the original template (the one on which the new template is based).

Another reason for deleting styles is to keep things from getting out of hand. Over a period of time, you may find that many old, unused styles creep into your documents and templates. Getting rid of them is like pruning dead branches from a tree: You're more likely to notice the ones that are left after the trimming is over.

Deleting a Local Style

When you delete a local style, *if there is no corresponding style name in the current template*, all those paragraphs that were assigned the style are then assigned the Body Text style. (This, of course, applies only to the current document since the style was local to that document.)

However, if there is a style with the same name in the template, it becomes visible to the document when the local style is deleted. The affected paragraphs are then reformatted using the specifications of the template style.

Deleting a Style in a Template

Deleting a paragraph style from a template is a much more serious business because other documents may be affected. When a paragraph style is deleted from a template, any affected paragraphs, even in other documents, revert to Body Text style. The paragraphs in the current document revert immediately. On the other hand, those paragraphs in another document will revert when you open the document and the program discovers that the style assigned to those paragraphs no longer exists.

For example, suppose that documents A and B are stored on disk, and both use the same template. Let's also suppose that both documents used the style called Head1 in that template. Now, suppose you delete Head1 from the template while A is open. The paragraphs assigned to Head1 immediately revert to Body Text. The next time you retrieve B, you'll find that all the paragraphs that had been assigned the Head1 style have reverted to Body Text.

However, you can recover if you act quickly enough. If you recreate the Head1 style in either document, each affected paragraph in that document (*only*) will be reassigned that style, *provided* you haven't assigned another style (either local or global) to that paragraph. This means that Professional Write Plus actually remembers the name of the last style assigned to each paragraph, even after that paragraph reverts to body text.

Here are the steps for deleting unwanted paragraph styles of either type:

1. Select Format/Change Template & Active Styles. The dialog box shown in Figure 7.1 will appear.

2. Highlight the style you want to remove. This can be any style in either column, except for Body Text in the template, which can't be removed.

3. Click on Remove.

4. Repeat steps 2 and 3 for each paragraph style you want to remove.

5. Click on OK to make your deletions permanent. (If you click on Cancel instead of OK, the deletions you made are nullified.)

You can't delete the Body Text paragraph style from a template. Since this style represents the majority of text appearing in a document, it's a fundamental part of every template. Moreover, since there must always be at least one style attached to a document, and since paragraphs revert to Body Text when their style is deleted, Body Text must remain.

Creating New Styles

The topic of creating new styles was covered in depth in Chapter 6. There it said that any new style you create is automatically attached to the current document. (As explained above, this means it is created as a local style.) The following material assumes you have read Chapter 6 and are familiar with the process of creating new styles. If not, you should read that chapter before going on.

In some cases you may want to create a new style and leave it as local. In other cases you will want to make the style global by attaching it to the current template. Creating a new global style is a two-step process. First, you create the new style, assigning it whatever characteristics you want. Then, you transfer that style to the current template, making it global.

Figure 7.4 illustrates the process for creating the new style Style2. In part a, the style has been created and is attached to the current document. Then part b shows the situation after the style has been transferred to the current template.

Changing Style Types

You can transfer a local style to the current template, making it global. Conversely, you can copy a style from the current template into the document, making it local.

When creating documents, should you keep all your styles in the attached template, or should you make them all local? There are pros and cons to each. There's an inherent danger and weakness involved with keeping all your styles global—that is, attached to templates rather than within the individual documents. Here's why: If you (or someone else) changes one or more styles in a template, those changes may affect many documents. Worse yet, if a style is accidentally deleted from a template, the formatting of many documents could be severely affected. This is certainly an argument in favor of keeping styles within the documents themselves.

Figure 7.4
Before (a) and after (b) moving a local style to the current template

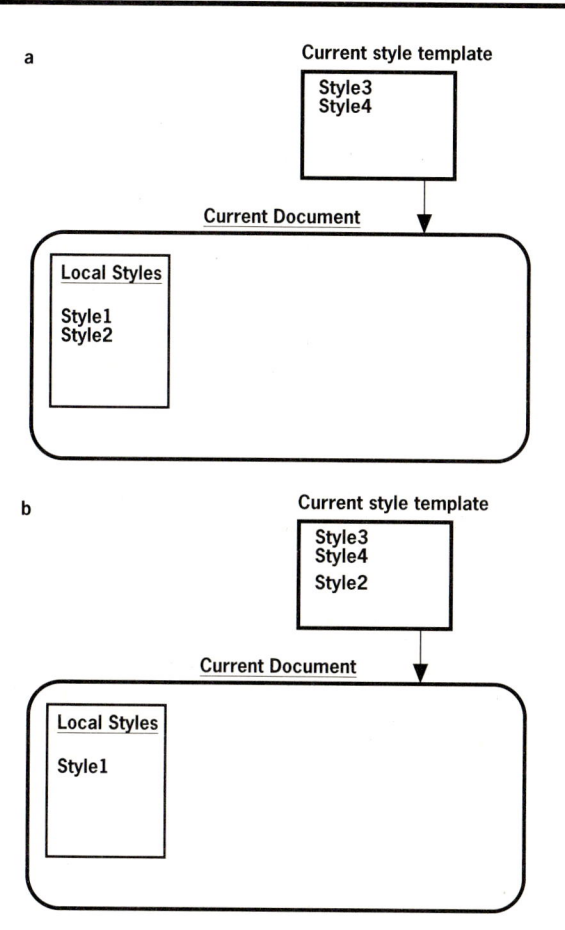

a

Current style template
Style3
Style4

Current Document
Local Styles
Style1
Style2

b

Current style template
Style3
Style4
Style2

Current Document
Local Styles
Style1

The other side of the argument is that by keeping all your styles in templates, rather than in the individual documents, you can make global changes to your documents simply by updating the templates. This argument may carry a good deal of weight in an organization that benefits from consistent formatting. Possibly a good compromise in this type of situation would be to maintain separate backups of your templates, making sure they're updated as the templates change. Then, if a template is accidentally changed or wiped out, the backup will save the day.

Here's another reason (although perhaps not a strong one) for keeping styles local. When you copy a document from one computer to another, you must also copy the formatting information. If the styles are maintained in a template, it will have to be copied as well. However, if the styles are all local, only the document needs to be copied.

Copying Styles from a Template to a Document
When you copy a style from a template to a document, the style becomes local. However, the original style remains in the template, although the document can't see it because the local version takes precedence. But maintaining the original style in the template keeps it available to other documents. Here's how to copy a paragraph style from the current template to the document:

1. Select Format/Change Template & Active Styles.

2. When the dialog box appears (Figure 7.1), in the right-hand column highlight the name of the style you want to copy to the document.

3. Click on <<Move<<. The style name will appear in the left column. It will also to continue to appear in the right column, although it's dimmed, indicating that it's now invisible to the document.

4. Click on OK, and the transfer is carried out.

Copying All the Styles A shortcut is available for copying all the paragraph styles from the current template into the document. Here's how:

1. Select File/Save As.

2. When the Save As dialog box appears, click on the option labeled "Keep Styles With Document".

3. Click on OK, then verify that you want to overwrite the current version of the document.

Saving the file in this way has a two important effects. First, all the styles in the current template are immediately made local to the document. Second, the current template is detached from the document. You can see this by displaying the Styles box: The word "Styles" appears at the top, indicating that no template is attached. You can also see that no template is attached by displaying the Change Template dialog box. The word "(none)" appears in the edit box labeled "Current Template".

The next time you retrieve the document, all the styles will be local, and no template will be attached. However, at any time you can attach either the original template or another one to the document.

Moving Styles from a Document to the Current Template
Here's how to move a local paragraph style from the current document to the attached template:

1. Select Format/Change Template & Active Styles.

2. When the dialog box appears (Figure 7.1), in the left-hand column highlight the name of the style you want to transfer to the template.

3. Click on >>Move>>. The style name will disappear from the left column and appear in the right one.

When a style is moved from the document to the template, the original local style is deleted from the document, so that only the new global version exists. This is quite different from the situation in which a global style is *copied* to the document. In that case both the original and the new copy of the style continue to exist.

Renaming Paragraph Styles

You can't rename a paragraph style directly. However, with a little bit of effort you can effectively rename a *local* paragraph style, as follows:

1. First create a new style, using the one you want to rename as a model, and naming the new style whatever you want. (Chapter 6 describes how to create a new style.)

2. Assign this new style to all the paragraphs that were assigned the original style. This is easily done by using the Find & Replace feature. (See "Switching Paragraph Style Assignments," later in this chapter.)

3. Delete the original style.

This technique is best confined to a local style. If you try to apply it to a global one, you'll have to go through every document affected by the template containing the style, using Find & Replace to assign the new style to the affected paragraphs.

Editing Paragraph Styles

As you work with a document, you can edit any of the paragraph styles—either those in the attached template or those you've created as local styles. Chapter 6 described the details of making various types of changes to a paragraph style. You use exactly the same procedures to edit either a global or local style.

This section focuses on the *consequences* of making any type of change to either a local or global style, that is, how your changes affect the current document and possibly others as well. There are two very important points to remember, relevant to modifying an existing paragraph style of either type. First, when you modify a paragraph style in any way, the changes immediately affect every paragraph in the current document that has been assigned that style.

For example, suppose you have created a document with many headings, and you have assigned a style called Head1 to each of these. Now further suppose that during the editing process you decide to change the font size of all the headings. To accomplish this, all you need to do is assign a different size to the Head1 style, and the change will be immediately "telegraphed" to every heading in the document.

The second, and even more important point, is that the changes you make to a style *of either type* affect only the current document. *They do not immediately affect the style in the current template in any way.* This seems contradictory: How can you change a global style without changing it?

If you want to make a change to a style in the template *itself,* you must take additional steps. The reason for this is that changing a template could affect many other documents—even those already in existence—so the program forces you to think twice before making any kind of template change.

Editing a Style in a Template

When you edit a global style, some very subtle and tricky things happen. It's very important that you understand this process, so that you can work with global styles effectively.

Suppose you make some type of change to a style contained in a template. For example, you could change the typeface or font size. Several things happen when you make the edits:

- First, a duplicate of the original paragraph style is created, and it is assigned as a local paragraph style to the current document.

- This new paragraph style is given the same name as the original paragraph style.

- The original style remains in the template.

- The changes you make are applied to the new local paragraph style, *not to the original paragraph style in the template.*

The reasoning behind this is that you'll often want to make a change to a style, but usually only for the current document. For example, you might want to change the body text size to 10 points for a particular document, without making that change to the Body Text style in the current template.

Remember, the local paragraph style takes precedence over the corresponding one in the template. That is, the original paragraph style in the template becomes invisible to the current document, and the document can only see the local style. To illustrate this behavior, Figure 7.5 shows the before and after situations when the style named Style3 is edited. Initially, Style3 is contained in the current template. After the style has been modified, it becomes attached to the document as a local style. The *unchanged* version of Style3 continues to exist in the template, although it can't be seen by the document (this is indicated in the figure by placing Style3 in parentheses).

Figure 7.5
Before (a) and after (b) modifying a style in the current template

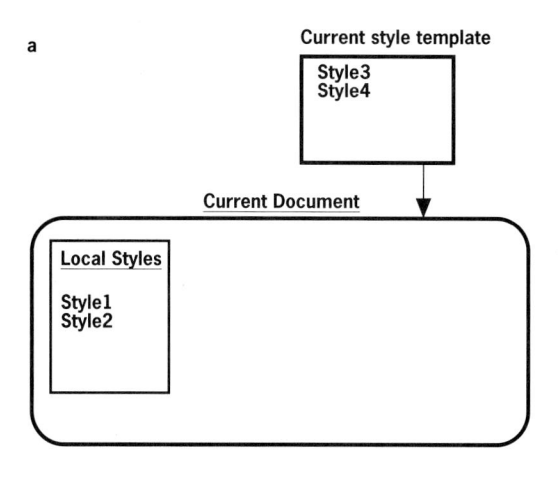

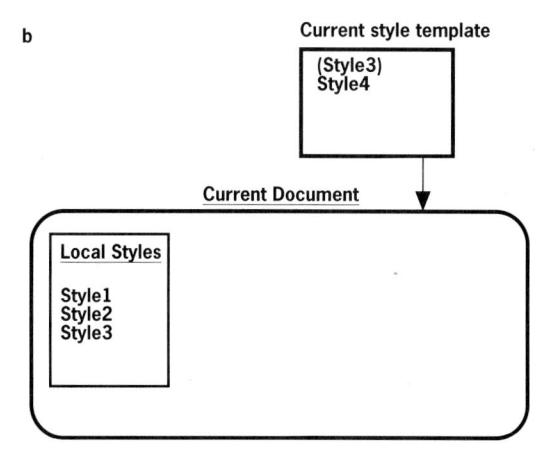

[Diagram (a): Current style template containing Style3, Style4, linked to Current Document which contains Local Styles: Style1, Style2]

[Diagram (b): Current style template containing (Style3), Style4, linked to Current Document which contains Local Styles: Style1, Style2, Style3]

This invisibility is reflected in the Change Template dialog box. The name of the modified paragraph style appears in both columns, but it's dimmed in the right column, indicating that it's invisible to the current document. You can also note this effect in the Styles box (press Ctrl-X to display it), where the name of the paragraph style now appears with a leading period, indicating that it's local.

Making the Changes Global

The changes you make to a style affect only the local style. However, you can also make those changes to the global copy of the style in the attached template. To do this, you transfer the local paragraph style back into the template. This is a simple process, and it was described in "Moving Styles from a Document to the Current Template," earlier in this chapter.

Reverting to the Original Style Options

When you modify a global style, a new local style is created that contains your changes, and the original style remains unchanged in the template. In some cases you may wish to delete these changes and revert to the original style. For example, suppose you change the font size of the Body Text style from 10 points to 12 points. The new, local Body Text style will be assigned a font size of 12, while the original Body Text style in the attached template remains at 10 points.

Here's how to revert back to the original paragraph style:

1. Select Format/Change Template & Active Styles.

2. When the new dialog box appears, click on the style in the *left column* that you want to undo.

3. Click on Revert in the middle column.

4. Click on OK to have the change take effect.

The modified style is deleted from the document, and the original style in the template takes effect again.

Switching Paragraph Style Assignments

Suppose that a group of paragraphs is assigned to one paragraph style, Style A, and you want to change these assignments to another style, Style B. To do this manually in a large document would take you forever and a day. However, you can do it in one or two minutes with the Find & Replace feature. You simply enter the name of the old and new styles, and the program will automatically make the reassignments. If you wish, you can even select which paragraphs you want to reassign. To reassign a group of paragraphs from one style to another, follow these steps:

1. Select Edit/Find & Replace, and the Find & Replace dialog box will appear (Figure 7.6).

2. In the edit box labeled "Find", enter the name of the style to be replaced. You must enter the *exact* spelling, including the proper case and any blanks.

3. In the box labeled "Replace With", enter the name of the new style. Again, be sure to use the exact spelling and case.

4. Click on Find & Replace Style.

5. Click on Replace All.

Figure 7.6
Enter the names of the original and new paragraph styles

Remember, a style name can contain spaces, and capitalization within a style name is also significant. You must get the spelling exactly right, or the program won't be able to find the style assignments.

If you want to selectively replace style assignments, click on OK instead of Replace All in step 5. As each paragraph is found, it will be highlighted and the program will pause. You can then choose whether or not to change the style assignment of that paragraph.

Here's a handy tip that can save you some time and trouble when reassigning styles. In step 2 and 3 above, if the style you're using has been assigned a function key, you can simply press that key instead of entering the style name, and the program will automatically enter the name for you. This also eliminates the possibility of misspelling a style name.

Templates and Page Layouts

When you create a new template, the page layout parameters for the current document are included as an integral part of the template. These parameters include values for the page size and orientation, margins, tabs, headers, footers, gutters, lines around the page, and number of columns per page. (Chapter 3 describes how to work with the various page layout parameters.) Each time you assign that template to a *new* document, those layout parameters become the defaults for the document. For example, the margins in the DEFAULT.STY template are set to 1 inch all around, and the page size is set to 8 1/2 by 11 inches. These become the default values for each new document that's assigned this template.

As you work with a document, naturally you can change any of the default page layout values. And when you make these changes, they are automatically restricted to the current document. That is, these changes do not affect the corresponding page layout values stored in the attached template.

However, you can also change the layout values stored in the template. And thereafter, these new values will become the defaults for each new document that uses the template. For instance, you *could* change the left and right margin settings in DEFAULT.STY from 1 to 2 inches each (*but don't do it*—leave the default template intact).

Changing the Current Document Layout

When you create a new document, its page layout values are determined by the Page Layout in the assigned template—until you make any layout changes. (Remember, the Page Layout of a document consists of the specifications that control the layout of every page.) This situation is illustrated in Figure 7.7a. Likewise, if you switch to a different template, its Page Layout values will become those of the new document. Again, this is true as long as you haven't made changes to any of the layout features (margins, tabs, and so on) since the document was first created.

However, as soon as you make any type of layout change, *a local Page Layout* is created for the document, as shown in Figure 7.7b; and this local layout then controls the document. Subsequently, any layout changes you make are to the local Page Layout, but the layout in the template remains unchanged.

Changing the Page Layout in a Template

If you want to create a standardized Page Layout that can be used for many documents, you need to add it to one or more of your templates. To change the Page Layout of a template, follow these steps:

1. If the layout changes you plan to make will *not* apply to the current document, save the document, and then start a new one (using the New option on the File menu).

2. Attach the template you want to modify.

3. Make the layout changes you want. These changes will affect only the current document, until you carry out steps 4 and 5.

4. Select Format/Save As a New Template. The dialog box shown in Figure 7.3 will appear, and the current template name will appear in the File Name edit box.

5. Click on OK, and then click on Yes to verify that you want to overwrite the template. When you save the template, the local Page Layout is copied as part of it.

If you want the new layout values to apply to the current document as well, you can skip step 1. However, note that in this case when you execute steps 4 and 5, any local paragraph styles will also be saved to the template. If you wish, you can then copy those styles back as local styles, using the Change Template & Active Styles option on the Format menu.

Figure 7.7
The template controlling the Page Layout (a), and the local Page Layout controlling the current document's layout (b)

Deleting a Template

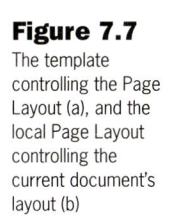

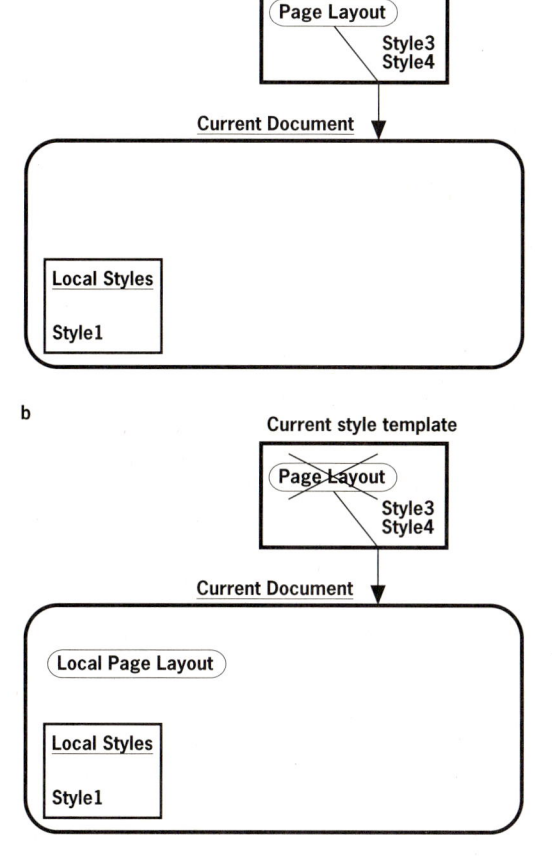

Deleting a template is truly a dangerous operation. Fortunately, you have to do a little work to accomplish it, which gives you time to consider your action carefully. Since each template is stored in a separate file, all you need do is delete that file. You can do this from within Professional Write Plus (use the File Manager option on the File menu), from within Windows (by using the Windows File Manager), or from DOS (using the DEL command).

By now, you should appreciate the hazards of this type of operation. If you delete a template, any document to which it was attached will lose all the paragraph formatting generated from that template. But here are some safeguards you can use to prevent this type of disaster:

- Keep regular backups on floppy disks of all your template files. If you perform regular backups of any type, make sure that all of your templates are included.

- Consider also keeping backups of your templates in separate files on your hard disk. Usually, you'll be using only a few templates on a regular basis, and because each template takes up only a few thousand bytes, the amount of required disk space is not very significant.

- Think twice before deleting a template file. Then think once again. Ask yourself: Are there really no documents that reference this template?

Using Styles and Templates: Hints and Tips

Paragraph styles and templates are among the most valuable word processing tools at your disposal. However, not understanding how styles work can lead to a lot of difficulty, particularly since you are dealing with both *local* paragraph styles and page layouts and *global* styles and page layouts within templates.

This section reviews the more important points about using styles and templates and offers a few helpful hints.

Switching Templates

At any time while you're working on a document, you can attach a different template. Usually, the reason for doing this is to access paragraph styles other than the ones currently available. However, there are a few pitfalls to be aware of when switching templates. And not being aware of them can produce a lot of trouble and confusion.

As mentioned earlier, the page layout of a new document is initially set by the Page Layout in the attached template. If you switch to another template, and if you haven't made any layout changes to the current document since it was first created, the page layout characteristics of the new template will be assigned to the document. However, if you have made any layout changes, a local Page Layout is created. In that case, switching to a new template will have no effect on the page layout of the document, because the local Page Layout takes precedence.

When a new template is attached to a document, all the paragraph styles in the template become available to the document, but there are various possible complications, as shown below.

Situation 1: Duplicate Names

The document contains a *local* paragraph style with the same name as one in the new template. In this case, the new, global paragraph style becomes invisible to the document because a local style always takes precedence over one with the same name in a template.

Situation 2: An Unmatched Name

The old template contains a paragraph style for which there is no equivalent style name in the new template. In this case, when the new template is selected any paragraphs that were assigned to the original paragraph style will be reassigned to Body Text.

For instance, suppose that several paragraphs have been assigned to the style Bullet in the original template. If Bullet is not a style in the new sheet, all those paragraphs will be reassigned to Body Text and reformatted accordingly.

This example illustrates one of the dangers in switching templates, but there's a simple way to avoid this: Before switching to a different template, copy all the styles in the template into the document, using the Change Template & Active Styles screen (Figure 7.1). That way, it won't matter if the new template is missing any of the old styles, because they'll continue to exist as local styles.

There's another way in which you can recover from the loss of a style. When a paragraph reverts to Body Text, the name of the original style (in this example, Bullet) is remembered for that paragraph by the document, *until the next time you save the document.* If before then, you create a style for that document with the same name, the paragraph will be formatted to the specifications you set up for that style.

Situation 3: No Matching Local Style

The new template contains a style with the same name as one in the old template, and there is no local style with the same name. In this case, the paragraphs assigned to this style will be reformatted according to the specifications in the new template.

For instance, suppose that the original template contains the style Title, which specifies a 14-point Helvetica font. The new template also contains a Title style, but it specifies an 18-point Times Roman font. When this new template is selected, all associated headings in the document will be reformatted to 18-point Times Roman.

However, you may or may not want this to happen. If you don't want any paragraphs to be reformatted, then copy all the styles from the original style into the document (make them local) before switching templates. Your document will ignore any styles in the new template with names the same as those in the original template.

As a general rule, make all the current paragraph styles local before switching templates. This will protect against any of the hazards just described. You wouldn't do this, of course, if you were deliberately changing templates in order to reformat your entire document by using the styles in the new template.

Manipulating Styles with Caution

Before moving any styles in or out of a template, make sure of the consequences. Will other documents be affected? If so, is that what you want? Remember, there are several operations that can move styles in and out of documents and templates:

- Using the >>Move>> and <<Move<< options in the Change Template dialog box
- Selecting Save As a New Template on the Format menu
- Using the File/Save As option, and then choosing the option Keep Styles with Document

If there's any question at all about adverse effects on other documents, keep all style changes local to the current document. You don't have to work too hard to do this, because all changes are kept local automatically. In fact, you have to take one of the extra steps described earlier to have any style changes transferred to the template.

Remembering Page Layouts

When you make changes to the page layout of a document, they are confined to the current document. That is, the Page Layout in the attached template is not affected. However, when you use the Save As a New Template option, either to update an existing style or to create a new one, the current Page Layout settings are copied to the template. This could have a dramatically adverse effect on other documents that use that template.

If you want to copy the local styles of the current document to the template without copying the Page Layout values as well, use the Change Template & Active Styles dialog box, not the Save As a New Template option.

Recovering from an Accidental Style Deletion

If you accidentally delete a style from a template, you can recover before any documents are permanently affected, but the timing is critical. To illustrate this, let's suppose that documents A and B use the same template for their paragraph formatting, and that both documents use the style called Indent in that template. Now suppose that you accidentally delete the style Indent from the template while using document B.

Later, when you retrieve document A into Professional Write Plus, any paragraphs assigned the Indent style immediately revert to Body Text because the style Indent no longer exists. However, for each of those paragraphs, the name of the original assigned style (Indent) is remembered by the document—unless you assign another style to that paragraph.

To recover from this accident, create a new style called Indent, with the same name as the one accidentally deleted, and then assign to this new style the same paragraph characteristics the original Indent style had. Each paragraph originally assigned to Indent will then automatically be reassigned to the new Indent—again, provided you haven't in the meantime assigned any other style to the paragraph.

Setting Template Defaults

Each time you create a new document, a template is attached to it. This happens in one of two ways:

- The *default template* is automatically attached to the document.

- You select the template you want to be attached.

Normally, the first of these methods is used. (When Professional Write Plus is first installed, the template named DEFAULT.STY is used as the default template. However, you can change the default to any other template that you have created.) Alternatively, you can also select an option so that the second method is used.

When you create a new template, it's stored in the *default template directory*. Similarly, whenever you want to attach a different template to a document, your selection is limited to the templates stored in the default template directory. When Professional Write Plus is first installed, the default template directory is set to \PWPLUS\STYLES (assuming that the program files are stored in the directory \PWPLUS).

However, you can select a different default template directory. This can be any existing directory on any disk drive, but for ease of use you should create a unique directory whose only purpose is to contain your own templates. Just make sure that whatever directory you select as the default contains *all* the templates you plan to use. If it doesn't, you can use the File Manager to copy or transfer the templates into that directory.

Selecting the Default Template Directory

You can select *any existing directory* as the storage area for any templates you create. If you want to create a new directory, you'll have to do so either from within the Windows File Manager or from DOS—you cannot create a new directory from within Professional Write Plus.

To assign a directory as the default for saving your templates, select Options/Default Paths. When the next dialog box appears (see below), enter the full path name of the directory in the box labeled "Template". This default will remain in effect until you change it. Any new templates you create will automatically be stored in this directory.

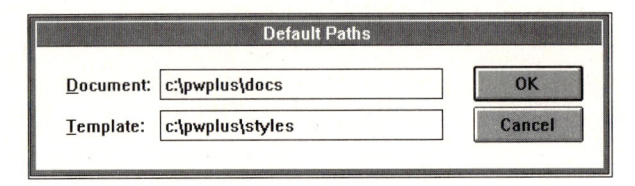

```
                    Default Paths
  Document:  c:\pwplus\docs            OK
  Template:  c:\pwplus\styles          Cancel
```

Selecting the Default Template

You can easily change the default template from DEFAULT.STY to any other one that's stored in the default template directory. Remember, whenever you create a new document, the program looks in the default directory for the template you have selected as the default. If you want to use a template as a default, but it's not in the default directory, use the File Manager to copy or move the template into that directory.

To select a new default template, follow these steps:

1. Select Options/Default Template, and the dialog box shown in Figure 7.8 will appear. The list box displays all the templates stored in the default template directory.

Figure 7.8
Select the default template

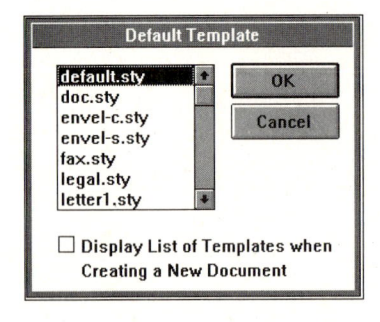

```
        Default Template
  default.sty      OK
  doc.sty
  envel-c.sty     Cancel
  envel-s.sty
  fax.sty
  legal.sty
  letter1.sty

  ☐ Display List of Templates when
     Creating a New Document
```

2. Click on the template you want to be the new default, then click on OK.

3. If you want to be able to select a template other than the default each time you create a new document, click on the option labeled "Display List of Templates when Creating a New Document".

If you click on this last option, then the default template is *not* automatically assigned to each new document. Instead, when you open a new document a list box similar to that in Figure 7.8 appears, and you can then select the template you want.

Including Text as Part of a Template

When you create a new template, you can optionally include the text that appears in the current document. For example, you could create a template for your normal correspondence, and as part of this template you could include your company heading. Then, each time you begin a new document with this template the text can be inserted as part of the document.

Creating the Template

Here's how to create a template with text:

1. Start a new document (select New from the File menu), and select a template that contains some or all of the styles you'll be using in the new template.

2. If necessary, add new paragraph styles, and customize them as needed.

3. Set the Page Layout options the way you want them (margins and so on).

4. Enter the text to be included as part of the template. Format this text the way you want it to appear on your documents.

5. Select Format/Save As a New Template.

6. Enter a name for the new template. This must be a valid file name, with a maximum of eight characters, including letters and digits.

7. Click on the Include Document Contents option, and then click on OK. The new template will be saved.

The template will contain all the styles in the original template (unless you changed them), any new styles you created, the page layout specifications, and whatever text you entered.

Using the Template

You can use this new template to create new documents, each of which will contain the text saved as part of the template. In order to access the text saved with the template, as well as the template itself, you must take a couple of special steps. First, you must set the default that displays a list of available templates each time you create a new document. This is described in the earlier section "Selecting the Default Template." Then you must use the displayed list to attach the template when the document is first created.

Here are the steps for using this special type of template with a new document:

1. Select File/New.

2. When the Style Template dialog box appears (Figure 7.9), click on Copy Template Contents.

3. Click on the name of the template and then click on OK.

Figure 7.9
Use the Copy Template Contents option to include any text as part of the selected template

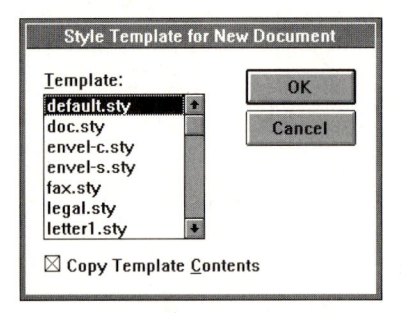

The new template will be selected, and the text saved with the template will appear on the screen, formatted as it was originally. You can then create the rest of the document.

If you want to use the template for a new document *without* the accompanying text in the sheet, simply do not click on Copy Template Contents (step 2).

Generating Rough Drafts

Rough drafts are usually double- or triple-spaced. One way to output this type of draft is by temporarily modifying one or two styles. To begin, create your document using single-spacing (double-spacing wastes space on the screen, requiring you to scroll twice as often as necessary). Then, to output a draft with double- or triple-spacing, simply change the line-spacing option for the most common paragraph styles in the document. (Typically, you'll need to change only Body Text.) Then, after you print the draft, change the style or styles back to their original settings.

A more streamlined way to generate rough drafts is to use a separate template designed specifically for this purpose. When creating this type of template, which you can call something like Draft, use your standard template as a model. Then, assign double- or triple-spacing to the Body Text style for this new template, and make any other necessary changes to the various styles.

Use the standard template for creating and editing the document. Then, when you want to generate a rough draft, switch to the other template, make your printout, and then switch back to the standard template.

Using the Built-In Templates

The Professional Write Plus software includes a wide assortment of built-in style templates, each of which is designed for a particular type of document. Most of these templates are fairly simple, and you may find some useful ideas by browsing through them.

These templates are originally stored in the directory \STYLES, which is under the directory containing the Professional Write Plus program files. Here's a list of them, along with a brief description of the purpose of each one:

Template Name	Type of Document
DEFAULT.STY	General purpose
DOC.STY	Books and manuals
ENVEL-C.STY	Center-feed envelopes
ENVEL-S.STY	Side-feed envelopes
FAX.STY	Fax transmission cover sheet
LEGAL.STY	Legal size documents
LETTER1.STY	Formal letters
LETTER2.STY	Formal letters
LETTER3.STY	Formal letters
MEMO1.STY	Memos
MEMO2.STY	Memos
MEMO3.STY	Memos
MEMO4.STY	Memos
NEWSLTR1.STY	Newsletters
NEWSLTR2.STY	Newsletters
NUMBERS.STY	Bulleted and numbered lists
OVERHEAD1.STY	Overhead projection master
OVERHEAD2.STY	Overhead projection master
PRESSREL.STY	Press release
PROPOSAL.STY	Proposal
REPORT1.STY	Reports
REPORT2.STY	Reports
REPORT3.STY	Reports
REPORT4.STY	Reports

To view the contents of any of these, first make sure that:

- You have set the option to display a list of templates each time you create a new document (for details, see "Selecting the Default Template" earlier in this chapter).

- The default template path is set to the directory \STYLES, which is under the directory containing the Professional Write Plus program files.

Then, select File/New. When the list of templates appears (Figure 7.9), select the template you want, select the option "Copy Template Contents", and then click on OK. Each template contains explanatory text, which will be displayed for your inspection. By reading this text and studying the various characteristics of the template, you may gain some insight as to how to build your own.

Summary

Paragraph styles and templates are among the sophisticated features that raise Professional Write Plus above run-of-the-mill word processors. Moreover, as you gain a bit of experience with styles you'll find that they are quite easy to use and can make an enormous difference in the quality of your documents.

Although the term *desktop publishing* is seldom used in reference to Professional Write Plus, up until very recently the use of paragraph styles was restricted to desktop publishing software. The presence of styles in state-of-the-art word processors such as Professional Write Plus is a dramatic development that has helped to raise the standards of word processed documents.

Frames are the other significant desktop publishing feature included as an integral part of Professional Write Plus. This dynamic tool is discussed in Chapters 10 and 11.

CHAPTER 8

Customized Letters and Mailing Labels

Creating Customized Letters

Using Data from Other Sources

Mailing Labels

Creating Customized Letters

LIKE MOST POPULAR WORD PROCESSORS, PROFESSIONAL WRITE PLUS CONtains a feature that allows you to merge name and address information in a data file with a standard form letter to generate customized letters. This same merging process can be used for any type of customized documents you care to create. For example, you can use name and address information from a data file to generate a group of bills or invoices.

To create a group of customized letters, you must first create a data file. This file contains a group of records, each of which consists of name and address information, along with any other bits and pieces of data you care to include. To generate the customized letters, you merge the contents of the data file with a standard letter. As each customized letter is created, you can send it directly to the printer, or you can first review it on the screen. You can also output all the letters to a disk file for later editing.

After you have created a data file, you can use it repeatedly for different groups of customized letters. You can also edit the data file, adding and deleting records to keep the information up to date.

Professional Write Plus can read information from several different types of data files. This handy feature allows you to create customized letters by using information from other software packages, such as database managers and spreadsheets, as well as other word processors.

Although Professional Write Plus doesn't contain a special feature for generating mailing labels, you can easily set up one or more name-and-address files to use for printing groups of labels of any size. Although this method contains a few restrictions, you can still use the program to simplify your bulk-mailing routine.

Creating Customized Letters

Suppose you want to create a group of customized letters similar to the one shown in Figure 8.1. To do this, you must create both a data file and the standard letter.

A *data file* contains the names, addresses, and other custom information to be used in the different letters. Figure 8.2 shows a typical data file. Each row in this file (except the top two, which contain special information) consists of one *record*, which contains the information about a particular person. Each record consists of a group of *fields*, and the *field names* appear in the second line of the data file. For example, in Figure 8.2 the field names are TITLE, FIRST, LAST, and so on.

The *standard letter* contains the basic content of the customized letters you want to print. However, in place of the actual name and address, a group of field names appears. For example, instead of showing a last name, a field name something like <LAST> appears. Figure 8.3 illustrates the standard letter that was used to create the customized letter shown in Figure 8.1.

CUSTOMIZED LETTERS AND MAILING LABELS

Figure 8.1
A personalized letter

```
January 15, 1992

Mr. Sam Spade
14 Falcon Court
San Francisco, CA 94107

Dear Mr. Spade,

On behalf of our organization, Save The Mammals Now, I would like to thank
you for your most generous contribution. Our organization is dedicated to
the preservation of all forms of warm-blooded life, and your gift will help
us to perpetuate this activity.

Sincerely yours,


Needlepoint Abercrombie
Chairman of the Board
```

Figure 8.2
A data file

```
$@
TITLE$FIRST$LAST$ADDRESS$CITY$STATE$ZIPCODE$COUNTRY@
Mr.$Sam$Spade$14 Falcon Court$San Francisco$CA$94107$USA@
M.$C. Auguste$Dupin$38 Rue Morgue$Paris$$75014$France@
Mr.$Philip$Marlowe$777 Morpheus Blvd.$Los Angeles$CA$90055$USA@
Mr. and Mrs.$N.$Charles$8467 Delgado Ave.$San Francisco$CA$94111$USA@
Mr.$Sherlock$Holmes$221B Baker Street$London$$$UK@
```

To create the customized letters, you *merge* the contents of the the data file and the standard letter. During this process, the information in each record in the data file is combined with the standard letter to produce a customized letter, as illustrated in Figure 8.4.

The following sections describe the process for creating a group of customized letters similar to that shown in Figure 8.1. This is a three-step process:

1. Create the data file.

2. Create the standard letter.

3. Merge the data file with the standard letter to create the customized letters.

Once you have created a data file of names, addresses, and so on, you can skip the first step above.

Figure 8.3
This standard letter was used to create the letter in Figure 8.1

```
<TITLE> <FIRST> <LAST>
<ADDRESS>
<CITY>, <STATE> <ZIPCODE>

Dear <TITLE> <LAST>,

On behalf of our organization, Save The Mammals Now, I would like to thank
you for your most generous contribution. Our organization is dedicated to
the preservation of all forms of warm-blooded life, and your gift will help
us to perpetuate this activity.

Sincerely yours,



Needlepoint Abercrombie
Chairman of the Board
```

Figure 8.4
Merging information to generate personalized letters

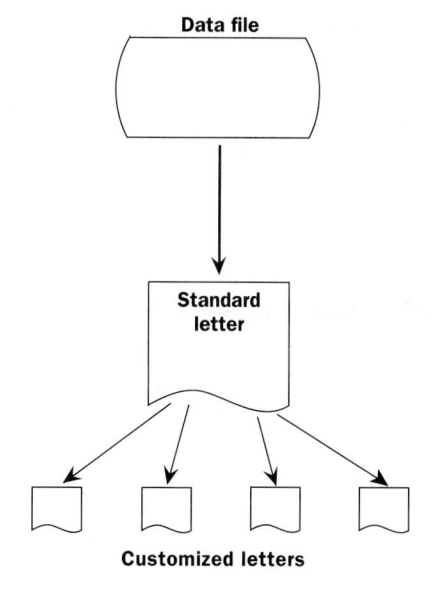

Creating a Data File

A data file is a normal Professional Write Plus document file, in which information is grouped into records and fields. Each record contains information about a particular person or organization. You can use the same data file for many different personalized letters, groups of mailing labels, or other types of documents.

To create a data file, you begin with a new, empty document. The information is entered and organized as a group of records, each of which contains the same number of fields, and each of which starts with a new paragraph.

Each field ends with the special character of your choice, which is called the *field delimiter*. Each record ends with another special character of your choice, called the *record delimiter*.

Figure 8.2 shows a typical data file in delimited format. In this figure, the $ character is used as the field delimiter, and the @ character as the record delimiter.

The top line of the data file must contain the two special characters used as the field and record delimiters, in that order. The second line must contain the names of the fields, separated by the field delimiter. This line must end with the record delimiter. The top two lines in Figure 8.2 illustrate these features.

Each record in the file must begin a new paragraph, or the program won't be able to read the data properly. You can omit a field value in a record, provided that you insert a field delimiter to indicate that a value is missing. (If the empty field is the last one in a record, this is optional.) For example, in Figure 8.2 the last record is missing values for both the STATE and ZIPCODE fields.

CAUTION! *Do not insert any text into a data file other than exactly what you want to merge, since the program might then misinterpret the contents of the file.*

Here are the steps for creating a new data file (when following these steps, you can refer to Figure 8.2 as a guide):

1. Start with a new, empty document.

2. On the first line, enter the characters to be used as the field delimiter record delimiter, then press the Enter key. *Do not* insert any blanks between these two characters.

3. On the second line, enter the names of the fields to be used in the records. Separate the field names with the field delimiter character, and end the line with the record delimiter.

4. On the third and following lines enter the data records (see the following section).

5. Save the data as a regular Professional Write Plus document, naming it something like MYDATA, or any other name you can easily remember.

Rules for Entering Records

As you enter the records into a data file (step 4 above), follow these guidelines:

- You must include the field delimiter (the first character on the first line) between each pair of fields.

- Each record must end with the record delimiter (the second character on the first line).

- You can leave the value for a field blank, but make sure to insert a field delimiter to indicate the presence of the blank field (unless it's the last one).

- A record can extend across multiple lines. You can let Professional Write Plus select where to break the lines (according to the document's layout), or you can break them yourself with hard returns between fields. In the latter case, make sure you press the Enter key *before* you enter the field delimiter. For example, entering the following would not work correctly:

    Mr. Philip Marlowe$<hard return>

    777 Morpheus Blvd.$Los Angeles$CA$90055

    Whereas the following would work:

    Mr. Philip Marlowe<hard return>

    $777 Morpheus Blvd.$Los AngelesCA90055

Creating a Standard Letter

A standard letter contains two parts:

- The standard text that will appear in each of the customized letters.

- A group of field names. Each name represents an item from the data file to be merged with the standard text.

As part of creating a standard letter, you must specify the name of the data file to be used in the merge process. Then, as you enter the text for the letter, you can insert the names of any of the fields in the data file.

To see how this works, let's go through the steps for creating the standard letter shown in Figure 8.3. These steps fall into two sections. First, you display the names of the fields to be used (which the program retrieves from the data file you specify). Then you enter the standard text, inserting field names wherever you wish. To begin, here are the steps for displaying the field names for your data file:

1. Start with a blank screen.

2. Select Edit/Insert Variable, and the dialog box shown in Figure 8.5 appears.

Figure 8.5
Select the Merge Field option from this dialog box

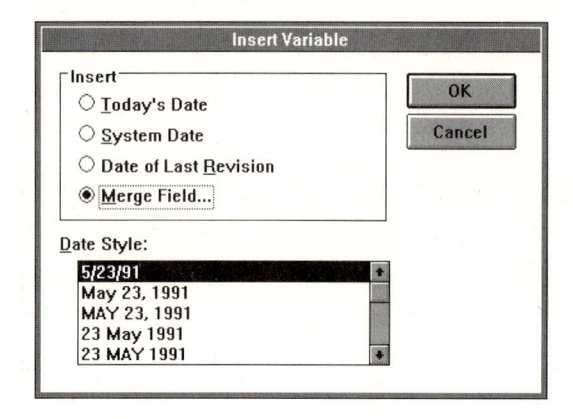

3. Click on Merge Field, then click on OK.

4. When the next dialog box appears (similar to Figure 8.6), click on the Data File button.

Figure 8.6
The Insert Merge Field dialog box

5. In the next dialog box (see Figure 8.7), enter the name of the data file you want to use, or select it from the list boxes, then click on OK. Note that in this dialog box, the directory selected is the default document path.

6. The Insert Merge Field dialog box will reappear, this time displaying the names of the fields in the data file you selected, as shown in Figure 8.8.

This dialog box is a true Windows window. It will remain on the screen while you create the standard letter, making it easy for you to insert field names anywhere in the text. You can reposition this window anywhere on the screen, although you can't change its size.

Figure 8.7

Enter the name of the data file to be used

Figure 8.8

This dialog box displays the names of the fields you can use

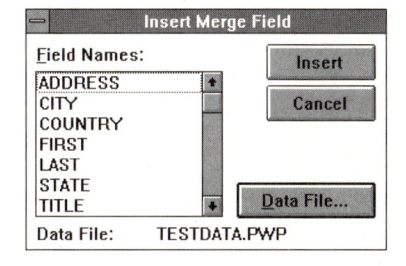

To insert a field name in the standard document, move the text cursor to where you want the name to appear, then select that name from the Insert Merge Field dialog box. For example, here are the steps for creating the standard letter shown in Figure 8.3:

1. Enter the date on the first line, then skip a line so that the text cursor is at the beginning of the third line.

2. Double-click on the field name TITLE in the Insert Merge Field dialog box.

3. Reposition the text cursor: Click to the right of where <TITLE> appears in the document.

4. Press the spacebar once. This creates a space after <TITLE>.

5. Double-click on FIRST in the field name dialog box.

6. Reposition the text cursor by clicking on the end of the first line in the text.

7. Repeat steps 4 and 5, but using the field name LAST.

8. Press Enter to go to the next line.

9. Continue entering text and field names, following the technique illustrated in the preceding steps. (Be sure to enter a comma and space between the city and state fields.)

10. When you have finished the letter (which should look like that shown in Figure 8.3), you can remove the Insert Merge Field dialog box from the screen by double-clicking on the control box in the upper-left corner or by clicking on Cancel.

11. Save the document to a disk file. Even if you plan to use the letter immediately you should save it, just in case something goes wrong when you perform the merge operation.

Tips on Creating a Standard Letter

There are a number of things to consider when creating standard letters:

- You can freely intermix regular text with field names, for example, the comma and blank space between the city and state field names. Also, you can use the same field name as many times as you wish within a standard document.

- You must use the Insert Merge Field dialog box to enter field names. That is, you can't just type in the field names where they should appear on the screen.

- Don't worry about leaving enough space for long field values. When the merge process takes place, each letter will be formatted as necessary to make room for field values of any size.

- You can use the standard block operations to copy or move field names once they are entered in the text. You can also delete field names from the text, using either the Del or Backspace keys. Just keep in mind that a field name behaves like a single character. For example, if you position the text cursor just to the left of a field name and then press the Del key, the entire field name will be deleted. Similarly, if you position the text cursor to the left of a field name and then press the Right Arrow cursor key, the cursor will jump to the right of the name. If a field name is within a block of text that's deleted, the name is also deleted (with no warning message).

- You can save a standard letter as a regular Professional Write Plus document, so that you can use it at a later time. When you save the letter (using the File/Save As option), enter a short identifying comment in the Document Description box. This will help you to find the correct file later on.

Merging the Data and the Standard Letter

After you have created a standard letter, you can merge it with the information in a data file to generate the customized letters. As each customized letter is generated, it will appear on the screen for your inspection. You can then edit it, print it, and go on to the next one. Alternatively, you can have the letters sent directly to the printer or to a disk file.

To begin the merge, make sure that the standard letter is displayed on the screen. Then follow these steps:

1. Remove the Insert Merge Field dialog box from the screen if it's still displayed.

2. Select File/Merge, and the Merge dialog box, shown in Figure 8.9, will appear. Note that the name of the data file you selected earlier is displayed in this box.

Figure 8.9
Use this box to set the merge options

3. Click on Merge, View & Print, then click on OK.

The first customized letter will then appear on your screen, along with this dialog box:

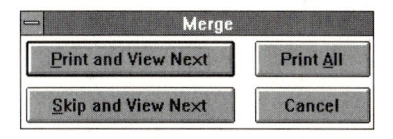

You can edit the letter in any way you wish, then select one of these merge options. Table 8.1 summarizes the options and their functions.

Using an Existing Standard Letter

Above it was assumed that you're creating a new standard letter each time. However, you can also merge a data file with an existing standard letter. The only requirement is that the field names in this letter must be the same as those in the data file you select.

Table 8.1   Merge Options

Option	Function
Print and View Next	Prints this letter, then displays the next one
Print All	Prints the remaining letters—select this option when you're sure no changes are needed in the remaining letters
Skip and View Next	Does not print the letter, but continues displaying subsequent ones
Cancel	Terminates the merge process

Here's an outline of the steps to follow when using an existing standard letter:

1. Retrieve the letter into Professional Write Plus.
2. Click on File/Merge.
3. When the next dialog box appears (Figure 8.3), click on the Data File button, then select the name of the data file you want to use. If it's an ASCII file (see "Using Data from Other Sources," below), the screen will then prompt you to enter the name of the corresponding description file.
4. Proceed with the merge as described earlier.

The biggest difference between this process and that described above is that you supply the name of the data file *after* the standard letter is displayed on the screen.

Tips on Merging

If a data field has no value, then no space will be taken up on the customized letter. This could produce unexpected output. For example, if the title name field for a record were blank, the corresponding letter could have a salutation "Dear Charles" instead of "Dear Mr. and Mrs. Charles."

Using the Other Merge Options

Using the steps described above, each letter is displayed before being printed. As an alternative to this procedure, you can bypass the viewing option and have the letters printed directly. Or, if you want to create the letters now, but review and print them at some later time, you can have the letters output to a disk file instead of the printer.

To send the customized letters directly to the printer without viewing them, click on the Merge & Print option in the dialog box (Figure 8.9) instead of using Merge, View, & Print. The letters will go directly to your printer. Each letter will begin at the top of a new page.

To output the letters to a disk file: In the edit box labeled "Merge & Save As" (in Figure 8.9), enter the name of the file to be used. If necessary, include the name of the disk drive and directory to contain the file. This file will be in regular Professional Write Plus format, so that you can subsequently edit it. After you enter the file name, click on the Merge & Print option. All of the merged letters will be written to the file you named.

Using Data from Other Sources

To provide access to information generated by other software packages, Professional Write Plus can merge data from a file in any of the following formats (in addition to the standard format for data files described earlier): fixed-field ASCII, comma-delimited ASCII, and DIF. When using any of these types of data files, you must also create a special *description file,* which contains information Professional Write Plus needs about the data file.

DIF formats are not covered in this book since it's very unlikely that you'll encounter them. (For details about these types of data files, refer to the User's Manual that accompanies the Professional Write Plus software.) The two types of ASCII files are described below, along with information on creating the corresponding description file.

Files in Fixed-Field ASCII Format

In a file with fixed format, all the *values* that go in a particular field must be the same length, but different fields can be of different lengths. Also, each record must end with a hard return. Figure 8.10 illustrates a file with this type of format. For example, the TITLE field is 13 characters long, the FIRST field is 12, and so on.

Figure 8.10
A data file in fixed-field format

```
Mr.            Sam           Spade      14 Falcon Court     San Francisco   CA 94107   USA
M.             C. Auguste    Dupin      38 Rue Morgue       Paris              75014   France
Mr.            Philip        Marlowe    777 Morpheus Blvd.  Los Angeles     CA 90055   USA
Mr. and Mrs.   N.            Charles    8467 Delgado Ave.   San Francisco   CA 94111   USA
Mr.            Sherlock      Holmes     221B Baker Street   London                     UK
```

If you're using this type of file, make sure that it conforms to the following rules:

- Every record must be exactly the same length.

- Each record must end with a hard return.

- The values in each particular field must all be the same length, even if the field value for a particular record is blank. (Remember, spaces here count as characters.)

This type of data field is easy to create using a monospaced font such as Courier. You simply line up the columns on the screen, as indicated in Figure 8.10.

In order to use a fixed-field ASCII file, you must create a description file (an ordinary Professional Write Plus file) that contains the names and lengths of the fields. Figure 8.11 illustrates this type of description file, which must conform exactly to the following rules:

- The first line of this file must contain the word "FIXED," followed by a hard return.

- Each field name must be followed by a comma and the number of characters the field contains.

- Empty fields must be indicated by an extra comma.

- Each field name and corresponding length must be on a separate line that ends with a hard return.

- Do not insert any spaces anywhere in any line of this file.

Figure 8.11
A description file for a data file in fixed-field format

```
FIXED
TITLE,13
FIRST,12
LAST,15
ADDRESS,20
CITY,15
STATE,6
ZIPCODE,10
COUNTRY,10
```

Files in Comma-Delimited ASCII Format

In a comma-delimited ASCII file, the field values are separated by commas. The value of any field can be any length, because a comma indicates where each field value ends. If a field value is missing, the comma must still be inserted. Each record must end with a hard return. Figure 8.12 shows a file of this type.

Figure 8.12
A data file in comma-delimited ASCII format

```
Mr.,Sam,Spade,14 Falcon Court,San Francisco,CA,94107,USA
M.,C. Auguste,Dupin,38 Rue Morgue,Paris,,75014,France
Mr.,Philip,Marlowe,777 Morpheus Blvd.,Los Angeles,CA,90055,USA
Mr. and Mrs.,N.,Charles,8467 Delgado Ave.,San Francisco,CA,94111,USA
Mr.,Sherlock,Holmes,221B Baker Street,London,,,UK
```

A variation on this type of format is one in which the individual values are enclosed in double quotes. This type of format is useful if, for example, some of the text values include commas. By enclosing a text value in quotes, the comma is "shielded" and is not considered a field separator.

In order to use a comma-delimited ASCII file, you must first create a description file (as an ordinary Professional Write Plus file) that contains the names of the fields. Figure 8.13 illustrates this type of description file, which must conform exactly to the following rules:

- The first line of this file contains the word "COMMA" followed by a hard return.

- The field names are then listed one per line, each one ending with a hard return.

Figure 8.13
A description file for a data file in comma-delimited ASCII format

```
COMMA
TITLE
FIRST
LAST
ADDRESS
CITY
STATE
ZIPCODE
COUNTRY
```

Merging Data from a File in Either Fixed or Comma Format

Before you use a data file in either fixed-field or comma-delimited format, make sure that

- The data file conforms to the structure specified above. If there is any deviation from this structure, Professional Write Plus won't be able to interpret the information in the file.

- You create the appropriate description file.

To merge data from a file in either fixed or comma format, you follow the same steps that were described earlier, except that you must also supply the name of the corresponding description file. Here are the steps in more detail:

1. Begin creating the standard letter (select Edit/Insert Variable/Merge Field).

2. Specify the name of the data file, including its full path name and extension, if any. Remember that neither type of file will be in Professional Write Plus format, so make sure you do not include the .PWP extension with the file name. The program will recognize that the data file is in either fixed-field ASCII or comma-delimited format, and ask you to specify the description file.

3. Enter the name of the description file or select it from the edit boxes for the screens. The names of the fields will then appear, as shown in Figure 8.8.

4. Carry on creating the standard document and performing the merge, as described earlier.

Using Other ASCII File Formats

You're not necessarily restricted to the types of ASCII file formats described above. In many cases you may be able to use other formats. The basic technique is first to open the file as an ASCII file. Then, using any of Professional Write Plus's editing features, convert the file into one of the two ASCII formats described in this chapter.

Often the Find & Replace feature will be invaluable for this purpose. For example, suppose that you want to use the data in an ASCII file, but the field separator in the file is a semicolon. You can transform this file into a comma-delimited file as follows: Using the Find & Replace feature, replace every semicolon in the file with a comma. To use the transformed file, all you then need do is create a description file.

Mailing Labels

Professional Write Plus doesn't have a simple built-in feature for generating mailing labels. However, with a little bit of work you can create a file of names and addresses that can be used for printing your labels. By necessity, the method described here is a bit clumsy since the program lacks a true label-printing capability. In addition, there are several shortcomings to this technique:

- You won't be able to conveniently use a label data file for generating customized letters, because the file isn't in the correct format.

- You'll be able to use label sheets or rolls with only one label across the page. This shouldn't present too much of a problem, because this format is available for all types of printers.

- When you create the data file, you'll have to customize it for one label size. If you want to use a different size, you'll have to modify the entire file.

- There's no way to automatically sort the records in a file, say by zip code or last name. If you want the records sorted, you'll have to do it manually as you enter the records, or afterwards by cutting and pasting. Or, you could get very sophisticated: Export the file either to Lotus 1-2-3 or Microsoft Excel, sort the records there, and then import the sorted file back into Professional Write Plus.

The end result of the method described here is an ordinary Professional Write Plus document that contains name-and-address information in a format suitable for printing labels. You can update the list of names in this document by using the program's Find & Replace feature.

Creating the Name-and-Address File

Before creating the file, you must decide on the size of label you'll be using because this will determine the spacing of the data in the file. For example, a typical mailing label dimension is 1 by 3 inches. Make sure of the exact label size before beginning.

The most crucial measurement is the vertical distance from the top of one label to the top of the next, as indicated in Figure 8.14. You must be sure of this measurement, or the printed information will get out of sync with the labels. This isn't as hard as it sounds; label-to-label dimensions are usually simple fractions (1 inch, 1.5 inches, and so on).

After you've determined the label-to-label vertical dimension, you can begin to create the data file. Here are the basic steps:

1. Start with a new blank document.

2. Select a font size of approximately 10 to 12 points.

3. Select a line spacing that divides exactly into the label-to-label spacing. For example, if the label spacing is exactly 1 inch, you could use a line spacing of 0.20 inches. The easiest method is to assign the line spacing to the paragraph style used for the information you enter.

4. Turn on the vertical ruler and the tab ruler. These will help you to use the correct record spacing.

5. Set the top and bottom margins (see the following section).

6. Enter the first record (name and address).

Figure 8.14
Measure the label dimensions carefully

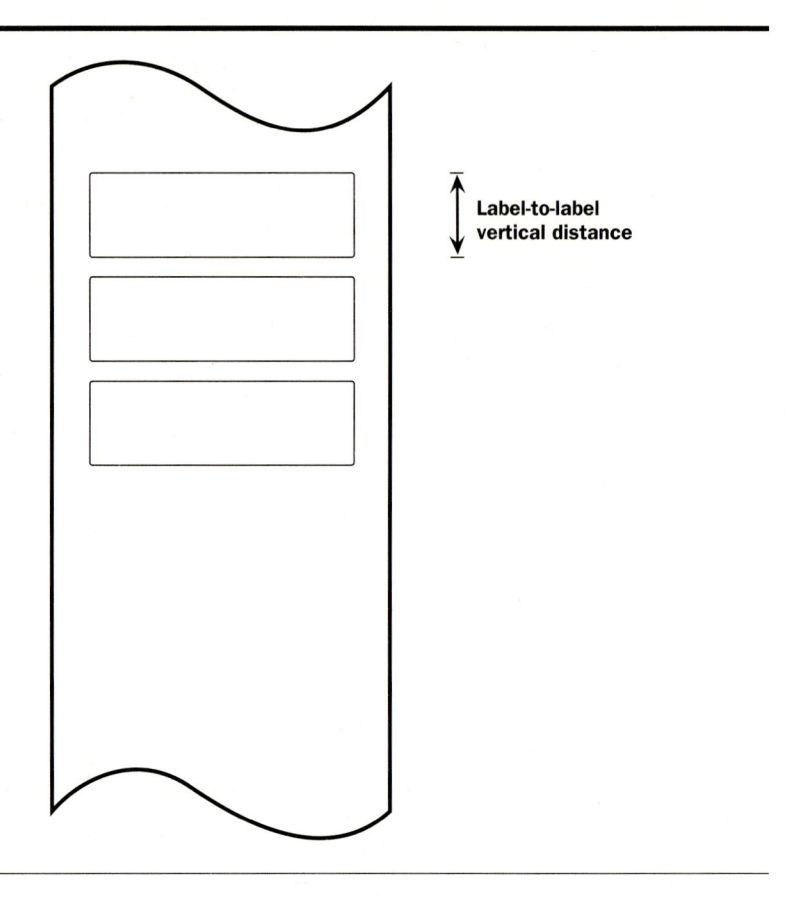

Label-to-label vertical distance

7. Enter as many blank lines as necessary to fill up the vertical distance equal to one label (for details, see "Spacing the Records," below).

8. Continue entering as many records as will fit fully on the page. If a record won't fit entirely, enter it on the next page.

9. When you're done entering records, save the document.

Setting the Top and Bottom Margins
The top and bottom margins you set will depend on both the printer and the label sheets or rolls you're using. You may need to use a bit of trial and error to determine the correct margins. The following steps may help you to adjust the margins:

1. Set the top and bottom margins to zero.

2. Print a sheet or two of labels. Or, if you're using a continuous roll, print at least the equivalent of one full sheet (11 inches, for example, for an ordinary page length). For continuous-roll printers, take special note of the position of the first label (relative to the print head, for example) so that you can duplicate it each time you print a group of labels.

3. Examine the output to see which, if any, records didn't print completely (or at all).

4. Reset the top and bottom margins as necessary.

Many printers leave a sizable margin at the top and bottom of each page (this includes many dot-matrix printers, as well as laser printers). For some printers this will mean that the top label on each page—or the equivalent label on a continuous roll—can't be printed on. If this is the situation with your printer, adjust the top margin of the document so that the printing begins on the second row of labels instead of the first. Similarly, if necessary set the bottom margin so that the last label on the page is completely skipped. This may seem like a waste, but there's nothing you can do about the blank space some printers leave.

Spacing the Records

Each record must occupy exactly the correct amount of vertical space, namely the label-to-label vertical distance indicated in Figure 8.14. As an example, let's suppose that your labels are spaced exactly one every inch (a very common spacing). As indicated above, you must choose a line spacing that divides evenly into 1 inch. Actually, you don't have too many choices. For instance, if you're using a 10- or 12-point font you're pretty much limited to a line spacing of either 0.20 or 0.25 inches.

A line spacing of 0.20 inches will allow you up to five printed lines per label, although five is actually pushing it, because that leaves nothing for the space between labels.

Let's say that you select a line spacing of 0.20 inches. This means that every record must occupy *exactly* five lines, whether or not those lines contain text. For instance, if a record contains only three printed lines, you must enter two blank lines at the end. Using the vertical ruler will help you to remember these blank lines. A quick glance will tell you whether the records on a page are lined up properly.

Printing the Labels

Once you have established your data file, printing the mailing labels is quite straightforward. First, set up the labels in the printer. For printers using a continuous roll, make sure that you position the first label exactly right in the printer. Then, simply retrieve the name-and-address file and print it.

Editing the File

You can easily add or delete records in the file, using Professional Write Plus's various editing features. To delete a record you must first locate it, and the Find & Replace feature makes this a breeze. Select Edit/Find & Replace, and then enter part or all of the name you want to find, making sure that the Find Whole Word Only option is turned off if necessary.

When you delete a record, make sure to delete all the blank lines between that record and the next one. Otherwise, the next time you print labels, the output will be out of sync. Likewise, you can add a new record anywhere you want in the file. Just make sure to add the proper number of blank lines at the end of the record (see "Spacing the Records").

If you're maintaining the file in sorted order, by zip code, last name, or whatever, use the Find & Replace feature to locate the part of the file where the new record is to be entered. For example, if the records are in zip code order and you want to enter a new record with a zip code of 12345, just search for the string "12345". You can then manually scroll through the records with this zip code to determine exactly where you would like to place the new one.

Summary

Once you have established a data file of names and addresses, printing a group of customized letters or mailing labels will be as easy as rolling off a log. If you plan to print both letters and labels on a regular basis you'll need to set up two different data files. This may be a bit of a nuisance, but the long-term dividends will pay off handsomely.

If you have name-and-address data stored in a database or spreadsheet, you can almost certainly use that information to create customized letters and labels. Output the data as an ASCII file, import the file into Professional Write Plus, and then transform it into one of the formats described in this chapter. The only difficulty here is that whenever you update the original data you'll also need to update the Professional Write Plus data file, so that the two data sets are synchronized.

One word of warning: Creating a data file often requires hours or even days. Make sure you create a backup of each data file, so that a hard disk crash doesn't cost you unnecessary work.

CHAPTER 9

About Printers, Typefaces, and Fonts

Typeface, Font, and Other Vocabulary

Printer Capabilities

The Types of Fonts Available

Screen Fonts

Special Print Options

Working with More Than One Printer

Getting Even Higher Print Quality

THE CORNERSTONE OF WORD PROCESSING IS THE TYPE THAT YOU SEE. The end result of all your work is the printed document, the appearance of which is determined to a large extent by the quality of the printed type. Moreover, as you create your documents you're constantly looking at type on the screen, and the quality of this type can make a significant difference in your perception of how wonderful word processing is.

Professional Write Plus, in conjunction with Windows, offers you the ability to print with a wide range of different styles and sizes of type. In principle, you can have as wide a selection of choices as with any desktop publishing software. However, in practice you may be limited by your printer's capabilities and also by the particular software installed for your computer under Windows. If you want to expand your printing capability beyond the limitations of your own printer, you can send your printer output to a disk, which can later be copied to a high-quality printer somewhere else.

By itself, Windows offers a very modest assortment of type sizes and styles for a wide range of printers. But a good deal of off-the-shelf software is available for increasing the potential of your printer, and if you have a laser printer, your type-printing capabilities are limited only by how much of this software you have installed.

Because Professional Write Plus is a graphics oriented program, your screen can display virtually any size and style of text. Again however, in practice you're limited by the software installed under Windows.

By becoming familiar with the range of text styles and sizes available to you, and understanding how different products function, you can improve Professional Write Plus's performance—both on the screen and on the printed page.

Typeface, Font, and Other Vocabulary

In order to understand the capabilities of Professional Write Plus and your printer, you need to be familiar with some commonly used terminology. Unfortunately, computerized typography changes so rapidly that this terminology is in a constant state of flux, and often the same term is used in several different ways. The following sections define some of the most important terms using their most current meanings.

Typefaces

Typeface refers to the general features that apply to a complete set of characters. There are hundreds of different typefaces, each of which has applications for which it is best suited. For example, one of the most common typefaces is Times Roman. It, or a similar typeface, is commonly used as the main text in books, magazines, newsletters, and so on. Another popular typeface is Helvetica. It is often used for headings and other applications that benefit from a simple, clean look.

Figure 9.1 illustrates a few different typefaces. Remember, these are just a small sample of the dozens of typefaces in common use, not to mention the hundreds of others that are less popular.

Figure 9.1
A sample of different typefaces

This is Times Roman

This is larger Times Roman

Still larger Times Roman

This is Helvetica type

This is Courier (a monospaced typeface)

This is Script (can you see why?)

Monospaced and Proportionally Spaced Typefaces

Typefaces can be separated into two general categories: *monospaced* and *proportionally spaced*. Each character in a monospaced typeface occupies the same amount of horizontal space. These typefaces tend to look unsophisticated, but they have their applications. For example, a monospaced typeface can be very useful when printing financial information, because columns of digits line up nicely. One of the more common monospaced typefaces is called Courier (see Figure 9.1).

In a proportionally spaced typeface, each character takes up only as much horizontal space as it requires. For example, a lower case "i" takes up less than half the space of a lower case "m." A page of proportionally spaced text can be more easily read than a page of monospaced text, primarily because there is less white space between characters. Many of the examples shown in Figure 9.1 are proportionally spaced.

Serif and Sans Serif Typefaces

One of the distinguishing characteristics of a typeface is whether or not it has *serifs*, the tiny strokes at the ends of the horizontal and vertical lines that make up the letters. For example, Times Roman is a serif typeface. On the other hand, Helvetica is a *sans serif* typeface, meaning that it has no serifs. Compare, for example, the capital "T" in the examples of Helvetica and Times Roman typefaces shown in Figure 9.1.

Some typefaces fall into neither category. The Script typeface shown in Figure 9.1 illustrates this.

Generally, a large amount of serif text is easier to read than the equivalent text in a sans serif typeface. Nevertheless, sans serif typefaces have many uses. For example, large sans serif typefaces are often used for titles and column headings.

Type Size

The size of characters is expressed as a measurement of how much space they occupy on the printed page, both vertically and horizontally. Character size is most often measured in terms of *points*. There are 72 points per inch. The point size refers to the maximum amount of *vertical* space that can be occupied by a line of text. For example, a line of 12-point text occupies 12 points, or $\frac{1}{6}$ of an inch (see Figure 9.2). This distance is measured from the top of an ascender (as in the letter "t") to the bottom of a descender (the letter "g"). Generally speaking, as the size increases the amount of space required increases both horizontally and vertically.

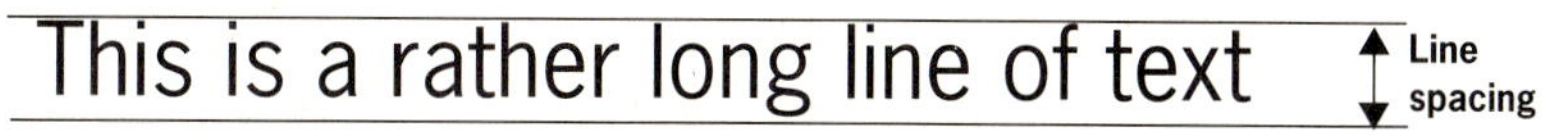

Figure 9.2
Point size is the vertical space occupied by each line of text

This is a rather long line of text   ↕ Line spacing

As a point of reference, many books are written in 10- or 11-point text. This size is small enough so that a reasonable amount of text fits on a single page and the lines justify well. On the other hand, the text is large enough to be read comfortably. Large headers in books may be in 18-point text or slightly larger, depending on the available space on the page. Newspaper headlines are usually in 36-point type and larger.

Type size can also be measured in terms of its *pitch,* which is the number of characters that occupy one inch horizontally. For instance, the draft mode of most printers uses a 10-pitch (or *pica*) typeface, which prints at ten characters per inch.

Pitch and point size are distinct but somewhat related measurements. The smaller the point size, the larger the pitch. But there is no direct relationship, since point size is a vertical measurement, whereas pitch is horizontal.

The type size you select within Professional Write Plus refers to the *printed* text; it has little to do with the size displayed on your screen. You can select different views (from the View menu), each of which will display the same text in a different magnification.

Text Attributes

As mentioned in earlier chapters, the term *attribute* refers to modifications made to the style of a particular typeface. For example, bold and italic are attributes commonly used to enhance particular bits of text within a document. Text without any modifying attributes is referred to as *normal*.

Professional Write Plus offers a wide range of attributes (available through the Text menu) for enhancing text in various ways. All these attributes will appear on your screen in Layout mode. However, whether they can be printed depends on the limitations of your printer. For example, some older dot-matrix printers cannot print double underlining or strikethrough.

Orientation

Printing can be done using either of two orientations: *portrait* or *landscape* (see Figure 9.3). Most printing is done using portrait orientation, and all printers can output in this mode. The great majority of newer printers can also output in landscape orientation.

Because on most printers each character is printed as a series of dots, in principle one orientation is as easy to output as another. However, the amount of intelligence built into a printer determines whether it can output in landscape orientation.

Fonts

The term *font* is one of the most commonly used—and overused—words in computerized typography. Historically, a font refers to a group of characters that share the same typeface, size, and attribute. For example, Times Roman 12-point italic is a particular font: the typeface is Times Roman, the size is 12-point, and the attribute is italic.

In computerized typesetting, *font* has a slightly different meaning. Suppose you purchase a piece of software that generates a particular group of fonts. Each individual font refers to a specific typeface, size, attribute, *and orientation*. For instance, a particular software package might include the Times Roman and Helvetica typefaces with sizes of 8, 10, 12, and 14 points; normal (or roman), italic, boldface, and bold-italic attributes for all four sizes; and portrait and landscape orientation for all sizes and attributes. Thus, the total number of fonts is 64 (32 for each typeface).

Often, the term *font* is used more loosely to refer simply to a particular typeface and size, without reference to attributes or orientation. Professional Write Plus uses this terminology. For example, if you select the Font option on the Text menu, the dialog box shown in Figure 9.4 appears. You select only the typeface and size from this box (not the attributes or orientation). To select specific attributes, you make various other selections from the Text menu. To select an orientation, you select Page Layout from the Format menu.

Figure 9.3
(a) Portrait and
(b) landscape
orientations

(a)

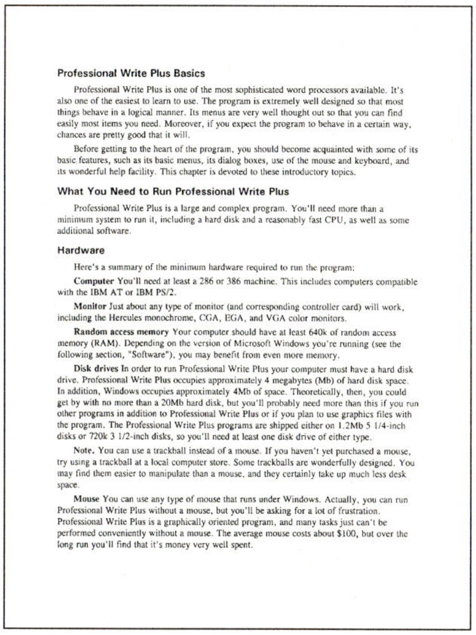

Professional Write Plus Basics

Professional Write Plus is one of the most sophisticated word processors available. It's also one of the easiest to learn to use. The program is extremely well designed so that most things behave in a logical manner. Its menus are very well thought out so that you can find easily most items you need. Moreover, if you expect the program to behave in a certain way, chances are pretty good that it will.

Before getting to the heart of the program, you should become acquainted with some of its basic features, such as its basic menus, its dialog boxes, use of the mouse and keyboard, and its wonderful help facility. This chapter is devoted to these introductory topics.

What You Need to Run Professional Write Plus

Professional Write Plus is a large and complex program. You'll need more than a minimum system to run it, including a hard disk and a reasonably fast CPU, as well as some additional software.

Hardware

Here's a summary of the minimum hardware required to run the program:

Computer You'll need at least a 286 or 386 machine. This includes computers compatible with the IBM AT or IBM PS/2.

Monitor Just about any type of monitor (and corresponding controller card) will work, including the Hercules monochrome, CGA, EGA, and VGA color monitors.

Random access memory Your computer should have at least 640k of random access memory (RAM). Depending on the version of Microsoft Windows you're running (see the following section, "Software"), you may benefit from even more memory.

Disk drives In order to run Professional Write Plus your computer must have a hard disk drive. Professional Write Plus occupies approximately 4 megabytes (Mb) of hard disk space. In addition, Windows occupies approximately 4Mb of space. Theoretically, then, you could get by with no more than a 20Mb hard disk, but you'll probably need more than this if you run other programs in addition to Professional Write Plus or if you plan to use graphics files with the program. The Professional Write Plus programs are shipped either on 1.2Mb 5 1/4-inch disks or 720k 3 1/2-inch disks, so you'll need at least one disk drive of either type.

Note. You can use a trackball instead of a mouse. If you haven't yet purchased a mouse, try using a trackball at a local computer store. Some trackballs are wonderfully designed. You may find them easier to manipulate than a mouse, and they certainly take up much less desk space.

Mouse You can use any type of mouse that runs under Windows. Actually, you can run Professional Write Plus without a mouse, but you'll be asking for a lot of frustration. Professional Write Plus is a graphically oriented program, and many tasks just can't be performed conveniently without a mouse. The average mouse costs about $100, but over the long run you'll find that it's money very well spent.

(b)

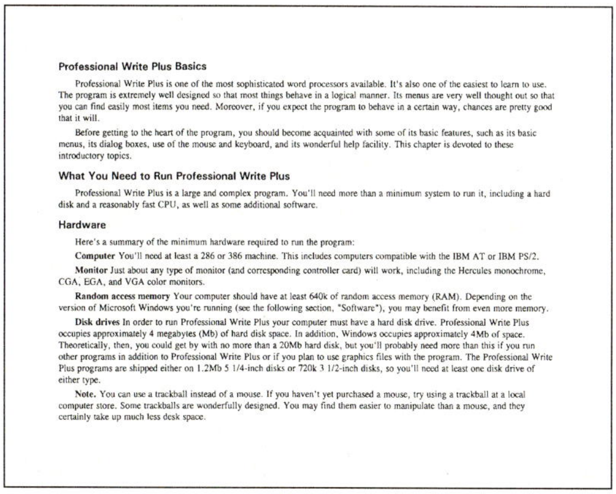

Professional Write Plus Basics

Professional Write Plus is one of the most sophisticated word processors available. It's also one of the easiest to learn to use. The program is extremely well designed so that most things behave in a logical manner. Its menus are very well thought out so that you can find easily most items you need. Moreover, if you expect the program to behave in a certain way, chances are pretty good that it will.

Before getting to the heart of the program, you should become acquainted with some of its basic features, such as its basic menus, its dialog boxes, use of the mouse and keyboard, and its wonderful help facility. This chapter is devoted to these introductory topics.

What You Need to Run Professional Write Plus

Professional Write Plus is a large and complex program. You'll need more than a minimum system to run it, including a hard disk and a reasonably fast CPU, as well as some additional software.

Hardware

Here's a summary of the minimum hardware required to run the program:

Computer You'll need at least a 286 or 386 machine. This includes computers compatible with the IBM AT or IBM PS/2.

Monitor Just about any type of monitor (and corresponding controller card) will work, including the Hercules monochrome, CGA, EGA, and VGA color monitors.

Random access memory Your computer should have at least 640k of random access memory (RAM). Depending on the version of Microsoft Windows you're running (see the following section, "Software"), you may benefit from even more memory.

Disk drives In order to run Professional Write Plus your computer must have a hard disk drive. Professional Write Plus occupies approximately 4 megabytes (Mb) of hard disk space. In addition, Windows occupies approximately 4Mb of space. Theoretically, then, you could get by with no more than a 20Mb hard disk, but you'll probably need more than this if you run other programs in addition to Professional Write Plus or if you plan to use graphics files with the program. The Professional Write Plus programs are shipped either on 1.2Mb 5 1/4-inch disks or 720k 3 1/2-inch disks, so you'll need at least one disk drive of either type.

Note. You can use a trackball instead of a mouse. If you haven't yet purchased a mouse, try using a trackball at a local computer store. Some trackballs are wonderfully designed. You may find them easier to manipulate than a mouse, and they certainly take up much less desk space.

Character Sets

A *character set*, sometimes called a *symbol set,* refers to the group of characters available in a particular font. For example, when you use a dot-matrix printer you are limited to the character set built into the printer for whatever font you select. Alternatively, a font cartridge for a laser printer typically contains a few dozen fonts. When you print with any of these fonts, you are limited to the character set built into the cartridge.

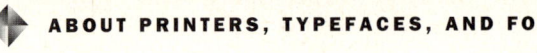

Figure 9.4
Use this dialog box to select the typeface and size

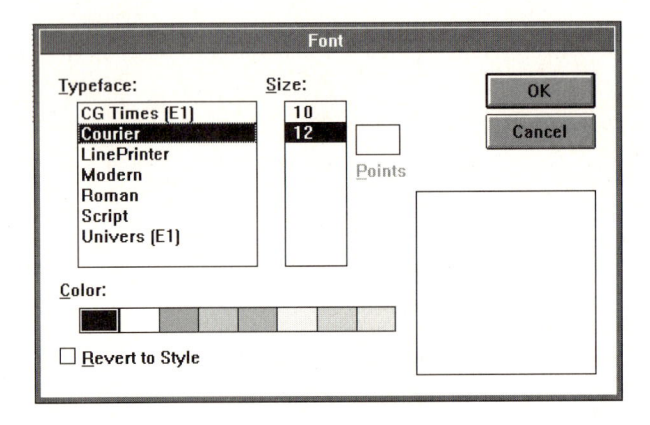

Each character set is designed for a specific purpose. For example, many of the fonts marketed commercially consist of the character set called ASCII, which is made up of the characters most often used in ordinary word processing:

- The letters A through Z and a through z
- The digits 0 through 9
- The special characters available on a standard keyboard (?, ", and so on)

Some sets consist of characters specific to a particular language. For example, Hewlett-Packard's German character set includes special characters, such as ü, and the French character set includes the character é. Other character sets contain special symbols for special purposes. For instance, Hewlett-Packard's Math character set contains various arithmetic symbols, such as ± and ≈, as well as several Greek characters.

When shopping for type-generating software, you should carefully examine the specifications of each program to see exactly which character sets, as well as fonts, are included.

Printer Capabilities

Professional Write Plus can output to a large variety of printers. In fact, because of the basic design of Windows you can use any printer that Windows recognizes. But since printing is one of the more important aspects of generating good-looking documents, it's useful to understand the differences between the various types of printers. In particular, you need to understand the limitations of your own printer, so that you'll know what to expect from it.

Print Quality

Nearly all printers these days generate output by placing dots on the page. However, each printer has certain built-in limitations that determine its best possible print quality. This quality is determined by several factors:

- The *resolution*—the number of dots printed per linear inch
- The *accuracy* with which the dots are placed on the page
- The *saturation* of the images on the page, a measure of the darkness of each dot

Each printer has its own particular capabilities in each of the above areas, but laser printers generally perform better than dot-matrix printers in all three categories.

Resolution is one of the most important factors in determining print quality. Most laser printers print at a resolution of 300 dots per inch (dpi) or more. Many dot-matrix printers also print at 300 dpi or better, but since other factors are involved, the quality of dot-matrix printout doesn't equal that of laser printers.

The accuracy with which the printed dots are placed is equally as important as the resolution. Laser printers position each dot electronically, which is one of the reasons for the high quality of laser-printed text and graphics. In dot-matrix output, the accuracy of dot placement is determined by the mechanical positioning of the printer's paper roller and print head. Because of the difficulty of rapidly and accurately positioning these relatively large, heavy objects, dot-matrix output is not nearly as sharp as that of laser printers. Because of the complexity of mechanical factors, print quality can vary a good deal among dot-matrix printers, even those of exactly the same model.

Dot-matrix printers come in two basic types: 9-pin and 24-pin. As a general rule, 24-pin printers produce a much better quality. Most 9-pin printers can't print at a very high resolution, resulting in poor- to medium-quality output.

Although some 24-pin printers claim to have resolution of as much as 360 dpi, there will always be some error in the positioning of these dots due to mechanical limitations. However, if you have a 24-pin printer of fairly recent vintage, it may be able to generate quality sufficient for your desktop-publishing needs.

Another important factor in determining print quality is the saturation of each dot. Laser printers generally deliver a good deal more ink (or toner, actually) per dot than do dot-matrix printers, which is one reason for the sharper appearance of laser printout. Moreover, the amount of ink delivered per dot remains relatively constant throughout the life of the toner cartridge, resulting in a uniformly high print quality up until nearly the end of the cartridge's life.

On the other hand, dot-matrix printer ribbons start to degrade from the first time you use them. This degradation is hard to notice because it happens uniformly and slowly. But as your eyestrain worsens from reading your printout, you'll slowly get the message that it's time to replace the ribbon.

Using a variable dot size is a recent laser-print development that enormously enhances print quality. With this feature, a program built into the printer determines the optimum size to use for each printed dot. The result is a significant improvement in the smoothness of curved and diagonal lines, even for very large letters, which normally exhibit noticeable jaggedness.

Tips on Optimizing Your Printer's Capabilities

The print quality of most laser printers is determined by internal factors over which you have little or no control, except for an adjustment for the print darkness. However, you can often improve the print quality of a dot-matrix printer by making a few simple adjustments.

As mentioned earlier, the ribbon in a printer degrades gradually, as it slowly gives up its ink. One way to improve the print contrast is to use one-pass-only carbon ribbons, which produce the darkest possible print. Because these ribbons aren't inexpensive, and because they can be used only once (unlike other types of ribbons, which circle around endlessly), you may want to use the following strategy to limit the load on your checkbook: Use an ordinary ribbon for all the early drafts of a document, then switch to a high-quality ribbon for the final printout.

Many dot-matrix printers have both friction and tractor feed, and one feed method may generate more slippage between the paper and the print roller than the other. Try experimenting with each feed method to see if the print quality from either is superior. If so, use that feed method as much as possible.

There's also a subtle point that can have a strong effect on the quality of output from a dot-matrix printer. If you are using continuous-feed paper, the drag caused by the paper feeding into the printer may cause a small amount of slippage between the paper and the print roller, which can be enough to noticeably affect the print clarity. If you suspect this may be a problem, try feeding sheets in one at a time to see if the print quality improves. If so, use this paper-feed method for your final drafts. Or you can try decreasing the distance between the stack of paper and the printer.

The Types of Fonts Available

The fonts available to you within Professional Write Plus are those that are accessible to Windows. These fall into two categories: fonts built into Windows for your printer, and additional fonts that have been installed on your system. These additional fonts can be further subdivided into three types:

- Printer font cartridges
- Soft fonts
- Scalable fonts

Fonts Built into Your Printer

Note. As originally installed, Windows can utilize only those fonts built into your printer. To use additional fonts, you must install type-generating software under Windows.

Many printers come with a number of *built-in fonts,* which reside in the printer's permanent read-only memory (ROM). Some printers, such as PostScript-compatible laser printers, are equipped with a wide variety of built-in fonts. Other printers may come with very few fonts. For example, the Hewlett-Packard LaserJet II is equipped with only two built-in typefaces, Courier and Line Printer, each of which is available in a single type size. Both of these typefaces are monospaced, and although they do have some uses, in general they are not well suited for producing quality documents.

Windows can access some, if not all, of the built-in fonts of many printers. When you customize Windows for a particular printer, these fonts become accessible to any program running under Windows. For example, suppose you customize Windows for an NEC Pinwriter P2200, which is a common 24-pin printer. This printer has a large number of built-in fonts, and the information for most (but not all) of these fonts is built into Windows. Thus, when you customize Windows for that printer, those fonts become available to Professional Write Plus.

As another example, suppose you customize Windows for a Hewlett-Packard LaserJet III. This particular printer has several built-in *scalable typefaces,* which means that the printer is able to print *any* size of any of these typefaces. Windows can take advantage of this capability, which means that you can use Professional Write Plus to print in any character size for any of these typefaces.

Font Cartridges

Many printers are equipped with one or two slots into which you can insert a *font cartridge.* Each cartridge contains a variety of different fonts, thereby increasing the total number of fonts at your disposal. When you insert a cartridge into the printer, the fonts built into that cartridge become available to the printer, provided that the software controlling the printer knows about these fonts.

Windows contains built-in information about a variety of font cartridges for many different printers. In order to make use of a particular cartridge, it must either be on Windows' list of cartridges for your printer, or it must be compatible with a cartridge on this list. Thus, when you customize Windows for a particular printer, you must indicate what font cartridges, if any, are installed.

Font cartridges are rapidly losing popularity with Windows users. One of the reasons for this is that each cartridge contains only a few typefaces in a small number of sizes, which limits their usefulness. Additionally, many type-generating software packages are available for Windows, which generally offer many more fonts than a cartridge, and for less money per font. If you currently own a laser printer, don't even think about purchasing font cartridges. Type-generating software is a far more economical and convenient way to enlarge your repertoire of fonts. This software comes in two types:

- Groups of soft font files packaged and sold as a unit
- Programs that generate scalable typefaces

Soft Fonts

A *soft font* is a separate file that resides on your hard disk and contains the information necessary to print the character set for a particular font. Each specific font requires a separate file. For example, to be able to print 12-point Times Roman portrait-oriented text in normal, italic, and bold, you would need to install three different soft fonts. To print these same fonts in landscape orientation would require three additional soft fonts.

Before you can print a document that contains one or more soft fonts, the corresponding soft font files must be copied from your hard disk to the printer's memory. This copying process, often referred to as *downloading,* is carried out automatically by Professional Write Plus as needed, so normally you don't have to be concerned with it. If you sometimes notice that an unusually long time is needed to print the first page of a document, one possible explanation is that the soft font files needed for that document are being downloaded to your printer.

Soft fonts are generally sold in sets, each of which contains a collection of related fonts. Usually, each set contains one or two typefaces in several sizes and with various attributes in both orientations.

Although soft fonts offer a way to increase your choice of fonts, they have two drawbacks, the first of which is that they are not inexpensive. To build up a reasonable library of font sizes and typefaces requires a substantial financial investment.

The other problem with soft fonts is that they require a great deal of hard disk space. Table 9.1 lists the approximate disk space required for a few different font sizes. (These numbers are only estimates, but they are close enough for this discussion.) Each entry in this table is for a *single font,* that is, one size, attribute, and orientation of a typeface. To build up even a modest library of fonts can easily require several dozen megabytes of disk space.

Table 9.1 **Disk-Space Requirements for Soft Fonts**

Point Size	Space Occupied
10	25k
12	30k
18	60k
24	100k
30	140k
48	380k

Note. Fonts are installed for a particular printer, so be sure to select the correct printer if you have more than one.

Displaying the Available Soft Fonts

You can easily display the names of any soft fonts that have been installed in Windows using the following steps:

1. Select File/Printer Setup, and a dialog box will appear.

2. Highlight the current printer, then click on Setup (or double-click on the printer name), and a dialog box will appear. The exact contents of this box will depend on the printer you selected.

3. Click on Fonts, and the dialog box shown in Figure 9.5 will appear.

The box in the left part of this display lists all the soft fonts installed for the printer you selected. These fonts will also appear in the Fonts dialog box (Figure 9.4), along with any other fonts available to Professional Write Plus.

Scalable Typefaces

The most flexible and popular type of type-generating software offers *scalable typefaces.* The great advantage of this class of typeface is that you can select *any* print size from within Professional Write Plus, and the software instantly creates the correct fonts. Scalable typefaces for Windows have been developed quite recently, but they have quickly come to overshadow software types that generate individual font files.

Figure 9.5
Use this dialog box to display existing soft fonts or to add new ones

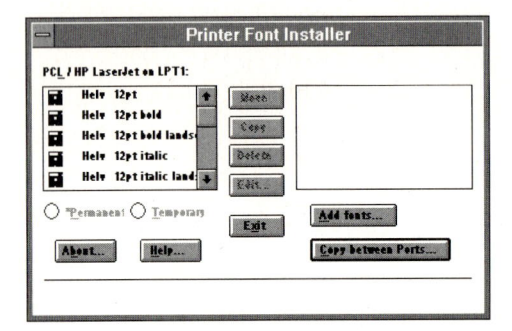

A typical typeface set that you would purchase might include two or three scalable typefaces at a modest cost. After installing these typefaces in Windows, you could then generate any size type in either portrait or landscape orientation, in normal, boldface, italic, or bold-italic.

The information about each typeface is contained in a separate file on your disk, called an *outline font file*. Each file is quite small, so that the total amount of disk space required even for several of these files is virtually negligible.

The installation of any of these software packages is generally quite straightforward—you usually need only follow a set of simple instructions on the screen. After installation, the new typeface names appear on the Fonts dialog box (Figure 9.4).

Printing a document containing scalable typefaces may require more time than with other types of fonts, since the detailed structure of each printed character must be sent individually to the printer. This is a *lot* of information—much more than is required for any other type of font.

Sources of Scalable Typefaces

Several vendors currently market scalable-type software. Some packages are more expensive than others, but they all generate good quality type. Here are a few of the vendors currently competing in this market.

Product	Publisher
Adobe Type Manager	Adobe Systems Inc. 1585 Charleston Road P.O. Box 7900 Mountain View, CA 94039 (415) 961-4400
Bitstream FaceLift	Bitstream, Inc. 215 First Street Cambridge, MA 02142 (617) 497-6222
Glyphix	Swfte P.O. Box 219 Rockland, DE 19732 (302) 429-8434
Publisher's Powerpak	Atech Software 5964 La Place Court, Suite 125 Carlsbad, CA 92008

Many other packages are commercially available. Those listed above have been personally tested by the author and found to generate good quality type. The absence of other packages from this list by no means implies a lack of quality. It simply means that not enough time or opportunity was available to test them.

Displaying the Available Fonts

You can easily display a list of *all* the fonts available for your printer within Professional Write Plus. To begin, you must select the desired printer—if you have a choice. (For more information about selecting printers, see "Working with More than One Printer," later in this chapter.) Then, select Font from the Text menu. In the Fonts dialog box (Figure 9.4), the list box labeled "Typeface" shows a list of all the available typefaces. This includes soft fonts, scalable typefaces, printer cartridges, and built-in fonts.

In the Fonts dialog box, there is no way to distinguish between the soft fonts, scalable typefaces, and built-in typefaces. However, this doesn't matter a great deal because what is most important is how the different typefaces work for you, regardless of their source.

After you have selected a typeface in the Fonts dialog box, the available sizes appear in the list box labeled "Size". When you select a size in this box, the box in the lower-right corner displays a sample of the text as it will appear on the screen. This may or may not bear any resemblance to the printed text (for more details, see "Screen Fonts").

If you select a scalable typeface, you're not restricted to the sizes listed in the Size box. In fact, you can enter any desired size (within limits) in the small box labeled "Points". The range of allowable sizes is dictated by the source of the scalable typeface. For example, some type-generating software allows sizes ranging from 1 to several hundred points.

Screen Fonts

Up to now, the discussion on typefaces, fonts, and so on has focused on printed characters. However, there are actually two different classes of type: that which is printed and that which appears on your screen. If life were perfect, there would be no difference between the two, and there would be no need for this section. Unfortunately, this is not the case.

For several reasons, the characters on your screen never look exactly as they do when printed (and vice versa). The main source of this discrepancy is that the printer and the monitor are entirely different pieces of hardware. In fact, the resolution of many printers is far better than that of nearly all monitors.

Whenever you select a particular typeface and size (using the Font option on the Text menu), Windows chooses the *screen font* that's the closest match, so that what you see on the screen more or less resembles what will be printed. This screen font contains the information necessary to display the characters in the selected typeface and size.

The screen font that Windows chooses depends on the particular view you're using. For example, text displayed on a VGA monitor in the Enlarged view is approximately twice as large as in the Standard view, so a different screen font is needed for each. Even in the same view, however, not every combination of typeface and size has a corresponding unique screen font. In many cases the same screen font is used for several different sizes, or even several different typefaces. One of the consequences of this is that the *relative* text sizes on the screen may be quite different from what appears on the printed output.

A screen font has several functions. First of all, it must display characters in readable form, and as much as possible in the correct relative size. For example, 20-point text should appear on the screen approximately twice as large as 10-point text. A screen font should also approximate the style of the text. For instance, serif and sans serif text should appear quite different on the screen.

Another important function of the screen font is to maintain the correct relative spacing between words and lines. Moreover, exactly the same words should appear on each screen line and its corresponding printed line, and the contents of each screen page should be exactly the same as the corresponding printed page.

Sources of Screen Fonts

The screen fonts used to display text on your monitor come from two sources:

- Those built into Windows
- Those supplied as part of a type-generating software package

The screen fonts supplied with Windows correspond to the printer typefaces and sizes also supplied with Windows. Similarly, when a type-generating package is installed in Windows, screen fonts are included as well.

Some Windows screen fonts are first rate, as are some supplied with type-generating software. But the quality of screen fonts varies tremendously. Consequently, some screen fonts are noticeably better than others. For example, Figure 9.6 shows samples of 72-point type displayed with screen fonts from Windows and Adobe Type Manager, one of the leading type-generating packages.

Figure 9.6
Screen fonts from (a) Windows and (b) Adobe Type Manager

(a) This is 72-point Helvetica

(b) This is 72-point Helvetica

Some software packages (such as Adobe Type Manager) are "smart enough" to automatically substitute their own screen fonts for those built into Windows. You don't have to worry about this, because it's all done automatically when you install the software package into Windows. You can simply sit back and reap the benefits of better-looking text on the screen.

Selecting Screen Fonts

The range of screen fonts available to you is one of the most important aspects of word processing because these fonts are what you're constantly looking at when working with the computer. Some fonts look extremely good on the screen, whereas others can give you a quick case of eyestrain.

In one sense, you have no control over the screen fonts that are displayed: Within a document, you select each font on the basis of what you want to be printed, and then the program selects the closest matching screen font. It seems as though what you see is what you get, but this isn't necessarily the case.

With a little subterfuge, you may be able to avoid looking at screen fonts that strain your eyes. The basic trick is as follows: For your rough draft work, use *any* screen font that looks good. Then, when you're ready to finalize a document, switch to the correct font.

To illustrate this point, suppose you want the body text of your document printed using 10-point Times Roman. Let's also suppose that the corresponding screen font looks pretty awful on your monitor. However, by trial and error, you've discovered that the screen font for 12-point Times Roman is much more attractive, easy to read, and so on.

To improve your life while you're working with this document, select 12-point Times Roman for the body text font. Then, when you get ready to do your final document design and printing, substitute 10-point Times Roman for the body text.

Take a little time to experiment with the different screen fonts available to you. As you're doing this, also test out the different view options on the View menu (Working, Standard, and Enlarged). Different screen fonts are used for the different views, so you have many options from which to choose. You'll probably find a few combinations of screen fonts and views that are distinctly superior to the others. When you find a combination that works well for you, use it for your rough work.

Avoiding Horizontal Scrolling

As you're experimenting with different views and fonts, keep in mind that you want to avoid scrolling left and right to view your text. That is, when a line appears on the screen, it should *all* be visible. If you need to use the horizontal scroll bar very much, you'll soon give up word processing and go back to your typewriter.

Suppose you find a combination of screen font and view that's really great, but the text is so large that some of the lines don't fit entirely on the screen. To solve this problem, increase the right margin until the lines are short enough to be completely visible on the screen. You can use the tab ruler at the top to help determine a reasonable value for the margin, then use the Page Layout dialog box to reset the margin.

Again, these margins are just temporary, while you're working on rough drafts. For the final document, you'll have to change back to the margin setting you really want to use for the printout.

Other Screen Display Problems

As mentioned earlier, the characters that make up a particular screen font never appear exactly the same as the corresponding printed characters. For example, the character widths used on screen fonts may differ from those that are printed. This can cause either too much or too little spacing to appear between words on the screen, because each line on the screen must contain the same characters as the corresponding printed line.

Having too much space between words on the screen isn't a serious problem, as long as that space doesn't also appear on the printed output (it usually doesn't). On the other hand, some screen fonts may generate lines in which the words are squeezed together to the extent that you may have difficulty reading them. This is usually the result of Windows using a screen font that's a poor match to the printed font. If this occurs, you can try using a different typeface to see if the screen font improves. Or, you can switch to Draft mode when necessary.

Automating Font Changes

The preceding techniques can help to optimize your enjoyment of working with Professional Write Plus, but it would be nice to avoid switching fonts and margins for each document. You can automate all of this switching by using two different templates—one for your draft work and another for finalizing the documents.

The template for the draft work should contain the body text font that offers you the best viewing, as well as the margin settings needed to display each line fully on the screen. The other template should contain the margins and body text font for the final output. (For information on creating and modifying templates, see Chapter 7.)

When you begin working on a new document, use the draft template. Then, when you're ready to finalize the document, simply switch to the other template. The program will automatically reformat the entire document, so you may want to scan through it on the screen, just to make sure that the reformatting hasn't generated anything that needs fixing.

Special Print Options

Printing a document created with Professional Write Plus is usually a straightforward process. You select Print from the File menu, click on OK, and the entire document is printed. However, the program offers a wide range of printing options, which gives you a good deal of flexibility.

You can print selected pages of a document, or you can print multiple copies of either the entire document or the selected pages. When printing multiple copies, the standard option is to print all the copies of the first page, then those of the second page, and so on. The reason for printing in this order is that usually the total print time is minimized (this is especially true for laser printers). However, you can optionally have the copies collated.

You can choose to print the pages of a document in reverse order—beginning with the last page rather than the first. Another option offers the printing of crop marks on each page. This can be useful if you plan to send your output to a typographic-quality printer.

If your printer has more than one paper bin, you can have the first page printed from the paper in one bin, and the remaining pages from the paper in another, on letterhead and plain paper, respectively, for example.

When printing rough drafts, you can often reduce the print time by specifying a lower print resolution. For example, many Hewlett-Packard LaserJet printers can produce output at either 75, 150, or 300 dots per inch. Printing at the lowest resolution can drastically reduce the print time, especially when a document contains graphics.

Selecting the Options

To select any of the print options described above, begin by selecting Print from the File menu. When the Print dialog box appears (Figure 9.7), you can select the following options:

- **Page Range**   Either click on All (the default), or enter the page numbers you want printed.

- **Number of Copies**   Enter the number of copies of the selected pages to be printed (default is 1).

For the remaining print options, click on Options. The dialog box shown in Figure 9.8 appears, offering the following options.

Special Print Options

Figure 9.7
Use this dialog box to select the pages and number of copies to print

[Print dialog box showing:
Number of Copies: 1
Page Range:
● All
○ From: 1 To: 9999
Printer:
HP LaserJet III
Buttons: OK, Options..., Setup..., Cancel]

- **Collate** If you select this option, the pages of each copy will be collated. (The default option is to print all copies of each page together.)

- **Crop Marks** If you want crop marks printed on each page, select this option. For this option to work, your document must have at least $1/2$-inch margins all around.

- **Bin Options** Use these options to select which paper tray to use for the first page and remaining pages.

Figure 9.8
Use this dialog box to select print options

[Print Options dialog box showing:
Print Options:
☐ Reverse Order
☐ Collate
☐ Crop Marks
Bin Options:
First Page: Upper Tray / Lower Tray / Manual feed
Rest: Upper Tray / Lower Tray / Manual feed
Buttons: OK, Cancel]

Once you have selected any of the print options described above, they will remain in effect for the remainder of your word processing session. This can be very handy, but it can also create minor irritations under certain circumstances. For example, you might have draft paper in one bin and a higher quality in the other. If you forget to change the Bin Options selections back, you may have to reprint, possibly wasting some expensive paper. You could, of course, cancel the print job in the middle (press Esc), change the selection, and start again.

Speeding Up Your Printout

With many printers, you can speed up the print process by specifying a lower-than-maximum print resolution. Because there are fewer dots to be printed, less time is needed for printing. The time savings is especially noticeable when some of the pages contain graphics, which can take forever and a day to print.

If a document contains only text, the amount of time saved depends on the printer and the fonts involved. There are so many different types of printers and fonts that no accurate generalization is possible. Your best bet is to experiment with your own printer, using different resolutions and noting which ones require the least time to print.

Here are the steps for changing the print resolution for your printer:

1. Select File/Printer Setup.

2. When the next dialog box appears (Figure 9.9), highlight the printer you are currently using, then click on Setup. A dialog box will then appear, corresponding to your printer, similar to that shown in Figure 9.10.

Figure 9.9
Select the current printer

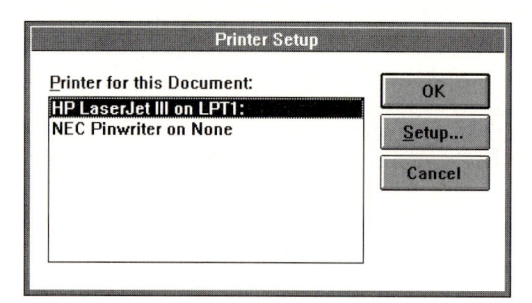

3. In the box labeled "Graphics Resolution", click on the resolution you want. For rough drafts choose the lowest value, and for final drafts choose the highest.

The resolution you select will be kept in Professional Write Plus's permanent files, and it will be used for all subsequent documents. To change the resolution again, repeat the above steps.

Changing the Paper Size and Orientation

In order to change either the paper size or the orientation of a document, you must modify the page layout, as described in Chapter 3. In addition, you must change the setup for the printer assigned to the document. Otherwise,

◆ **Working with More Than One Printer** 269

when you attempt to print the document Professional Write Plus may send the wrong instructions to the printer.

Figure 9.10
Use this dialog box to select various printer options

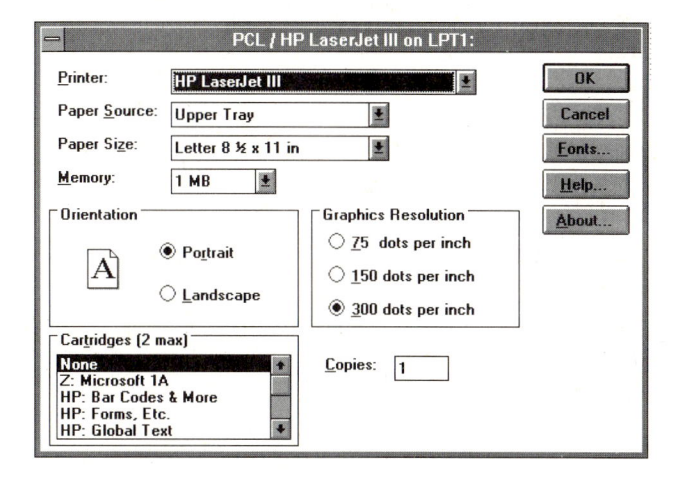

![Figure 9.10 - Printer setup dialog box showing PCL / HP LaserJet III on LPT1: with options for Printer, Paper Source, Paper Size, Memory, Orientation, Graphics Resolution, Cartridges, and Copies]

Here are the steps for changing the printer setup for a new paper size or orientation:

1. Select File/Printer Setup.
2. When the Setup box appears, click on Setup, and a dialog box similar to Figure 9.10 will appear.
3. To change the paper size, click on the arrow in the box labeled "Paper Size", then click on the desired size.
4. To change the orientation, click on the corresponding button in the Orientation box.

In some cases, none of the paper sizes listed in the dialog box (step 3) will correspond exactly to the size you selected when modifying the page layout. Just select the size that's closest to the actual paper dimensions being fed to the printer.

Working with More Than One Printer

You can install as many printers as you wish under Windows. Then, for any particular application you can select which printer you want to use. Of course, each printer you select must be attached to the port (the connection on the back of the computer) that you specify as part of the installation process. (For details about printer installation, refer to Appendix C.)

When using Professional Write Plus, you can switch back and forth between two or more printers that have previously been installed under Windows. For example, if you are sharing a high-quality laser printer with several others, you could print your rough drafts on another printer, then switch to the laser printer for the final copy.

There are two types of printers you need to be concerned with:

- The printer that is currently active in Windows
- The printer that is assigned to the current document

These may or may not be the same printer. The *active printer* is the only one you can print with, since only one printer at a time can be the active Windows printer. You can make a printer active only from within Windows, not from Professional Write Plus. Normally there is only one active printer although there may be two or more.

Each document you create with Professional Write Plus is always assigned a printer. When you first create a new document, the printer that's currently active is automatically assigned to the document. However, you can change the printer assignment at any time. Once you have assigned a printer to a document, it remains assigned unless you change it. In particular, the printer assignment remains the same even if you change the active printer.

For example, suppose that printers A and B are installed under Windows, and let's assume that you have made A the active printer. As you work with a document, you can assign to it either printer A or B. If you assign A to it, you can immediately print the document because A is the active printer. However, if you assign printer B to the document, you won't be able to print it until you make B the active printer.

Selecting the Active Printer

To make a printer the active one, you must temporarily exit from Professional Write Plus to Windows, run the Windows Control Panel, and then make a few dialog box selections. Here's how to activate any printer that's installed under Windows (assuming that you're running Professional Write Plus):

1. Press Ctrl-Esc. The Task list box, shown in Figure 9.11, appears. This box lists all the tasks currently running under Windows.

2. Double-click on Program Manager.

3. Locate the window for the Main program group. If it's reduced to an icon, double-click on that icon.

Working with More Than One Printer　　　　　　　　　　　　　　　　　　　　**271**

Figure 9.11
This box lists the Windows tasks currently running

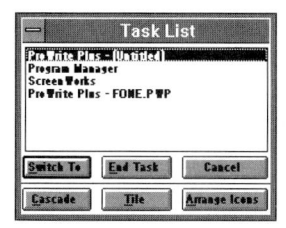

4. When the window for the Main program group appears, double-click on the Control Panel icon, and the display shown in Figure 9.12 appears (see below for additional information).

Figure 9.12
The Control Panel

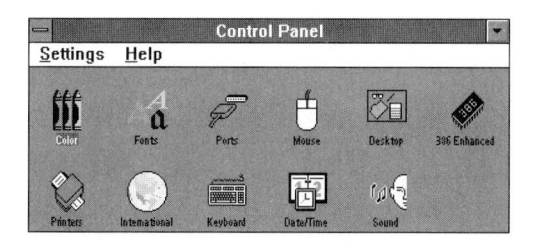

5. Double-click on the Printers icon, and the dialog box shown in Figure 9.13 appears.

Figure 9.13
Use this dialog box to select the active printer

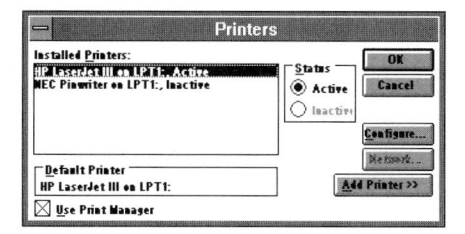

6. Click on the printer you want to activate.

7. Click on the Active option in the Status box, and then click on OK.

8. Find your way back to the Professional Write Plus program. One way is to press Ctrl-Esc, then double-click on Pro Write Plus in the Task list box that appears (Figure 9.11).

When Windows is initially installed, the Control Panel icon is located in the Main program group. If you can't find the icon there, it's probably been moved to another program group. You'll have to search around to find it, or perhaps get assistance from whoever manages your Windows system.

Assigning a Printer to a Document

In order to print a document, its assigned printer must also be the active printer. For example, if printer A is assigned to a document, but printer B is active, you can't print the document. If you try to print a document whose assigned printer is not the active printer, you'll see a message on the screen that reads "Cannot print this document. Install the correct printer driver and try again". In order to print it, you have two options:

- Change the printer assigned to the document to B.
- Change the active printer to A.

To change the printer assigned to a document, follow these steps:

1. Select File/Printer Setup, and the dialog box shown in Figure 9.9 will appear.
2. Click on the printer you want to select, then click on OK.

What Happens When You Change the Assigned Printer

Each printer is assigned its own selection of fonts, and these will vary from one printer to the next. For example, the available fonts for a laser printer will be entirely different from those for a dot-matrix printer. As a result of this fact, there are important consequences when you change the printer assigned to a document.

As an example, suppose that when you create a new document the currently active printer is a Hewlett-Packard LaserJet II, so it's the one automatically assigned to the document. As you build the document, you'll assign various fonts, all of which are available under Windows for this printer.

Now suppose you change the assigned printer to an NEC Pinwriter P2200, which is a 24-pin dot-matrix printer. None of the fonts originally assigned to the document are available on this new printer. As a result, Professional Write Plus reassigns all the fonts in the document, making the best matches it can from the fonts available on the new printer. To make sure these fonts are reasonable from your point of view, you should take a bit of time to check them out.

If you select the Modify & Create Styles option from the Format menu after changing the printer assignment, you'll probably see a message similar to that shown in Figure 9.14. This indicates that the font originally assigned to the current style is no longer valid, and you should pay attention to the substitute font selected by Professional Write Plus and perhaps change it.

Figure 9.14
This message reminds you to check the new fonts resulting from a printer change

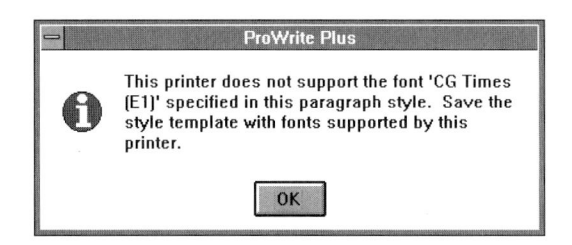

Getting Even Higher Print Quality

You can obtain even better print quality than is possible with your own printer if you output your document to a floppy-disk file, carry that floppy to a computer attached to a high-quality printer, and then copy the file to that printer. This is actually quite easy because many commercial printing shops own laser printers, or even higher quality printers, and offer this type of service.

If you don't own a laser printer, you can use this technique to get laser printer quality for $1 or less per page. Or, if you want to generate truly professional quality, use a Linotronic, Compugraphic, or similar printer, all of which output at resolutions of 1200 or more dots per inch. The cost for using these devices can run as high as $5 or more per page.

The technique for performing this wizardry is quite straightforward. To illustrate how to accomplish it, let's suppose that you have a 24-pin dot matrix printer, but you would like to print some documents on the Hewlett-Packard LaserJet III printer that's available at your local print shop. To do this, you must set up both Windows and Professional Write Plus to output to this printer, then send the final "printout" to a floppy-disk file. Here are the steps:

1. Install the HP LaserJet III to run under Windows. As part of this installation:

    - Assign the printer to the port named FILE:.

    - Make sure that the printer is assigned Active status. (Appendix C contains complete details on installing new printers.)

2. Select the HP LaserJet III as the printer for the document (select File/Printer Setup, then click on HP LaserJet III).

3. Create the document as you would normally.

4. Insert a blank, formatted disk in one of your floppy drives.

5. Select File/Print, then click on OK when the Print dialog box appears.

6. When the next dialog box appears (Figure 9.15), enter a file name where the document will be written. Make sure to include the disk drive as part of the file name.

Figure 9.15
Enter the name of the output "print" file

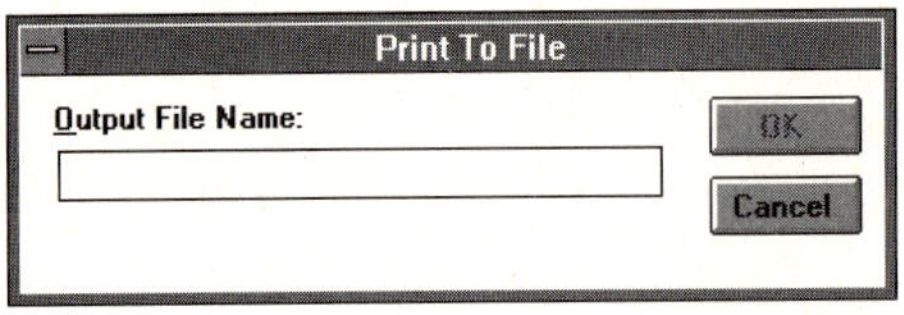

7. Take the floppy disk to the computer with the LaserJet III printer.

8. Copy the file you created to the printer. For example, if your file is named DOC1, and if the logical name of the printer is LPT1:, enter a command such as:

```
COPY A:DOC1 LPT1:
```

9. Before creating any other documents with Professional Write Plus, be sure to reassign the printer you normally use.

You don't need to select the printer before creating a document, as described in these steps, although doing so may save you a considerable amount of time. You can create a document with one printer assigned, and later switch the printer assignment to the LaserJet III. However, when you switch printers your document will probably change considerably. For example, the fonts available for the LaserJet will most likely be different from those available for any other printer, and this will change the line lengths throughout the document. If you do switch printers in this way, make sure to proofread your document *carefully*.

Summary

Understanding the different types of fonts and printers will help you get the best possible quality for your documents. Windows comes equipped to handle most of the fonts built into most printers. In addition, you can also take advantage of a wealth of commercially available computerized typefaces. Many of these are modestly priced, and they can greatly enhance the variety and quality of your printed documents.

Although Professional Write Plus is a WYSIWYG system, there will always be some difference between the screen display and the printed page, largely due to the limited number of screen fonts available. WYSIWYG is a powerful and indispensable feature, but you need to supplement it with periodic printouts during the design of a document so that there won't be any last-minute surprises.

CHAPTER 10

Using Frames

Basic Frame Operations

*Working with
Multiple Frames*

*Working with Text
in a Frame*

*Setting the
Frame Options*

Working with Frames

A FRAME IS A RECTANGULAR BOX THAT YOU CAN INSERT ANYWHERE within a document, and in which you can place either text or graphics. Frames can be a tremendously powerful tool, and they're one of Professional Write Plus's desktop-publishing cornerstones. With frames, you can transform an ordinary-looking document into a sophisticated presentation.

Using a frame, you can import a picture from just about any graphics-generating computer program, including drawing programs and software that transforms a scanned image into a computerized file.

You can also use frames to customize the layout of text within a document. Once you have entered a block of text into a frame, you can then resize and reposition the frame anywhere on the page. This gives you the ability to compose page layouts that are limited only by your imagination—and good taste. For example, the page layout shown in Figure 10.1 was created by creating several frames on the page, then inserting text into the individual frames.

A frame can contain either text or graphics, but not both. However, you can overlap frames, so that the contents of one appears to be inside another. For example, you can create a frame containing a picture, then insert another small frame at the bottom to contain the picture caption. By inserting this caption within its own frame, you can then precisely adjust its position relative to the picture.

After having created a frame, you can reposition it on the page simply by using the mouse to drag it to a new location. You can also change the size of an existing frame. These two features, plus the program's ability to automatically wrap text around a frame, allow you to perform on-the-spot page layout. Because Professional Write Plus is a WYSIWYG (what you see is what you get) program, you can easily work with frames to create attractive page layouts.

Basic Frame Operations

You can create one or more frames in any part of a document, including in the middle of existing text. After creating a frame, you can resize it, reposition it on the current page, move it to another part of a document, or delete it. Using the Windows clipboard, you can even copy a frame from one document to another.

In general, when *frame* is referred to in this book, the *contents* of the frame are included, whether text or graphics. For example, when you reposition a frame, its contents are also moved. Or, when you delete a frame, its contents are also deleted.

Figure 10.1
Using frames to enhance a page layout

Bay Hiking

Published Quarterly   Volume 5, no. 2

Hiking East and West

If you're a resident of any part of the greater San Francisco Bay Area, you have access to a nearly unlimited array of hiking possibilities. And, you can suit your hiking to the weather. This is a decided advantage, considering the wide variety of weather patterns that frequent the area.

If you want to be in sunshine as much as possible you'll need to be flexible, because yesterday's prediction for clear weather may not materialize. Especially during the summer, the offshore fog has a way of coming and going seemingly at will, but you can't ever be sure that today's fog will still be there tomorrow. An early morning weather forecast is usually the best way to maximize your chances of figuring out where the sun will be, but even then you'd better bring several layers of clothing, just in case.

The hills in Marin County, which form the last vestige of the Coastal Range, offer hiking that's as beautiful and varied as any in the Bay Area. Most of the hiking trails are attached in one way or another to Mount Tamalpais and its surrounding hills, and countless dozens of trails and miles dot these wonderful slopes. On the western edge of the hills lies Stinson beach, and rugged trails like the Dipsea offer spectacular views leading from the beach all the way up to the peak of Tamalpais.

When to Hike Where

For those times during the sprint, summer, and fall when the fog is present in Marin, plan to hike in the East Bay. On the other hand, when the temperatures east of the Oakland hills climb into the 80's or 90's, you may want to go over to Marin, where it's likely to be 20 or 30 degrees cooler. For those days when it's foggy in Marin and Roasting on Mount Diablo in the East Bay, the Regional Parks bounding on Berkeley and Oakland may be your best bet for temperate hiking.

On the way from Stinson to Tamalpais you can pay a visit to Muir Woods, which contains one of the most beautiful and well-known redwood groves in the country. You'll pay a price for this beauty, because the hiking is hilly and arduous.

On the eastern slopes of the hills lie several lakes, and although artificial they nevertheless offer many beautiful hikes and views. East of these lakes lie the Marin suburbs, so you don't need to worry about getting lost. Just head east from wherever you are, and sooner or later you'll come up hard against civilization.

If your planned hiking day turns out to be foggy in Marin, several lovely hiking alternatives are available in the East Bay Regional Parks. Considering the proximity of so many large urban areas, such as Oakland, Berkeley, and Concord, the existence of this large complex of parks is truly a miracle. Literally hundreds of miles of trails dot the region, covering a wide variety of terrain ranging from flat, yet not boring, to hilly, strenuous, and beautiful. Even when the Marin hills are fogged in, these parks are as likely as not to be in clear sunshine.

Creating a Frame

Creating a new frame is a a straightforward process. You can place the frame *anywhere*, including the middle of existing text. Position the cursor approximately where the frame is to be placed, then create the frame by using the mouse to select its size. Here are the steps:

1. Select Frame/Add a Frame, and the mouse cursor will take on the appearance of a small box.

2. In your mind's eye, picture the frame (a box) on the screen, then move the mouse cursor to any corner of that frame. (The upper-left corner of the cursor should be positioned at the starting point.)

Basic Frame Operations

3. Press the mouse button and hold it down.

4. Drag the mouse cursor across the screen. As you do, you'll see the frame grow.

5. When the frame is about the right size, release the mouse button.

When you release the mouse button, the position of the frame will be indicated by a a box drawn around the perimeter. You'll also see eight *handles* around the outside of the frame, as shown in Figure 10.2. When these handles are displayed, it indicates that the frame is *selected*, which means that you can work with it.

Figure 10.2
Creating a frame

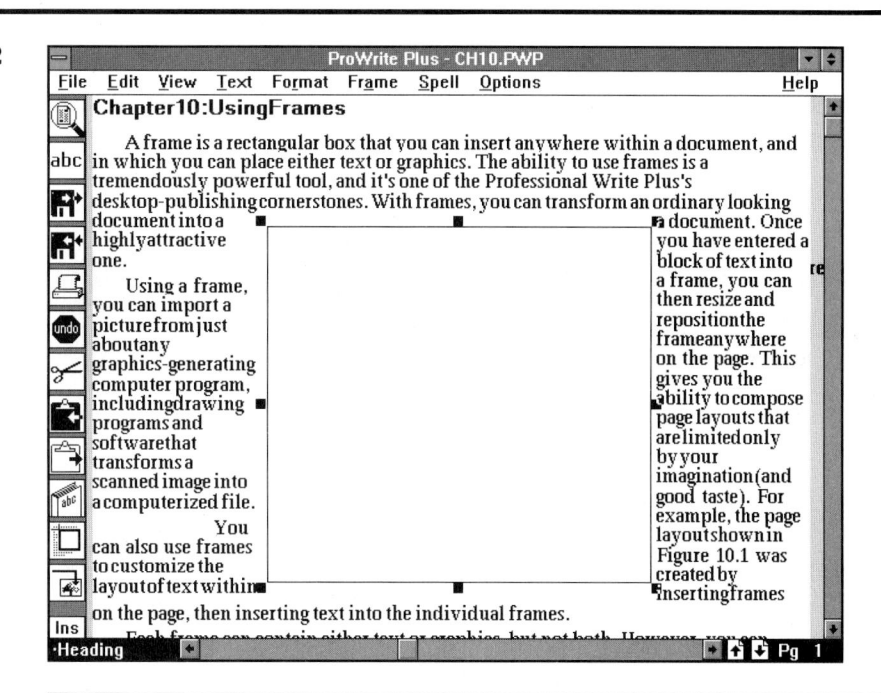

If you create a frame in the middle of existing text, that text is automatically wrapped around the frame, as shown in Figure 10.2.

Selecting a Frame

When you first create a new frame, it's automatically selected, which means you can perform various operations on it such as moving, resizing, and so on. When you want to work with another part of a document, click the mouse cursor there. This deselects the frame, hiding the eight handles in the process.

USING FRAMES

To select an existing frame, just click on it. The handles become visible and you can then work with the frame. When you select a frame, be careful not to double-click on it. If you do, the *contents* of the frame are selected, rather than the frame itself. For instance, to edit text within a frame, you double-click on the frame. When you double-click on a frame, the handles are dimmed, indicating that the contents of the frame have been selected.

If you do accidentally double-click on a frame, you can quickly recover by clicking anywhere outside the frame. Then (single) click on the frame again to select it.

Resizing and Repositioning Frames

Note. Full Page view is often the most effective view for repositioning or resizing frames.

Two of the most basic frame operations involve changing a frame's size and position. These operations are essential to good page design, and you should have little trouble using them. You can use these operations regardless of the contents of a frame. For instance, if you reduce the size of a frame, the contents may no longer be entirely visible, but it's still all there.

To resize a frame, *grab* a handle (click on it and hold the mouse button down) and drag it to a new position. As you do so, the frame will expand or contract, depending on the direction you drag the handle.

The handle you grab determines in which direction the frame is resized. For example, to increase or decrease the size on the right side of the frame, use the middle handle on that edge. If you want to increase the size both to the right and down, use the handle in the lower-right corner.

You can reposition a frame *on the same page* simply by dragging it around with the mouse. Click on any part of the frame (except any of the handles), hold the mouse button down, and drag the frame to its new position. When you reposition a frame, any surrounding text is automatically reformatted to wrap around the frame (unless you have turned off the wrap-around option within Frame/Frame Layout).

Moving and Copying Frames

Note. When a frame is copied or moved, the Windows clipboard is used as a temporary storage area. This means that you can just as easily move (or copy) frames to another document as to another page in the same document.

To copy or move a frame from one page to another within a document you must first select it, and then use the various options on the Edit menu. Alternatively, you can use either the corresponding speed keys or the icons on the side bar. When a frame is copied or moved from one page to another, it reappears at the same position on the new page as on the original. You can then drag it to wherever you want it on the new page. To copy or move a frame from one page to another, follow these steps:

1. Select the frame by clicking on it.

2. Select either Copy or Cut from the Edit menu, depending on whether you're copying or moving the frame.

Basic Frame Operations

3. Scroll to the page where you want the new copy to appear.
4. Select Edit/Paste, and the frame (with its contents) will appear.
5. Reposition the new frame to where you want it.

If you copy a frame to another page, the new frame will initially be a duplicate of the original. However, the two are completely independent of each other, and modifications to one will have no effect on the other.

You can use the Copy and Paste options to make a copy of a frame on the same page. However, when you paste the frame onto the page, it will exactly overlap the original frame, so you won't be able to see it. To separate the two frames, click on the visible one and drag it to a different location. The other frame will remain in place.

Copying to Another Document

Using a technique similar to that described above, you can copy a frame from one document to another:

1. Select the frame to be copied.
2. Select Edit/Copy. A copy of the frame and its contents will be copied to the clipboard.
3. Open the new document. You can either save the existing document and then open the new one, or you can open the new one as a second document.
4. Display the page on which you want to paste the frame. Then select Edit/Paste.
5. Drag the frame to where you want it on the page.

Deleting Frames

When a frame is deleted, its contents are deleted as well. This makes deletion an operation not to be undertaken lightly—particularly if you have spent a lot of time working on the frame. To help minimize the possibility of catastrophic error, save your document before deleting a frame. Then if you change your mind, you can recover from the saved copy of the document.

To delete a frame, you first select it, then do any of the following:

- Press Del.
- Select the Cut option from the Edit menu.
- Press Shift-Del.

The method you choose depends on whether you think you might want to undo the deletion. Normally, use the Del key for deleting a frame that you're absolutely sure you won't want to recover. However, if you think that there's even a small chance you might change your mind about the deletion, use either of the last two options listed above. Here's why: With either of these options, the frame is copied to the clipboard. You can then later recover the frame from the clipboard by using the Paste option from the Edit menu, provided that you haven't in the meantime copied something else to the clipboard. However, remember that if you use Paste, the frame will be pasted onto the current page, not the original one.

If you accidentally delete a frame by using the Del key, you may still be able to recover by using the Undo feature, which remembers the last few changes made to the document. If you can recover, the frame will be pasted back onto the page from which it was deleted, not on the current page.

Locating Hidden Frames

One of your options is to create a frame without an enclosing box. In this case, when the frame is empty, and if there's no surrounding text, the frame will be difficult to locate because it's basically invisible. To solve this dilemma, you can use the Go To function, which can locate each frame on the current page. Here's how it works:

1. Position the text cursor at the top of the page.

2. Select Edit/Go To, and the dialog box shown in Figure 10.3 will appear.

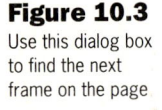

Figure 10.3
Use this dialog box to find the next frame on the page

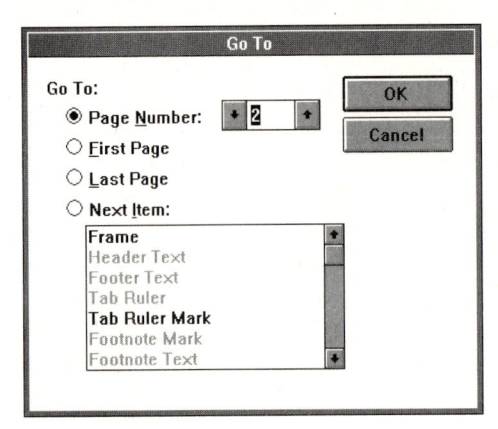

3. Select Frame in the list box, and then click on OK. The first frame on the page will be selected.

4. To find the next frame on the page, you can either press the speed key Ctrl-H or click on the Go To side bar icon. (When the program is first installed, the Go To icon isn't displayed on the side bar. For details about making it visible, see Appendix B.)

Invisible frames can also make a document appear longer than necessary. For example, if your document contains only two pages of text, but Professional Write Plus thinks the document is five pages long, there may be invisible frames on any of the last three pages. In order to get rid of these pages you must first delete any frames there.

Here's one other point to keep in mind: The Edit/Go To/Frame option will locate frames only on the current page. If you have several suspect pages, you must move the text cursor to the top of each one and then use Edit/Go To/Frame to search for frames.

Working with Multiple Frames

Most of the frame operations described in the preceding sections can be applied to several frames at the same time. For example, you can select two or more frames on the same page at the same time (Figure 10.4). You can then delete, copy, or move them all in a single operation. Note, however, that you can't select two frames on different pages at the same time.

Here's how to select two or more existing frames on the same page:

1. Select one of the frames by clicking on it.

2. To select another frame without deselecting the first one, click on the new frame while holding down the Shift key.

3. Follow the same procedure for selecting additional frames.

To delete, cut, or copy all of the selected frames, use the same keys and menu selections that you would for a single frame. For example, to delete all the selected frames press the Del key or select Edit/Cut.

If two or more frames are selected at the same time, you can't change the layout of any of them (using the Frame/Frame Layout option). To change the layout of any of the frames, reselect it by itself: Click on it, and the other frames will be deselected. You can then select Frame/Frame Layout and then make changes to the layout. See "Setting the Frame Options", later in the chapter for details on changing the frame layout.

Grouping Frames Together

Sometimes it's convenient to treat two or more frames on the same page as a group. Then, whatever action you perform on any frame in the group is

USING FRAMES

automatically performed on all others. These actions include selecting, moving, copying, or deleting. All the frames in a group must be on the same page.

Figure 10.4
Two frames selected at the same time

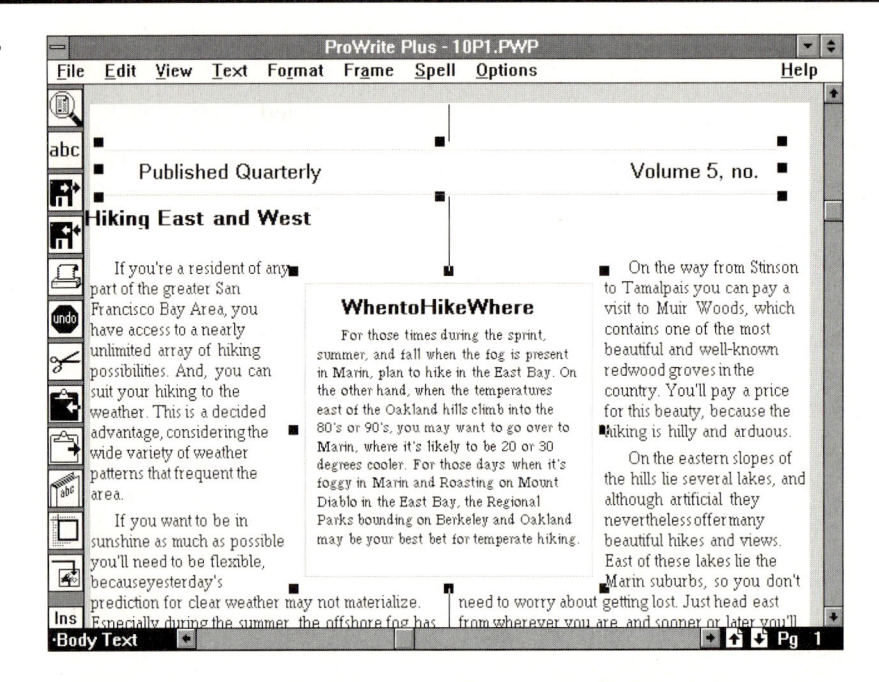

The most important use of frame groups is for moving two or more frames simultaneously. For example, suppose you create one frame that contains a picture, and another frame directly underneath for the caption. It would be convenient if when you repositioned either of the frames the other would be dragged along as well. Grouping the frames together accomplishes this.

To create a group, select the frames and then use the Group Frames option on the Frame menu. A check mark will then appear next to this option. To deselect the group, select any frame in the group and then select Frame/Group Frames again.

To familiarize yourself with the process of grouping frames, follow these steps:

1. Create two or three frames on a page. You could place either text or graphics in these frames, but for now leave them empty.

2. Select all the frames by holding down a Shift key and then clicking on each frame.

3. Select Frame/Group Frames. The selected frames will now be treated as a group.

Working with Multiple Frames

4. Click anywhere outside the frames, so that they are all deselected (the handles will disappear).

5. Now click on any one of the frames. When you do, notice that all the frames in the group are automatically selected.

6. Reposition any one of the frames by dragging it with the mouse. Notice that all the selected frames are dragged along as well.

7. Deselect the group: Click on any of the frames, then select Frame/Group Frames.

   Here are a few things to keep in mind with respect to grouped frames:

- If you delete any frame in a group, the rest are also deleted—which is another reason to be especially careful with deletions. However, you can recover the frames by using the Undo feature.

- All the frames in a group must be on the same page.

- You can't change the layout of a frame (using the Frame/Frame Layout option) that's part of a group. To change the layout of any frame in a group, first deselect the group. After making the layout changes, you can then regroup the frames.

- You can't select the contents of a frame (by double-clicking on the frame) that's part of a group. For example, you can't edit the text in a grouped frame.

Overlapping Frames

In some circumstances it's convenient to create two or more frames that are partially or totally overlapping. Frames that overlap are useful when you want to combine text and graphics frames that can be manipulated as a unit. There are also special effects you can create with overlapping frames. (See Chapter 11 for details.)

Here are the rules for working with overlapping frames:

- The frame most recently created will be the top one.

- If you click on an area that's common to both frames, the one in front is selected.

- If two or more frames overlap, holding down the Ctrl key and clicking (slowly!) repeatedly on the overlapped area will select each frame in turn.

When two or more frames overlap, it's just about impossible to edit text in a frame that's not in front because every time you try to move the text cursor by clicking the mouse cursor, that click selects the frame in front.

To illustrate this problem and how to deal with it, consider the overlapping frames in Figure 10.5. If you click anywhere in the area common to both frames, the frame that's selected will be the one that happens to be in front (it could be either one, depending on the order in which the frames were created). Now suppose that FRAME2 happens to be in front, but you want to edit the text in FRAME1. As part of the editing, you may click somewhere in the area common to both frames, in which case FRAME2 will immediately be selected, and you're no longer editing FRAME1.

Figure 10.5
Two overlapping frames

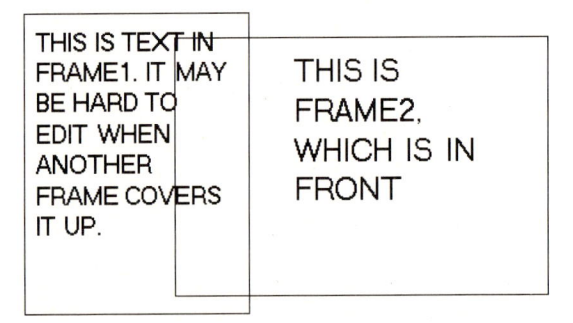

```
THIS IS TEXT IN
FRAME1. IT MAY          THIS IS
BE HARD TO              FRAME2,
EDIT WHEN               WHICH IS IN
ANOTHER                 FRONT
FRAME COVERS
IT UP.
```

To solve this dilemma, you can bring FRAME1 to the front. Then when you click anywhere in the common area, FRAME2 won't be selected. To bring a frame to the front, first select that frame, then select Frame/Bring to Front.

Suppose that you want to select a frame that's completely underneath a larger one. You can't bring it to the front because you can't see it to select it. In this situation, you can do either of the following:

- Select the frame that's in the front, then select Frame/Send to Back. The order of the frames is reversed, so that the one that was in back is now in front where you can work with it.

- Hold down the Ctrl key, then click on the overlapping area until the frame you want is selected.

If there are more than two overlapping frames, you can use either of the above to bring any frame to the front.

Working with Text in a Frame

After you have created a new frame, you can enter either text or graphics into it. This section illustrates how to work with a text frame. Figure 10.6

shows a frame containing text. Notice that the text wraps around within the frame, just as it does within a page.

Figure 10.6
A frame containing text

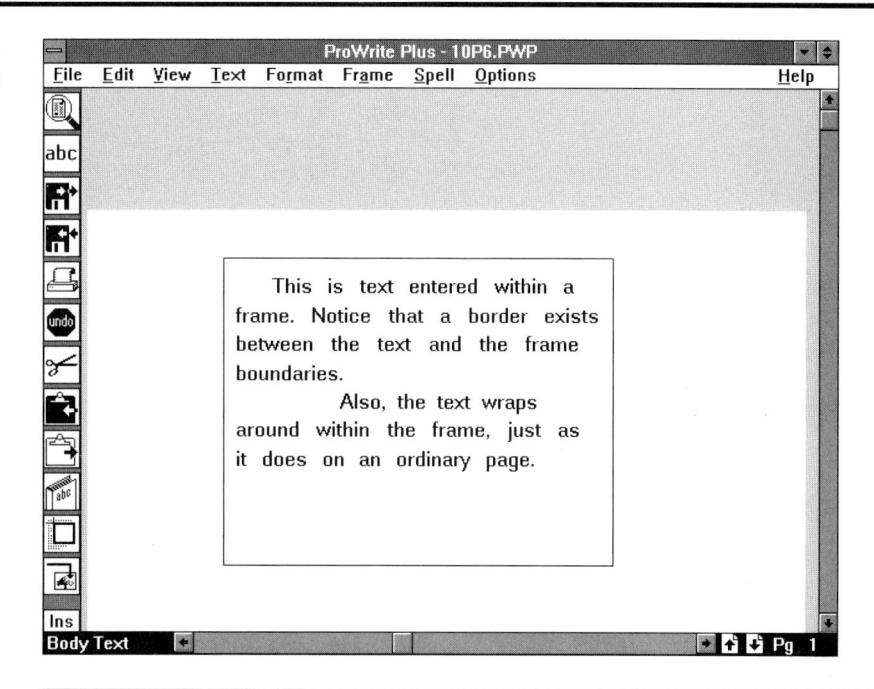

To enter text into a new frame, follow these steps:

1. Double-click anywhere inside the frame. Or, click once on the frame and then press the Enter key. The handles will be dimmed, and the text cursor will appear at the upper-left corner of the frame.

2. Begin entering whatever text you want.

3. When you're finished entering text, you can move the text cursor outside the frame by clicking wherever you want it to go. Or, you can press Esc twice, in which case the text cursor will appear at the position it occupied prior to entering the frame.

As you enter text, it will automatically wrap around when it reaches the right edge of the frame. You can enter and edit text using the same features you normally do. This includes

- Entering and deleting text using the standard editing keys
- Using the Text menu to select different fonts, alignments, and line spacings

- Using block operations to copy, move, and delete text
- Copying or moving text between a frame and the main part of a document, using block operations

The last item is possible because when you perform a block operation the Windows clipboard is used as a temporary holding area. Generally, you can perform any text operation within a frame that you can with ordinary text.

If you continue entering text after you've run out of room within the frame, that excess text will be saved as part of the frame, even though it's not visible on the screen. If you want to make this text visible, you'll have to expand the frame size.

Setting the Frame Options

There are various ways in which you can customize the look of a frame. For example, you can change the style, position, and color of the line drawn around the frame; or you can completely eliminate the line. You can also create a border of white space between the contents of a frame and the text on the page outside the frame.

You can choose if and how text should wrap around the outside the frame. By default, text is wrapped around each frame that's created. However, this can be changed in either of two ways:

- You can completely turn off the automatic wraparound, so that the text flows under the frame.
- You can set the wraparound so that the text flows only from the top to the bottom of the frame, but not on either side.

A frame can also be set to either transparent or opaque. This is a handy feature that allows you to create many interesting graphic effects. For example, by overlapping two or more frames and selectively making some of them opaque and others transparent, you can create shadow boxes, reverse text, and so on.

If a frame is being used for text, you can customize its format by setting the tabs and the number of columns within the frame. This high degree of tailoring gives you a great deal of flexibility in creating page layouts.

To customize a frame, you begin by selecting the frame, then choosing Frame Layout on the Frame menu. The dialog box shown in Figure 10.7 appears, and you can then select the options you want.

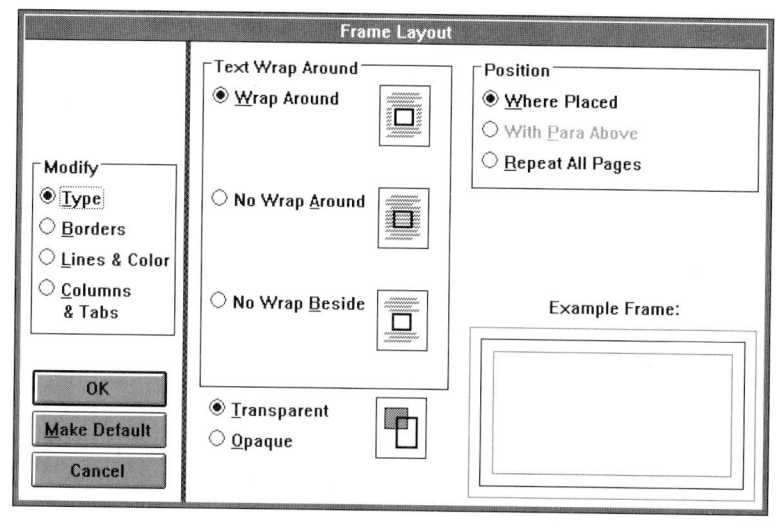

Figure 10.7
The dialog box for customizing a frame

[Frame Layout dialog box showing Modify options (Type, Borders, Lines & Color, Columns & Tabs), Text Wrap Around options (Wrap Around, No Wrap Around, No Wrap Beside), Transparent/Opaque options, Position options (Where Placed, With Para Above, Repeat All Pages), and Example Frame, with OK, Make Default, and Cancel buttons.]

Creating Borders

A *border* is the blank space surrounding the contents of a frame. A border has two purposes. First, it creates space between the line drawn around the frame and the frame contents. Second—and just as important—you can use a border to separate the contents of the frame from the adjacent material on the page.

By default, the border for each new frame is set at 0.1 inches, which is the size used in Figure 10.6. However, you can customize the space on the four sides of the frame individually. That is, you can choose one size for the top border, another for the bottom, and so on. You can even eliminate the border on any or all sides of the frame.

To illustrate the effect of changing a border, Figure 10.8 shows the same frame as that in Figure 10.6, but with a wider border drawn around the frame.

To change the width of the borders in a frame, follow these steps:

1. Click on Borders (in the box labeled "Modify"), and the Frame Layout dialog box will change to that shown in Figure 10.9.

2. In the box labeled "Borders", enter the values for the four different borders.

For each border, you can enter the value directly. Alternatively, you can click on the arrow at the right end of the edit box. Each click adds 0.05 inches to the border.

The default unit for the border values is inches. However, you can also use centimeters, picas, or points instead. (There are 6 picas to the inch, and

12 points to the pica.) To change the units, click on the word "inches" at the bottom of the Borders box. Each click will change the units.

Figure 10.8
The frame in Figure 10.6 with wider borders

> This is text entered within a frame. Notice that a border exists between the text and the frame boundaries.
> Also, the text wraps around within the frame, just as it does on an ordinary

Figure 10.9
Use this dialog box to insert borders

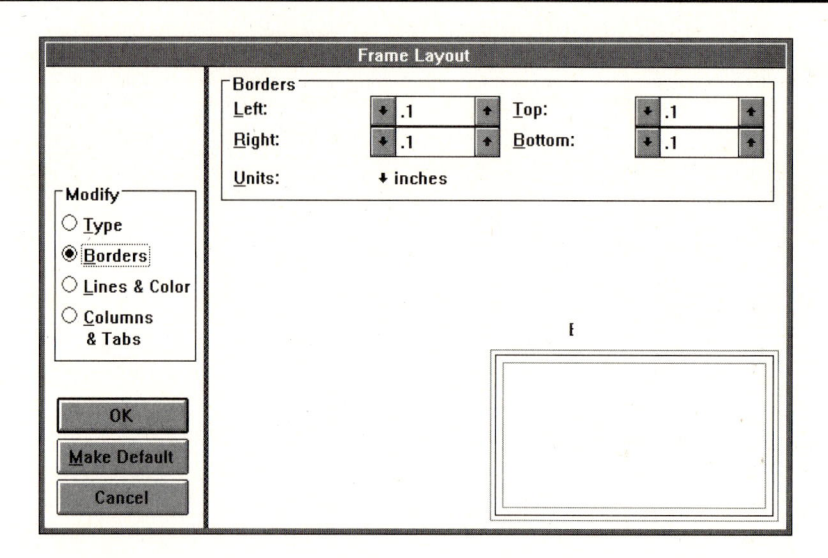

Frame Layout dialog box
- Borders
  - Left: .1
  - Right: .1
  - Top: .1
  - Bottom: .1
- Units: inches
- Modify:
  - ○ Type
  - ● Borders
  - ○ Lines & Color
  - ○ Columns & Tabs
- OK / Make Default / Cancel

The box at the lower-right of the dialog box shows a schematic of the border (defined by the outer and inner lines), the frame contents (the blank inner space), and the line drawn around the frame (the line somewhere between the inner and outer border lines). This may make more sense after reading the next section, where the options for positioning the line around the frame perimeter are described.

Creating Lines Around a Frame

By default, when a frame is created a line is drawn completely around it. However, you can delete the line on any or all sides of the frame, or you can change it in various ways. For example, you can select from a wide variety of line sizes, styles, and colors (for color monitors or printers).

You can also control the placement of the lines, relative to the inner and outer edge of the frame border. Here's how to modify the line drawn around a frame:

1. Select Lines & Color in the box labeled "Modify", and the Frame Layout dialog box will change to that shown in Figure 10.10.

Figure 10.10
Use this screen to select the options for lines around a frame

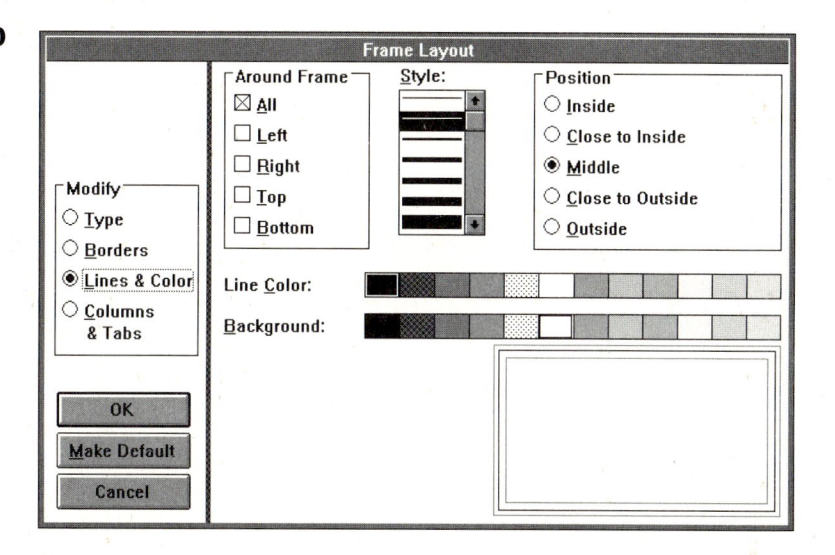

2. Select on which sides of the frame you want lines drawn. Make your selection in the box labeled "Around Frame". To remove the line entirely, just make sure that no option is selected in the box. (To deselect an option, click on it.)

3. Choose the desired style of line by clicking on your selection in the box labeled "Style". There are many different choices, so it would be a good idea first to scroll through the entire group to see what's available.

4. Select the color of the line by clicking on one of the selections on the line labeled "Line Color". This option is meaningful only if you have a color monitor, of course.

5. Select the position of the line relative to the border (see below for details).

6. To have your selections take effect, click on OK.

Selecting the Line Position

When you select the position of the line drawn around the frame (step 5, above), this position is relative to the existing border, if one exists. (For details about creating a border, see the section "Creating Borders".) The little box at the bottom-right of the dialog box shows this line position, as well as the boundaries of the border. Figure 10.11 illustrates these features. Here, the blank section in the middle represents the actual frame contents, and the shaded area represents the border, which is bounded by the inner and outer lines. The middle line is the one actually drawn around the frame.

Figure 10.11
A schematic showing the border and line drawn around the frame

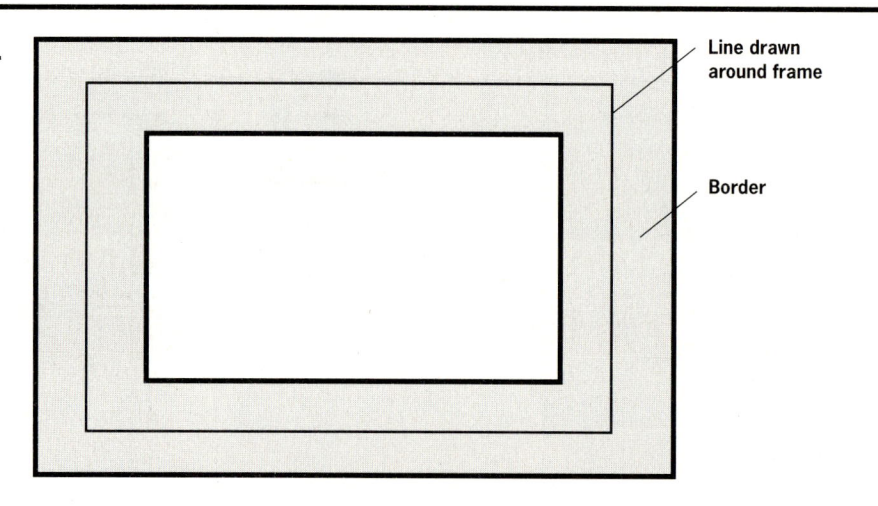

Table 10.1 shows your choices when selecting the position of the line.

The Middle option is frequently the most useful, because it divides the border into two separate parts. The inner part of the border separates the line from the contents of the frame, and the outer part of the border separates the line from the text outside the frame. Essentially, by selecting the Middle option you're creating inner and outer borders of the same width.

On the other hand, you can create inner and outer borders of different widths by selecting either Close to Inside or Close to Outside, and then choosing an appropriate border size. For example, if you select Close to Inside, a relatively wide border will be created between the drawn line and the rest of the page, and a narrow border between the line and the frame contents. Figure 10.12 illustrates this situation.

Table 10.1   **Line Position Options**

Option	Line Placement
Inside	On the inner edge of the border
Close to Inside	Not quite on the inner border edge
Middle	Midway between the inner and outer edges of the border
Close to Outside	Not quite on the outer border edge
Outside	On the outer edge of the border

Figure 10.12
Selecting the Close to Inside option

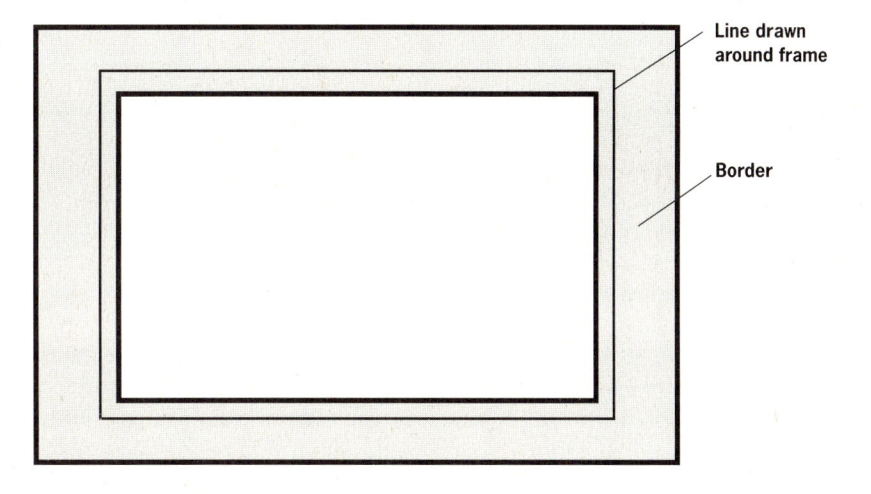

Choosing a Frame Position

When you create a frame, its default position on the page is wherever you position it, and it won't move unless you drag it to another place on the page. However, you can optionally attach, or *anchor,* a frame to the paragraph above it. This means that if the paragraph moves (as result of editing, for example), the frame will move as well, so that it's always right under the same text.

Here's how to anchor a frame to a paragraph:

1. Select the frame and position it directly under the paragraph it relates to.
2. Select Frame/Frame Layout.
3. When the Frame Layout dialog box appears, click on With Para Above, then click on OK.

The frame will remain anchored to the paragraph, even if it moves from one page to another as a result of editing changes. If you delete that paragraph, the frame will become attached to the preceding one. By the same token, if you position the text cursor at the end of the paragraph and then add a new one (by pressing Enter and then entering text), the frame will become attached to the new paragraph instead of the original one.

When a frame is anchored to a paragraph, you can't move the frame vertically on the page. However, you can drag it back and forth horizontally.

If you want to detach the frame from the selected paragraph, select the Where Placed option on the Frame Layout dialog box. The frame will then remain at its current position, unless you intentionally reposition it.

Setting Tabs and Columns

In many ways, you can treat a frame as though it were a minipage within the current page. For example, earlier you saw that you could add and edit text within a frame. Similarly, if you're working with a text frame you can assign a multicolumn layout within the frame. This allows you enormous flexibility in creating page layouts. For example, Figure 10.13 shows a text frame with a two-column layout. The frame itself is on a page containing a three-column layout.

You can also assign tab settings within a frame. Both the column layout and the tabs within a frame are completely independent of the layout of the rest of the document. By default, you can assign up to eight columns within a frame, and as many tab settings as you wish (within reason) within each column.

Here are the steps for assigning either a multi-column frame layout or new tabs:

1. Select the frame.
2. Select Frame/Frame Layout.
3. Click on Columns & Tabs, and the dialog box will change to that shown in Figure 10.14.
4. Select the number of text columns by clicking on the desired number under the Number of Columns option. The tab ruler at the top of the dialog box will then display the margins of each column with the symbols ▶ and ◀ .

Figure 10.13

A multi-column frame layout

> **Chapter 10: Using Frames**
>
> A frame is a rectangular box that you can insert anywhere within a document, and in which you can place either text or graphics. The ability to use frames is a tremendously powerful tool, and it's one of the Professional Write Plus's desktop-publishing cornerstones. With frames, you can transform an ordinary looking document into a highly attractive one.
>
> Using a frame, you can import a picture from just about any graphics-generating computer program, including drawing programs and software that transforms a scanned image into a computerized file.
>
> You can also use frames to customize the layout of text within a document. Once you have entered a block of text into a frame, you can then resize and reposition the frame anywhere on the page. This gives you the ability to compose page layouts that are limited only by your imagination
>
> (and good taste). For example, the page layout shown in Figure 10.1 was created by inserting frames on the page, then inserting text into the individual frames.
>
> Each frame can contain either text or graphics, but not both. However, you can overlap frames, so that the contents of one
>
> > Creating a frame is a fairly easy process. Basically, all you have to is draw the frame with the mouse.
> > The frame size you create isn't encased in stone. You can change the frame dimensions at any time simply by dragging a frame handle in the desired direction, either to increase or reduce a frame dimension.
> > You can also reposition the frame anywhere on a page by using the mouse to drag it around.
>
> appears to be inside the other. For example, you can create a frame containing a picture, then insert another small frame at the bottom to contain the picture caption. By inserting this caption within its own frame, you can then precisely adjust its position relative to the picture.
>
> After having created a frame, you can reposition it on the page, simply by using the mouse to drag it to a new location. You can also change the size of
>
> an existing frame. These two features, plus the feature that automatically wraps text around a frame, give you the ability to perform on-the-spot page layout, because the composition appearing on the screen is really what will be printed out.
>
> Because Professional Write Plus is a WYSIWYG (what you see is what you get) program, you can easily work with frames to create attractive page layouts. You can create as many frames as needed on each page, some of which can be used for graphics and others for text.
>
> **Basic Frame Operations**
>
> You can create one or more frames in any part of a document, including the middle of existing text. After creating a frame, you can resize it, reposition it on the current page, move it to another part of a document, or delete it. Using the Windows clipboard, you can even copy a frame from one document to another.
>
> When we refer to a *frame*, the contents of the frame are included as well, whether it is text

5. Select the amount of space between the columns by entering the number (in inches) in the Gutter Width edit box.

6. If you want unequal column or gutter widths, use the mouse to reposition the corresponding margin symbols in the tab ruler at the top of the dialog box.

7. To draw lines between the columns, click on the Line Between Columns option, then select the line style and color.

8. To assign tab settings, click on the appropriate position in the tab ruler. (For more information about assigning tab settings, refer to Chapter 3.)

Figure 10.14
Use this dialog box to select tabs and a multi-column layout within a frame

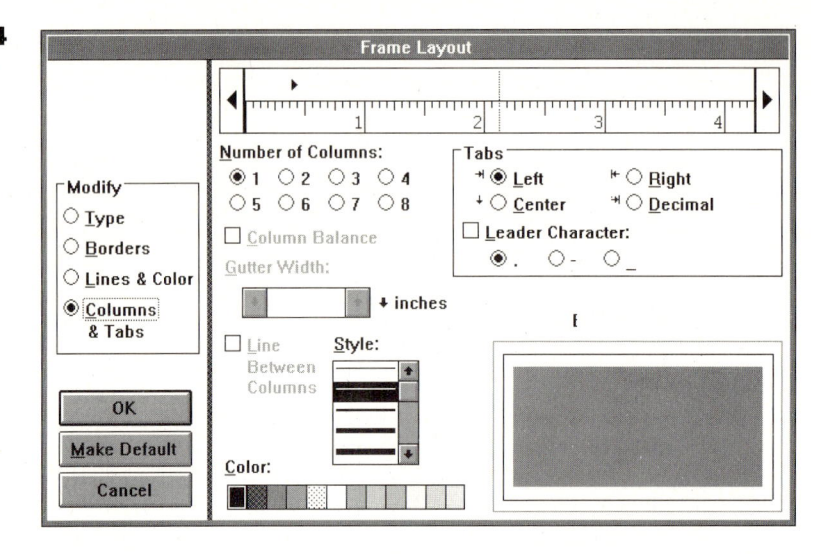

If you reposition any of the margins (step 6), the Gutter Width option becomes dimmed, because it applies only to evenly spaced columns. To restore the columns to uniform widths and spacings, simply click on the appropriate number under the Number of Columns option.

The box in the lower-right corner displays the current frame layout, including the relative sizes of the columns and gutters. As mentioned earlier, it also shows any lines and borders you create for the frame.

Adjusting the Frame Background

If you're using a color monitor, you can select a color for the frame background other than the default, which is white. Select Lines & Color, then select the color you want from the line labeled "Background". The box in the lower-left corner will display the color as it will appear in the frame.

The background color will extend out only to the position of the line drawn around the frame. If there is no line drawn, the color will extend to the position where the line would be, as determined by your selection in the box labeled "Position".

Making a Frame Transparent or Opaque

In addition to choosing the background color for a frame, you can also select whether the frame is transparent or opaque. When a frame is transparent, the contents of another frame underneath will be visible. Also, if you turn off the text wraparound option, so that text flows underneath the frame, that text will be visible. On the other hand, if a frame is made opaque, then nothing underneath will be visible.

Numerous special effects can be achieved by making frames either transparent or opaque (Chapter 11 gives various examples). Here's how to make a frame either opaque or transparent:

1. Select the frame, then display the Frame Layout dialog box.

2. Click on Type in the box labeled "Modify".

3. Click on either Transparent or Opaque at the bottom of the screen.

Note that, in order for the Transparent option to be available, the background color (under the Lines & Color option) must be white.

Creating a Repeating Frame

It's possible to have the same frame automatically appear on every page of a document. This is an *exact* duplicate of the frame, including its position on each page and also its contents. This could be useful if, for example, you wanted to create a fancy header or footer, perhaps containing graphics. If could also be a convenient way to incorporate a repeating page element, such as a logo or other feature.

You cannot use a repeating frame to create frames in the same position on each page but with differing contents. Every duplicate of a repeating frame contains the same contents. Use these steps to create a repeating frame:

1. Create a frame on any page of the document, and insert whatever text or graphics you want into the frame.

2. Select the frame; then select Frame/Frame Layout.

3. In the Frame Layout dialog box, click on Repeat All Pages.

The frame and its contents will automatically appear on each page in the document. If you insert a new page anywhere within the document, the frame will appear there as well.

If you modify the contents of the repeating frame *on any page,* those changes will appear in each copy of the frame. Similarly, if you change the size of any copy of the frame, or reposition it on the page, those changes will affect the corresponding frames on each page of the document. Likewise, if you delete the frame on any page, all the corresponding frames will be deleted.

If you insert a frame into a header or footer, it's automatically repeated on each page, so in this case you don't need to select the Repeat All Pages option.

Setting Default Frame Options

You can set any of the options described above to be defaults, so that each new frame that is created is automatically assigned these default options. For example, you could set a default so that each frame is assigned a 0.25 inch border all around. Here's how to set default frame options:

1. Select an existing frame, or create a new one.
2. Select Frame/Frame Layout, then select *all* the options you want to be defaults.
3. Click on Make Default.

From then on, every new frame will be assigned the defaults you selected. Moreover, these defaults will be remembered by the program in subsequent word processing sessions.

Working with Frames

The preceding sections described various frame options, such as using lines and borders around a frame. This section uses a couple of examples to illustrate how to use some of these options. First you'll see how to create a text frame within a page. Then this example will be expanded on by going through the basic steps for creating a simple one-page newsletter.

Creating a Text Frame

Placing text within a frame is a handy design device. After the text has been entered, you can reposition the frame anywhere you like on the page, or you can move the frame to another page within the document.

Figure 10.15 illustrates a text frame embedded within a page with a two-column layout. Notice that a small white border separates the main text from the frame, which is itself outlined with a light line. Also, a small white border surrounds the text within the frame.

This section outlines the steps needed to create a page similar to the one shown in the figure. Many of these steps will refer to features described in the section "Setting the Frame Options". You may want to refer to that section for details.

1. Starting with an new, empty document, create a two-page layout. (Select Format/Page Layout, then click on 2 for the Number of Columns option).
2. Enter whatever text you like on the page. It needn't be the same as that shown in Figure 10.15, but it should fill up most of the page.

Figure 10.15
A text frame can liven up a page

Hiking East and West

If you're a resident of any part of the greater San Francisco Bay Area, you have access to a nearly unlimited array of hiking possibilities. And, you can suit your hiking to the weather. This is a decided advantage, considering the wide variety of weather patterns that frequent the area.

If you want to be in sunshine as much as possible you'll need to be flexible, because yesterday's prediction for clear weather may not materialize. Especially during the summer, the offshore fog has a way of coming and going seemingly at will, but you can't ever be sure that today's fog will still be there tomorrow. An early morning weather forecast is usually the best way to maximize your chances of figuring out where the sun will be, but even then you'd better bring several layers of clothing, just in case.

The hills in Marin County, which form the last vestige of the Coastal Range, offer hiking that's as beautiful and varied as any in the Bay Area. Most of the hiking trails are attached in one way or another to Mount Tamalpais and its surrounding hills, and countless dozens of trails and miles dot these wonderful slopes. On the western edge of the hills lies Stinson beach, and rugged trails like the Dipsea offer spectacular views leading from the beach all the way up to the peak of Tamalpais.

On the way from Stinson to Tamalpais you can pay a visit to Muir Woods, which contains one of the most beautiful and well-known redwood groves in the country. You'll pay a price for this beauty, because the hiking is hilly and arduous.

On the eastern slopes of the hills lie several lakes, and although artificial they nevertheless offer many beautiful hikes and views. East of these lakes lie the Marin suburbs, so you don't need to worry about getting lost. Just head east from wherever you are, and sooner or later you'll come up hard against civilization.

If your planned hiking day turns out to be foggy in Marin, several lovely hiking alternatives are available in the East Bay Regional Parks. Considering the proximity of so many large urban areas, such as Oakland, Berkeley, and Concord, the existence of this large complex of parks is truly a miracle. Literally hundreds of miles of trails dot the region, covering a wide variety of terrain ranging from flat, yet not boring, to hilly, strenuous, and beautiful. Even when the Marin hills are fogged in, these parks are as likely as not to be in clear sunshine.

When to Hike Where

For those times during the sprint, summer, and fall when the fog is present in Marin, plan to hike in the East Bay. On the other hand, when the temperatures east of the Oakland hills climb into the 80's or 90's, you may want to go over to Marin, where it's likely to be 20 or 30 degrees cooler. For those days when it's foggy in Marin and Roasting on Mount Diablo in the East Bay, the Regional Parks bounding on Berkeley and Oakland may be your best bet for temperate hiking.

---

3. Create a new frame on the page, then position it approximately as shown in the figure. Notice that much of the text on the page is right up against the frame edges.

4. Select Frame/Frame Layout, then select the Wrap Around option so that the text on the page will flow around the frame instead of under it. (This option is automatically assigned unless the default frame options have been changed in your program.)

5. Create a 0.2 inch border all around the frame. This will serve to separate the text on the page from the edge of the frame, and it will also create space between the edge of the frame and the enclosed text.

6. Create a line around the frame. As you can see in the figure, the line serves to outline the contents of the frame and set it off from the rest of the page. Use a relatively thin line since you don't want it to dominate the page. Select Middle for the position of the line. This will place it in the middle of the border created in step 5, so that there is equal space inside and outside the line around the frame.

7. To begin adding text, double-click on the frame. The handles will be dimmed, and the text cursor will appear in the upper-left corner.

8. Enter a paragraph or two of text into the frame. Notice that the text will remain inside the border created in step 5.

9. After you have finished entering the text, readjust the size of the frame to minimize the amount of blank space at the bottom. You can stretch or shrink the frame in any direction, and the included text will automatically be reformatted to accommodate the new size. If you shrink the frame too much, some of the text at the bottom will become invisible, although you can make it reappear by increasing the frame size again.

10. Reposition the frame so that it's centered both horizontally and vertically on the page. To help you with this adjustment, turn on the tab and vertical rulers.

Your page should now look something like that shown in Figure 10.15. In the next section we'll carry on with this example and describe some additional techniques for using text frames effectively.

A Basic Newsletter Design

The example described in the previous section can be used as the basis of the simple newsletter design you saw in Figure 10.1. To modify the page shown in Figure 10.15 into the form shown in Figure 10.1, follow these steps:

1. Create a frame for the banner at the top of the page. Make sure that the frame extends the entire width of the page. If you leave any space between the frame and either margin, text from below might "squeeze" into it. Make the frame about 1 inch high. (Use the vertical ruler as a guide.)

2. Create a border of about 0.2 inch at the bottom of the frame. You don't need to create borders on any of the other three sides.

3. Select the Wrap Around option for the frame.

4. Create a line around the frame. Select a double line or something equally bold, to make the title stand out.

5. Double-click on the frame so that you can enter text.

6. Select a text size of approximately 48 points, then enter a short title. Due to shortcomings in some screen fonts, some of the letters may overlap others on the screen. This is no cause for concern, because they'll print out without the overlap. (This is one example of where what you see isn't what you get!)

   However, if the top or bottom part of every letter is cut off, you need to take corrective action, because this *will* print out as displayed. You can usually fix this problem by selecting the entire line as a block, then assigning it Single Spacing from the Text menu.

7. Create another frame below the one containing the title. This will be for the volume and issue number. Extend this frame across the entire width between the left and right margins, and make it about 1/2 inch high. Select the Wrap Around option for this frame. Then draw a line of medium thickness across the top and bottom. Assign a top border of about 0.2 inch.

8. Enter some descriptive text into this frame, as shown in the Figure 10.1.

9. Center the line of text vertically in the frame as follows:

   - First adjust the space between the text and the top of the frame by changing the top frame border.

   - Then adjust the space at the bottom by using the middle handle at the bottom to change the size of the frame (drag the handle up or down to decrease or increase the size).

10. To finish up the page layout, you can resize and adjust the positions of the top two frames to achieve the best possible appearance. In fact, the main reason for creating these frames is just that—to allow you to individually adjust these text elements on the page. For example, to create a little more space between the banner and the line below it, just drag the lower frame down a bit.

Summary

Frames are an essential part of creating sophisticated and attractive page layouts, and the techniques presented in this chapter cover the essential of frame manipulation. There are many more refinements concerning the layout and fine-tuning of page designs. These are addressed in Chapter 13.

CHAPTER

11

Working with Graphics

The Types of Graphics Files You Can Import

General Notes About Importing Graphics

Importing a Graphic Image

Working with a Graphic Image

Fitting a Graphic Image into a Frame

Techniques for Working with Frames

The Types of Graphics Files You Can Import   303

CHAPTER 10 DESCRIBED HOW TO CREATE AND MANIPULATE FRAMES, and also how to use them for working with text. Frames, however, have another important use, which is to act as a vehicle for importing graphics into your documents.

If you've been impressed so far with Professional Write Plus's features, you'll be even more impressed by its graphics capabilities. Using a frame, you can import graphics in just about any of the common graphics file formats and incorporate them into your work. After inputting a picture, you can then resize it, crop it, and place it anywhere in a document. If this sounds like desktop publishing, it is. One of Professional Write Plus's unadvertised strong points is the ability to perform many functions usually expected only from much more costly desktop publishing software.

Graphic images can come from many different sources: painting and drawing programs, image-scanning systems, and computerized art or *clip art*. Clip art consists of one or more graphic images stored in a disk file. The majority of this art is stored in file formats acceptable to Professional Write Plus, which means that an enormous wealth of graphics is available to you.

To access any type of graphic image stored on a disk file, you simply select a blank frame in your document, then tell Professional Write Plus the name of the disk file to import. After the image has been imported into your work, you can resize and crop it to suit the needs of the page. The entire process has been simplified to the point that you may find it hard to resist using graphics in your documents.

The Types of Graphics Files You Can Import

There is no single file format for graphic images. Instead, many different formats exist, largely due to the rapid rise of microcomputers. Because computer graphics has developed so rapidly, several different graphics standards have emerged. In order to remain competitive, designers of today's software (such as Professional Write Plus) must accommodate as many of these standards as possible. The result is a boon for users like yourself.

With regard to importing graphics, Professional Write Plus is extremely flexible, in that it can read just about all the popular graphics formats. This section briefly outlines what these formats are, so that you'll have a good overview of the types of graphics files available.

Bitmapped and Vector Graphics

All graphics images fall into one of two general categories: *bitmapped* and *vector,* and both types can be imported into Professional Write Plus.

An image in bitmapped format is composed of a large number of dots, or *pixels*—perhaps as many as several hundred thousand. This type of format is relatively easy for software to manipulate. For example, Professional Write Plus can resize, rotate, and invert (black goes to white and vice versa) bitmapped graphic images, all of which give you a good deal of control over the page appearance.

However, whenever a program changes the size of a bitmapped image, some distortion inevitably results because of the difficulty in transforming the relative positions of the dots making up the image. An added difficulty exists when a bitmapped image on the screen is printed. Because of the difference in resolution (number of dots per inch) between the screen and the printer, some translation must be performed during the print process, which results in a loss of clarity. Consequently, although bitmapped images are easy to manipulate, there is often a loss in clarity in the printed image.

On the other hand, graphic images written in vector format don't have these difficulties. Each part of a vector image is written as a mathematical description. This is much more complicated than a simple bitmapped image, but there's a good reason for the complexity. When you resize a vector image, the mathematical description of each part of the image changes proportionally, so that there is no loss of resolution or distortion. On the negative side is the fact that it's very difficult for a program to manipulate a vector image. For example, Professional Write Plus can't rotate or invert this type of graphic (although it can resize these images). Generally speaking, when you manipulate a graphic in vector format you can expect little if any distortion in the end result.

Usable Graphics Formats

Professional Write Plus can import graphics images in either vector or bitmap format. The following sections give information about the specific formats Professional Write Plus can use.

PCX Format

PC Paintbrush (PCX) is one of most popular file formats for graphics. The name comes from the PC Paintbrush drawing program, which generates output in this format. Many other drawing programs also use the same file format. Files in this format usually have the extension .PCX, and they are often referred to as "PCX files." A PCX image can be either monochrome or color.

Windows Bitmapped Format

Windows Bitmapped is one of the two formats used by Windows applications to transfer graphic images via the Windows clipboard. When a program that uses bitmapped images copies or cuts an image to the clipboard, this type of format is used. A graphic in Windows Bitmapped format can be in either monochrome or color.

Windows Metafile Format

Windows Metafile format (WMF) is the other type of graphic file format that can be used by applications running under Windows. When a program that works with vector graphic images cuts or copies an image, the graphic copied to the clipboard is in Windows Metafile format. A file containing this type of image has the extension .WMF.

TIF Format

Tagged Image File (TIF) is another popular style for graphic files. These files are frequently generated by image-scanning systems and are referred to as "TIFF" files. The standard extension for this type of file is .TIF. There are several different flavors of TIF formats, and the *Professional Write Plus User's Guide* lists the following as being acceptable to the program:

- RLE (Run Length Encoding)
- CCITT3 compression
- Byte and word-aligned images with no compression

EPS Format

Encapsulated PostScript (EPS) is a popular graphic image format used by software generating output for PostScript-compatible printers. Files of this type usually have the extension .EPS, and they can be either monochrome or color. The EPS file format, which was developed by Adobe Systems, Inc., generates a very high-quality image.

But why does the program create a file if it is just sending output to a printer? The answer is that some users may not own a PostScript printer, so instead they generate their output to an EPS file, which can later be copied to a PostScript printer somewhere else.

The primary use for this file format is to produce extremely clear output for PostScript printers. However, some software packages output an additional image in each graphic file, which is in either TIF or Windows Metafile format. This extra image can be used for displaying the file contents on your screen. It can also be used for generating printout on a non-PostScript printer. In other words, even if you don't have a PostScript printer you can print the contents of an EPS file, provided that a TIF or Windows metafile image is included as well.

HP PCL Format

Hewlett-Packard Printer Command Language (HP PCL) is used for creating output on a Hewlett-Packard printer (or compatible). Many programs that can print to an HP printer can alternatively send the printer output to a file in HP PCL format. This file, which usually has the extension .PCL, can later be copied directly to an HP-compatible printer (with a DOS

COPY command, for instance). However, you can also import the contents of a .PCL file into Professional Write Plus.

There are a couple of restrictions on using this type of file. First, you can't import a file in *compressed* PCL format. Also, a PCL file may contain both text and graphics, but unless the text is in graphics form it will be ignored when the file is imported into Professional Write Plus. Finally, only monochrome images can be generated in a PCL file.

ANSI CGM Format

Ansi Computer Graphics Metafile (CGM) conforms to the ANSI standard format for graphical data exchange, a standard that has been adopted by many of the leading graphics software packages. This is a high-quality color vector format that allows you to do perform scaling without losing picture quality. For more details about using this type of file, refer to the *Professional Write Plus User's Guide*.

PIC Format

Lotus Picture or PIC is the format of graphics generated by the popular Lotus software packages. This type of file has the extension .PIC. It's a vector format, which means that you can rescale this type of graphic in Professional Write Plus and still retain the high-quality image. However, when this type of graphic is printed the text fonts may be changed due to various technical differences between Lotus and Windows.

SDW Format

Ami and Ami Professional, which are high-end word processing programs, can generate graphic images and store them in files with an .SDW extension. These images can be either in monochrome or color.

MAC Format

MAC is a popular graphic format, generated by MacPaint and other Macintosh paint programs. It is a monochrome bitmapped format, and files generally have the extension .MAC. Note that you can't directly use a file created by a Macintosh program. Instead, you'll first have to copy the file to a floppy disk in IBM PC-compatible format. This service is commonly available in most cities.

ART Format

Not surprisingly, Professional Write Plus can import graphic images in any of the file formats generated by products marketed by Software Publishing Corporation. First Publisher, which is a low-cost desktop publishing program, is one of these products. It can generate monochrome graphic images in either high- or low-resolution bitmapped format. These clip art files generally have the extension .ART.

SYM Format

Harvard Graphics is another of Software Publishing's popular graphics products. It generates high-quality monochrome or color vector images that can be imported into Professional Write Plus. These so-called symbol files use the extension .SYM.

Two different types of formats can be imported: those generated by Harvard Graphics versions 2.3 and those generated by earlier versions (called "pre-2.3" by Professional Write Plus). For further details about importing this type of image, refer to the *Professional Write Plus User's Guide*.

General Notes About Importing Graphics

Whenever you import a graphic image, a certain amount of luck and faith are involved. In the large majority of cases, the quality of the imported graphic will be acceptable, perhaps even as good as the original image. However, there are a great many different types of graphic software currently in use, and as indicated in the previous section there are many types of graphic file formats. A software package may output a file that it labels as a particular format (PCX, for instance), but there's no guarantee that the file is completely compatible with the accepted standard for that format. For example, some types of so-called PCX files can't be imported by Professional Write Plus.

If and when you encounter a situation in which either you can't import a graphic at all, or the quality of the imported image is too awful to bear, there's not a great deal you can do about it from within Professional Write Plus. What you get is what you're stuck with.

You do have a couple of recourses, however. First, you could try to get the source program (the one that generated the image) output in a different file format. If this isn't possible, you'll have to find another source of graphics.

These remarks aren't meant to discourage you from trying to import graphics. On the contrary, most of the time things will go very smoothly, and you'll be very pleased with the quality of the imported images. Most of the popular software that generates files in any of the standard graphics file formats, such as PCX or TIF, do a good job of conforming to the accepted format standards, and you'll be able to import these files without any difficulty.

Screen and Printer Output

There are many complex paths between a graphics file on your floppy disk, the image appearing on your screen, and the printed image. A great deal of internal translation goes on to paint the final picture on the screen—particularly with color images. The quality of the screen picture is determined to a large extent by the type of control board (technically called a *graphics adapter*) your computer uses to process the image and send it to the screen. In addition, the image quality depends to some extent on the caliber of your monitor.

There is a great variation in the quality of graphics adapters, and again this is particularly true of color. If your control board is relatively inexpensive, you shouldn't expect to see really high-quality color on the screen.

Another important factor in this scheme is the *device driver* for your monitor. This is a program used by Windows to communicate information to your control board and monitor. Windows contains several built-in device drivers for different types of monitors, and it may be using one of these for your system. On the other hand, some monitors come with their own drivers, which must be installed under Windows in order to get the most out of the monitor.

If you suspect that your screen isn't generating the best possible picture, you may want to investigate which driver is being used by Windows. In addition, you may be able to obtain a more up-to-date driver from the manufacturer of the monitor. Unfortunately, details about this topic are beyond the scope of this book. If you're not well acquainted with the internal operation of Windows, try to find someone who is.

These remarks are equally true for color printing, which is a highly complicated process. Again, a lot of translation goes on between your computer and the printer. At the risk of stating the obvious, print quality is primarily dependent on the caliber of the printer, and good color printers are extremely expensive. A high-quality monochrome printout, which will include well-proportioned gray scales, often looks a lot better than a mediocre color printout.

As it does with monitors, Windows uses a device driver to communicate with your printer. It's important that the correct driver for the printer be installed under Windows. Otherwise, the output will be either poor or nonexistent. Again, if the quality of the output isn't what you expect, find out exactly which driver is being used by Windows.

Importing a Graphic Image

The actual technique for importing a graphic image is surprisingly easy, considering the high degree of complexity going on behind the scenes. To import a picture, you first create a frame in the general vicinity of where you want the image to be placed. Then you simply select the type of image to be imported and the name of the file where it's located; Professional Write Plus does the rest. You can then get to work and adjust the image to fit into your document.

To import a graphic, follow these steps:

1. Draw a frame somewhere in the general location of where you want to place the picture. The size of the frame isn't critical at this point, because you can adjust it later on.

2. With the frame still selected, select File/Import Graphics, and the dialog box shown in Figure 11.1 will appear. Note that if no frame is selected, the Import Graphics option is not available.

Figure 11.1
Select the type of graphic file and the file name

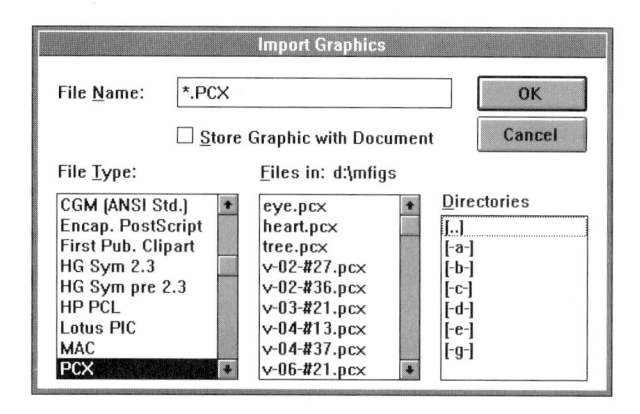

Import Graphics
File Name: *.PCX
☐ Store Graphic with Document
File Type: / Files in: d:\mfigs / Directories
CGM (ANSI Std.) / eye.pcx / [..]
Encap. PostScript / heart.pcx / [-a-]
First Pub. Clipart / tree.pcx / [-b-]
HG Sym 2.3 / v-02-#27.pcx / [-c-]
HG Sym pre 2.3 / v-02-#36.pcx / [-d-]
HP PCL / v-03-#21.pcx / [-e-]
Lotus PIC / v-04-#13.pcx / [-g-]
MAC / v-04-#37.pcx
PCX / v-06-#21.pcx

3. In the list box labeled "File Type", click on the appropriate file format. If you don't know which to select, you can try selecting each file type in turn, until the file you want appears in the list box labeled "Files in".

4. Select the name of the file to be imported. You can either use the list boxes labeled "Directories" and "Files in", or you can enter the full file name (including the disk drive and directory) in the File Name edit box.

5. If you want a copy of the file stored with the current document, click on Store Graphic with Document (see the next section for more information).

6. Click on OK, and the image will be copied into the selected frame.

Saving a Graphic with Your Document

If you select the Store Graphic with Document option in step 5 above, a copy of the original graphic file is created in the same directory as your document. This new file is given the same name as your document file, but with a Gxx extension. For example, the first graphic file saved with the document MYSTUFF.PWP will be named MYSTUFF.G00, the second one MYSTUFF.G01, and so on.

When displaying or printing a document, Professional Write Plus refers to the original graphic file, unless you created a copy in step 5. In that case, the program refers to the copy, not the original.

There are advantages and disadvantages to storing a graphic file with your document. One of the main disadvantages is that the extra file takes up disk space. If you're importing several graphic images into a document, the copied images could exhaust your hard disk.

The main reason for storing a graphic image with the document is that your document then isn't dependent on the original file. For example, if a drawing program alters the original file, those changes will be reflected in your document, unless you created a copy of the file in step 5. This may or may not be an advantage, depending on whether you want your document to reflect the latest changes to the image.

If you copy your document to another disk, the associated graphics files can easily be copied as well, provided that you store the graphic with the document. If you don't include the graphic, the document in the new location may not have access to the original graphic file.

As a rule, if you don't plan to move your document to another disk, don't use the Store Graphic with Document option.

Working with a Graphic Image

After a graphic has been imported into a frame, there are several ways you can customize it:

- Reposition the frame on the page

- Change the size of the frame, which may or may not alter the size of the image, depending on other selected options

- Change the size of the image within the frame (as opposed to change the frame size)

- Move the image within the frame

- Crop the image

- Delete the image from the frame

For details about the first two of these operations, refer to Chapter 10. Before describing the remaining options, let's first discuss the difference between selecting a frame and selecting its contents.

Selecting a Frame Versus Selecting Its Contents

As described in the previous chapter, you select a frame by clicking anywhere within its boundaries. You can then move the frame, delete it, and so on. On the other hand, you can also select just the graphic image within a frame. This is useful when you want to manipulate the image relative to the

Working with a Graphic Image   311

frame boundaries. For instance, you can reposition an image within a frame by selecting the image and then dragging it with the mouse.

To select the image within a frame, just double-click inside the frame. The frame handles will be grayed out, and the mouse cursor turns into a four-way arrow, like this:

To deselect the contents of a frame, click anywhere outside the frame. If you want to select the frame itself, but the image within is currently selected, you must first deselect the contents by clicking outside, then click (once) again within the frame.

Remember, when a frame is selected the handles appear in black on the screen. On the other hand, when the frame contents are selected the handles appear in gray.

Adjusting Image Size

You have complete control over the size of the image within a frame. Generally, you adjust the image size as part of the overall process of page design and layout.

When adjusting the image size, you have the following options:

- Leave the image at its original size. These are the original dimensions of the imported image, that is, without any scaling by Professional Write Plus.

- Set the image to a percentage of its original size.

- Set custom vertical and horizontal dimensions.

- Adjust one of the two dimensions of the image, and let the program set the other so as to retain the original proportions.

- Let the program adjust the size so that as much as possible of the image fits within the frame.

Options for Resizing

To adjust the size of the image, begin by selecting the frame. Then select Frame/Graphics Scaling, and the dialog box shown in Figure 11.2 will appear. (The Frame/Graphics scaling option is not available until a frame is selected.) Use the following options to adjust the size of the image:

- To keep the image at its original size, select Original Size.

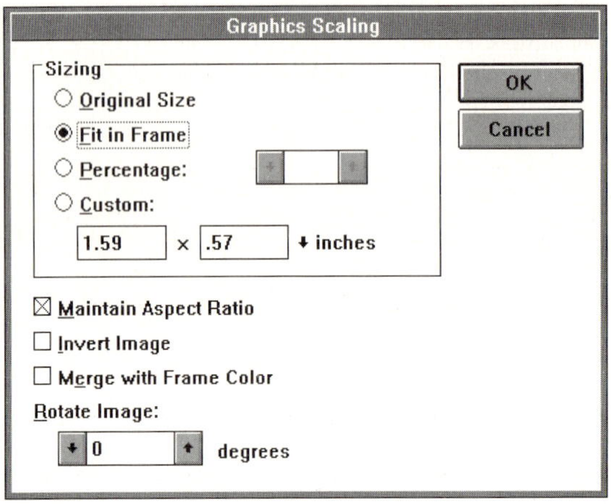

Figure 11.2
Use this box to adjust the size and appearance of a graphic within a frame

- To fit the entire original image in the frame, use the Fit in Frame option. When this option is selected, the image will automatically be resized as you adjust the frame size. If the Maintain Aspect Ratio option is also selected, the original proportions of the vertical and horizontal dimensions of the image will be maintained during this fitting process. If Maintain Aspect Ratio is not selected, the program will do its best to keep the frame filled in both dimensions. If the frame becomes too small, some of the image will be pushed outside the frame and won't be visible.

- To select a particular image size, click on the Custom option, turn off Maintain Aspect Ratio, then enter the dimensions you want in the associated edit boxes. The box on the left is for the width, and the other for the height. By default, the numbers you enter are in inches, but you can also use centimeters, picas, or points as the unit of measure. To change units, click on the word "inches". Each click changes the units, and the numbers in the edit boxes are automatically recalculated.

- To select an image size and also maintain the original proportions, turn on the Maintain Aspect Ratio option, then enter only one number in either Custom edit box. The other number will be automatically calculated to maintain the same aspect ratio.

- To select a particular image size as a percentage of the original size, click on the Percentage option, then enter the percentage in the associated edit box.

Cropping

You can also control exactly which portion of an image is in the frame, a process called *cropping*. There are two ways in which you can crop an image:

- By moving the image within the frame, you can crop two adjacent sides of the image.

- By repositioning the frame edges, you can crop the corresponding edges of the image.

To get some practice with these two operations, follow these steps:

1. Import a graphic image into a frame.

2. With the frame selected, choose Frame/Graphics Scaling.

3. When the Graphics Scaling box appears (Figure 11.2), click on original size, then click on OK.

4. Double-click on the image inside the frame (the handles will be dimmed).

5. Holding down the mouse button, reposition the image within the frame. Experiment to see the limits of movement.

6. Click anywhere outside the frame, then single-click on the frame to select it.

7. Drag the right edge of the frame in toward the center of the frame. As you do, note that the right edge of the image is cropped.

8. Crop the bottom edge of the image by repositioning the lower edge of the frame.

9. Now drag the top edge of the frame down about an inch, and notice what happens to the image.

10. Drag the left edge of the frame in about an inch, and again notice what happens to the image.

Here are some guidelines to follow when cropping:

- The Fit in Frame option should not be selected. Instead, use one of the alternative options (Original Size, Percentage, or Custom). The reason is that with Fit in Frame selected, the program tries to keep the entire image displayed inside the frame as you change the frame dimensions.

- To crop the left or upper edge of an image, reposition the image within the frame.

- To crop the right or bottom edge, move the right or bottom frame edge.

Here's the reason for these rules: As long as Fit in Frame is not selected, the image remains fixed relative to the left and top frame edges, regardless of which frame edge you reposition. On the other hand, if Fit in Frame is selected, the program tries to keep the entire image visible by resizing it. This means that you can't effectively crop when Fit in Frame is selected.

Deleting an Image

To delete the image from a frame, double-click on the image, then press Del or select Edit/Cut. The image is deleted, but the empty frame remains. Note that this is different from deleting the entire frame, in which case both the frame and its contents are deleted.

In some cases it's actually faster to delete a frame plus its contents, rather than just the image itself, even though you must then create a new empty frame. This is true particularly with large and complex graphic images, which take a while to disappear.

Fitting a Graphic Image into a Frame

The previous sections described how to move a graphic image within a frame, resize the image, and crop it. However, these features become powerful tools only when you put them all together to fit an image into a frame and the frame to the page.

There are many aspects to fitting an image into a frame. The exact steps you use depend on the particular situation. Here are two possible scenarios:

- An image must fit into a frame with predetermined dimensions. For example, you may be designing a newsletter page, and you need a picture of specific dimensions to fit in a particular location. In this type of circumstance you'll need to resize and crop the picture to fit the frame.

- The frame dimensions are to some degree flexible, so that you can crop an image exactly the way you want it, and then adjust the frame dimensions to match the cropped image.

Each of these cases requires special treatment.

Fitting to a Frame of Specific Dimensions

When you need to customize an image to a frame of specific dimensions, you must resize and reposition the image as best you can. In this type of situation two types of adjustments can be made:

- Vary one or both dimensions of the image

- Reposition the image within the frame

Here's an outline of the steps you can follow:

1. Set the exact frame size you want.

2. In the Graphics Scaling box (Figure 11.2), select the Original Size and Maintain Aspect Ratio options.

3. Study the image in the frame, and estimate how much to increase or decrease its size. For instance, if the image is much too large you might begin by reducing it by 50 percent.

4. In the Graphics Scaling box, use either the Percentage or Custom option to enter the estimated new size. For example, if you want to reduce an image by 50 percent, you could do either of the following:

- Enter **50** in the Percentage edit box.

- Replace the number in either Custom edit box. For example, if the original width is 10, you would replace it with **5**. You need only enter one value, because the Maintain Aspect Ratio option will automatically recalculate the other value.

5. Again study the image in the frame, moving it around to get the best possible placement.

6. Continue repeating steps 3 through 5 until the image is the right size, is cropped the way you want, and is positioned properly in the frame.

If you can't get the correct cropping by using the above steps, you may need to give up on maintaining the image aspect ratio. If this is the case, deselect the Maintain Aspect Ratio option. Then, repeat steps 3 through 5, except that each time you perform step 4 enter *both* a new vertical and horizontal dimension. As you go through this process, the image will become somewhat distorted. A good idea is to print out the page after several adjustments, just to make sure the distortion isn't getting out of hand.

If the image does become too distorted, you can either try to backtrack or you can start over by selecting the Original Size option. This restores the image to its original dimensions, and you can try again, perhaps being a little more cautious when adjusting the individual dimensions.

In the long run, you may need to compromise to find the best balance of cropping, sizing, and amount of distortion.

Letting the Program Do the Fitting

There's a simple way to have the program fit a graphic into a frame of specific dimensions. Select the frame, then select the option Frame/Graphics Scaling/Fit in Frame. The program then adjusts the dimensions of the graphic so that it is entirely visible within the frame. At the same time, the original aspect ratio of the graphic is maintained. Note that by using this option you give up control over the exact size of the picture, although you can perform limited cropping by selecting the graphic within the frame and then repositioning it.

Exact Cropping

The previous section described how to adjust an image to fit into a frame of specified dimensions. This isn't always the case, and many times you'll be able to be flexible about the relative frame dimensions. In that case, you can crop the image exactly the way you want, adjusting the frame dimensions accordingly. Here's how to proceed:

1. First set the size of the frame so that you can distinguish the various elements of the image. (Don't worry yet about the exact frame sizing.)

2. Double-click on the image in the frame.

3. Display the Graphics Scaling box (select Frame/Graphics Scaling), click on the Original Size option, and make sure that Maintain Aspect Ratio is turned on.

4. Reposition the image within the frame, so that the upper-left corner *of the part you want to keep* is next to the upper-left corner of the frame. In other words, the left and top parts of the image *that you don't want* are pushed outside the frame.

5. Deselect the image (click outside the frame), then select the frame itself (click once inside, so that the handles reappear, undimmed).

6. Using the mouse, adjust the lower and right edges of the frame so that the unwanted parts of the image on the bottom and right side are squeezed out of the frame.

The frame should now display just that part of the image you want. However, the frame size probably won't be correct, and that can now be adjusted.

7. Using the vertical ruler, measure the vertical dimension of the frame.

8. Calculate the ratio of the existing vertical dimension to the dimension you actually want. For example, if the frame is now 2 inches tall, but you want it to be 4 inches, the calculated ratio is then 2. *Remember this number!* (Ratio in this sense of the word is simply the result of dividing the desired measurement by the existing one.)

9. Using the vertical and horizontal rulers as guides, expand the frame size by using the bottom-right handle. For example, if the calculated ratio is

2, and the existing frame dimensions are 2 by 2.5, expand the frame so that its new dimensions are 4 by 5. (In other words, multiply the existing frame dimension by 2.)

10. Display the Graphics Scaling dialog box.

11. The Custom edit box on the right contains the present vertical dimension of the image. Multiply this number by the ratio you calculated above (2 in the example), then enter that number in the edit box on the right. For example, if the number in the box is 3.5 and your calculated ratio is 2, enter 7 in the box. Finally, click on OK.

12. When the edit screen reappears, double-click in the frame, then readjust the image so that just the part you want is visible.

Figure 11.3 illustrates the various stages of this process. Figure 11.3a shows the original image in the frame, with the Fit in Frame option selected. Figure 11.3b shows the image with Original Size selected and the image moved so that the left and top edges have been adjusted. Figure 11.3c shows the result after resizing both frame and the image.

The above example used the vertical dimension to resize the image and frame. This was for illustration only; the horizontal dimension could just as easily have been used. With the Maintain Aspect Ratio option selected, you can enter a number in either the vertical or horizontal edit box and the program will recalculate the other dimension.

If you're more comfortable working with percentages instead of absolute numbers, you can use the Percentage option rather than entering the image dimensions in step 11. For instance, in the above example the length ratio was 2:1, so you would click on the Percentage option in the Graphics Scaling box and then enter **200**. This would double the original dimensions of the image.

Automatic Resizing

You can use the Fit in Frame option to have the program help you resize an image within a frame. With this option selected, the visible part of an image will grow or shrink as you increase or decrease the frame dimensions. You can use this procedure with the Maintain Aspect Ratio option either on or off. The advantage of this method is that the image is automatically resized for you. However, this method suffers in that it offers only a limited amount of cropping.

Here's a simple exercise to illustrate how to use this feature:

1. Retrieve a graphic image into a frame.

2. Adjust the frame to the proper size.

Figure 11.3
(a) The original image and frame; (b) after the new top left corner of the image has been established; and (c) the resized frame and image

3. In the Graphics Scaling dialog box, select the Fit in Frame and Maintain Aspect Ratio options.

4. Double-click in the frame, then move the image to achieve the best position.

5. Reposition either the lower or left edge of the frame. The visible image will expand and contract in the same proportion as the frame, as long as the aspect ratio can be maintained. When the aspect ratio can no longer be maintained the image will stop changing size.

This method is fine for quick and dirty adjustments, but for detailed cropping avoid the Fit in Frame option.

Techniques for Working with Frames

Using the various frame options available to you, different types of interesting effects can be created to enhance your documents. For example, you can create a shadow box effect around a frame, helping to set it off from the rest of the page. You can also create special borders around frames, again to create an eye-catching impact.

Rotation and inversion are two techniques for creating special effects. Although Professional Write Plus is designed to rotate only graphics frames, with a little help from Windows you can also use these operations on text frames. You can rotate the contents of a frame from 0 to 360 degrees, using 1-degree increments. You can also invert the black and white colors of a frame, a technique that can produce interesting and unusual effects.

Using the Group option, you can attach a caption to a frame, so that whenever you manipulate the frame the caption goes along as well.

Adding a Caption to a Frame

You can add a caption to a frame, and as an added convenience you can attach the caption so that when you move the frame the caption moves as well. The trick is to place the caption in a frame of its own and then group the two frames together. (You may remember this from Chapter 10.) Figure 11.4 illustrates this situation, showing the two frames selected together.

Here are the steps for attaching a caption to a frame:

1. Directly below the frame containing the picture, create a new frame that's wide enough to hold the caption. Don't worry if your dimensions aren't perfect; you can resize this frame later on.

2. Create a small border around the new frame, perhaps 0.1 to 0.2 inch all around. This border will separate the caption from the graphic frame, and it will also create space between the caption and any surrounding text. If this border size isn't perfect, you can readjust it later.

Figure 11.4
A caption attached to a frame

The magnifying glass is a powerful tool

3. Unless you have a particular reason for doing otherwise, turn off the lines drawn around the new frame: In the Frame Layout box click on Lines & Color, then make sure that none of the options are selected in the box labeled "Around Frames".

4. Double-click in the new frame, then enter the caption text.

5. Select the caption as a block. Then using the Text menu, select a typeface and size for the caption. A size of between 9 and 12 points is usually about right.

6. Adjust the position of the caption, either by moving the block or changing the top border.

7. Select *both* the graphic and caption frames together by holding down the Shift key while selecting each frame.

8. Select Frame/Group Frames.

The two frames are now linked together, so that when you reposition either one the other is moved as well. Remember that if you delete either frame the other will also be deleted. However, if you do accidentally delete the frames, you can use the Undo option to recover, provided that you do so immediately after the deletion.

If you want to delete the caption but not the picture, you must first ungroup the frames by clicking in either one and then selecting Frame/Group Frames.

Creating Shadowed Frames

Shadow boxes to highlight frames have become the rage, now that everybody and his brother seems to have access to high-quality word processors or desktop publishing systems. As shown in Figure 11.5, a shadowed frame adds an extra dimension, making the frame really stand out. This effect is actually quite easy to create, taking only a few steps.

Figure 11.5
A shadow box adds a third dimension

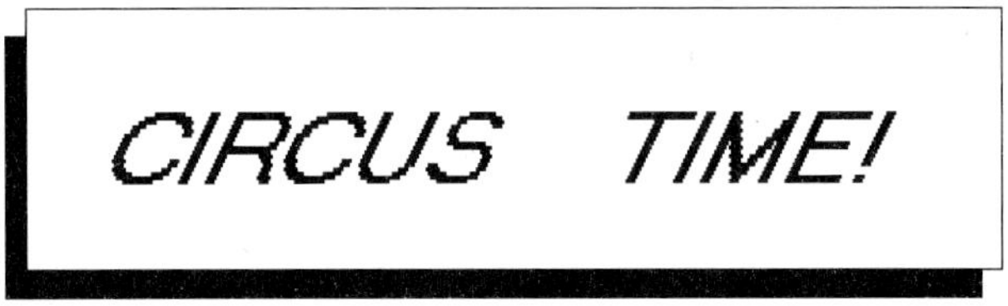

You can use the shadow box effect with any type of frame (text or graphics). Here are the steps (refer back to Chapter 10 for details of working with frames):

1. Select the frame for which you want to create a shadow box.

2. Make a copy of the frame: Select Edit/Copy, then select Edit/Paste. The new copy is pasted directly on top of the original.

3. Drag the new frame away from the original, so that you can select either one.

4. Select the *original* frame, then assign it a black background color (using the Frame Layout dialog box). This frame should now appear as a solid black box.

5. Select the *new* frame, make it opaque, and add a line drawn completely around the frame, using the Outside option for the line position.

6. Reposition the new frame back over the old one, so that it looks like Figure 11.5.

7. Select both frames at the same time (by holding down the Shift key as you select them), then click on Frame/Group Frames.

The frame plus its shadow are now linked together, so that when you move one the other will also be moved. Moreover, if you delete either one, both will be deleted.

This technique works equally well for graphics and text frames. It also works whether or not the original frame has any borders, as long as you position the line on the outer edge of the frame (step 5 above).

Instead of using a black background for the shadow frame, you can try using some of the other colors and patterns. Different printers handle the various tones in different ways, so you'll have to experiment with your own printer.

Creating Thick Border Lines

If the line options offered in the Frame Layout dialog box aren't heavy enough for your purpose, you can create an extra-heavy line around a frame by using a variation on the theme described above. Figure 11.6 shows an example of this. Here are the steps to create this effect:

Figure 11.6
A heavy line around the border

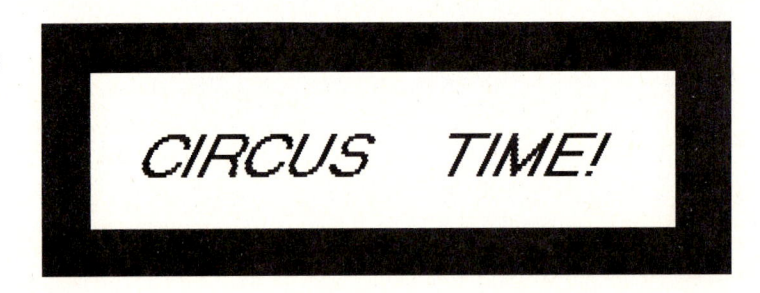

![CIRCUS TIME!]

1. Create the frame and contents——either text or graphics.

2. Using the Frame Layout dialog box, assign this frame to be opaque, and draw a thin line entirely around it. This line will help you with alignment in the following steps.

3. Create a new frame that's somewhat larger than the original one, and assign it a black background color.

4. Position the new frame over the old one, then select the Frame/Send to Back option to place the new frame behind the original one.

5. Resize the black frame so that the border line is the thickness you want.

As with shadow frames, you can try using different background colors and patterns for the larger frame. If your printer can handle them, you may be able to create some interesting effects.

Using this technique, you can create more complex effects by overlaying several frames, as shown in Figure 11.7.

Figure 11.7
Overlaying several frames can generate an unusual effect.

> CIRCUS TIME!

Rotating and Inverting Graphics Frames

When you invert a graphics frame, all the black is transformed to white, and vice versa. You can also rotate a graphics frame in 1-degree increments. These operations are reserved for graphics frames, but with a little ingenuity you can also use them for text frames. Figure 11.8 shows an image before and after a 90 degree rotation; and Figure 11.9 shows an image and its inversion.

Due to software limitations, not all types of graphics can be rotated or inverted. Generally, these operations can be applied only to bitmapped images, which encompass the following types of imported graphics:

- PC Paintbrush (.PCX)
- Tagged image format (.TIF)
- Bitmap images on the Windows clipboard
- First Publisher ClipArt (.ART)
- Hewlett-Packard Printer Command Language (.PCL)
- MacPaint (.MAC)

To rotate a graphic image in a frame, use the following steps:

1. Select the frame.
2. Select Frame/Graphics Scaling.
3. When the Graphics Scaling dialog box appears, click in the edit box labeled "Rotate Image", then enter the amount of rotation you want, in degrees.
4. Click on OK. After a short pause the rotated image will reappear in the frame.

Figure 11.8
(a) An image before and (b) after being rotated 90 degrees

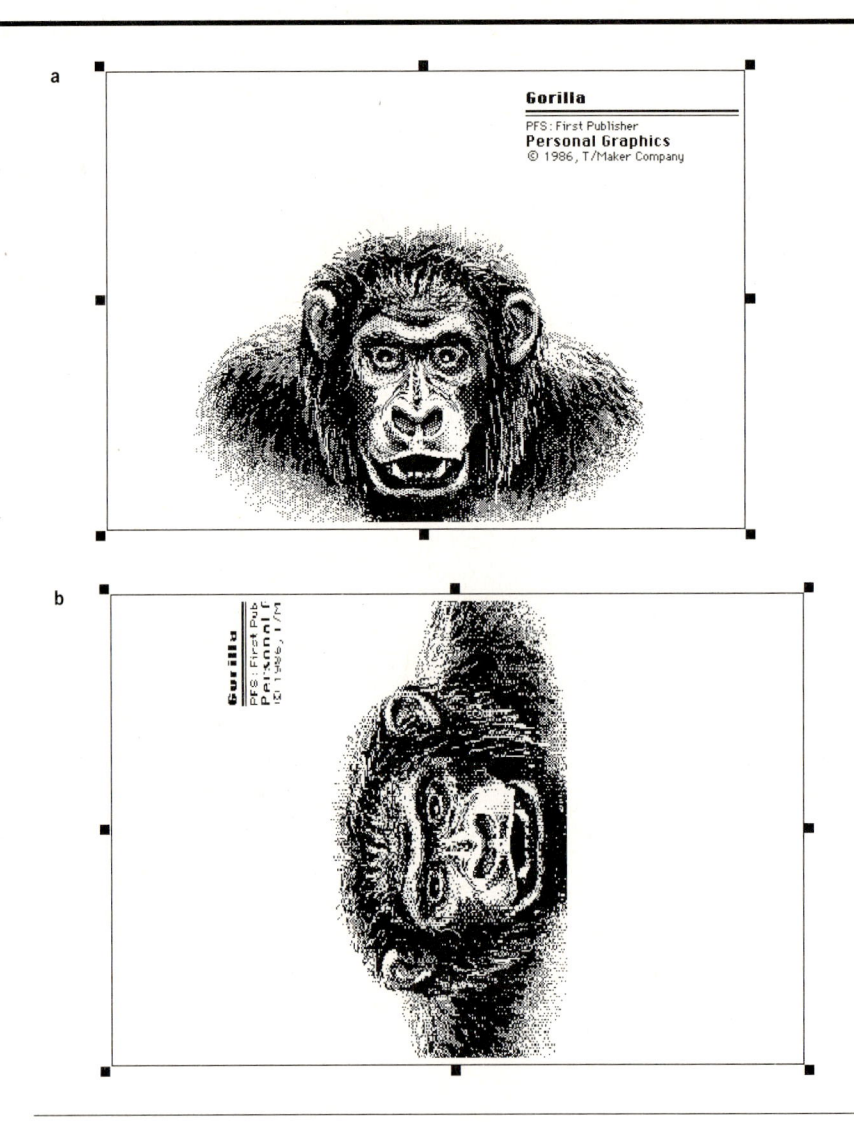

A rotated image often will suffer from some degree of distortion, as you can see in Figure 11.8. You can compensate for this by turning off the Maintain Aspect Ratio option and then adjusting one or both of the image dimensions. However, remember that whenever you change the dimension of an image there's some loss in clarity.

To invert an image, follow steps 1 and 2 above, click on Invert Image, then click on OK. There's generally no distortion or loss of clarity when an image is inverted.

Figure 11.9
The original image (a) and the image after inversion (b)

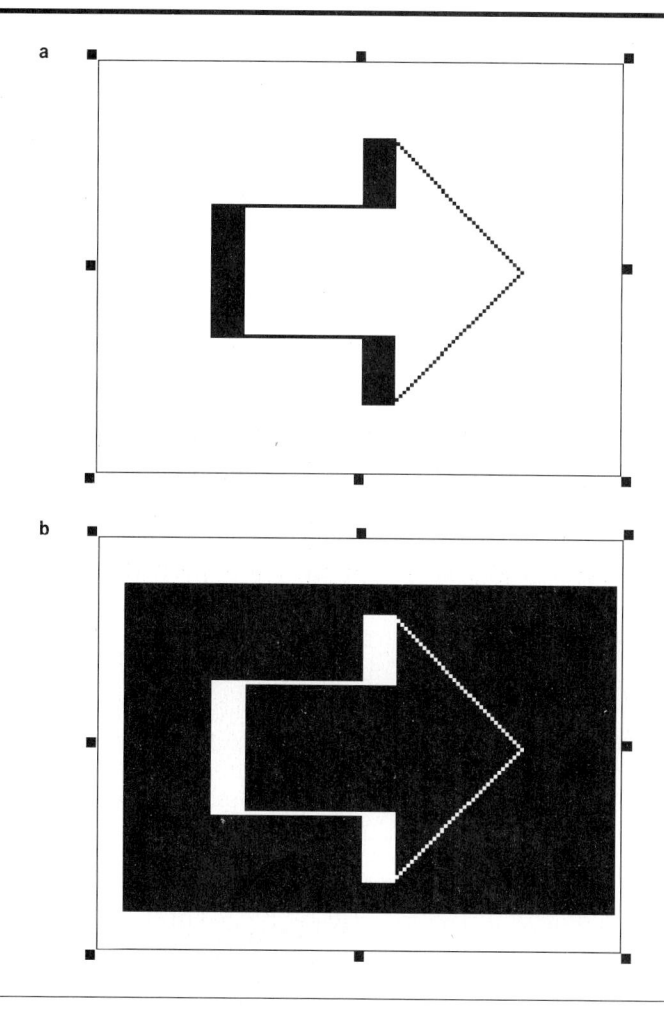

WARNING! *These operations can make a total mess out of the contents of your frame, and you can't undo a rotation or inversion. Before attempting either rotating or inverting save a copy of your document.*

Rotating and Inverting Text

Professional Write Plus does not support rotation or inversion of text frames. However, by making use of the Windows clipboard you can effect these operations by converting a text block into the equivalent graphics frame. To do this, you begin by taking a "snapshot" of your screen and copying it to the Windows clipboard. Then you create a new frame and paste the snapshot back into it. This is now a graphics frame, which can be cropped, rotated, and inverted.

To get some practice performing this type of operation, follow these steps:

1. On a blank screen, enter some text. Use the largest font that will fit on the screen, perhaps 24 or 36 points (see Figure 11.10a).

2. Press Alt-PrtSc. This transfers a bitmapped image of the *entire screen* to the Windows clipboard.

3. Delete the text from the screen, then create a new frame.

4. With the frame selected, click on Edit/Paste, and an image of your entire screen will appear in the new frame (Figure 11.10b).

5. Crop the image in the new frame, so that only the original text is displayed (as shown in Figure 11.10c).

This new frame now contains the contents of the original frame, but in bitmapped graphic form. That is, as far as Professional Write Plus is concerned it's a genuine graphic frame. You can invert the contents of this frame, or rotate it by any desired amount. Figure 11.11 shows the frame in Figure 11.10c rotated by 90 degrees and inverted.

This technique gives you the ability to create all kinds of interesting effects, but you pay a price (as usual, there's no free lunch). When you print the graphics frame resulting from the conversion to the Windows clipboard format, you may notice a substantial loss in resolution, particularly for larger letters. Here's why: When you print ordinary text, the printer uses the highest possible resolution, which is the result of using either internally generated fonts or high-quality bitmapped fonts.

On the other hand, when you output text in graphics form, the printer is printing a bitmap corresponding to the entire text frame. This involves a translation from the screen bitmap to one that can be handled by the printer, and this process generates text that's bound to be miles away from the high-quality text the printer is capable of producing. To minimize this effect, use the largest possible font size when generating the original text and experiment to find the best-looking screen font, since that's what will be reproduced.

Summary

Graphic images can add the extra touch that transforms an ordinary document into one that catches the eye. With a little practice, you'll find that retrieving, resizing, and cropping graphics requires very little effort, and the end result is well worth the little time that is involved.

Summary

Figure 11.10
(a) The original text on the screen; (b) the new frame with an image of the entire screen; and (c) the new frame cropped to contain just the contents of the original frame

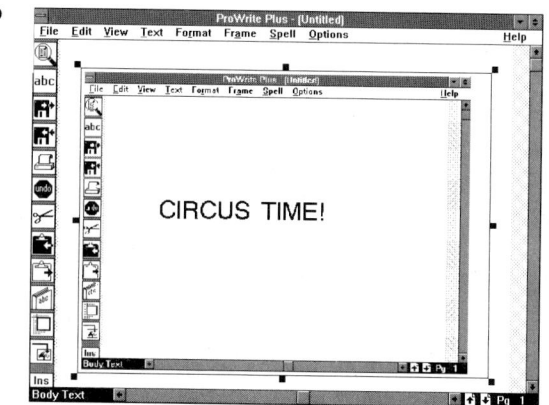

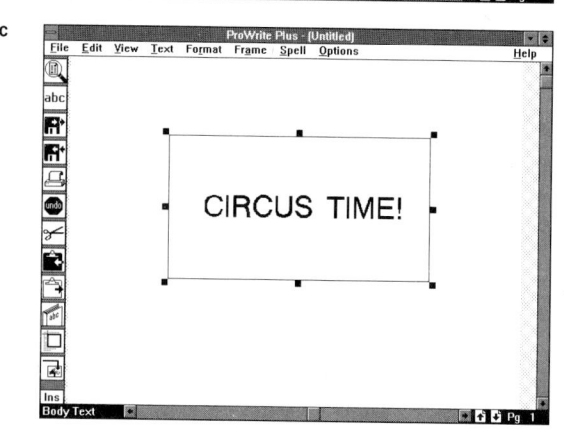

Figure 11.11
The inverted contents of the frame in Figure 11.10c (a) and the same contents rotated by 90 degrees

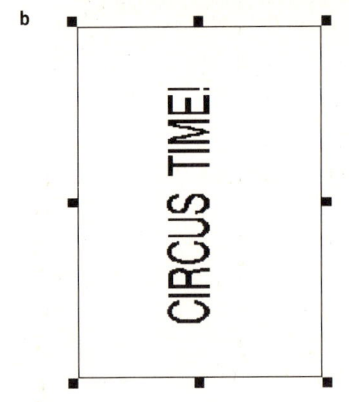

a

CIRCUS TIME!

b

CIRCUS TIME!

    A small library of graphic images can be an important resource. Many packages of clip art are commercially available, some of which are very reasonably priced. In addition, drawing programs such as Corel Draw offer you the tools to create your own art images. With a little artistic ability, you can use this type of program to create a graphic image for a particular need. You can then retrieve the image into a Professional Write Plus document, and also save the image for future use.

    Once you have gotten into the habit of using graphics as part of your documents, you'll wonder how you got along with simple text-oriented word processing.

CHAPTER

12

Grammar Checking and Electronic Mail

Checking Your Grammar

Using Electronic Mail

TWO HIGHLY SOPHISTICATED FEATURES NOT USUALLY ASSOCIATED WITH word processors are grammar checking and electronic mail or *e-mail*. Professional Write Plus includes both of these features, which are very definitely frosting on the word processing cake.

Professional Write Plus contains a special version of the popular program Grammatik, which you can use to check the grammar of any document. The grammar checking is impressively thorough, using thousands of built-in rules to check for correct sentence structure and punctuation. For example, it will tell you if a sentence contains two verbs whose tenses don't agree. It will also check for more subtle types of problems. For example, it will inform you if it thinks that your writing is too long-winded, or if you're using too many clichés.

Using the grammar checker can be a double-edged sword. Though efficient, its checks can be perhaps too thorough—you may be discouraged when you find out how many things the grammar checker finds wrong with your writing. Fortunately, you can temper the checker's diligence by adjusting it to ignore certain types of situations. For example, if you happen to like clichés, you can have them ignored during proofreading.

This version of Grammatik can proofread only documents in Professional Write Plus format. If a document is in ASCII or some other word processing format, you must first import it and save it as a Professional Write Plus document. (For more information about how the grammar checker works, refer to *Grammatik Windows for Professional Write Plus User's Guide*.)

If your computer is part of a system that operates a Novell/Action Technologies Message Handling Service (MHS), you can use Professional Write Plus to transmit electronic messages to other users on the system. You can also use your MHS to transmit messages to users of other MHS systems. As part of this mail system, an electronic address book is provided to help you keep track of remote users with whom you correspond.

Checking Your Grammar

The grammar checker is actually a separate program that's called up by Professional Write Plus. When you invoke the grammar checker, Professional Write Plus is unloaded from the computer's memory. Then, when you exit from the grammar checker, Professional Write Plus is loaded back into memory.

To see how to use the grammar checker you'll use a sample document that comes with the Professional Write Plus software. The name of this document is GRAMTOUR.PWP; it is initially stored in the PWPLUS\DOCS directory. (If you don't have access to this document, use one of your own to follow along in this section.)

Getting Started

To check the grammar of a document, first retrieve it into Professional Write Plus. Then, select Spell/Grammar. If you've made any changes to the document since retrieving it, the program automatically saves the document to disk. Then Professional Write Plus is unloaded from memory and the grammar checker is loaded.

After a few seconds pause the proofreading begins. As soon as the grammar checker encounters what it considers to be a grammar problem (referred to here as *problem,* for short), it pauses, displaying a screen like that shown in Figure 12.1. This is the screen you'll see during most of a proofreading session, so before going on let's explore its various parts.

Figure 12.1
The proofreading screen of the grammar checker

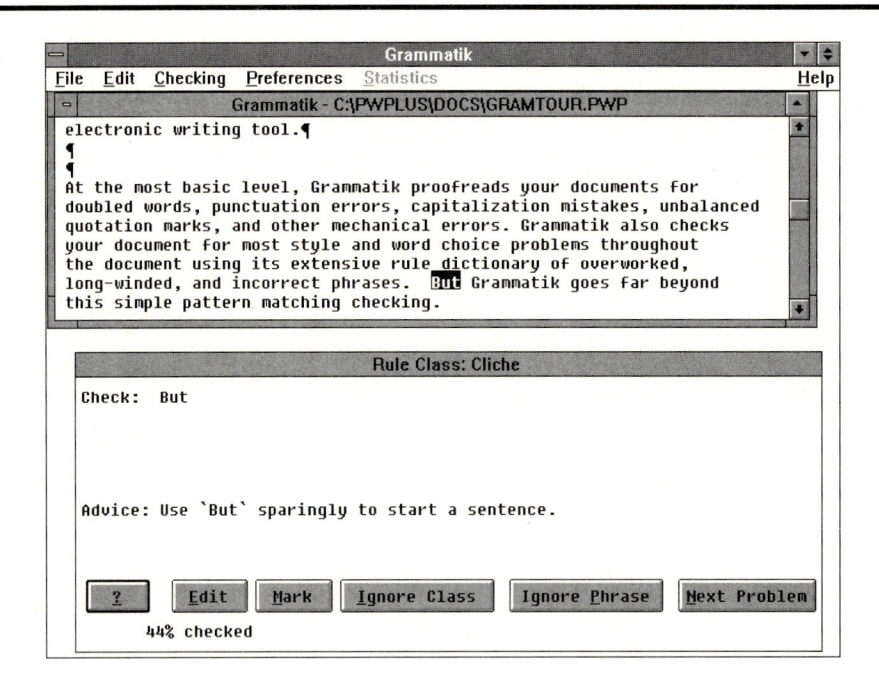

Menu Bar This is located at the top of the screen. The menus contain options for saving files, customizing the grammar checker to your preferences, and displaying various statistics.

Edit Window This is the top window on the screen. It displays the document text in the vicinity of the most recent problem, which is highlighted. For example, in Figure 12.1 the word "But" is highlighted. When a problem is encountered, you can sometimes fix it up by clicking in this window and then editing the text, using the standard editing keys.

Problem Window   This is the window in the lower part of the screen. It describes the nature of the current problem. For example, in Figure 12.1 the window contains the advice "Use 'But' sparingly to start a sentence."

Rule Class   This is the line in the middle of the screen (at the top of the problem window). It shows the general type of rule that has been violated by the current problem. For instance, in Figure 12.1 the rule class displayed is "Cliche", meaning that the grammar checker considers the current use of the word *but* a cliché.

Command Buttons   These six Windows-style buttons are located at the bottom of the screen. You use these buttons to tell the grammar checker how to deal with each problem it encounters in your document.

Dealing with a Grammar Problem

When the program encounters a grammar problem, you can deal with it in several different ways. Some of your options can be exercised by using the command buttons at the bottom of the screen. Other options are accessed from the menus in the menu bar. Your command button options are as follows:

Note. You can neither delete an existing hard return nor enter a new one during a grammar check.

- To get on-line help about the current rule class you've apparently violated, click on the ? command button. For example, if you click on this button for the situation shown in Figure 12.1, the help screen shown in Figure 12.2 will appear. You can use the vertical scroll bar to view the entire text for this topic. To exit from the help screen, click on Cancel. To explore other parts of the help system, use the Prev and Next options.

- To edit the document in order to eliminate the current problem, click on the Edit button or click anywhere in the edit window. Then make whatever changes are needed to the text. You can use the standard editing keys, as well as the Cut and Paste options on the Edit menu. Alternatively, you can skip editing for the time being and do it later in Professional Write Plus.

- To insert a mark (the # character) in the text at the place where the problem occurs, click on Mark. In addition to the mark, advice about the problem is also inserted in the text, unless you turn off the Include Advice When Marking option (see "Other Options," later in the chapter). After inserting the mark, the program then searches for the next problem in the document.

Figure 12.2
A help screen describing clichés

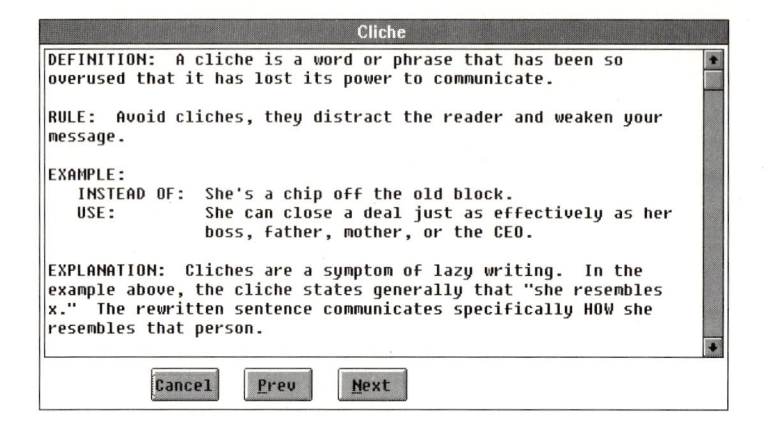

```
┌─────────────────────────── Cliche ───────────────────────────┐
│ DEFINITION:  A cliche is a word or phrase that has been so   │
│ overused that it has lost its power to communicate.          │
│                                                              │
│ RULE:  Avoid cliches, they distract the reader and weaken your│
│ message.                                                     │
│                                                              │
│ EXAMPLE:                                                     │
│    INSTEAD OF:  She's a chip off the old block.              │
│    USE:         She can close a deal just as effectively as her│
│                 boss, father, mother, or the CEO.            │
│                                                              │
│ EXPLANATION:  Cliches are a symptom of lazy writing.  In the │
│ example above, the cliche states generally that "she resembles│
│ x."  The rewritten sentence communicates specifically HOW she│
│ resembles that person.                                       │
│                                                              │
│           [Cancel]    [Prev]    [Next]                       │
└──────────────────────────────────────────────────────────────┘
```

- To ignore the current error for the remainder of the proofreading for this document, click on Ignore Phrase. Clicking on this option also causes the program to search for the next problem.

- To ignore the rule class that's currently displayed, Click on Ignore Class. When you select this option, the program will ignore any rule falling in this class for the remainder of the document proofreading. In addition, the program will immediately search for the next grammar problem.

- To search for the next problem in the document, click on Next Problem. Note that you won't need this option when you click on Mark, Ignore Class, or Ignore Phrase.

Going On

After you deal with the current problem, as described in the preceding section, the program then searches for the next problem. As each problem is encountered, it's displayed on the screen, and you can then deal with it using any of the options discussed above.

If you continue scanning the GRAMTOUR.PWP file, you'll eventually encounter the problem shown in Figure 12.3. The problem is the phrase "your own", which the program considers redundant.

Here, a new option for dealing with certain kinds of problems is shown: the Replace feature, located on the right side of the problem window. This option offers you possible replacements for the offending text. In this example the only alternative found by the program is the word *your*, which appears within the Replace box. To use this option, you can do either of the following:

- Make a selection in the Replace box, then click on Replace. The offending phrase is replaced by your selection.

Figure 12.3
The Replace feature

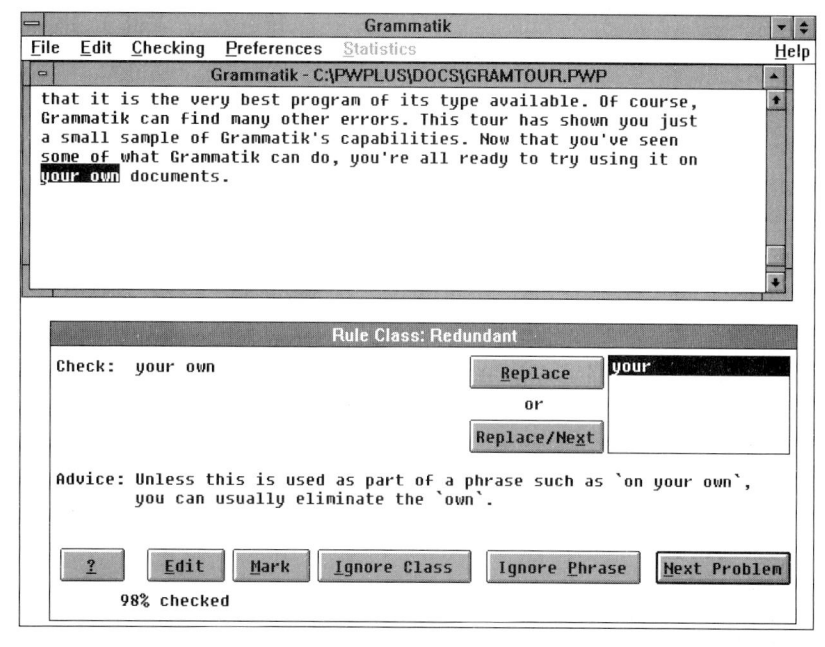

- Make a selection in the Replace box, then click on Replace/Next. The phrase in the text is replaced with your selection, and the program then scans the text for the next problem.

Interrupting the Proofreading

If you find that the proofreading is taking too long or isn't useful to you, you can terminate the process at any time:

1. Select File/Close.

2. When the next screen appears (see below), click on Yes if you want to save any changes made to the document during the proofreading. If you don't want to save the changes, click on No.

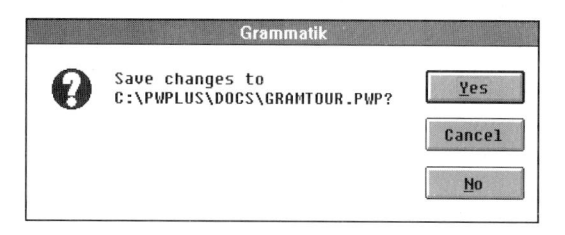

3. If you want to abort the cancellation and continue proofreading, click on Cancel.

Finishing Up

When the interactive grammar checking session has finished, the program gives you a chance to save the document—including any changes you've made—to the original file. The dialog box is shown in Figure 12.4.

Figure 12.4
Saving the checked file

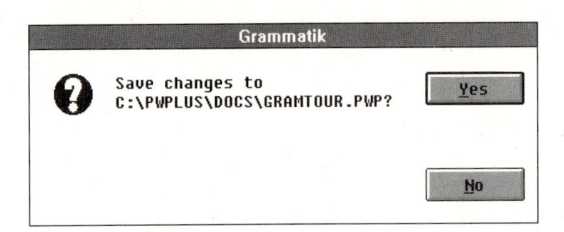

If you click on Yes, the file and its changes will overwrite the existing document. However, the original document (without any changes) is saved to a file with the same name, but with the extension .GBK. For example, a copy of the file MYWORK.PWP would be saved to MYWORK.GBK.

After saving your file, the program displays a summary of readability statistics, as shown in Figure 12.5.

After browsing through these numbers, you can erase the display from the screen by double-clicking on the control box in the upper-left corner of the display. Make sure you click on the control box for the document summary—not the control box for Grammatik. The screen shown in Figure 12.6 is then displayed. This is the grammar checker's main information screen. Among other things, it shows the name of the original file, the name of the file to which the proofread version has been stored, and the name of the backup of the original file.

If you choose not to save your file (Figure 12.4), the screen shown in Figure 12.6 is still displayed, even though in this case the screen is misleading because it implies that your file has been saved, whereas in fact it has not.

Note that in order to save your edits you must save the file. If you do not, the changes you made are lost.

Exiting Back to Professional Write Plus

When you're finished proofreading a document, you can exit from the grammar checker back to Professional Write Plus by selecting File/Exit. When the normal edit screen appears, the document that you proofread will reappear—

Checking Your Grammar

Figure 12.5
The readability statistics for a proofread document

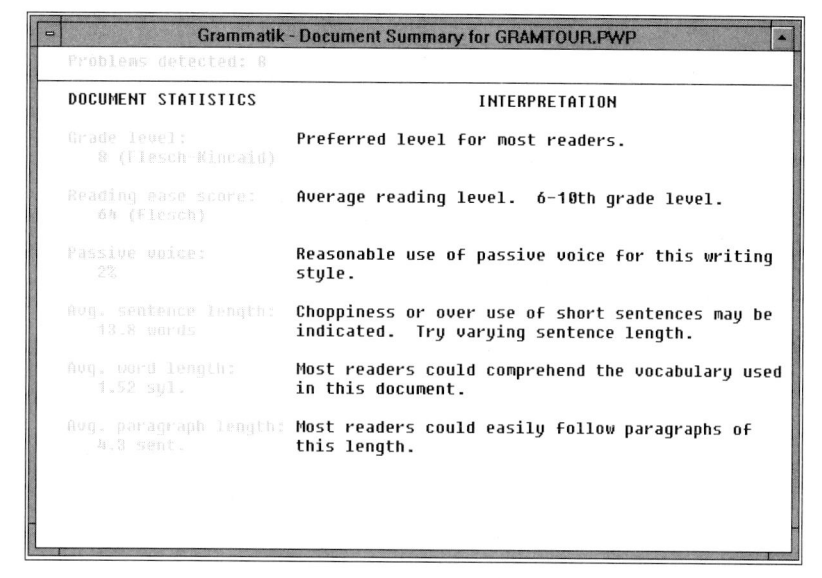

```
  Grammatik - Document Summary for GRAMTOUR.PWP
Problems detected: 8

DOCUMENT STATISTICS              INTERPRETATION

Grade level:              Preferred level for most readers.
  8 (Flesch-Kincaid)

Reading ease score:       Average reading level.  6-10th grade level.
  64 (Flesch)

Passive voice:            Reasonable use of passive voice for this writing
  2%                      style.

Avg. sentence length:     Choppiness or over use of short sentences may be
  13.8 words              indicated.  Try varying sentence length.

Avg. word length:         Most readers could comprehend the vocabulary used
  1.52 syl.               in this document.

Avg. paragraph length:    Most readers could easily follow paragraphs of
  4.3 sent.               this length.
```

Figure 12.6
Information about the proofreading process

```
                           Grammatik
File   Edit   Checking   Preferences   Statistics                  Help

                  PROFESSIONAL WRITE PLUS EDITION

        Word Processor:    Professional Write Plus

        Writing style:     Custom

        Preferences:       Standard Preferences



        File to Proofread: GRAMTOUR.PWP

        File Saved As:     GRAMTOUR.PWP

        Backup File:       GRAMTOUR.gbk
```

337

including any changes, marks, and advice added during the proofreading (assuming you saved the changes).

If you didn't make any editing changes to the document while checking the grammar, you can do so from within Professional Write Plus by using these marks and advice. Scan for each occurrence of the string "[#" (the marks and comments are automatically enclosed in brackets, although a mark by itself is not), and then make the necessary changes to the text. After each change, you can delete the brackets, marks, and accompanying advice.

If your document is long, however, this can be a *very* tedious process. If you decide you don't want to fix all the errors, you can retrieve the backup document generated by the grammar checker, which is a copy of your original document—the version before the addition of any changes made during proofreading.

Retrieving the Unchanged Document

If you save the changes you've made to a document during grammer checking, a copy of the original document is saved to another file with the .GBK extension. To retrieve .this document into Professional Write Plus at a later time, you must first rename it with the .PWP extension. You can then use the File/Open option to retrieve and work with the file. Probably the easiest way to rename the file is by using Professional Write Plus's File Manager (the File/File Manager option). Or you can temporarily exit to DOS from Windows and then use the DOS RENAME command.

Other Methods of Proofreading

The proofreading method described above is called *full interactive* because it involves your active participation for each grammar problem the program encounters. For long documents this could be extremely tiresome since hundreds or perhaps thousands of problems might be found.

In this type of situation you may prefer to let the program automatically scan the document, inserting marks and comments wherever problems are found. Then you can later examine the document at your leisure, making whatever corrections you feel are necessary.

You can have the grammar checker automatically proofread a document in three different ways:

- Inserting a mark (#) wherever a grammar problem is encountered

- Inserting both a mark and a short piece of advice at each encountered problem

- Scanning the document without inserting anything

In all three cases, the program will finish by displaying a screen of readability statistics, like the one shown in Figure 12.5.

To use any of these three proofreading methods, begin as described earlier: Retrieve the document to be checked, then select Spell/Grammar. When the main screen appears (Figure 12.1), pull down the Checking menu and then choose one of the following:

Stop, Mark Rest of Document   If you select this option, the program will automatically check the document, placing a mark (the # character) wherever a grammar problem is found.

Stop, Mark Rest of Document with Advice   The program will automatically check the document, inserting both a mark (#) and a piece of useful advice where each error is encountered.

Stop, Show Statistics   The document will be scanned for errors, but no marks or advice is inserted in the text. Only the screen of statistics (Figure 12.5) is displayed.

When you select either of the first two options, the document is automatically saved when the grammar checking finishes. This save is to the file containing the original document. However, a backup of the original is saved to a file with the same name but with the extension .GBK. For the last option, no save is needed since the file isn't changed.

Protecting Your Documents

Checking your documents for grammar is potentially dangerous because the grammar checker may insert a great deal of advice into the document. If a document is long, and if you use any of the options that insert marks or advice into the document, you could wind up with a document with hundreds or even thousands of suggested changes.

Normally, the backup copy generated during proofreading is adequate protection against losing the original document. However, if you proofread the same document twice, your original document will be lost because the second time around the original backup will be replaced by the document that was proofread the first time.

To guard against losing a large document, before proofreading save it to a file with a different name, or to a file with the same name but on a different directory.

Strategies for Grammar Checking

There are two basic strategies you can use for proofreading documents:

- Using interactive proofreading, make whatever changes you need as each problem is found using the Edit option. Do not insert any marks or advice into the document.

- Use one of the program's options for automatically scanning the document, inserting either just marks or advice and marks wherever problems are found. Then later use Professional Write to make the necessary corrections.

The first option is fine for short documents, but the second may often be more suitable for longer ones. If you use the second option, there are two different ways in which you can proceed:

- Using Professional Write Plus, go through the document and correct each error, deleting the accompanying mark and advice.

- Print a rough draft of the proofread document. Then restore the original copy of the document from the backup made by the grammar checker. Scan through the printed draft, making only those changes you feel are appropriate on the original.

Except for fairly small documents, you'll probably want to use the second option or a variation on it. For example, suppose you proofread the document stored in the file WORK.PWP. After proofreading, this file will contain any marks, advice, and edits you make. The original document will be stored in the file WORK.GBK, in the same directory as the original file.

To restore the original file, first rename the proofread file. For example, you could rename WORK.PWP to WORK1.PWP. Then, rename the backup file to its original file name—in this example, WORK.GBK becomes WORK.PWP.

Proofreading Other Documents

The previous section described how to use the grammar checker to proofread the document you're currently working with in Professional Write Plus. However, while you have the grammar checker loaded you can also check the grammar of other documents in Professional Write Plus format. Select the file to be checked, then use either the interactive or automatic proofreading mode.

By default, the directory used for selecting documents is the directory in use by Professional Write Plus when you called the grammar checker. You can select another directory as the default as follows.

1. Select Preferences/Document Path. (Note that this option is not available while you're checking the grammar of a document.)

2. When the dialog box appears (see Figure 12.7) enter the full path, including the name of the disk drive and directory.

Figure 12.7
Select the default document path

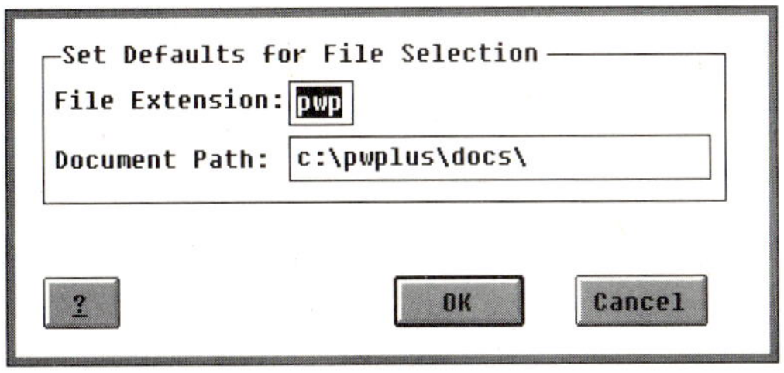

```
─Set Defaults for File Selection──────
File Extension: [pwp]
Document Path:  [c:\pwplus\docs\            ]

  [?]                    [ OK ]   [Cancel]
```

3. Click on OK to finish.

Note that even if a file you want to proofread has an extension different from .PWP, it must still be in standard Professional Write Plus format, or the grammar checker won't be able to proofread it.

To select a different file for proofreading, select File/Open, then enter the full name of the file, including the disk drive and directory. Or you can use the list box to select the correct disk drive and directory. Then highlight the name of the file you want to check and click on OK.

When you use either of these methods to select a document for proofreading, you can save the changes to a different file, instead of overwriting the original file: After you open the file and before you begin proofreading, select File/Save As, and then enter the name of the new file to be used for holding the proofread document. In this case the original file will remain unchanged.

Note that in this case there is no .GBK file associated with the file you've checked. Moreover, you can't use the Save As option after a file has been checked.

Displaying Statistical Output

The grammar checker has many different ways of analyzing the results of a proofreading session. You can view these various analyses by making the appropriate selections from the Statistics menu. Note that these options become available only after you have finished proofreading a document.

A detailed description of each type of analysis is beyond the scope of this book. However, this section outlines the various displays available. After proofreading a document, pull down the Statistics menu. Its options are as follows.

Document Summary This is the same screen that appears at the end of each proofreading session, as shown in Figure 12.5. It displays various statistics relating to the readability of a document, including a measure of its reading level.

Document Statistics This screen displays various statistics relating to the document, including three different types of readability scores. Some of this information is also displayed in the Document Summary.

Comparison Charts This screen displays various attributes of your document in comparison to those of three standard texts. By default, these are the Gettysburg Address, a short story by Ernest Hemingway, and a typical life insurance policy. You can change these defaults to any other three documents of your choice. (See the following section for details.)

You can scroll through the various charts by clicking on Previous and Next at the top of the displays.

Document Summary, Document Statistics, and Comparison Charts are true Windows screens. You can move between them either with the mouse or by pressing Alt-F6. You can also move, resize, and maximize any of them. You can display two or three at the same time by making selections from the Statistics menu. When you first display two at the same time, one will hide the other. However, by resizing them you can make parts of each visible at the same time. To erase one of these windows from the screen, select the appropriate Hide option on the Statistics menu or double-click on the control box of that window.

To print a copy of any chart displayed on the screen, select the corresponding Print option on the File menu. For example, if the Comparison Charts are displayed, select File/Print Chart. You can also save a copy of the document statistics to a separate file. Select Save Statistics in File from the Statistics menu, then enter the full name of the new file. The program will automatically add the .SUM extension to the file name you choose. This file is in ASCII format, and you can later retrieve it as an ASCII file into Professional Write Plus.

Customizing the Comparison Charts

The comparison charts use three standard works, stored as a permanent part of the program, to contrast with the document you're checking. You can replace one or more of these with your own special documents to use as the bases of comparison. Here's how:

1. Proofread the document you plan to use as a new comparison document. (Please reread the last sentence carefully.)

2. Select Statistics/Customize Charts, and the screen shown in Figure 12.8 will appear.

Figure 12.8
Select the standard comparison work you want to replace

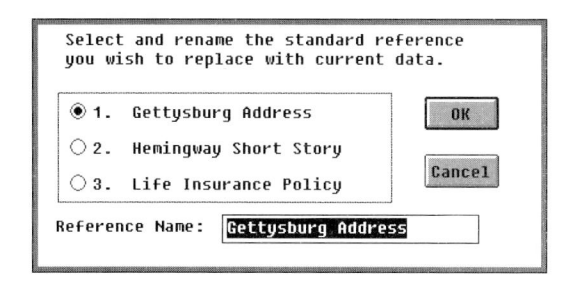

```
Select and rename the standard reference
you wish to replace with current data.

● 1.  Gettysburg Address           [ OK ]
○ 2.  Hemingway Short Story
○ 3.  Life Insurance Policy        [ Cancel ]

Reference Name: [Gettysburg Address]
```

3. Click on the standard reference you want replaced.

4. In the edit box labeled "Reference Name", enter the name you want associated with the new document, then click on OK.

The document you proofread (step 1) becomes one of the new standard references. The name you enter in step 4 will be used to refer to that document.

You can save your customizing for use in later proofreading sessions. For details, see "Saving Your Customizations" in this chapter.

To restore the original comparison works at some time later, select Statistics/Restore Default Comparison. The originals will be restored the next time you start the grammar checker.

Customizing the Grammar Checker

When proofreading your documents, the grammar checker makes use of a large number of rules. In using these rules, the checker also considers the following:

- The writing style being used

- A set of options describing those situations to be considered and those to be ignored

- Which general classes of rules are to be used and which are to be ignored

- Which rule dictionaries are to be used

When you first start using the grammar checker, a set of defaults are used for controlling the proofreading. For example, all of the built-in rule dictionaries are used. However, you can change many of these defaults to customize the proofreading so that it is tailored to your particular writing style and needs. For example, you would want to treat your business correspondence differently from your fiction masterpieces. At best, however, this customizing process is only approximate, because of the complexity of proofreading and the difficulty of pigeonholing an individual style.

You can save the custom settings you choose so that they can be used in future proofreading sessions. You can even save different groups of custom settings. For example, you might want to create one group for your business documents and another for freelance nonfiction writing.

Selecting the Rule Dictionaries

The multitude of rules used by the grammar checker are categorized into four different dictionaries: Standard Rules, Strict Rules, Business Rules, and Commonly Confused Words. By default, all four dictionaries are used, but you can deselect any that you don't want, depending on the writing style you use in a particular document. To choose the dictionaries you want to be used, select Preferences/Rule Dictionaries, then make your selection in the dialog box shown in Figure 12.9.

Figure 12.9
Select the rule dictionaries to be used

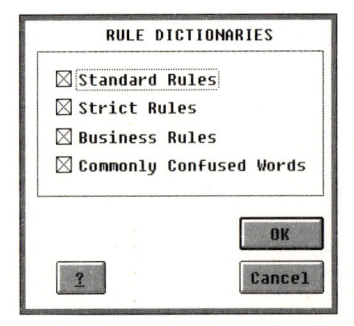

```
RULE DICTIONARIES
☒ Standard Rules
☒ Strict Rules
☒ Business Rules
☒ Commonly Confused Words
                    [ OK ]
  [ ? ]             [ Cancel ]
```

For documents with a formal tone, such as business correspondence, select all four dictionaries. For documents with an informal flavor, use only the Standard Rules and Commonly Confused Words dictionaries.

Instead of choosing the dictionaries directly, you can select the writing style you want (see "Setting the Writing Style," below). The grammar checker will then automatically select the dictionaries best suited to that style.

Selecting the Rule Classes

The grammar rules encompassed in the checker's four dictionaries are divided into 42 *rule classes*. You can select which of these classes to use, depending on the style of writing you're using.

To select the classes you want, choose Preferences/Rule Classes. The display that appears (see Figure 12.10) has three different screens for Grammatical, Mechanical, and Style rule classes.

The rules in the Grammatical class deal with the proper use of the different parts of speech, sentence structure, homonyms, and possessives. The

Mechanical rules are concerned with correct punctuation, capitalization, double words, and spelling. The Style rules deal with more subjective areas such as sentence length, split infinitives, passive versus active voice, and so on.

Figure 12.10
Select the rule classes to be used

```
                    RULE CLASSES
         ● Grammatical   ○ Mechanical   ○ Style
                 Grammatical Rule Class
    ☒ Relative pronoun        ☒ Adverb
    ☒ Infinitive              ☒ Number agreement
    ☒ Incomplete sentence     ☒ Verb agreement
    ☒ Possessive form         ☒ Article
    ☒ Homonyms                ☒ Comparative
    ☒ Pronoun                 ☒ Preposition
    ☒ Double negative         ☒ Incorrect verb form

         [ ? ]              [ OK ]    [ Cancel ]
```

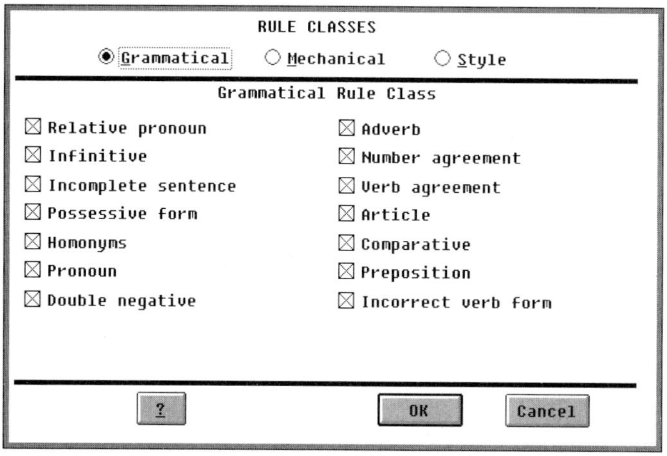

To select each of the three groups of rules, click on the corresponding button at the top of the Rule Classes screen. Then, select which individual rule classes you want turned on or off.

To find out about the meaning of a particular rule, click on ?, and then click on the rule. A help screen will appear, describing how the grammar checker uses the rule.

Instead of directly choosing the rule classes to be used, you can select the writing style you want (see "Setting the Writing Style," below). The grammar checker will then automatically select the rule classes that match that style.

Setting the Writing Style

Instead of selecting the rule classes and rule dictionaries individually, you can choose from five different writing styles. The grammar checker will then select the rule classes and dictionaries that best match that style. Choosing a writing style doesn't offer the fine control that's available when selecting from among the 42 rule classes, but on the other hand it's a good deal easier.

To choose a writing style, select Preferences/Writing Styles. When the dialog box appears (see Figure 12.11), make your selection from the choices that follow.

Figure 12.11
Select the style appropriate to your writing

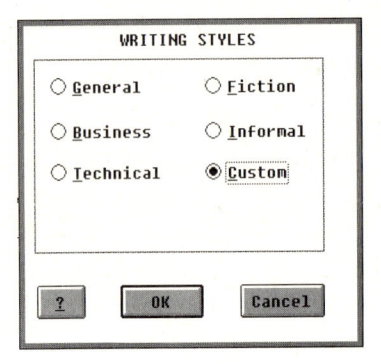

General If your documents don't fall into any of the other categories (below), use the General writing style. It uses all the rule dictionaries, as well as all the rule classes.

Business Select this style for business correspondence, reports, or any other documents that require a degree of formality. When you select this style, all the rule dictionaries and rule classes are used.

Technical This is also a formal writing style, suitable for manuals, technical papers, and other similar documents. This style uses all of the rule dictionaries except Business Rules.

Fiction When you select this style, all the rule dictionaries except Business Rules are used. However, the grammar checker turns off many of the rule classes, allowing a good deal of license in sentence structure, grammar, and so on.

Informal This style imposes the fewest restrictions on your writing. Only the Standard and Commonly Confused Words dictionaries are used. Furthermore, a great many of the rule classes are turned off. For example, the grammar checker allows you unlimited license in using clichés and jargon.

Custom This option is automatically selected when you make individual choices for rule classes and rule dictionaries.

Other Options

In addition to the grammar and style rules, the grammar checker also contains a set of options that are used when proofreading. To view these options, select Preferences/Options, and the display shown in Figure 12.12 will appear.

Figure 12.12
The options used by the grammar checker

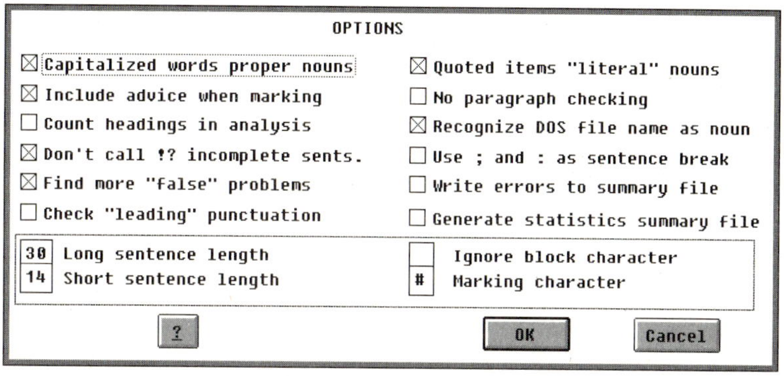

```
                              OPTIONS
 ☒ Capitalized words proper nouns    ☒ Quoted items "literal" nouns
 ☒ Include advice when marking       ☐ No paragraph checking
 ☐ Count headings in analysis        ☒ Recognize DOS file name as noun
 ☒ Don't call !? incomplete sents.   ☐ Use ; and : as sentence break
 ☒ Find more "false" problems        ☐ Write errors to summary file
 ☐ Check "leading" punctuation       ☐ Generate statistics summary file

  [30] Long sentence length           [ ]  Ignore block character
  [14] Short sentence length          [#]  Marking character

        [?]                        [  OK  ]        [ Cancel ]
```

Notice that some of these options require that you enter a number. For example, if you think that any sentence over 20 words is too long, enter **20** next to "Long sentence length".

Most of these options are quite cryptic. However, you can find out the exact meaning of any option as follows: Click on ? and then click on the option. A help screen will appear, describing exactly how the option will function when selected. For example, Figure 12.13 shows the help screen for the option labeled "Capitalized words proper nouns".

Unlike other customizations, these options are not affected by your choice of writing style.

A Systematic Approach to Customization

Because there's a strong connection between the options you select for the rule classes, rule dictionaries, and writing style, a methodical approach to customization is helpful. Here are some guidelines:

1. Begin by selecting the writing style that most closely fits your own. This creates a set of choices for the rule classes and rule dictionaries.

2. Check the Rule Dictionaries screen, making any additional selections you want.

3. Display the Rule Classes screen, and make any additional selections you feel are consistent with your writing style.

4. Display the Options screen and make your choices there.

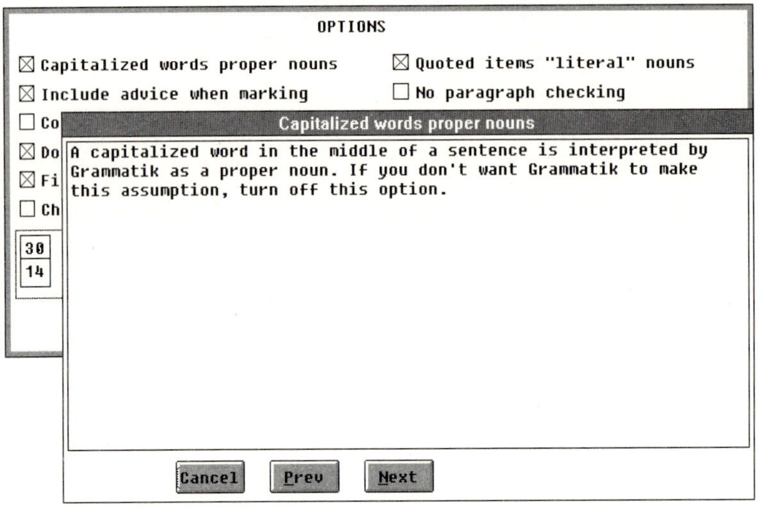

Figure 12.13
A help screen for one of the grammar options

```
                          OPTIONS
☒ Capitalized words proper nouns    ☒ Quoted items "literal" nouns
☒ Include advice when marking       ☐ No paragraph checking
☐ Co┌─────────────────────────────────────────────────────┐
☒ Do│ Capitalized words proper nouns                      │
☒ Fi│ A capitalized word in the middle of a sentence is interpreted by
☐ Ch│ Grammatik as a proper noun. If you don't want Grammatik to make
    │ this assumption, turn off this option.
 30 │
 14 │
    │
    │        Cancel    Prev    Next
    └─────────────────────────────────────────────────────┘
```

If you prefer, you need not select the options (step 4) last, since these choices aren't affected by any of the other selections.

Saving Your Customizations

You can create a special file that contains the customizations you have made during a proofreading session. This includes changes to the following:

- Comparison Charts
- Rule classes
- Rule dictionaries
- Writing style
- Options
- Document path

In later proofreading sessions, you can retrieve this file so that your custom settings are used instead of the defaults normally used by the grammar checker. To save your custom changes, follow these steps:

1. Select File/Save Preferences.

2. When the dialog box appears (see below), enter a directory and file name for saving your customizations. Don't include an extension, since .PRF is automatically appended to the file name. Finish by clicking on OK.

◆ **Using Electronic Mail**

```
Save preferences              c:\pwplus
    C:\PWPLUS\GMK.prf      [ Save   ]
                           [ Cancel ]
```

CAUTION! *Don't overwrite the GMK.PRF file which contains the original defaults for rule classes, dictionaries, etc. Instead, keep your .PRF files in a separate directory—perhaps where the Professional Write Plus program files are stored.*

3. In the next dialog box (Figure 12.14), enter a phrase that identifies the custom changes. When you retrieve this file in later proofreading sessions, this message will appear in the main information screen of the grammar checker (Figure 12.6).

Figure 12.14
Enter a descriptive phrase for your custom preferences

```
Enter identification message for
preferences file. This message is used to    [ OK     ]
help you identify the preferences file.
                                             [ Cancel ]
ID message (up to 31 characters)
Standard Preferences
```

To retrieve your customizations in a later session, select File/Load Preferences, then click on the name of the file you saved earlier. All of your custom settings stored in the file will be retrieved, taking the place of the standard defaults.

Using Electronic Mail

If your computer is part of system that operates a Novell/Action Technologies Message Handling Service (MHS), you can use Professional Write Plus to transmit messages to other users on the MHS. You can also use your MHS to transmit messages to users on another MHS system that can communicate with yours. Professional Write Plus's E-mail electronic address book furnishes a convenient place to keep the names and electronic addresses of these people.

As an attachment to a message, you can include the current Professional Write Plus document or just a selected part of it. Or, you can send any other file to which you have access.

NOTE. *A complete description of an MHS is beyond the scope of this book. If your local area network system operates an MHS, you can obtain information from the person who administrates it. If your computer doesn't operate an MHS, you can skip this section.*

Logging in to E-Mail

Each time you start a new session with Professional Write Plus you can either manually or automatically log in to the program's electronic mail system. If you plan to log in manually during a session, you must do so before opening any documents. If you open a document first, you won't be able to log in during the remainder of that session.

Here's how to log in manually:

1. Select Options/E-Mail Options. You'll see the screen shown in Figure 12.15.

Figure 12.15
The E-Mail options

2. Select Enable E-Mail (unless its already selected) and then click on OK. The E-Mail menu will appear in the menu bar at the top of the screen.

3. Click on the E-Mail menu, then click on Read Mail or any other option. The Login dialog box will then appear, as shown here:

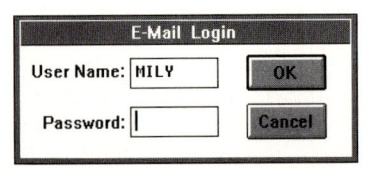

Using Electronic Mail 351

4. Enter your user name and then your password.

5. Click on OK.

The user name and password must be on the approved list for your MHS. If you don't have either, see your MHS administrator.

Once you're logged in, you remain so until you exit from Professional Write Plus. After you select the Enable E-Mail option (step 2), it remains in effect for subsequent Professional Write Plus sessions. This means that the E-Mail menu will automatically appear in the menu bar during each session.

Setting the Options

Using the E-Mail Options dialog box (Figure 12.15) you can set various options that influence your interactions with E-Mail. Once set, these options remain in effect for all subsequent word processing sessions, or until you change them. The options are as follows:

MHS E-Mail Path   Enter a valid MHS E-Mail path name in this edit box. You must enter this path name before you can use any of the other options in the dialog box. If you don't know which path name to use, consult your MHS network administrator.

Enable E-Mail   To have the E-Mail menu appear on the menu bar each time you start up Professional Write Plus, click on Enable E-Mail. This menu lists the various features available to you.

Auto Login   To automatically log into E-Mail each time you begin a Professional Write Plus session, click on Auto Login.

New Mail Notification   To have E-Mail automatically inform you about waiting mail, click on New Mail Notification. With this option selected, Professional Write Plus will periodically check E-Mail to see if any new mail has arrived for you. When a message arrives, an envelope icon (see below) will appear in the upper-left corner of your screen. After you read the mail, the icon will disappear.

The remaining options, in the box labeled "Defaults", affect the way in which Professional Write Plus documents are transmitted on E-Mail.

Send Text as ASCII   When this option is selected, each Professional Write Plus document file is converted to ASCII format before being transmitted.

This is a useful option if the recipient of your message is running a word processor other than Professional Write Plus.

Keep Graphics with Text   Using this option, when an entire Professional Write Plus document is transmitted, any associated graphics files are sent as well. This option and the next are useful when the recipient of your mail is running Professional Write Plus.

Keep Styles with Document   With this option selected, when an entire Professional Write Plus document is transmitted, any associated paragraph styles are converted to local styles and sent along with the document.

Transmitting the Current Document

You can transmit either the entire Professional Write Plus document you're currently working on or just a selected part of its text. To send the entire document:

1. Select E-Mail/Send Current Document, and the Send Document dialog box appears (see below). This shows the current defaults for transmitting documents, as described in the preceding section.

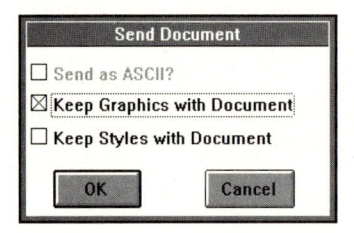

2. Make any changes you want to the options in this dialog box then click on OK. Remember that if you send the document as ASCII, all the formatting will be stripped from the text as it's transmitted.

3. If the document is new and you haven't yet saved it, or if you've made any changes since the last save, the Save As dialog box will appear, and you can select a file name in which to save the document.

4. The E-Mail Send dialog box will then appear. Overlaid on top of this is the E-Mail 'TO:' List dialog box, shown in Figure 12.16. Enter the names of the users to receive the document (see "Selecting User Names," below). Click on OK, and the E-Mail Send dialog box will become entirely visible, as shown in Figure 12.17.

5. To send "carbon"copies to additional users, click on the cc button, then select their names (for details, see "Selecting User Names," below).

Figure 12.16
Select the recipients for your mail

Figure 12.17
Select the options for transmitting a message and document

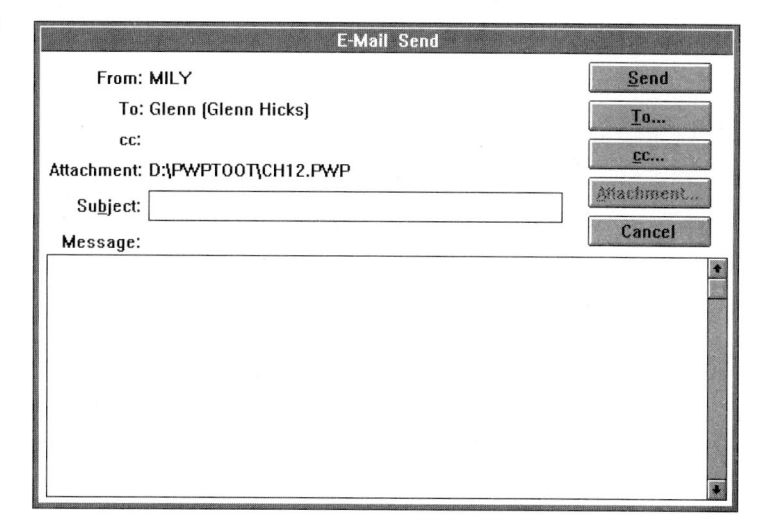

6. In the box labeled "Subject", enter a short phrase that describes the message or document you're sending.

7. In the edit box labeled "Message", add an informative message about the document you're sending. You can make this message as long as you wish.

8. Click on Send. The message will be sent, and the document will be included as an E-Mail attachment file.

Selecting User Names

To select recipients for your document, use the E-Mail 'TO': List dialog box (Figure 12.16). The names you select will appear in the box on the right labeled "Current TO: Names:". To select names for this list, you can use any combination of the following:

- Enter one or more names in the Mail Address edit box. These must be valid user names on your local MHS.

- Select names from the list box labeled "Local E-Mail Users" (this list includes all valid users of the MHS). To add each name to the Current TO: Names list, click on the name, then click on Add.

- Select names from the list box labeled "E-Mail Address Book". These are names of nonlocal MHS users with whom your MHS can communicate. To add each name to the Current TO: Names list, click on the name, then click on Add.

- From the list box labeled "Distribution Groups", select any entries to whom you want copies sent.

When you have finished selecting and adding names, click on OK. Or you can erase all the selected names by clicking on the Clear button and then begin again.

You can also use the above steps to select names of users to be sent copies. For instance, to send "carbon" copies of your document, click on the cc button on the E-Mail Send screen (Figure 12.17), and then select the names of the copy recipients from the lists on the screen. (This distinction between regular names and "cc" names seems artifical and not useful.)

Sending a Selected Part of a Document

Rather than sending an entire document, you can send just part of it. Simply select the text block you want to transmit, then click on E-Mail/Send Selected Text. When the next dialog box appears (see below), choose whether to send the text in standard Professional Write Plus format or as straight ASCII text. (Remember, if you send the text as ASCII all the formatting will be stripped from it as it's transmitted.)

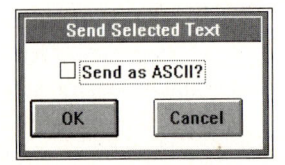

To finish transmitting the text, follows steps 4 through 8 in the previous section.

Transmitting Other Types of Files

You can transmit files other than those in Professional Write Plus format by including them as attachments to an E-Mail message. For details, see the following section.

Transmitting E-Mail Messages

One of the main functions of an e-mail system is to act as a courier for delivering messages from one user to another. The main advantage of this system is that the recipient doesn't have to be present when a message is sent. The message will simply be waiting when he or she gets around to checking the electronic mail.

As part of a message, you can include as an attachment a file of any type, such as a word processed document in Professional Write Plus or some other format, an ASCII file, a database or spreadsheet file, and so on.

Follow these steps to send a message:

1. Select E-Mail/Send a Message, and the E-Mail Send dialog box will appear, overlaid by the E-Mail 'TO:' List dialog box (Figure 12.16).

2. Enter the names of the users to receive the document (see "Selecting User Names", above). Then click on OK, and the E-Mail Send dialog box will then become entirely visible (Figure 12.17)

3. To send "carbon" copies to additional users, click on the cc button, and then select the names of the users (for details, see "Selecting User Names," above).

4. In the box labeled "Subject", enter a descriptive phrase regarding your message.

5. In the Message edit box, enter whatever text you want to send.

6. To send a file as an attachment, click on the Attachment option. In the dialog box that appears (see Figure 12.18), either enter the name of the file to be transmitted or select the name of the file from the list boxes. Make sure to include the disk drive and directory as part of the file name.

7. Click on Send, and the message will be sent. If you selected a file in step 6, it will be sent along as an attachment.

You can send any type of file as an attachment. If however, you want to send a file in Professional Write Plus format *and* include any associated graphics and paragraph styles, you can't use this method. Instead, you must retrieve the document into Professional Write Plus and then use the method described earlier in "Transmitting the Current Document."

Figure 12.18
The dialog box for transmitting an attachment file

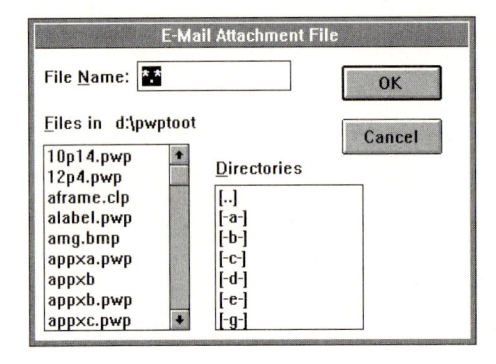

Reading Your Mail

To view the mail, select E-Mail/Read Mail and the E-Mail List screen will appear (see Figure 12.19). This includes any new mail, as well as old mail you haven't deleted. Note that if you selected the New Mail Notification in the E-Mail Options dialog box (Figure 12.15), an envelope icon will appear in the upper-left part of your screen whenever mail is sent to you while you're working with Professional Write Plus.

Figure 12.19
A list of E-Mail messages

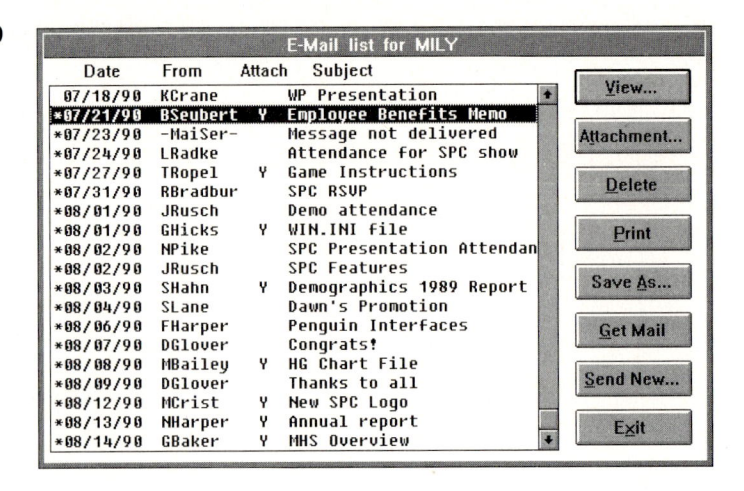

The E-Mail List screen displays a list of your mail messages. A leading asterisk indicates that a message has not yet been read. If a new message is

Using Electronic Mail 357

sent to you while you're using this dialog box, the envelope icon appears at the top of the screen.

Each line in the main part of the dialog box corresponds to one mail message. Each message has four parts, indicated by the column headings:

Date   The date the message was sent
From   Who sent the message
Attach   Whether the message is accompanied by a file
Subject   A short description of the message

The options on the right side of the dialog box offer you a variety of choices for dealing with your mail. These options will be described later on.

To read any particular message, either double-click on the corresponding message line or click on the message line in the dialog box, then click on View or press Enter.

The complete message appears on the screen, as shown in Figure 12.20. If the entire message doesn't fit on the screen, use the vertical scroll bar on the right to move through the text. The buttons on the bottom represent various options you can exercise for any particular message. Some of these are the same as the options available to you on the E-Mail List screen (Figure 12.19).

Figure 12.20
A complete E-Mail message

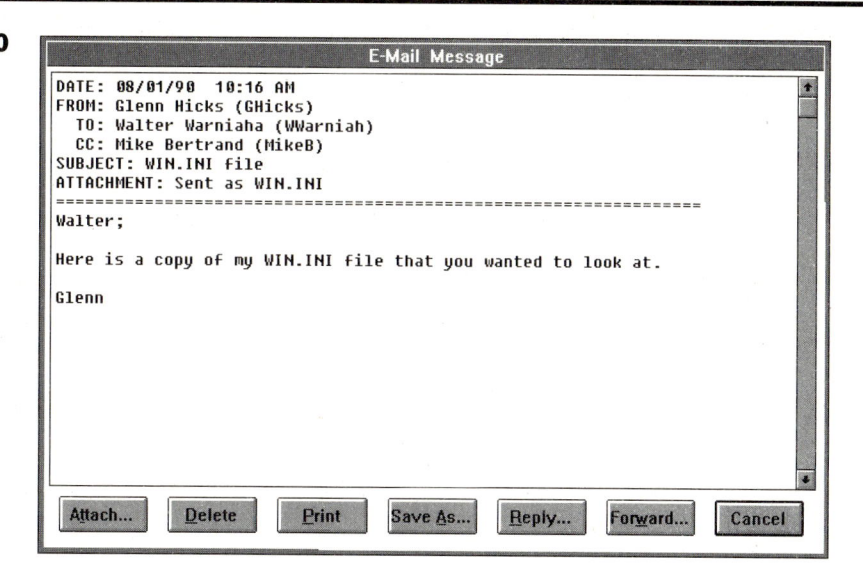

```
E-Mail Message
DATE: 08/01/90  10:16 AM
FROM: Glenn Hicks (GHicks)
  TO: Walter Warniaha (WWarniah)
  CC: Mike Bertrand (MikeB)
SUBJECT: WIN.INI file
ATTACHMENT: Sent as WIN.INI
================================================================
Walter;

Here is a copy of my WIN.INI file that you wanted to look at.

Glenn
```

[Attach...] [Delete] [Print] [Save As...] [Reply...] [Forward...] [Cancel]

After you have read a message, you have the following options:

- View the attachment to the message

- Delete the message
- Print the message
- Save the message as a Professional Write Plus document for later reference
- Issue a reply to the sender
- Forward the message to someone else on the network
- Cancel the message

Viewing an Attachment

Whenever a message is sent to you, it may be accompanied by an attachment file. If so, the column labeled "Attach" in the E-Mail List dialog box (Figure 12.19) will contain the letter "Y".

If the attachment file is text, you can view it by clicking on the Attachment button on this screen. If the full message is being displayed, click on the Attach button at the bottom.

The program automatically opens another window and retrieves the attached document, using whatever word processor is appropriate for the document. For example, if the document is in standard Professional Write Plus format, another copy of Professional Write Plus is loaded. Other types of documents will cause Windows Write or the Windows Notepad to be opened.

If the retrieved file is another type of file, such as a Windows Paintbrush .PCX file, the corresponding software package will be opened, if possible.

If the retrieved document is in Professional Write Plus format, you can then edit it, print it, and in general treat it like any other Professional Write Plus document.

While your cursor is in this new window you can do the following:

- Move back and forth between the document window and the window that's working with your mail.

- Save the attachment file under a different file name, using the Save As option. Note that when the Save As dialog box first appears, the name of the file containing the attachment appears in the File Name edit box. It doesn't serve any purpose to save to this same file, since nothing new will happen.

- Minimize the window by clicking on the minimize icon in the upper-right corner of the window.

- Close the window by double-clicking on the Control icon in the upper-left corner of the window.

Deleting Messages

You can delete a message in either of two ways. If the E-Mail List dialog box is displayed (Figure 12.19), click on the message and then click on Delete. If the E-Mail Message dialog box is displayed, just click on Delete.

When you delete a message, the attachment file disappears as well. Note that it's not erased (which might make the sender very unhappy). It's just not accessible to you as an attachment. If you want to save the attachment, retrieve it by selecting the Attachment option, then save it under a different file name.

Until you delete a message, it remains on your mail list. To save a message for later use and at the same time clean out your mail list, you can copy the message to a separate disk file as an ordinary Professional Write Plus document. (See "Saving Messages", below). You can then delete the message from the mail list.

Printing Your Mail

You can generate a hard copy of any of your mail messages. From the E-Mail List screen, select the message to be printed, then click on Print. You can also print the message that's displayed on the E-Mail Message screen by clicking on Print. The format of this printed output is plain vanilla, but it's clear enough for archival purposes.

Saving Messages

You don't have to do anything special to save a message. Just don't delete it. It will remain on your mail list until you decide you don't need it anymore.

To save a message as a Professional Write Plus document file, click on Save As from either the E-Mail Message screen or the E-Mail List screen. When the next dialog box appears (Figure 12.21), enter the name of the file in which the message is to be saved. To save to a directory different from the current one, do one of the following:

- Enter the new disk drive and directory as part of the name that you enter in the File Name edit box.
- Select the new drive and directory from the list boxes on the screen.

Issuing a Reply

To send a response to a message, follow these steps:

1. Display the complete message, as shown in Figure 12.20.
2. Click on Reply, and the screen shown in Figure 12.22 will appear.
3. Enter whatever text you want in the edit box labeled "Message".

Figure 12.21
You can save a message as a Professional Write Plus file

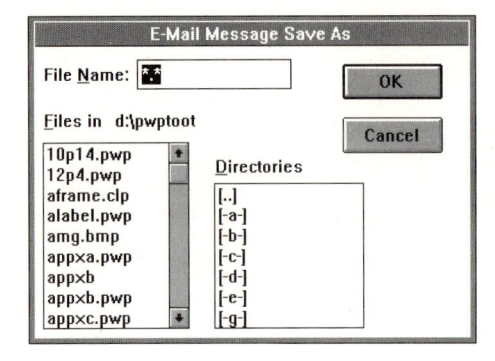

Figure 12.22
Use this screen to send a reply to a message

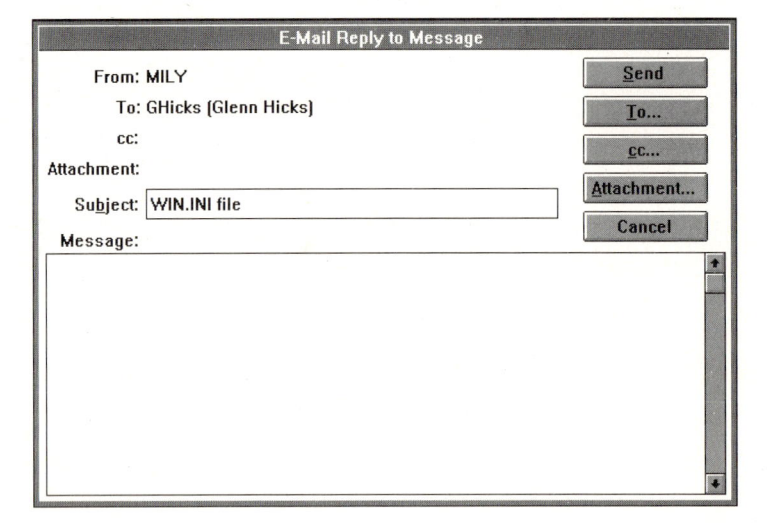

4. You can change the name of the recipient by clicking on the To button. The E-Mail 'TO:' List box then appears (Figure 12.16), and you can then select other recipients or change the name of the current recipient (the sender of the original message). For details about selecting names, see "Selecting User Names," earlier in this section.

5. To send "carbon" copies to other people on the network, click on the cc button. When the list of names appears, select the recipients.

6. To send your reply to the people you have specified, click on Send.

Forwarding a Message

After reading a message, you can forward it to one or more people on the network. Here's how:

1. Click on the Forward option in the E-Mail Message screen (Figure 12.20). The dialog box shown in Figure 12.23 will appear, overlaid by the E-Mail 'TO:' List dialog box.

Figure 12.23
Use this box to forward a message to others on the network

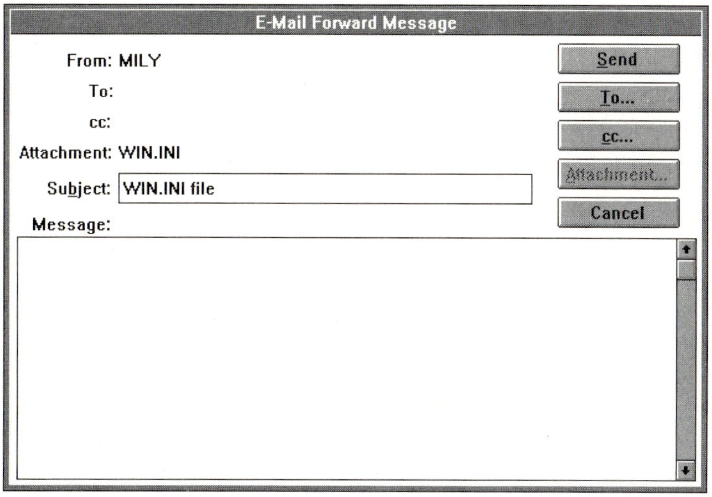

2. Select the names of those you want to get a copy of the message. (For details, see "Selecting User Names" earlier in this chapter.) Then click on OK, and the screen shown in Figure 12.23 will become completely visible.

3. In the box labeled "Message", enter whatever text you want to append to the message being sent.

4. If you like, modify the contents of the Subject edit box. (Initially, this contains the subject attached to the message sent to you.)

5. Click on Send, and the original message will be forwarded.

In addition to the original message, any attachment will also be forwarded, as will any text you entered in the Message box (step 3).

Sending New Messages

You can also send a new message from the E-Mail List screen (Figure 12.19). Just click on the Send New option, then follow the steps described in the section "Transmitting E-Mail Messages." There's no particular advantage to sending a message this way, as opposed to using the Send Message option on the E-Mail menu. It's just a convenience for you when you're reading mail and decide to send a new message to someone.

Using an E-Mail Address Book

You can create a special address book for those people who are valid users on a remote MHS that can communicate with your local MHS. Then when you send messages and files, you can select recipients from this address book in addition to local recipients.

Adding New Names

Use these steps to add a new name to the address book:

1. Select E-Mail/E-Mail Address Book. The dialog box shown in Figure 12.24 will appear.

Figure 12.24
The E-Mail Address Book

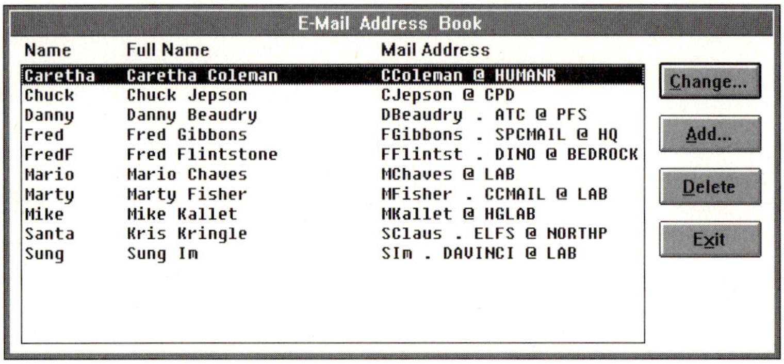

2. Click on Add, and the dialog box shown below will appear.

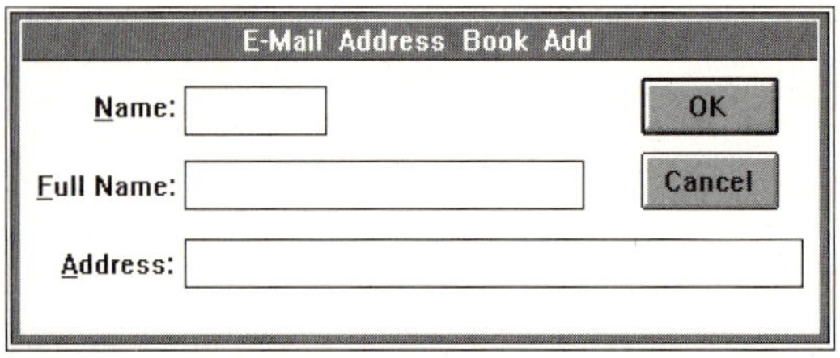

3. Enter a name with no more than eight characters. This name will appear when you select names for sending a message.

4. In the box labeled "Full Name", enter the complete name for this entry.

5. In the box labeled "Mail Address", enter the MHS address. This must be a valid address for the MHS at this person's site.

6. Click on OK, and the name will be entered in the address book.

Changing and Deleting Entries

You can alter the contents of an address book entry, as follows:

1. Click on the entry you want to change, then click on Change.

2. When the next dialog box appears (see below), change either the full name, the address, or both.

```
┌─────────── E-Mail Address Book Change ───────────┐
│                                                   │
│      Name: Caretha              ┌──────┐          │
│                                 │  OK  │          │
│ Full Name: Caretha Coleman      └──────┘          │
│                                 ┌──────┐          │
│                                 │Cancel│          │
│   Address: CColeman @ HUMANR    └──────┘          │
│                                                   │
└───────────────────────────────────────────────────┘
```

3. Click on OK.

If you change the Address portion of the entry, the new address must be a valid MHS address at the user's site. Also, note that you can't change the Name part of the entry. To modify the Name, you must delete the entire entry in the address book, then enter a new one using the new value for the Name part of the entry.

To delete an entry in the address book, click on that entry and then click on Delete.

Summary

If your computer system doesn't run an MHS, you won't be able to use Professional Write Plus's E-Mail feature. However, you can utilize the grammar checker with any computer that runs Professional Write Plus. Although grammar checking takes a fair amount of time, especially with long documents, it can help you polish whatever type of documents you generate.

Use the grammar checker as an aid and a guide—not as a law enforcement officer. Remember, the checker offers suggestions on how to improve your writing, but you always have the final say in how to structure your work.

CHAPTER

13

Creating Different Types of Documents

Selecting the Right Typeface

Page Design Tips

Technical Tips

Letterhead

Business Cards

Greeting Cards and Invitations

Newsletters

TRADITIONALLY, A WORD PROCESSOR HAS BEEN SIMPLY A TOOL FOR creating letters, reports, and other similar types of documents. If you stop to think about it, your mental image of these documents is probably that they all contain text and look pretty dull.

As shown in the preceding chapters, this image isn't necessarily valid when you use a modern word processor like Professional Write Plus. You can now make even a simple memo or note appear interesting by including little touches like ruling lines and different size text.

Moreover, beyond memos and notes you can create a wide variety of different types of documents, ranging from business cards to multipage newsletters. This chapter will explore some of these possibilities by describing the basic steps for creating different types of documents.

Selecting the Right Typeface

Some of the following sections will make specific suggestions of typefaces and sizes to use. These suggestions will be limited to the standard fonts most likely to be available on your system. However, each Windows installation is different, and the suggested fonts may not be available to you. On the other hand, your installation may offer a wide variety of fonts, and you may want to use some of those instead of the ones suggested here.

Regardless of the fonts available to you, keep the following points in mind when selecting a particular typeface and size in a given circumstance:

- The character of a publication should be a factor in selecting typefaces. For instance, an annual company report should have a more formal appearance than the announcement of a birthday party, and the typefaces should be selected accordingly.

- To emphasize an item on a page, such as headings and banners, use large type sizes.

- Limit the number of different typefaces appearing on a single page or in a single document. Too many different typefaces tend to add confusion rather than clarity. You can, however, add variety by using different sizes of the same typeface.

- Use a serif font for the main body of text. The reason is that large amounts of text are more readable in a serif typeface, as opposed to sans serif. The most commonly used serif typeface is Times Roman and its many imitators.

Page Design Tips

Creating an attractive page design requires a good deal of planning, and a bit of experience—either your own or someone else's—can be a valuable asset. Here are a few tips that may help you to generate good-looking documents:

Use Similar Documents as Examples The world is filled with printed pages, and there's no reason for you to ignore this wealth of material. Borrow from the ideas available in various publications, such as magazines, journals, newspapers, and so on. When you come across a page design that appeals to you, make a sketch of it, including the main design elements and their relative positions. There's no copyright on a page design, and you're free to benefit from the work of others, as long as you don't copy someone else's logo.

Plan Ahead It's very tempting to do your design work at the keyboard because using the desktop publishing features of Professional Write Plus is so enjoyable. Resist this temptation. Use a pencil and paper to make a sketch of the basic layout for each page. If you are considering a nonstandard-size document, investigate the cost first. Some page sizes are much more expensive to print than others.

Don't Use Too Many Elements If you don't have a lot of experience with page design, your natural tendency may be to fill the page with too many different elements: graphics, typefaces, rules, and so on. This tendency is especially tempting if you have only recently been introduced to the program's desktop publishing features. Avoid this tendency and keep the design of each page relatively simple—too many different elements confuse the reader's eye. To some extent, less is better than more. Just a few tastefully positioned elements are sufficient to make a page appear interesting and attractive.

Use Your Own Judgment Your own creative ability and good taste may surprise you. After you have finished a page design, wait a few days and then take a fresh look at it, keeping in mind the following points:

- Does the page look interesting?
- Do the main points come across clearly, or are they hidden by other features?
- Is the page too cluttered? This may be one reason that some of the main features don't stand out.
- Does the page draw your eye easily from one topic to the next, or is it difficult for you to find the key items on the page?
- Does the page create the impression you intended?

Get Advice—and Listen to It Being critical of your own work can be very difficult. Don't be afraid to show your design to other people, but be prepared to take their advice, even though it may not be what you expect or want to hear. It's very easy to fall in love with your own designs, but remember that what appeals to you may leave everyone else cold.

Technical Tips

When working with page layouts, you'll be using a few standard techniques over and over. For example, you will usually need to adjust the spacings between the various elements on a page. And often a design involves working with overlapping text frames. Being familiar with common situations like these—and their pitfalls—can save you a good deal of time. This section lists a few tips and hints about techniques that can help simplify your design work.

Adjusting Text Spacing

Adjusting the spacing between the various lines of text can be one of the most difficult parts of the design process. You can use any of the following approaches to working with line spacing:

- Use the Text/Spacing option to adjust individual lines of text. You can also assign different paragraph styles to various text lines and then use the Paragraph Spacing Above and Below options to control the spacing between paragraphs.

- Place each text line in a different frame. Then adjust the spacing by repositioning the individual frames. Obviously, this makes sense only to a certain point.

- Use a combination of the above, placing groups of adjacent lines in different frames. Reposition the individual frames to adjust the spacing between groups of lines.

Generally, you will probably find the last approach to be the easiest to manage. Using too many frames becomes confusing because of the boundary overlaps. On the other hand, adjusting individual lines with the Text/Spacing and Paragraph Spacing options can be somewhat difficult and imprecise.

When using the Text/Spacing option to adjust the spacings between lines in a group, here are a few helpful guidelines:

- Use the Custom option in the Line Spacing submenu to choose a specific spacing for a line.

- When you select a spacing for a particular line, it affects both the space above and below that line.

- When working with a group of lines within a frame, start at the top and work your way down.

- Due to a minor bug in the program, once you have set the spacing for a particular line, you may not be able to change it again with the Custom option in the Modify & Create Styles dialog box. If this happens, reset the spacing for that line by selecting Revert to Style from the Line Spacing submenu. You can then select a new custom spacing for the line. If this problem persists in a particular circumstance, try assigning the problem text to a new paragraph style, then adjust the line spacing for that style.

Working with Large Text

When working with very large text, such as for banners and headlines, you may have difficulty in adjusting the line spacing. Or you may have trouble getting large text to appear in a small frame. Here are some useful tips to remember:

- If you have assigned a nonzero border to the frame, there is less space available for text than appears on the screen. Here's an extreme example: If you create a 1-inch by 1-inch frame with half-inch borders all around, there's no space for anything at all within the frame.

- If you don't leave enough room for text within a frame, some of the text won't appear, and in some cases you won't be able to retrieve it, even when you increase the frame dimensions. If this happens, delete the frame, create a new one in its place, then try again, this time leaving more room for your text.

- Many screen fonts for large text don't work well, and the letters on a line may appear to overlap. Usually, however, the text will print normally, even though it appears garbled on screen. If you have trouble reading large text, switch to draft mode.

Working with Multiple Frames

Many page designs require the use of two or more frames, and sometimes several frames may overlap. Overlapping frames are often used for holding text, and a few useful suggestions may help you to deal with these types of interacting frames:

- Generally, don't draw a line around a text frame unless you want that line to be part of the final design. You don't need a line around a text frame in order to find it, because the text itself shows the position of the frame.

- Remember that when two or more frames overlap, one of them is in front and the others are layered underneath. When you click on an overlapping area, the frame on top is selected. To select a frame that's underneath, hold down the Shift key and then click until the frame you want is selected. Then to work with that frame, click on Frame/Bring to Front.

- Make overlapping text frames transparent and turn on the No Word Wrap option for any frame that's on top of another one.

- You can set the borders for each frame either at zero or some other value. Sometimes a nonzero border can be an effective means of creating a separation between frames.

Letterhead

One of the simplest and most useful types of documents you can create is a letterhead for your business. The letterhead is stored as part of a template you create, and each time you want to generate a letter you simply retrieve that template. If you have a laser printer, the quality of the customized letters will be first rate.

You can even create a variety of letterheads for different purposes by creating a different template for each one. To create a new letter, you just retrieve the appropriate template.

You can use any number of different features to create a letterhead. If you have access to high-quality clip art, you can include a graphic image as part of a logo. Otherwise, a few lines of well-chosen text in a couple of sizes can make an attractive letterhead.

Creating a Letterhead Template

You create a letterhead by making a new template that contains the text and graphics you want to use. To illustrate the process, here are the steps for creating the letterhead shown in Figure 13.1.

Figure 13.1
A simple letterhead

CRUISING PLEASURES

"We cruise, you snooze"

1000 Waters Way San Francisco, CA 95102
(415) 654-8679   FAX (415) 654-8625

1. Clear the screen.

2. At the top of the page, create a frame that's the approximate size of the graphic image for the logo. Make sure that no line is drawn around the frame.

3. Import the image into the frame (in this example, a steamship).

4. Resize and crop the image.

5. Create a second frame just to the right of the picture, then enter the text **CRUISING PLEASURES,** using a 14-point typeface. Size the frame to just fit the text. For ease in making adjustments, set the frame borders to zero. Again, make sure no line is drawn around the frame.

6. Create another frame on the right side of the page. Again, assign zero borders. In this frame, enter the text for the address and phone number, using a 9-point typeface.

7. Create a new frame below the one containing the graphic image. Then enter the text for the logo (in Figure 13.1 the text is **We cruise, you snooze**), using 9-point italics.

8. Adjust the spacing between the various lines (see "Technical Tips," earlier in this chapter).

9. To create a line at the bottom of the heading, create a frame there that extends from margin to margin across the page. Make the frame height as small as possible, and then create a line at the frame bottom by selecting Frame/Frame Layout/Lines & Color/Bottom. Then select the style of line you want.

10. Adjust the positions of the various elements in the letterhead. When you have finished, save it as part of a new template: Select Format/Save As a New Template. Then enter the name of the new template and click on Include Document Contents.

The new template will be created, and it will include all the text and graphics of your letterhead.

Notice that because each individual element in the letterhead was created within a separate frame, repositioning them relative to one another is very easy. Just grab a frame and drag it to where you want it.

To best judge the letterhead appearance you'll need to make printouts because the screen often distorts the size and spacing of the text.

Tips on Designing Letterhead

When making your letterhead, remember that the design should be eye-catching, but it shouldn't dominate the page. If you don't have a lot of design experience, keep your design simple, and don't make the heading so large that there's hardly any room on the page for your correspondence.

You can run your "heading" down the side of the page or at the bottom instead of placing it at the top. This type of alternative design can be very effective, but remember that you still want to leave convenient room for the contents of each letter. With any type of design, choose a typeface and size that won't conflict with—or be confused with—the ordinary type you use for your letters.

As you develop the design, you can use the Full Page view option to get a fairly good idea of the page appearance. To use this view to best advantage, make sure the Display As Printed option is selected in the Layout Mode Options dialog box. In addition, you should make periodic printouts. What you on the screen is rarely exactly what will appear on the printed page, and close monitoring can save you a good deal of unnecessary work.

Using the Template

Each time you want to create a new letter on letterhead, you simply select the template containing your letterhead. In order to retrieve the contents of a template along with the template itself, you must set up the following default for selecting a new template:

1. Select Options/Default Template.

2. Click on the option labeled "Display List of Templates When Creating a New Document".

3. To have this option take effect, click on OK.

Once you have established the retrieval default by using these three steps, it will remain in effect for all subsequent sessions with Professional Write Plus. Note that if you do not establish this default, then whenever you select the template the included text and graphics will *not* be retrieved as well.

To create a new letter using your custom letterhead:

1. Select File/New.

2. When the dialog box shown in Figure 13.2 appears, use the list box to select the template containing your letterhead.

3. Click on Copy Template Contents, then click on OK.

When the template is retrieved, your heading and logo will appear at the top of the new document.

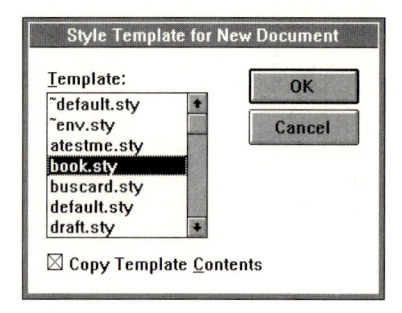

Figure 13.2
Select the template for a new document

Business Cards

You can easily use Professional Write Plus to create a master from which business cards can be printed, using the same techniques described for creating letterhead. Basically, you create a frame of the correct size, outline it with a border, then create and position your logo and text, using an individual frame for each.

Designing a Business Card

Before you try to design your own, study the cards of your friends, colleagues, and associates. Remember that your design capabilities are somewhat limited with Professional Write Plus, so try not to get delusions of grandeur. Whatever graphical logo you use is going to have to be premade. If you or a friend is proficient with a drawing program, you can use it to create the logo and then import it into a small frame that's part of the business card design.

When designing the card, here are a few guidelines to observe:

- Keep the design simple and to the point. Remember that a business card contains only a few square inches, not a football field.

- Use a larger or bold font for your name so that it catches the eye first.

- The smallest type size that's easily readable is approximately 7 or 8 points, depending on the typeface and the quality of the printing.

- For the smallest fonts, sans serif typefaces often work better than serif ones, especially for thermal processes that raise the ink on the cards. The reason is that this process tends to blur the fine ink edges, so that the serifs become fuzzy.

- What may look great when printed on your laser printer may not be attractive when duplicated by offset or some other professional printing process. For example, a shaded background may not look good when duplicated because some duplicating processes make some shadings appear uneven. Bring in a few sample designs to your local printer for advice and suggestions.

Creating a Business Card

There are many different approaches to the design of business cards, and you can use your ingenuity to create new and interesting ones. As an example, the following steps demonstrate how to create the card shown in Figure 13.3.

Figure 13.3
A simple business card design

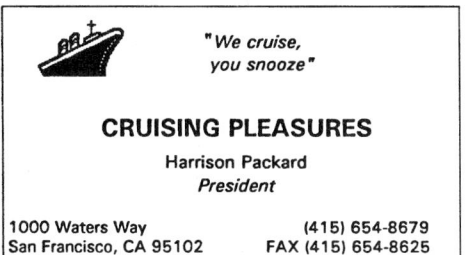

> "We cruise, you snooze"
>
> **CRUISING PLEASURES**
>
> Harrison Packard
> *President*
>
> 1000 Waters Way   (415) 654-8679
> San Francisco, CA 95102 FAX (415) 654-8625

1. Turn on the vertical ruler and the tab ruler.

2. Create a frame a tiny bit (about $1/32$ inch) larger than the exact size of the card you want to design. The most common card size is 2 by $3 1/2$ inches. You can use the Enlarged view for more accurate frame sizing.

3. Using the Frame/Frame Layout/Lines & Color option, create the thinnest possible line completely around the frame. Use the Outside option to place the line at the outer frame edge. This line will serve as the cropping guide for the printer; the extra space you allot is to allow for cutting the cards inside the border.

4. Create a frame for the logo picture (no lines around this frame), sizing it and placing it where you want it. The size and placement can be approximate, because they can be readjusted later. Note that in Figure 13.3 the logo (a steamship) is positioned in the upper-left corner of the card.

5. Import the logo into the frame.

6. Resize and crop the logo, and resize the frame if necessary.

7. Create a small frame in the upper-right corner for holding the text part of the logo.

8. Select a 9-point Helvetica font, then enter the text **We cruise, you snooze.**

9. Create a frame filling the lower half of the card frame.

10. Enter the three lines beginning with **CRUISING PLEASURES** and ending with **President**. Use 14-point type for the first line and 10-point for the other two. Center these three lines within the frame by using the Text/Alignment/Center option.

11. Enter the remaining two lines of text, using an 8- or 9-point font. To position the telephone number at the far-right edge, you can insert aright-justify tab there, then press Tab before entering the number.

12. Adjust the spacing of the text lines.

Greeting Cards and Invitations

You can use the program's desktop publishing features to create simple types of cards for announcements, invitations, and so on. With a little bit of creativity you can generate reasonably attractive designs, even without importing graphics from outside sources.

Because of Professional Write Plus's inability to print top-quality text upside down, your best approach to building a four-sided card is to separately create the four pieces shown in Figure 13.4. You can then paste them up as shown in the figure (or have your print shop do it for you). The pasted-up master can then be printed on heavy stock paper and the final prints folded as shown in the figure.

You can design whatever size card you like, but in order to use standard 8½ by 11-inch stock, each of the four pieces should be no larger than about 3¾ by 5 inches. This leaves adequate room for folding, as well as a comfortable border around the edge of each piece.

Here's an outline of the steps to create the lower-right section of the card in Figure 13.4:

1. Turn on the vertical ruler and the tab ruler.

2. On a blank page, create a frame no larger than 3¾ by 5 inches. (It can be smaller, depending on the dimensions you want for your cards.)

3. Using the Frame Layout dialog box (by selecting Frame/Frame Layout), use the Lines & Colors option to select a border for the perimeter of the frame. The selection isn't very large, but even a plain solid line around the edge of a page can be attractive. Select a black color for the line.

Greeting Cards and Invitations

Figure 13.4
The four pieces of a fold-out card

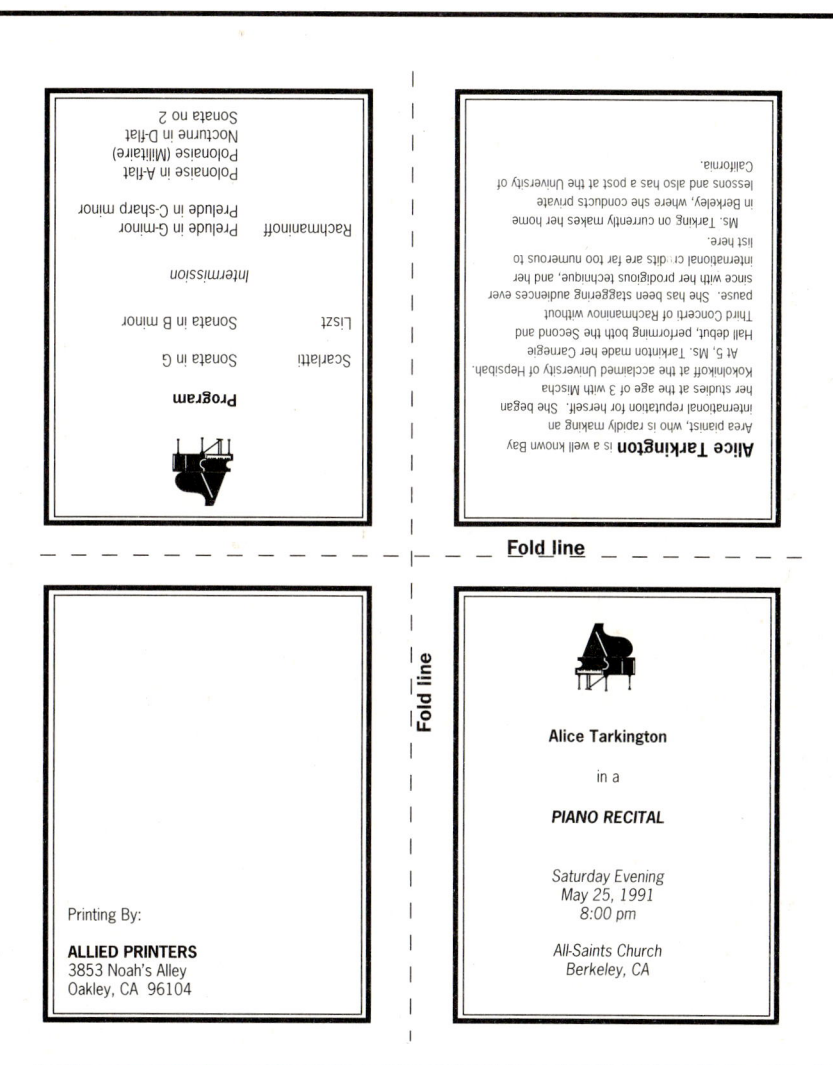

[Top-left panel (upside down): Program listing]

Program

Scarlatti — Sonata in G
Liszt — Sonata in B minor

Intermission

Rachmaninoff — Prelude in G minor
Prelude in C-sharp minor
Polonaise in A-flat
Polonaise (Militaire)
Nocturne in D-flat
Sonata no 2

[Top-right panel (upside down): Biography]

Alice Tarkington is a well known Bay Area pianist, who is rapidly making an international reputation for herself. She began her studies at the age of 3 with Mischa Kokolnikoff at the acclaimed University of Hepsibah. At 5, Ms. Tarkinton made her Carnegie Hall debut, performing both the Second and Third Concerti of Rachmaninov without pause. She has been staggering audiences ever since with her prodigious technique, and her international cr dits are far too numerous to list here.

Ms. Tarking on currently makes her home in Berkeley, where she conducts private lessons and also has a post at the University of California.

Fold line

[Bottom-left panel]

Printing By:
ALLIED PRINTERS
3853 Noah's Alley
Oakley, CA 96104

Fold line

[Bottom-right panel: Front cover]

Alice Tarkington

in a

PIANO RECITAL

Saturday Evening
May 25, 1991
8:00 pm

All-Saints Church
Berkeley, CA

---

4. Create another frame near the top of, but within, the first frame, then import the graphic image (in this case, a piano) into it.

5. Resize and crop the image, then center it near the top of the page by repositioning the frame.

6. Double-click within the first frame (not the one containing the piano image), then press Enter several times until the text cursor is positioned somewhat below the picture.

7. Enter the text for each line. Start each line at the left margin, using tabs to indent selected text.

8. Select all the text as a block, then center it with the option Text/Alignment/Center.

9. Adjust the spacing between the individual lines and, if necessary, readjust the position of the picture.

As with any other type of document, if you can't fine-tune the line spacing to your satisfaction, you can create different frames for the different groups of text lines. Then you can adjust the spacing between groups by repositioning the individual blocks.

Newsletters

Using Professional Write Plus's various desktop publishing aids, you can generate attractive and professional-looking newsletters. Single-page newsletters are easy to work with, but multipage newsletters are much more difficult because the program doesn't have any capabilities that allow you to control the text flow between columns and pages. You can create multipage newsletters, but you'll need to be extremely careful when entering and editing text.

By adjusting the page layout and inserting frames, you can produce just about any type of design you wish. If you have access to good-quality graphics, such as a collection of professionally drawn clip art, you can add spark to your newsletters.

Designing Newsletters

Before placing a finger to the keyboard, work out the entire design for each page with a pencil and paper. The layout you come up with should reflect the subject matter to be used and the intended audience as well as your own personal taste. Here are a few guidelines that may be helpful as you create your designs:

Number of Columns A newsletter should contain at least two columns per page for ease of reading. For variability and attractiveness, you can put different numbers of columns at the top and bottom. This type of flexibility is possible because you can create text frames with up to eight columns. For instance, if the first page is to contain two articles, you could place the top one in a two-column spread and the bottom one in three.

Headlines and Banners Leave adequate space at the top for the newsletter banner plus the accompanying logo, if any. A banner should be large enough to make a statement to your audience, yet not so large that it completely dominates the page. Also, plan on adequate space for any major headline to be included.

Positioning of Articles and Text Flow Unfortunately, you can't control the flow of text from column to column and page to page. Text flows from top to bottom and from left to right on each page. If one or more articles extends onto pages beyond the first, you'll have to enter the text manually on these pages in whatever columns you wish. This is a serious drawback, and you'll have to plan your work carefully in order to avoid massive headaches during editing. This issue is discussed in detail later on (see "Working with Multiple Pages").

Positioning of Graphics Because of Professional Write Plus's ability to import graphic art in a variety of popular formats, in principle you have access to an enormous range of computerized art. Well-chosen pictures can make a big difference in how a page strikes the reader, and even a fairly mundane graphic can liven up what would otherwise be an uninteresting format.

Carefully plan the position of each picture so that it's reasonably close to the accompanying article. Because of the flexibility in resizing and repositioning frames, you don't have to plan things down to the last millimeter. After all the text has been entered, you can make whatever adjustments are necessary.

Creating a Newsletter

The single-page newsletter shown in Figure 13.5 was created using Professional Write Plus, and the steps involved are listed below. Note that before performing any of these steps, you would first make a sketch showing the positions and sizes of the various elements on the page. Figure 13.6 shows a sketch for the newsletter.

Here are a couple of useful tips:

- Save your work frequently. It's very easy to make a mess when working with full-page designs, and having a ten-minute-old backup will often be a blessing.

- When creating a full-page design such as a newsletter, you can switch back and forth between Full Page view and Working or Standard view. (I prefer the Standard view because of the great screen fonts available for 10- and 12-point text.) Especially when creating and adjusting the various frames, Full Page view is invaluable.

- Make frequent printouts as you proceed. Unless you have a very high-quality monitor, you can't see the whole page clearly on the screen. Moreover, what you see on the screen is invariably somewhat different from what you get when you print.

Figure 13.5
A single-page newsletter

Bay Area Hiking

Fall, 1992 — *A Quarterly Publication*

Hiking East and West

If you're a resident of any part of the greater San Francisco Bay Area, you have access to a nearly unlimited array of hiking possibilities. And, you can suit your hiking to the weather. This is a decided advantage, considering the wide variety of weather patterns that frequent the area.

If you want to be in sunshine as much as possible you'll need to be flexible, because yesterday's prediction for clear weather may not materialize. Especially during the summer, the offshore fog has a way of coming and going seemingly at will, but you can't ever be sure that today's fog will still be there tomorrow. An early morning weather forecast is usually the best way to maximize your chances of figuring out where the sun will be, but even then you'd better bring several layers of clothing, just in case.

The hills in Marin County, which form the last vestige of the Coastal Range, offer hiking that's as beautiful and varied as any in the Bay Area. Most of the hiking trails are attached in one way or another to Mount Tamalpais and its surrounding hills, and countless dozens of trails and miles dot these wonderful slopes. On the western edge lies Stinson beach, and rugged trails like the Dipsea offer spectacular views leading from the beach all the way up to the peak of Tamalpais. On the way from Stinson to Tamalpais you can pay a visit to Muir Woods, which contains one of the most beautiful and well-known redwood groves in the country. You'll pay a price for this beauty, because the hiking is hilly and arduous.

On the eastern slopes of the hills lie several lakes, and although artificial they nevertheless offer many beautiful hikes and views. East of these lakes lie the Marin suburbs, so you don't need to worry about getting lost. Just head east from wherever you are, and sooner or later you'll come up hard against civilization.

If your planned hiking day turns out to be foggy in Marin, several lovely hiking alternatives are available in the East Bay Regional Parks. Considering the proximity of so many large urban areas, such as Oakland, Berkeley, and Concord, the existence of this large complex of parks is truly a miracle. Literally hundreds of miles of trails dot the region, covering a wide variety of terrain ranging from flat, yet not boring, to hilly, strenuous, and beautiful. Even when the Marin hills are fogged in, these parks are as likely as not to be in clear sunshine.

Starting with Tilden, Redwood, and Sibley Parks, you can work your way either east or south. Heading east, you'll discover the beautiful 13-mile loop around Briones Reservoir. Briones Park (no relation to the reservoir, which is actually maintained by the local utility company), contains many wonderful trails, and you're as likely to run into a wildcat as a blue jay or grazing cow. The cats aren't tame, and you'll never get closer than a good part of a mile.

Still further east lies Mount Diablo, one of the outstanding geological points of the area. You can spend days wandering around the trails that crisscross the slopes, and the views are always worth the effort.

When to Hike Where

For those times during the spring, summer, and fall when the fog is present in Marin, plan to hike in the East Bay. On the other hand, when the temperatures east of the Oakland hills climb into the 80's or 90's, you may want to go over to Marin, where it's likely to be 20 or 30 degrees cooler. For those days when it's foggy in Marin and Roasting on Mount Diablo in the East Bay, the Regional Parks bounding on Berkeley and Oakland may be your best bet for temperate hiking.

During the winter months, the Marin hills offer the warmest hiking because of the tempering effect of the Pacific Ocean.

Here are the steps for creating the newsletter:

1. Starting with a blank page, turn on the vertical and tab rulers.

2. Set the page layout: Click on Format/Page Layout, then click on 2 for the number of columns. Using the Lines option in the Page Layout dialog box, click on the Lines Between Columns option. To compensate for the large amount of white space at the top, set the top margin to 0.5 inches.

3. Create the blank frame to hold the banner text (frame 1 in Figure 13.6). Select the Wrap Around option for this frame and set the borders to zero. Make sure that the left edge of the frame is right up against the left

margin, or even a little beyond it. This prevents text you'll be adding later from leaking into the space between the left margin and the frame.

Figure 13.6
A sketch for the newsletter in Figure 13.5

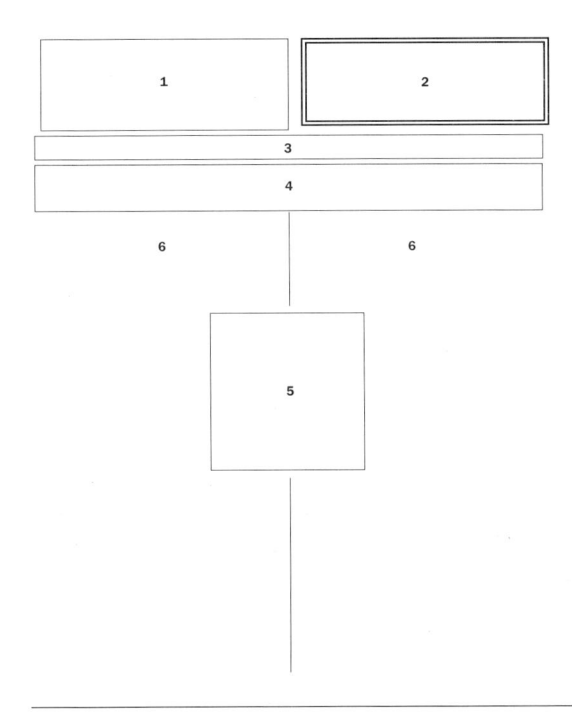

4. Enter the text for the banner, choosing a size that comfortably fills the allocated space. The banner in Figure 13.5 is 48-point Helvetica Italic. To space the text in from the left margin, use the spacebar. Or, to be more sophisticated, create a small border along the left edge of the frame.

5. Create a blank frame to hold the logo (frame 2 in Figure 13.6). Assign zero borders all around. Again, make sure that the right edge of the frame is against the right margin. Also, drag the left edge of the frame so that it's up against frame 1. These precautions are to prevent text you'll be creating later from leaking between the frames or between a frame and a margin.

6. Input the graphic image into the frame, and then resize and crop it.

7. Create a frame for the sub-banner (frame 3 in the figure), and assign thin frame lines at the top and bottom. Then enter the text for the sub-banner.

The reason for putting this text in a frame is to facilitate adjusting it in relation to the other page elements.

8. To center the sub-banner text between the top and bottom lines, create a small border at the top or bottom of the frame. Start by trying a small top border. If that doesn't work, use a small one at the bottom.

9. Create a frame for the main article heading (frame 4 in the figure), then enter the heading text. Adjust its size and center it—the text in the figure is done in 18-point bold. The main reason for using a frame here is to allow the heading to span both columns on the page, because a wide frame overrides the column settings on the page.

10. Create a frame for the boxed text—called a *sidebar*—in the middle of the page (frame 5 in Figure 13.6). Create a border of 0.25 inches all around and specify a line around the frame, placing it in the center of the frame border.

11. Enter the text for the sidebar. If there's too much text, increase the frame size. If the frame is too large, reduce its size so that there is no extra space at the bottom.

12. Enter the text for the main article. If necessary, begin by pressing the Enter key until the text cursor is positioned just below the article heading. When the text reaches the bottom of the first column it will automatically flow to the top of the second column. Alternatively, you can retrieve the text from another file. (See "Using Previously Created Text," below.)

13. Make the final adjustments to the positioning and sizing of the various frames.

If the text for the main article is either slightly too short or too long for the page, you can use any combination of the following to make adjustments:

- Change the size of the sidebar frame. As part of this adjustment you can also make small changes to the size of the text there.

- Make small changes to the size of the body text in the main article. Generally, the text size should be from 9 to 12 points.

- Readjust the four margins. A small change to the left or right margin can make a significant difference in the total column length of your text.

- Readjust the height of the frames at the top of the page.

If the text is so long that no combination of these adjustments is adequate, you'll need to create a second page for the article (see "Working with Multiple Pages," below).

Using Previously Created Text

When creating a newsletter, you can enter the text directly onto each page, as described in the preceding steps. However, you might prefer to create the individual articles at an earlier time, in a separate file. Then, as you're building the newsletter you can retrieve the articles and place them where you want them.

You can easily accomplish this by using Professional Write Plus's ability to work with multiple documents. For example, suppose you have created the text for one of your articles at some earlier time, and you now want to retrieve it into your newsletter. Here's how to accomplish this:

1. Retrieve the article into a second window running Professional Write Plus, by using the File/Open/Open Another option.

2. Select the entire article as a block.

3. Select Edit/Copy, which transfers a copy of the block to the clipboard.

4. Now click on the window containing the newsletter, positioning the text cursor where you want the article to be placed.

5. Select Edit/Paste. The article will be copied from the clipboard into the newsletter at the position of the text cursor.

Adding a Drop Cap

A *drop cap* is an extra large letter that appears at the beginning of a chapter or section. In Figure 13.5, the first letter of the main article is a drop cap. This special effect adds an extra touch of professionalism to a page, and it's surprisingly easy to create: Simply use a separate frame for just that single letter. Here are the steps:

1. Create a small frame, placing it in the vicinity of where you want the drop cap to be. Set all frame borders to zero and don't create any lines on the frame edges. Adjust the frame size so that it's a little larger than the size of the drop cap you want to create.

2. Double-click on this frame so that you can enter text into it.

3. Create a new paragraph style called Drop Cap, using the Body Text style as a model, and assigning the following characteristics:

- A font size of 55 points

- A line spacing of 0.4 inches

- No spacing above or below the paragraph

- Indentation for all lines set to zero

4. Enter the single letter you want to use as a drop cap.

5. If the drop cap isn't visible in the frame, increase the height of the frame until the letter appears.

6. To change the size of the letter, use the Font option in the Modify & Create Styles dialog box. (You can select a type size to suit your degree of flamboyance.)

7. Make the frame as short as possible: Reduce the height of the frame bit by bit, until the letter disappears. Then increase the frame size just enough to make the letter reappear.

8. Adjust the width of the frame so that the right edge just about touches the adjacent text. (You may need to make a sample printout or two in order to get this adjustment just the way you want it.)

9. Adjust the frame so that the left edge of the drop cap is up against the left margin and the top edge is about even with the top of the first full line of text.

10. Remember to delete the first letter of the paragraph—it has now been replaced by the drop cap.

Working with Multiple Pages

Professional Write Plus was not designed as a true desktop publishing tool, so its lack of certain conveniences in this area is not surprising. Its biggest shortcoming is the inability to automatically direct the text flow to specific columns that you select. Text *always* flows from top to bottom and left to right (with respect to columns on a page). When the text reaches the bottom of the rightmost column on the page, it then flows into the first column of the next page.

If you have two or more articles on the first page of a newsletter, and each of them will flow onto additional pages, you must manually enter the text into whatever columns you wish on the successive pages. This requires a bit of planning during text entry and editing.

A Working Strategy Here's the best strategy you can follow: enter as much text for each article as will fit onto page 1, but don't go onto the next pages yet. After entering the text for all the articles, fully edit them and then completely finalize the page layout details.

If, during these final stages for page 1, text from an article on the left overflows into the text for an article on the right, you'll have to delete the overflow, perhaps saving it for later insertion on a later page. On the other hand, if text from the article on the right overflows, it will spill over onto the second page. You can later reposition this overflow wherever you want it.

Only after you've completely finished with page 1 should you go on to page 2. Similarly, completely finish with page 2 before tackling page 3, and so on.

Changing the Page Layout   Remember that if you make *any* type of change to page 1, it will probably affect the layout of later pages since Professional Write Plus does not allow you to create different page layouts for different pages of a document. That is, the layout you select with the options in the Page Layout dialog box applies to every page in a document. This includes the number of columns on the page, the margins, and the other features in the Page Layout dialog box.

However, you can easily circumvent this restriction. For each page beyond the first, create a frame that fills the entire page. Then within each frame you can choose the layout you want.

For example, to create a three-column layout with wider margins for page 2, begin by creating a frame that fills the page. Then adjust the frame size so that its boundaries define the margins you want for the page. Alternatively, you can adjust the effective page margins by specifying the appropriate border sizes for the frame. When you've set your margins, select the number of columns you want using the Columns & Tabs option on the Frame Layout dialog box.

Summary

Word processing software has evolved rapidly, and you can now create documents that only a few years ago would have required extremely expensive and complex desktop publishing software. There's virtually no limit to the different types of documents you can create with Professional Write Plus, and those described in this chapter are only a small sample of what's possible.

Using the program's desktop publishing features, you can create highly attractive newsletters, brochures, and so on. The ability to incorporate frames into a page design offers unlimited design possibilities. This is further enhanced by being able to create multiple-column layouts within a frame. However, the program has definite limits on its usefulness for multipage, multicolumn publications.

After you have created a new design for a business card, newsletter, or whatever, save it for later use. Over a period of time you'll build up a repertoire of useful designs that will allow you to create documents with comparatively little effort.

APPENDIX A

Installing Professional Write Plus

If you're familiar with how to use Windows, you'll have little trouble installing Professional Write Plus. Installation can be done either from the DOS prompt or from within Windows.

NOTE. *In order to install Professional Write Plus, Windows 3.0 must be installed on your computer.*

Before installing Professional Write Plus, make duplicates of the original program disks (including duplicate labels), and then store the originals in a safe place. My philosophy is that original program disks should be used twice: once to make a set of backups and once to throw out when a new version of the software is released.

Insert the backup disk 1 into drive A or B of your computer. The entire installation takes from 5 to 15 minutes, depending on the speed of your computer.

Installing the Program Files

To install the program from DOS, enter the command **A:INSTALL** (or **B:INSTALL** if disk 1 is in drive B). Then follow the instructions on the screen (see "Installation Details," below).

To install the program from within Windows, follow these steps:

1. With Windows running, display the Program Manager window, which will look something like Figure A.1 (yours will probably look different, depending on your particular Windows setup).

2. Click on the File menu, then click on the Run option. The dialog box shown here will appear:

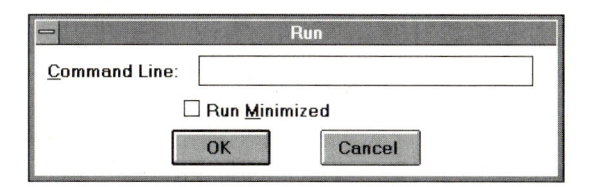

3. In the edit box labeled "Command Line", enter either **A:INSTALL** (or **B:INSTALL** if disk 1 is in drive B), then click on OK.

4. Follow the instructions on the screen as described in the next section.

Figure A.1
The Program Manager window

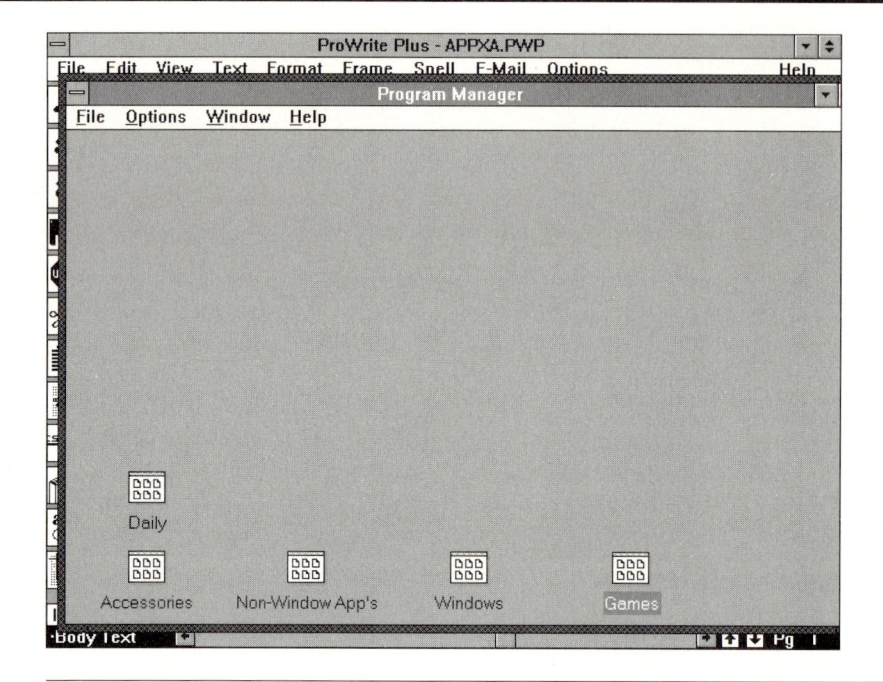

Installation Details

During installation, most of the instructions you'll see on the screen are self-explanatory. However, here are a few tips about those areas that may be confusing.

Professional Write Plus Directory   Normally, the installation process puts the Professional Write Plus programs in a directory named C:\PWPLUS. If this directory doesn't exist, the installation will create it. You can, however, have the programs installed in any disk drive and directory you wish. When the program asks, just enter the name of the disk drive and directory. If the directory you enter doesn't exist, the program will create it. If the directory does exist, make sure that it doesn't contain any other files (good practice is to keep all program files for each software package in a separate directory).

Windows Directory   The program files for Microsoft Windows are normally stored in the directory C:\WINDOWS. If this is not the case for your system, you must supply the correct name of the Windows directory when the program asks you to. *This is important.* If you don't know where the Windows programs are stored, find out before proceeding with the installation.

Modifying Your AUTOEXEC.BAT File As part of the installation, changes are made to a file named AUTOEXEC.BAT on your hard disk. When the installation program asks you if it can make these changes, enter **Y** unless you have a particular reason for not allowing this step. This modification inserts the name of the Professional Write Plus directory in your system's path (a list of easily accessible directories), which makes life simpler for Windows.

Creating a Program Icon

Before you can run Professional Write Plus you must create a program icon, along with suitable information, within Windows. Then, whenever you want to run the program you simply double-click on this icon. Assuming that Windows is running, here's how to create the icon:

1. Display the Program Manager window.

2. Select the group window in which you want to create the Professional Write Plus icon. If this window is reduced to an icon, double-click on the icon. If the group window is on the screen, click anywhere within that window.

3. Pull down the File menu, then click on the New option.

4. When the New Program Object box appears (see below), click on Program Item, then click on OK.

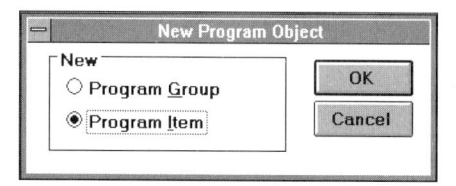

5. When the next dialog box appears (see below), fill in the two edit boxes as follows (you can use the Tab key or the mouse to move between these boxes):

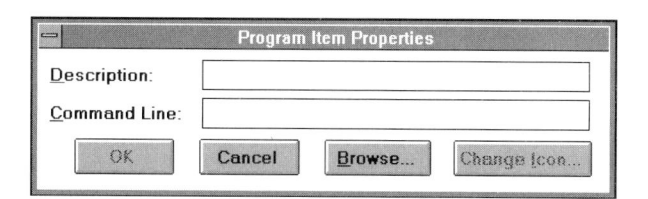

Description: Enter a short descriptive phrase, something like **ProWrite**. If you leave this box blank, "ProWrite Plus" will automatically be inserted.

Command Line: Enter **C:\PWPLUS\PWPLUS.EXE**. This identifies the name of the program file (PWPLUS.EXE), as well as its complete path.

6. Click on OK. A new icon for Professional Write Plus will now appear in the group window you selected.

Whenever you want to run Professional Write Plus, you first select the group window containing the icon you've created, then double-click on this icon.

APPENDIX B

Customizing Professional Write Plus

You can customize many of Professional Write Plus's options to suit your particular way of working. When you first install the program, these options are set at their default values—which is fine for your initial word processing efforts. However, as you gain experience with the program you'll probably want to change some of these options. How to do so is described in this appendix.

When you make any type of customization, it remains in effect for all future word processing sessions, or until you change it again. If you change an option while you're working with more than one document at the same time, the new option will affect only the window in which you make the change, not any of the others. That is, the new option will not have any effect during the current session on any other documents already open in other windows nor on any documents you subsequently open in other windows.

However, if you change an option and then open another document in the same window, that option will affect the document. Moreover, the option will affect all documents you work with in subsequent word processing sessions in all windows.

Customizing the Side Bar

The side bar (on the left side of the screen) displays a group of icons you can use to perform various types of operations. This icon bar is a great convenience, since clicking on an icon is usually much quicker than pulling down a menu and then selecting the option you want.

The icons initially shown on the bar aren't the only ones available. You can choose from a rather large selection (shown in Table B.1), placing icons on the bar for those operations you perform most frequently.

Here are the steps for customizing the icon bar:

1. Click on Options/Icons. The dialog box shown in Figure B.1 will appear. The left part of this box shows the icons currently displayed on the icon bar, as well as their relative placement. (The number of icons displayed in the icon bar depends on your particular monitor.) The right part of the figure contains a scroll box that lists all the available icons.

2. On the left part of the screen, click on the icon you want to replace. This icon will become highlighted.

3. Scroll through the list box on the right until the new icon you want appears, then click on that icon. It will then appear at the left in the highlighted position.

4. Continue with steps 2 and 3 for each icon you want to change.

Table B.1 The Icons That Can Be Placed on the Icon Bar

Icon	Function	Icon	Function	Icon	Function
	Full Page/Current View		Justify Text		New
	Draft/Layout Mode		Double Underline Text		Normal Text
	Open		Subscript Text		Bold Text
	Save		Superscript		Italic Text
	Print		Page Layout		Underline Text
	Undo		Modify & Create Styles		Word Underline Text
	Cut		Frame Layout		Left Align Text
	File Manager		Thesaurus		Right Align Text
	Find & Replace		Copy		Center Text
	Go To Next		Paste		Read Mail
	Insert Page Break		Spelling		Show/Hide Tab Ruler
	Insert Variable		Add a Frame		Show/Hide Pictures
	Insert Footnote		Import Graphics		Show/Hide Marks
	Insert Note		Import Text/Data		Grammar
	Change Font		Export Text		

5. Finish up by clicking on OK. If you click on Cancel, your changes are ignored.

Setting the Start-up Defaults

The start-up defaults are a small group of options that control, among other things, some of the ways in which the edit screen is displayed each time you begin a word processing session. These options control the following:

- Which display mode is selected
- The view

Setting the Start-up Defaults

Figure B.1
Use this dialog box to customize the icon bar

[Screenshot of ProWrite Plus - APPXB.PWP showing the Icons dialog box with Icons Available list: Leave Blank at this Location, Full Page/Current View, Draft/Layout Mode, Open, Save, Print, Undo, Cut. OK and Cancel buttons.]

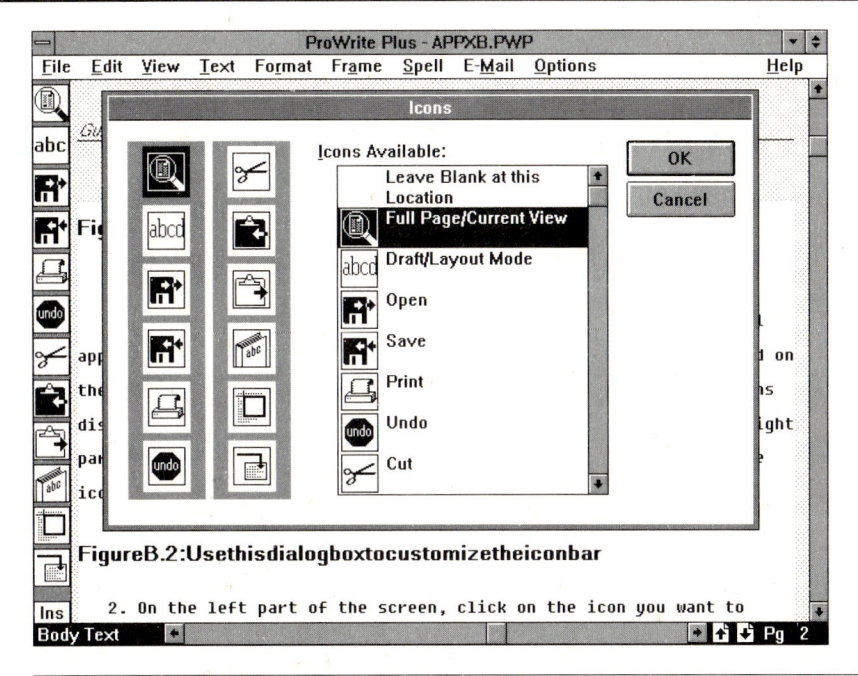

- The size of the window
- Whether the Styles box is displayed
- Whether the program's logo is displayed at the start of each session
- What happens to a selected text block when a key is pressed

The last of these options isn't really a start-up option, but for some reason the program groups it with the others.

To change any of these options, click on Options/Startup Defaults, and the screen shown in Figure B.2 will appear. Then make your selections as described below.

Display Mode   You can select either Layout or Draft as the default mode whenever you begin a session. Layout is the initial default set by the program when it's first installed.

Default View   You can select either Working or Standard view as the one selected at the beginning of each session. The initial default is Working view, which is set at 91 percent of the size of Standard view.

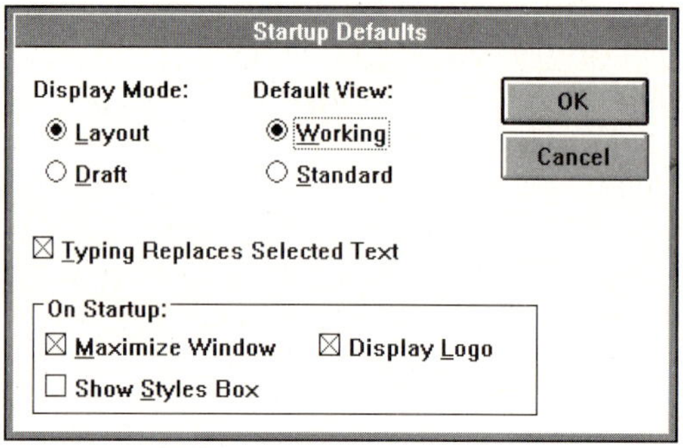

Figure B.2
The start-up options

[Startup Defaults dialog box showing:
Display Mode: ● Layout, ○ Draft
Default View: ● Working, ○ Standard
☒ Typing Replaces Selected Text
On Startup: ☒ Maximize Window, ☒ Display Logo, ☐ Show Styles Box
OK / Cancel buttons]

Typing Replaces Selected Text Normally, when you select a text block and then immediately type a character, the block is automatically erased. However, you can turn off this option by clicking on it in the dialog box so that the X is removed.

Maximize Window If this option is selected (the initial program default), the Professional Write window is maximized at start-up, meaning that it occupies the entire screen.

Display Logo If this option is selected (as it is when you first install the program), the program's logo appears briefly at the beginning of each session. You can save yourself a second or two each day by turning off this option.

Show Styles Box When this option is selected, the Styles Box is displayed at the beginning of each session. Initially, this option is turned off.

The Display Mode and Default View options can be changed during a word processing session by making selections from the View menu. You can change the size of the window during a session by clicking on the maximize button (at the top-right corner of the screen) and then adjusting the window size. You can also hide or display the Styles box during a session by using the Options menu. The other options can be changed only from the Startup Defaults dialog box.

Setting the Default Paths

You can select defaults for the following paths:

Document Path This is the path the program automatically accesses the first time you retrieve a document when starting a new session, unless you

Setting the Default Paths

specify another option. It's also the path used the first time you save a new document in each session, unless you specify otherwise. And when you access the File Manager, this is the default path the program assumes.

During any particular session, this default remains in effect until you select another path for retrieving a document. That new path then becomes the default *for that session only*.

When the program is first installed, the default document path is set to the directory \DOCS under the Professional Write directory. For example, if the program files are stored in C:\PWPLUS, the default document directory is C:\PWPLUS\DOCS. This directory contains a few sample documents you can use to help become familiar with the program.

Normally, you'll probably want to change this directory to wherever your most current documents are stored.

Template Path This is the path where Professional Write looks for your templates. It is the only directory from which a template can be retrieved. To use a template that's not in the default template path, you can either copy the template to the default template path or temporarily change the default path.

Initially you'll be using the templates supplied with the program, and these are all stored in the \STYLES directory under the directory containing the Professional Write Plus program files. Later, as you create your own templates, you can either continue to use this default directory or create another one.

Here's how to change either of these default directories:

1. Select Options/Default Paths. The dialog box shown below will appear.

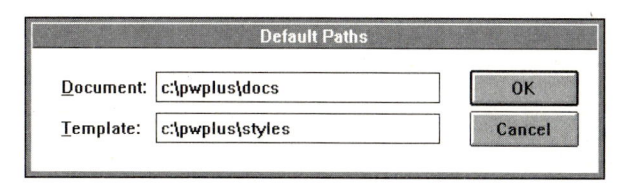

   ```
   ┌──────────────── Default Paths ────────────────┐
   │                                               │
   │   Document:  c:\pwplus\docs        [   OK   ] │
   │                                               │
   │   Template:  c:\pwplus\styles      [ Cancel ] │
   │                                               │
   └───────────────────────────────────────────────┘
   ```

2. Double-click in the edit box labeled "Document", and then enter the new path where you want to store and retrieve documents. Be sure to include the disk drive, as well as the full path name.

3. Double-click in the edit box labeled "Template", and then enter the path for the directory containing the templates you'll be using on a day-to-day basis.

4. Finish up by clicking on OK, or click on Cancel to void your selections.

Remember that the paths you select here are the ones initially selected at the beginning of each word processing session. During any particular session, you can change the default for either path by using the above steps.

However, you can also change the default document path simply by retrieving a document. The path from which it is retrieved becomes the new default document path for that session.

Changing the Default Template

Whenever you begin working on a new document (by selecting File/New), a template must be assigned to it. When the program is initially installed, it is set up so that one of its built-in templates, DEFAULT.STY, is assigned as the default template. That is, this template is automatically assigned to each new document you create.

You can change the template used as the default. For example, you might want to create a template specially designed for your daily correspondence and then assign it as the default. Or you can set up the program so that you select which template to use each time a new document is created.

The only templates directly available to you are those stored in the default template path. For details about assigning this path, see the preceding section.

Here's how to change the default template:

1. Select Options/Default Template, and the dialog box shown in Figure B.3 will appear. The templates displayed in the list box are those in the default template path.

Figure B.3
Use this box to select the default template

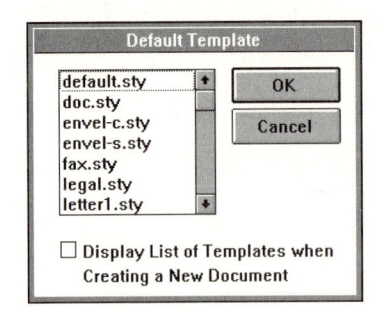

2. To select a new template as the default, click on its name in the list box, and then click on OK. The template you select will automatically be assigned to each new document you create.

Instead of automatically assigning a default, you can set up the program so that you select a template each time you create a new document:

1. Select Options/Default Template. When the dialog box appears, click on the option labeled "Display List of Templates when Creating a New Document".

2. Click on OK.

From then on, each time you begin a new document you'll select the template you want from a list box that appears on the screen. Note that you must use this option if you want to include the contents of a template as part of a new document.

Setting the Layout Mode Options

Layout mode is Professional Write's WYSIWYG (what you see is what you get) screen. This is the preferred mode to use whenever possible because it displays many features that aren't visible in draft mode. You can customize many options associated with layout mode by selecting Options/Layout Mode Options, then making your choices from the dialog box that appears (see Figure B.4).

Figure B.4
Display options for layout mode

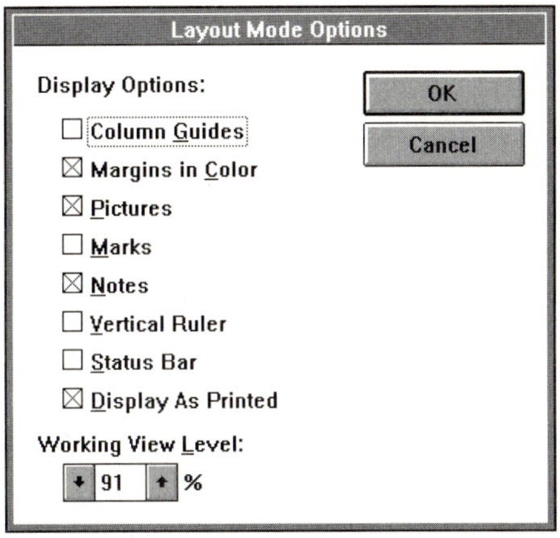

The purpose of these options is to customize your word processing environment. None of them has any effect on the printed output. Moreover, they have no effect on the draft mode display. (To change the draft mode display, see "Draft Mode Options," below.) Your options are as follows:

Column Guides Use this option to display dotted lines at the column margins. This option is particularly useful when working with multicolumn page formats because it shows the column boundaries.

Margins in Color When this option is selected, the margins are displayed in color (color monitors only) or as a light pattern of dots (on a monochrome monitor). The color that's displayed depends on the way various color options are established within Windows.

Pictures If this option is selected, each imported graphic image is displayed within its frame. When this option is *not* selected, each image is replaced with a large X, along with the name of the associated graphics file. Deselecting this option can save a good deal of display time when graphic images are complex, especially with a slower computer.

Marks When this option is selected, a little symbol is displayed for each hard return, tab, page break, and inserted tab ruler.

Notes When this option is turned on, each note you create within a document is displayed as a little box where the note is contained in the text. If you use a lot of notes you'll find this a handy way to locate them.

Vertical Ruler Select this option to display the vertical ruler on the left side of the edit screen. The ruler is essential for detailed page layout work.

Status Bar The status bar appears at the bottom of the screen. When this option is selected, the status bar displays the following information:

- The edit mode (either Insert or Typeover).
- The current line number.
- The current column position. For monospaced fonts, this corresponds to the character position on a line; for proportional fonts this number doesn't have much use.
- Whether caps lock is on or off.
- The full path name of the current directory.

Display as Printed When this option is selected, the line and page breaks appearing on the screen correspond exactly to those printed. This option should normally be selected, because otherwise the screen won't show you where these breaks will be when a document is printed.

Working View Level The number you enter for this option controls the size of the Working view relative to the Standard view. You can customize this option to suit your particular viewing needs.

Draft Mode Options

To set the various options available with draft mode, select Options/Draft Mode Options. The dialog box that appears (Figure B.5) shows the options available to you. As with the layout mode options, none of these has any effect on the printed page, nor do they have any effect on the layout mode display.

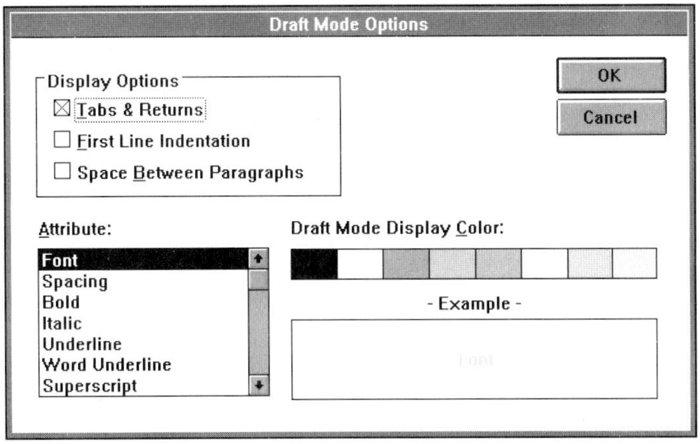

Figure B.5
Display options for draft mode

If you plan to use the draft mode to any significant extent (although I advise against it), you'll find some of these options invaluable:

Tabs & Returns With this option selected, each tab appears as --->, and each hard return as ¶.

First Line Indentation With this option turned on, the first line of each paragraph is indented five spaces.

Space Between Paragraphs To display a blank line between each pair of paragraphs, select this option.

Attribute Colors No attributes, such as boldface or italics, can be seen in draft mode, because all characters are displayed in the same typeface. However, you can identify the various attributes that may be assigned to text by assigning a different color to each attribute.

You can assign a color to any attribute that can be selected from the Text menu. However, these colors will not show for attributes that are assigned as part of a paragraph style. For example, if you assign the color red to the bold attribute, any text you make bold using the text menu will appear red on the screen. However, if you assign the bold attribute to the Heading paragraph style the headings will not show in red on the screen.

To assign a color to a particular attribute:

1. Click on the attribute you want in the list box at the bottom-left of the dialog box (under "Attribute").

2. Click on the color you want assigned to that attribute under "Draft Mode Display Color".

3. Click on OK to have your selections take effect.

Unless you have a phenomenal memory, begin by assigning colors only to the most common attributes, such as boldface and italics. Then, after you learn to recognize them automatically, add one or two more. Initially, a written list of color assignments might be helpful.

Backup, Speed, and Undo Options

Among the program's many options are two that allow you to create automatic backup files, helping you to protect your work. Two other options can be set to speed up spell checking and search-and-replace operations. Finally, you can set the number of operations that the program will remember and reverse with the Undo operation.

Setting the Backup Options

You can set up Professional Write so that it automatically saves whatever document you're working with after a preset time interval. This is an invaluable feature. For instance, let's assume that you set the program to save your work every ten minutes. Now suppose that while working with a document you manage to make a total mess of it—with an ill-considered search-and-replace operation, for example. To recover, simply select File/Open, and then select the same file again. (Make sure you answer No when the program asks if you want to save your latest changes!) You'll be back to where you were when the last automatic save occurred—no more that ten minutes before.

You can also set a program option that creates a separate backup file for each document you work with. Here's how it works: Let's suppose that you open an existing document, make several changes, and then save it back to the same file. When you make this save, a copy of the *original* document is saved in a file of the same name, but in a different directory, which you have previously selected. Subsequently, each time you perform a save, a copy of the document *as it was when you did the previous save* is saved to the backup file.

To set up either of these backup options, follow these steps:

1. Select Options/Backup Options, and dialog box shown in Figure B.6 will appear.

2. To set up the program to save your work automatically, click on the option Auto Timed Save. Then enter the desired time interval between saves. You can enter any number between 0 and 99 (minutes).

Figure B.6
Use this dialog box to set the backup options

WARNING! *This feature will not work with a new document that hasn't yet been saved to a file.*

3. To have the program create a backup file each time you do a save, click on the option Auto Backup. Then in the Path edit box, enter the complete path of the directory where you want the backup files saved. A good idea is to choose a directory that's not used for anything else. In particular, don't choose a directory that's used for saving your normal Professional Write Plus documents. If you do, the backup file will simply overwrite your ordinary file, accomplishing exactly nothing.

4. Click on OK to save your options.

If you implement the feature that creates backup files, you might want to periodically browse through the backup directory and delete those files you no longer need.

Setting the Speed Options

Two of the program's operations, spell checking and find and replace, can take considerable time, especially for long documents. You can reduce the operation time by forcing the program to enter draft mode before performing either of these tasks. Here's how:

1. Select Options/Speed Options, and the dialog box shown here will appear:

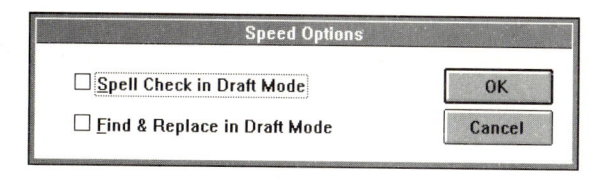

2. Click on the operation(s) you want speeded up, then click on OK to save your options.

Suppose that you have set the speed option for spell checking. Whenever you begin a spell check and you're in layout mode, the program will switch to draft mode, perform the spell check, and then switch back to layout mode.

Setting the Number of Undo Levels

The Undo feature allows you to reverse the last operation performed with Professional Write Plus. Not every operation can be undone, but most of the damaging ones can, including block moves and deletes.

When first installed, the program can undo only the last operation, but you can set an option so that it remembers up to four. Here's how:

1. Select Options/Undo Levels.

2. When the Undo submenu appears (see below), select the number of levels you want to be able to reverse.

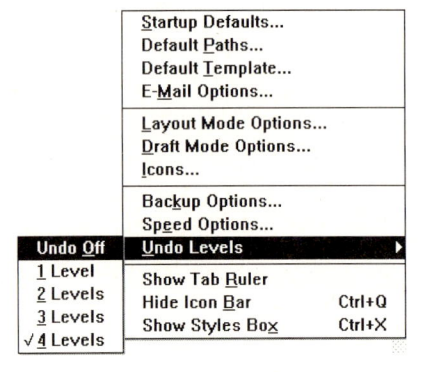

```
Startup Defaults...
Default Paths...
Default Template...
E-Mail Options...

Layout Mode Options...
Draft Mode Options...
Icons...

Backup Options...
Speed Options...
Undo Off      Undo Levels          ▶
1 Level       Show Tab Ruler
2 Levels      Hide Icon Bar    Ctrl+Q
3 Levels      Show Styles Box  Ctrl+X
√ 4 Levels
```

As with any other option, the program remembers this one forever, or until you change it again. For more details about using the Undo feature, see "Recovering from Accidents" in Chapter 4.

Other Options You Can Set

Whenever you start up a word processing session, the tab ruler and icon bar may or may not appear. If either of these is not displayed, you can make it visible by selecting either Show Tab Ruler or Show Icon Bar from the Options menu. Conversely, you can remove either the tab ruler or the icon bar from the screen by selecting the corresponding Hide option on the Options menu.

The advantage to hiding either the tab ruler or the icon bar is that more space is made available on the screen for displaying your documents.

However, being able to click on icons is a great advantage that you may not want to forgo.

Whether the icon bar is visible or invisible when you start a word processing session depends on the state of the last word processing window to be closed in the previous session. If the icon bar was displayed when the last window was closed, then it will be displayed at your next word processing session. The same is true for the tab ruler.

APPENDIX C

Customizing for a New Printer

Whenever necessary, you can use printers other than the ones already installed with Professional Write Plus. However, in order to do so you must customize Windows for that printer. This is the nature of things: Any program designed for Windows automatically has access to all printers installed for Windows.

Installing the Printer Under Windows

As a preliminary step, make sure that the printer is attached to one of the ports (connectors) on the back of the computer. Each port has a name, either LPT1:, LPT2:, COM1:, COM2:, COM3:, or COM4:. In order to customize Windows for the printer, you must know the name of the port, so if necessary find out before proceeding.

You'll need to use the Windows disks during customization. Make sure you use a duplicate of the original disks, rather than the originals themselves.

If you're currently working with Professional Write Plus, you must exit temporarily to Windows. Then you can run the Control Panel to perform the customization. Here are the steps:

1. If you're working in Professional Write Plus, press Ctrl-Esc to display the Task Manager (see Figure C.1).

Figure C.1
The Windows Task Manager

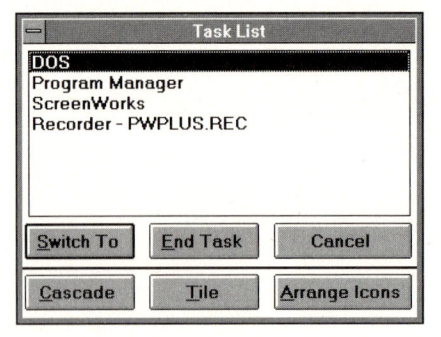

2. Double click on Program Manager.

3. Locate the Control Panel icon. It may be in the Main program group, or perhaps another one.

4. Double-click on the Control Panel icon, and the display shown in Figure C.2 will appear.

Figure C.2
The Windows Control Panel

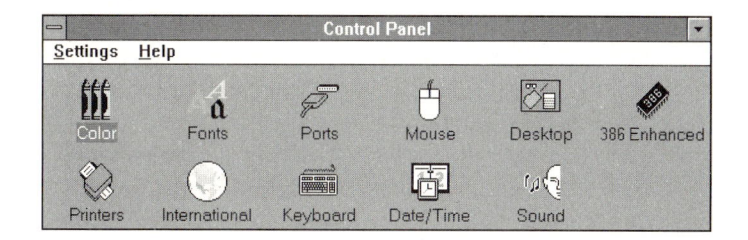

5. Double-click on the Printers icon, and the dialog box shown in Figure C.3 will appear.

Figure C.3
Use this dialog box to display the existing printers or customize for a new printer

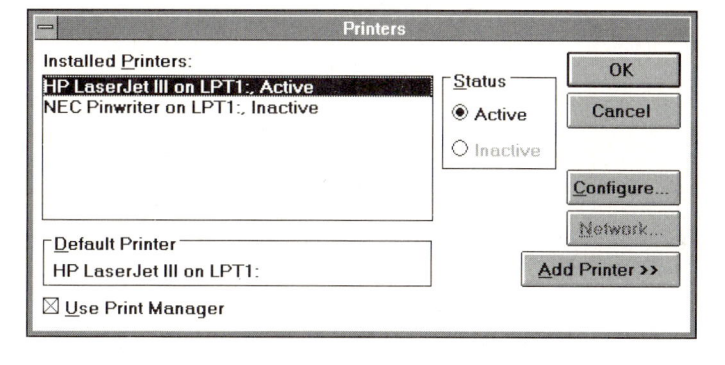

6. Click on Add Printer, and the dialog box shown in Figure C.4 will appear.

7. In the box labeled "List of Printers", highlight the desired printer name, then click on Install (see below for additional instructions). The dialog box shown in Figure C.5 will appear.

8. Insert the Windows disk containing the driver for the new printer into either disk drive A or B. Then enter the name of the disk drive in the edit box and click on OK. For example, if you're using drive B, enter **B:**. After a few seconds, the display shown in Figure C.4 will reappear, and the name of the new printer should appear in the list box labeled "Installed Printers". (For more information about this step, see below.)

9. Click on Configure, and the dialog box shown in Figure C.6 will appear.

10. In the box labeled "Ports", click on the name of the port to which the printer is attached (see below).

Figure C.4
Select the printer from the bottom list in this box

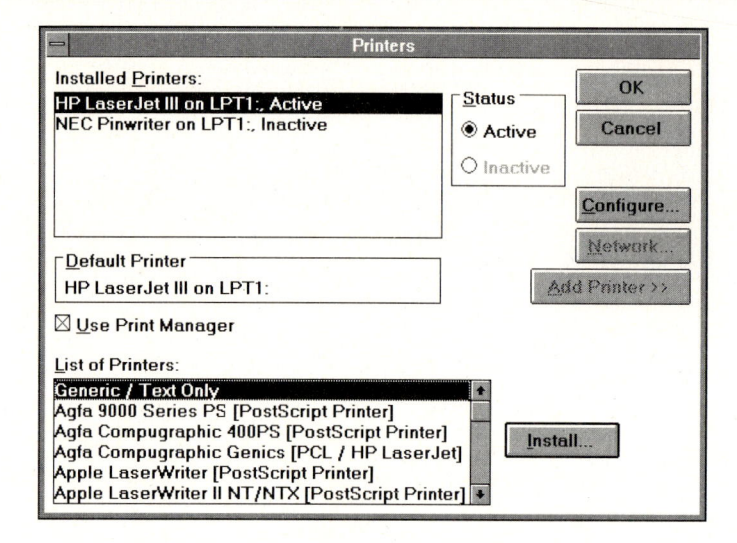

Figure C.5
Enter the name of the disk drive containing the Windows disk

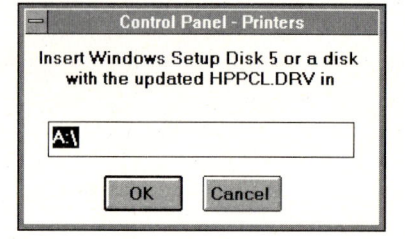

Figure C.6
Select the port to which the printer is attached

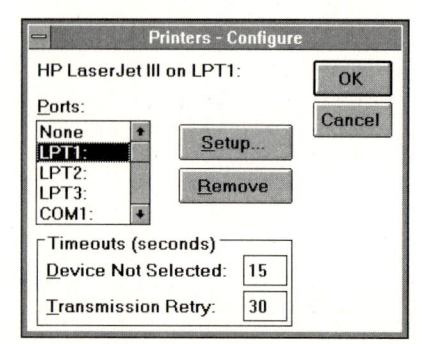

Installing the Printer Under Windows

11. Click on Setup. You'll then see a dialog box listing various configuration options for your printer. (This display will vary from one printer to another.)

12. Select the options you want for your printer (portrait or landscape orientation, printer resolution, font cartridges installed, if any, and so on).

13. Work your way back to Windows by clicking on OK in each dialog box.

If your printer isn't listed in the dialog box (step 7), you'll have to select one on the list that's close to yours. Your printer manual may indicate which popular printer your own emulates. If so, select that one in step 7. Otherwise, you may need to use trial and error to find a printer on the list that allows Windows to use your printer effectively.

As a starting point, here are some suggestions for each of the general types:

- Laser printers: HP LaserJet or HP LaserJet Series II
- 9-pin dot matrix printers: Epson FX-80, LX-80, MX-80, or IBM Graphics
- 24-pin dot matrix printers: Epson LQ 800 or Epson LQ 1500

In step 8 you must insert the appropriate Windows disk. Here again, you may need to use a little trial and error. Try the following disks first:

- 5 1/4 inch disks: For all printers try Disk 5
- 3 1/2 inch disks: For laser printers try Disk 7; for all other printers try Disk 6

If you get a message that Windows still needs another disk, it means that you've used the wrong one. Try again, starting with the highest numbered disk and working backwards until Windows finds the driver it's looking for.

If you don't know the name of the port to which your printer is attached (step 10), you can try using trial and error. Select a port, then see if Professional Write Plus can talk to the printer. Keep trying until you find the correct port.

When using trial and error, try the port names in the following order:

1. LPT1:
2. LPT2:
3. LPT3:
4. COM1:
5. COM2:
6. COM3:
7. COM4:

If none of these work with your printer, you'll need to get help from someone familiar with your hardware setup.

Improving the Printer Output Quality

In some cases, especially when you first install a printer, the quality of your printed output may be less than you expect. For example, if the printer has been generating better output with a non-Windows program, you should rightfully expect at least the same quality when printing under Windows.

Remember, several different types of fonts can be used with a printer: built-in fonts, those from font cartridges, Windows fonts, and scalable typefaces from third-party software. Not all fonts generate the same quality of printed output—in fact the variation may be quite surprising.

For dot-matrix printers, the best-quality fonts are usually those built into the printer itself. However, some scalable typefaces may look very good, and some may come close to the quality of the built-in ones. Windows fonts, on the other hand, usually generate only medium-quality output.

With a laser printer, you should settle for nothing less than very good output, especially at the smaller type sizes. If one particular typeface is generating particularly poor quality, don't use it—you can do better.

If you're convinced that your printer should be doing better, before doing anything else check the resolution being used by Windows for your printer. This is an easy procedure, and it's a lot less expensive than purchasing type-generating software. The easiest way to determine whether Windows is using the best possible printer resolution is to try them all. Most printers have only two or three to choose from.

Testing the Printer Resolution

From within Professional Write Plus, you can easily change the resolution Windows uses for your printer:

1. From the File menu, select Printer Setup/Setup.

2. When the Setup dialog box appears, select a different resolution for the printer.

After you select a new resolution, try printing some text to see if there is any improvement. If you find a resolution that's best for the printer, select it and leave it. Any selections you make in the printer Setup dialog box remain in Professional Write Plus's files until you change them later.

Using Type-Generating Software

If you don't get adequate output at any resolution, you may need to consider purchasing type-generating software from outside vendors. Many different software packages designed to run with Windows are currently on the market. Some of them are quite inexpensive, yet generate very good printed type.

If you're considering making a purchase, try to obtain a sample of the printout generated by a printer like yours or similar to it before making a decision. For example, if you have an Epson 24-pin printer, a sample from any model of 24-pin Epson will be adequate for the purposes of comparison.

APPENDIX D

Troubleshooting

This appendix lists some of the more common problems encountered while working with Professional Write Plus.

Problem   *A tab was changed in the Page Layout dialog box, but that tab doesn't seem to exist on the edit screen.*

Solution   There's very likely an inserted tab ruler somewhere in your document, above where you're working. The tabs on this ruler do *not* display in the Page Layout dialog box (which displays the tabs of the document's Page Layout). Any tabs you insert in the Page Layout dialog box go into the Page Layout, not the inserted tab ruler.
   Tabs on an inserted tab ruler take precedence over any Page Layout tabs, which is basically the heart of your problem. If you want to insert a tab, do it on the tab ruler on the edit screen.

Problem   *There is extra space between two words in the text, and this space can't be erased.*

Solution   Some or all of that blank space has been italicized or boldfaced or assigned a larger font size, thereby taking up more space. Select that blank space as a text block, along with a character or two on either side, then select the option Text/Normal. This may eliminate the bold, italic, or large-size blank, and the extra space should disappear. If this doesn't work, try assigning the block to the same font as the surrounding text.

Problem   *An existing document file can't be modified with the Save or Save As option.*

Solution   The Read-Write file attribute has probably been set to Read Only. This may have been done as a precaution during some type of system failure. Here's how to reset the attribute so that you can work with the file: Activate the File Manager, select File/Attributes, enter the name of your file, and then assign its attribute to be Read-Write. Alternatively, if you're running on a network someone else may be working with the document. Only one person at a time can modify and save a document.

Problem   *The last page or pages of a document can't be deleted.*

Solution   Most likely there are one or more empty frames on each recalcitrant page. All frames on a page must be deleted before the page itself can be deleted. To find a frame so that you can delete it, move the text cursor to the top of the page in question, then select Edit/Go To/Frame. The first frame on that page will be selected, and you can then delete it. When the page no longer contains any frames, you can delete it. Note that the Go To/Frame option works only on the current page, so you'll need to move the cursor to each page in turn.

Problem   As text is entered, it jumps around a space on the page as though there were an invisible object there.

Solution   There's a blank frame occupying that space. To delete the frame, click anywhere within the offending space. When the frame handles become visible, press the Del key to delete the frame.

Problem   The top or bottom of some text lines are clipped (not visible).

Solution   Here's the most likely explanation for this behavior: The line spacing for the lines containing the offending text has been set to a custom value. This could have been done either from the text menu or by assigning a custom spacing to the paragraph style. That custom spacing remains fixed, even when you enter text of a larger size, with the result that there isn't enough vertical space between lines for that text.

There are two possible ways to eliminate this problem. One approach is to select the offending lines as a block, then assign either Single Spacing or a custom line spacing large enough to accommodate the text size. Another possibility is to reassign Single Spacing to the paragraph style. The program will then automatically adjust the line spacing to accommodate larger text.

Problem   Sometimes the tab ruler appears at the start of each word processing session, and other times it doesn't. Who's in control here?

Solution   Whether or not the tab ruler is visible when you start up Professional Write Plus depends on the status of the tab ruler in the word processing window you exited last during your previous session. If the ruler was visible then, it will also be visible the next time you start the program. Note that this is also true of the icon bar.

Problem   How can the entire line width be made visible on the screen at the same time?

Solution   This problem occurs primarily when using a color monitor at the higher resolutions. Not having the entire line visible is a real nuisance, and you should definitely customize the program so that you don't have to scroll horizontally to see your text. There's no absolutely ideal solution to this situation, because the problem involves the way Professional Write Plus and Windows display text.

The approach to this problem that's built into Professional Write Plus is the Working view, which offers a text size that's a percentage of the size displayed in Standard view. When Professional Write Plus is first installed, this percentage is set to 91. If you select Working view set at 91 percent, and you then turn on the tab ruler, you'll see that just over 6 1/2 inches of paper width is visible on the screen—namely a full line width for 8 1/2-inch wide paper minus the 1-inch margins.

This is the simplest solution, and you should try it before any others. If you're satisfied with the quality of the text display, then that's as far as you need to go. Unfortunately, the problem with this approach is that on some color monitors the screen fonts for 10- and 12-point type (the size you'll probably use most often) don't look very good.

Here's a solution that may be more acceptable to you: Change the right margin to 1.5 inches for any document that you're working with. In addition, use Standard view and set the size of the font in the Body Text paragraph style to 10 or 12 points. On many Windows installations the screen font for this size—in Standard view—yields by far the best-looking screen output.

To make this solution easier to implement, assign a right margin of 1.5 inches to the templates you use for generating text-based documents. Then, each time you create a new document using one of these templates, the margins will be set automatically.

The only drawback to this solution is that you'll probably want to make the right margin smaller before making your final printout. At first, this may seem like a rather steep price to pay, but it really isn't. This is the approach I take with my Super VGA monitor: Just before generating the final output for a document, I change the right margin back to 1 inch. This process has become so routine that I don't give it a second thought; and the benefit of working with high-quality screen fonts is worth the small amount of time needed to change the margin.

Problem *Working with overlapping frames seems difficult and confusing, and it often seems impossible to manipulate text in some of these frames.*

Solution Here's a simple approach to working with overlapping frames: First select the frame you want to work with—if necessary, hold down the Ctrl key while clicking repeatedly until the correct frame is selected. Then click on the option Frame/Bring to Front. The selected frame will be shifted so that it's on top of all the others, and you can then work with the frame contents to your heart's content.

INDEX

*, 104-106
? command button, 333
?, 104-106
_, 397
¶, 106, 397
<PAGE BREAK> symbol, 54

A

Above and Below spacing options, 181-182
Accidents, recovering from, 115-116, 220-221
Accuracy, of printers, 255
Active printer, 270-272
Add a Frame icon, 390
Address book, E-Mail, 362-363
Adobe Type Manager package, 261, 263
After Paragraph page break option, 183
Alignment, 55, 174
    of headings, 171-172
    keeping for export, 145
    of text, 55-56, 156, 174-178
All indentation option, 176
Allow Page Break Within Paragraph option, 183
Alt keys, 5, 11
Alt-Backspace, 48, 116
Alt-F4, 57
Alt-PrtSc, 326
American dictionary, 88
Ami Professional files, 140-141
Anchoring frames, 293-294
Angle brackets <>, 106
ANSI CGM format, 306
ANSI character set, 135
ANSI files, 135
Appending documents, 132-133
Arrow keys, 5
ART format, 306, 323
ASCII File Export dialog box, 144-145
ASCII File Import dialog box, 138-140
ASCII files
    comma-delimited, 240-241
    exporting, 141-145
    fixed-field, 239-240
    importing, 133-135, 137-140
    opening, 140
    saving, 145
Aspect ratio, 312
Assigned printer, changing, 272-273
Associated template, 150

Associated text, 88, 100
Asterisk (*) wildcard character, 104-106
Attached template, 202
Attachments, to messages, 358
Attribute Colors option, 397-398
Attributes, read/write, 151
Attributes, text 49, 252
    assigning, 50-52, 53, 172-173
    changing, 99-100, 104, 107
    searching for, 99-100, 101, 108
    undoing, 51-52
Auto Backup option, 125, 127, 399
Auto Timed Save option, 125, 126-127, 131, 398
AUTOEXEC.BAT file, 387
Automatic hyphenation, 157, 178-179
Automatic numbering, 188
Automatic page layout setup, 202
Automatic resizing, 317-319
Automatic word-wrap, 28

B

Backspace key, 5, 28, 32
\BACKUP directory, 127
Backup options, 125-128, 398-399
Backward search, 100
Banners, 376-377
Basic font, 156
Before Paragraph option, 183
Bin print options, 267
Bitmapped graphics, 303-307
Bitstream FaceLift package, 261
Blank frames, 408, 409
Blanks, searching for, 98
Block operations, 43-48, 88-89
Blocks, 41-43
Body Text paragraph style, 160-161, 174, 207-208
Bold attribute, 49
Bold Text icon, 53, 390
Bookmarks, 101-102
Borders, creating, 289-290
Both Sides indentation option, 177
Built-in fonts, 257
Built-in templates, 225-226
Bulleted lists, 156, 184-187
Business cards, 372-374
Business Rules dictionary, 344
Business writing style, 346

C

Capitalization
    checking for, 92, 93
    searching for, 98-99, 103-104, 108
Caps Lock key, 4
Captions, adding, 319-320
Carbon copies, sending, 352, 354
Carbon ribbons, 256
Cards
    business, 372-374
    greeting 374-376
cc button, 352, 354
CCITT3 compression (TIF format), 305
Center alignment, 175
Center tab, 67
Center Text icon, 390
Centering, headings, 171-172
Change Font icon, 390
Change Template dialog box, 203
Character sets, 253-254
Check box, 14
Click on, 9
Clip art, 303
Clipboard, Windows, 42-43, 132-133, 280, 326
Collate print option, 267
Colors, assigning, 173
Column Balance option, 82
Column Guides option, 395
Columns
    selecting number of, 81-83, 376
    and tabs, in a frame, 294-296
Comma-delimited ASCII format, 240-241
Commonly Confused Words dictionary, 344
Comparison charts, customizing, 342-343
Context-sensitive help, 22-23
Control box icon, 7
Control menu, 7
Control Panel, Windows, 270-272, 402-403
Control Panel icon, 402-403
Copies, to print, 266
Copy icon, 48, 390
Copying
    files, 148-149
    frames, 280
    paragraph styles, 210
    text, 46-47, 131-133
Courier typeface, 250

Crop Marks print option, 267
Cropping, graphics, 313-314, 316
Ctrl keys, 5
Ctrl-B, 52, 53
Ctrl-C, 56
Ctrl-Enter, 106
Ctrl-H, 111, 283
Ctrl-I, 53
Ctrl-Ins, 48
Ctrl-J, 56
Ctrl-L, 56
Ctrl-M, 40
Ctrl-O, 16, 38
Ctrl-P, 37
Ctrl-PgDn, 18
Ctrl-PgUp, 18
Ctrl-R, 56
Ctrl-S, 35
Ctrl-Tab, 106
Ctrl-U, 53
Ctrl-W, 53
Ctrl-X, 160
Ctrl-Y, 161
Current template, 202
Cursors
    mouse, 8, 9
    text, 6
Cursor movement, 31
Custom edit box, 180
Custom Line Spacing dialog box, 55
Custom writing style, 346
Customization
    of grammar checker, 348-349
    of Professional Write Plus, 389-401
Customized letters, creating, 229-239
Cut icon, 48, 390
Cut option, 47
Cutting and pasting, 28

D

Data files, 229, 233, 237-242
Date variables, 117-118
dBase Import dialog box, 138, 139
DCA/FFT file format, 141
DCA/RFT file format, 141
Default directories
    document, 33, 121-122, 392-393
    template, 203, 221-222, 394

INDEX

Default frame options, setting, 298
Default paths, setting, 392-394
DEFAULT.STY template, 159, 201, 202, 221, 225, 394
Default tab settings, 71
Default template, 202, 221
    changing, 394-395
    selecting, 222-223, 394
    using, 158-159
Default view, 391
Defaults, start-up, 390-392
Del key, 5, 32
Deletion, undoing, 47-48
Description files, 241
Desktop publishing, 226
Device driver, monitor, 308
Dialog boxes, 13-17
Dictionaries
    American, 88
    Business Rules, 344
    personal, 88
    personal, editing, 92-94
    Standard Rules, 344
    Strict Rules, 344
DIF file format, for export, 141
Different fonts, using, 172-174
Direct entry, selecting the directory by, 123
Directories
    changing, 124
    creating, 221, 386
    default, 33, 121-122, 392-394
    selecting, 121-125, 146-147
    template, selecting, 221-222
Display Logo option, 392
Display modes, 40-41, 391
Display as Printed option, 396
DOC.STY template, 225
\DOCS directory, 121-122
Document descriptions, 112-113
Document directory, default, 33, 121-122 392-393
Document file, 121
Document path, 392-393
Document Statistics screen, 342
Document Summary screen, 342
Documents, 27
    appending, 132-133
    assigning a printer to, 272
    creating, 27
    erasing, 37
    locating, 113-114
    in multiple windows, 131
    multiple, working with, 128-133
    opening, 38-39
    printing, 36-37
    protecting, 339
    saving, 32-36, 128
    searching from beginning, 100
    transferring text between, 131-132
DOS text files, importing, 133
Dot-matrix printers, 255-256
Double CR files, importing, 135
Double indent, 178
Double Underline Text icon, 53, 390
Double words, 91-92
Double-click, 9
Downloading, soft fonts, 258
Draft mode, 40, 396-398
Draft/Layout Mode icon, 40, 390
Drafts, generating, 224-225
Dragging, 9
Drop capitals, 381-382
Duplicate names, of paragraph styles, 219

E

E. mail. *See* Electronic mail
E-Mail address book, 362-363
E-Mail List screen, 356-357
E-Mail Options dialog box, 350, 351
E-Mail Path option, 351
E-Mail Send dialog box, 352
Edit boxes, 14-15, 64
Edit button, 333
Edit menu, 45
Edit screen, 5-8
Edit screen tab ruler, 67-69
Edit window, grammar checker, 332-333
Editing
    data files, 246
    headers and footers, 78
    notes, 110-111
    page numbers, 80-81
    paragraph styles, 211-214
    text, 27-32
Electronic mail, 349-350
    address book for, 362-363

414 ◆ INDEX

    logging in, 350-351
    options, 351-352
    transmitting documents, 352-355
    transmitting messages, 355, 359-362
    viewing, 356-362
Elevator, 7, 18
Ellipses, 13
Enable E-Mail option, 351
Enable file format, for export, 141
Encapsulated PostScript (EPS) format, 305
End key, 5
Enlarged view, 41
Enter key, 5
ENVEL-C.STY template, 225
ENVEL-S.STY template, 225
EPS format, 305
Erasing, current work, 37
Escape key, 5
Exact attributes, in search, 101
Exact cropping, 316-317, 318
Existing, 57
Export Text dialog box, 144
Export Text icon, 390
Exporting, files to other programs, 141-145

F

Facing Pages view, 41
FAX.STY template, 225
Fiction writing style, 346
Field delimiter, 232
Field names, 229, 236
Fields, 229
FILE: port, 273
File formats
    graphics, 303-307
    text, 134, 141-142
File Manager, 146-152
File Manager icon, 390
File name specification, 122, 124, 147-148
File names, 33-34
File operations, standard, 148-151
File type, ASCII, 139-140
Files, 120. *See also individual file type*s
    deleting, 150
    exporting, 141-145
    importing, 133, 137-140
    moving and copying, 148-149
    renaming, 150-151

    printing to, 273
    retrieving, 38-39, 148
    saving, 35, 128
    selecting for display, 123-125
Find & Replace dialog box, 97, 98
Find & Replace feature, 96-108, 399
Find & Replace icon, 390
Find Backwards option, 100
Find Exact Attributes option, 99-100, 101, 108
Find Exact Case option, 99, 108
First Line Indentation option, 177, 397
First Publisher ClipArt (ART), 306, 323
Fixed-field ASCII format, 239-240
Font cartridges, 257-258
Font changes, automating, 265
Font file, outline, 260
Fonts, 52, 156, 252-253. *See also* Typefaces
    assigning, 53-54, 172-173
    built-in, 257
    displaying available, 261-262
    scalable, 259-261
    screen, 262-265
    selecting, tips on, 173-174
    soft, 258-259
    types of, 257
Fonts dialog box, 53-54
Footers, 72-78
Footnote Mark option, 115
Footnote Text option, 115
Formatting information
    in exported files, 142-143
    in imported files, 135-136
Frame Layout dialog box, 288-289, 296
Frame Layout icon, 390
Frame options, setting, 288-298
Frame/Bring to Front option, 286, 410
Frame/Send to Back option, 286
Frames, 277
    adding captions to, 319-320
    anchoring to paragraphs, 293-294
    background of, 296-297
    blank, 408, 409
    borders around, 289-290
    copying, 280-281
    creating, 278-279
        lines around, 291-293, 322
        repeating, 297

deleting, 281-282
fitting to specific dimensions, 314-316
grouping, 283-285
hidden, 282-283
inverting, 323-328
moving, 280-281
multicolumn, 294-296
multiple, 283-286, 368-369
overlapping, 285-286
placing graphics in, 314-319
resizing, 280
rotating, 323-328
selecting, 279-280, 310-311
setting options for, 288-298
shadowed, 321-322
text, 286-288, 296-297, 298-300
transparent, 296-297
Friction feed, 256
Full interactive proofreading, 338
Full justification, 55-56
Full page view, 41
Full Page/Current View icon, 390
Function key shortcuts, for assigning styles, 197-198
Function keys, 4, 197-198

G

.GBK extension, 336, 338
General writing style, 346
German character set, 254
Global styles
    deleting, 206-208
    editing, 212-213
    versus local, 155, 205-206, 208-211
Glyphix package, 261
GMK.PRF file, 349
Go To dialog box, 111, 114
Go To feature, 111, 114-115, 282
Go To icon, 283
Go To Next icon, 390
Grammar checking, 331-343
    customizing, 342-349
    strategies for, 340
Grammar icon, 390
Grammatical rules class, 344
Grammatik program, 331-349
GRAMTOUR.PWP document, 331
Graphics, 302
    cropping, 313-314, 316

deleting, 314
displaying, 396
fitting into a frame, 314-319
importing, 307-310
inverting, 323-325
positioning, 310, 377
rotating, 323-325
saving with document, 309-310
sizing, 311-312, 314-316, 317-319
Graphics adapters, 307-308
Graphics file formats, 303-307
Graphics files, moving with document, 149-150
Graphics frames. *See also* Frames
    rotating and inverting, 323-325
Greeting cards, 374-376
Group Frames option, 284-285
Grouping, frames, 283-285
Gutters, 82

H

Handles, 279-280
Hanging indent, 175, 177, 178
Hard hyphen, 179
Hard Pg Break option, 115
Hard returns, 28, 40
    searching for, 106-107
Hardware requirements, 1-2
Headers, 72-78
Headings
    fonts for, 174
    paragraph style for, 163-167
    placement of, 170-172, 376-377
Help, on-line, 20-23
Helvetica typeface, 250
Hewlett-Packard Printer Command Language (HP PCL) format, 305-306, 323
Hidden frames, locating, 282-283
Home key, 5
Horizontal scroll bars, 7, 19
Horizontal scrolling, avoiding, 65, 264-265
HP PCL format, 305-306, 323
Hyphenation, 157, 178-179

I

Icon bar. *See* Side bar
Icons, 389, 390
    assigning attributes with, 52, 53
Ignore Phrase option, 334

INDEX

Image size, adjusting, 311
Images. *See* Graphics
Import Graphics dialog box, 309
Import Graphics icon, 390
Import Text/Data dialog box, 137-138
Import Text/Data icon, 390
Indent paragraph style, 158
Indentation
    in bulleted lists, 186-187
    of text paragraphs, 156, 175, 176-178
Informal writing style, 346
Initial Caps attribute, 49
Initial Caps option, 51
Ins key, 5, 32
Insert editing mode, 31, 32
Insert Footnote icon, 390
Insert Merge Field dialog box, 234-236
Insert Note icon, 390
Insert Page Break icon, 390
Insert Variable icon, 390
Insert variables, 117-118
Installation
    printers, 402-406
    Professional Write Plus, 385-388
Interactive proofreading, 340
Introductory text, for paragraphs, 193-194
Invitations, 374-376
Italic Text icon, 53, 390
Italics attribute, 49

J

Justification, 55-56, 174-175
Justify Text icon, 390

K

Keep Graphics with Text option, 352
Keep with Next Paragraph option, 183
Keep with Previous Paragraph option, 183
Keep Styles with Document option, 352
Keyboard, 2-5
    making selections from, 11-12, 16-17, 44
    moving cursor with, 15, 30-31
Keyboard layouts, 3
Keyboard shortcuts, 11-12
Keypad, numeric, 4

L

Labels
    mailing, 242-246
    printing, 245-246
Landscape orientation, 60-63, 252, 253, 268-269
Large text, 368
Laser printers, 255-256
Last revision date of insert variable, 117
Layout. *See* Page layout
Layout mode, 40, 395-396
Layout views, 40-41
Leader character, 67, 68, 69
Leader Character option, 70
Left Align Text icon, 390
Left alignment, 175
Left indent, 175, 177-178
Left justification, 55-56
Left tab, 66
LEGAL.STY template, 225
LETTER.STY templates, 225
Letterhead, 369-371
Letters, mail merge, 229-239
Letterspacing, 179, 182
Line Between Columns, 82
Line endings, 139, 144-145
Line position around a frame, 293, 343
Line spacing, setting, 54-55, 156, 179-182, 367-368
Line Style list box, 194
Lines
    above or below paragraphs, 157, 167-170, 194-195
    around frames, 291-293, 322-323
    around pages, 83-84
    separate, adding, 196
List box, 14, 15-16
Lists
    bulleted, 156, 184-187
    numbered, 156, 187-193
Local styles. *See also* Paragraph styles
    deleting, 206-207
    editing, 211-212
    versus global, 155, 205-206, 208-211
    renaming, 211
    in template, 219-220
Logging in, to E-Mail, 350-351
Login dialog box, 350
Logo, turning off, 392
Lotus Picture (PIC) format, 306
Lowercase, attribute, 51

M

MAC format, 306, 323

INDEX

Mail merge, 229-242
Mail messages, 359-362
Mailing labels, 242-246
Margins, setting, 64-65, 244-245
Margins in Color option, 395
Marks, inserting, 333, 338
Marks option, 396
Math character set, 254
Maximize box icon, 7
Maximize Window option, 392
Meaning box, 95
Meaning Variations list box, 94, 95
Mechanical rules class, 345
MEMO.STY templates, 225
Menu bars, 7, 332
Menus, selecting from, 10-12
Merge Variable option, 115
Merging
    data files and standard letters, 229-239
    data from outside source, 239-242
Messages, mail, 359-362
MHS (Novell/Action Technologies Message Handling Service), 331, 349
Microsoft Windows 3.0 or later, required, 2
Microsoft Windows
    directory, 386
    installing printers under, 402-406
    screen fonts from, 263
    version required, 2
Microsoft Windows Write file format, 141
Microsoft Word file format, 141
Minimize box icon, 7
Misspellings, 90-91
Modify & Create Styles dialog box, 164
Modify & Create Styles icon, 390
Monospaced typefaces, 250
Mouse, 2, 8-10
    maintenance of, 10
    moving the text cursor with, 29-30
    selecting a block with, 43-44
    selecting menu items with, 10-11
    selecting directories with, 123
    using in dialog boxes, 14-16
Mouse button, 9
Mouse cursor, 6, 8, 9
Mouse pad, 8
Multicolumn layouts, 294, 295, 378-381

Multilevel numbered lists, 190-193
Multilevel styles, options for, 190-191
Multimate file format, 141
Multiple attributes, 51
Multiple frames, 283-286, 368-369
Multiple pages in a newsletter, 382

N

Name-and-address file, 243-246
Names, in E-Mail address book, 362-363
New icon, 390
New Mail Notification option, 351
New Program Object box, 387
Newsletters, 300-301, 376-383
NEWSLTR.STY templates, 225
Nondocument files, importing, 133-135, 138-140
Normal attributes, returning to, 51-52
Normal text, 252
Normal Text icon, 390
Note markers, 108
Note option, 115
Notes, 108-112
Notes option, 396
Novell/Action Technologies Message Handling Service, 331, 349
Num Lock key, 4
Number of copies option, 266
Numbered lists, 156
    creating, 187-189
    multilevel, 190-193
    types of, 187
Numbering, pages, 78-81
NUMBERS.STY template, 225
Numeric keypad, 4
Numeric tab, 67

O

Office Writer file format, 141
OK button, 17
Opaque frames, 296-297
Open dialog box, 122, 125
Open icon, 390
Orientation, page, 59-63, 252, 253, 268-269
Orientation box, 61
Original style options, reverting to, 214
"Out of system memory" error message, 129
Outline font file, 260
OVERHEAD.STY templates, 225

INDEX

Overlapping frames, 285-286
Overstrike attribute, 49

P

Page arrows, 7
Page breaks, controlling, 156, 182-184
Page design, tips on, 366-367
Page Layout dialog box, 59, 61, 69-72, 82
Page Layout icon, 390
Page Layout tab ruler, 65, 70-71
Page layout, 365-369
    changing, 54-56, 216-217, 383
    elements of, 59
    setup, automatic, 202
    and templates, 215-217, 220
Page margin area, 72-73
Page Numbering dialog box, 79-80
Page numbers, 78-81
Page orientation, 59-63, 252, 253, 268-269
Page Range print option, 266
Page Settings button, 60
Page size, setting, 59-62
Page Status box, 7
Page view, 280
Pages
    drawing lines around, 83-84
    going to particular, 114
    in newsletter, 382
    numbering, 78-81
Paper, 256, 267, 268-269
Paragraph returns, keeping, 139, 145
Paragraph styles, 155-162
    applying, 161-162, 166-167
    assigning to function keys, 197-198
    for automatic numbering, 188-189
    for bulleted lists, 185-186
    copying, 210-211
    creating, 162-172, 208
    deleting, 206-208, 220-221
    editing, 172, 211-214
    features assigned with, 156-158
    local versus global, 155, 204-205, 208-211
    renaming, 211
    switching assignments of, 214-215
    switching templates containing, 218-220
    viewing, 198
Paragraphs, 155
    adding introductory text, 193-194

    aligning, 174-177
    assigning styles to, 161-162, 214-215
    indenting, 174-178
    inserting between outline levels, 193
    spacing between, 180-182, 196
Parent, of current directory, 123
Paste icon, 48, 390
Path name, 34
Paths, setting default, 392-394. *See also* Directories
PC Paintbrush (PCX) format, 304, 323
Period (.), leader character, 68, 69
Personal dictionary, 88, 92-94
PgDn key, 5, 18
PgUp key, 5, 18
PIC format, 306
Pica typeface, 251
Picas, 55
Pictures option, 396
Pitch, 251
Pixels, 303
Pointing and clicking, 8-9
Points, 53, 251
Ports, printer, 269-270, 402, 404, 405
Portrait orientation, 60-61, 252, 253, 268-269
PRESSREL.STY template, 225
Print dialog box, 37, 267
Print icon, 390
Print options, 266-269
Print quality, 255-256, 273-274, 406-407
Print side bar icon, 37
Print speed, 268
Printers, 254-256
    assigning to a document, 272-273
    installing, 402-406
    multiple, 269-273
    and screen output, 307-308
    selecting the active, 270-272
Printer ports, 269-270, 402, 404, 405
Printer resolution, 406
Printer settings, 62-63
Printer Setup dialog box, 63, 268
Printers icon, 271, 403
Printing
    documents, 36-37
    to a file, 273
    mail messages, 359
    mailing labels, 245-246

INDEX

Problem window, 333
Professional Write (DOS version) file format, 141
Professional Write Plus directory, 386
Professional Write Plus icon, 387
Professional Write Plus window, 392
Program files, installing, 385-387
Program icon, creating, 387-388
Program Manager window, 385, 386
Proofreading. *See* Grammar checking; Spell checking
Proportionally spaced typefaces, 250
PROPOSAL.STY template, 225
Publisher's Powerpak package, 261
Push button, 14
.PWP extension, 122-123
PWPLUS.EXE, 2

Q

Question mark (?) wildcard character, 104-106
Quitting without saving, 37, 57

R

RAM (random access memory), 1
Read Mail icon, 390
Read/Write attributes, 151, 408
Readability statistics, 336, 337
Record delimiter, 232
Records, in data file, 229, 233
Relative tabs, 70
Repeating frames, 297
Repetitive jumping, 115
Replace box, 334-335
Replacement attributes, 104
Replacement capitalization, 103-104
Replacement string, 96, 102
Replies to messagages, 359-360
REPORT.STY templates, 225
Reset to Zero indentation option, 176
Resolution, printer, 255, 406
Rest indentation option, 177
Rich Text Format, for export, 141
Right Align Text icon, 390
Right indent, 175
Right justification, 55-56, 171-172, 175
Right tab, 66-67
RLE (Run Length Encoding) TIF format, 305
Rough drafts, 224-225
Rule classes, 333, 344-345
Rule dictionaries, 344

Ruler, vertical, 316
Ruling lines. *See* Lines

S

.SAM extension, 140
SAMNA Word IV file format, 141
Sans serif typefaces, 174, 250-251, 372
Saturation, of images, 255
Save As dialog box, 34, 125, 145
Save icon, 35, 390
Saves, automatic, 126-127, 398-399
Scalable typefaces, 173, 257, 259-261
Screen, and graphics output, 307-308
Screen display, problems, 265
Screen fonts, 262-265
Script typeface, 250
Scroll bars, 7
Scrolling, 18-19
SDW format, 306
Search string, 96
Search-and-replace operations, 96-108
Select Printer dialog box, 63
Selection box, 16
Send Document dialog box, 352
Serif typefaces, 174, 250-251
Serifs, 174, 250
Shadow effect, creating, 321-322
Shift keys, 4
    moving two or more tabs using, 68, 69
    selecting a block with, 44
    selecting multiple frames with, 283
Shift-Del, 47, 48
Shift-Ins, 48
Shortcuts, function key, for assigning styles, 197-198
Show Styles Box option, 392
Show Tab Ruler option, 67
Show/Hide Marks icon, 390
Show/Hide Picture icon, 390
Show/Hide Tab Ruler icon, 390
Side bar, 7, 19-20
    block operations with, 48
    customizing, 389-390, 391
    displaying, 400-401
Sidebar (text), creating, 380
Single CR files, 135
Single-level numbered lists, 188-190
Small caps attribute, 49
Small caps option, 51

INDEX

Snapshot, of screen, 325-326
Soft fonts, 258-259, 406-407
Space
    above and below a paragraph, 180-182
    below the heading, 170-171
    between words, 408
Spacing
    in document, 196
    of lines, 156, 367-368
    of records, in mailing labels, 245
Speed keys, 48, 52, 53. *See also individual key combinations*
Speed options, 399-400
Spell checking, 87-94, 399-400
Spelling dialog box, 89, 93
Spelling icon, 390
Standard letters, 229-231
    creating, 233-236
    merging data with, 237-239
    using existing, 238
Standard Rules dictionary, 344
Standard view, 41, 391, 410
Start up, 2
Start-up defaults, setting, 390-392
Starting over, 37-38
Statistical output, in grammar checker, 341-343
Status bar, 7
Status Bar option, 396
Stop, Mark Rest of Document option, 339
Stop, Mark Rest of Document with Advice option, 339
Stop, Show Statistics option, 339
Strict Rules dictionary, 344
Strikethrough attribute, 49
Strings, 98, 102-103
Style deletion, recovering from accidental, 220-221
Style names, keeping in file transmissions, 139, 145
Style options, reverting to original, 214
Style rules class, 345
Style types, changing, 208-211
Style-assignment keys, 197
Styles. *See* Paragraph styles; Templates
Styles box, 160
    displaying, 198, 392
    using, 159-160
\STYLES directory, 225, 393
Submenus, 12
Subscript attribute, 49

Subscript Text icon, 53, 390
Superscript attribute, 49
Superscript icon, 53, 390
SYM format, 307
Symbol set, 253-254
Synonyms list box, 94, 95, 96
System date insert variable, 117
System requirements, 1-2

T

Tab leaders, 67
Tab rulers
    deleting, 71
    displaying, 400-401
    on edit screen, 67-69
    in imported files, 136-137
    inserting, 71
    in Page Layout, 66, 70-71
    visibility of, 409
Tab symbol [---->], in draft mode, 40
Tabs, 66
    changing, 66, 70-71
    deleting, 68, 69
    default, 71
    in frames, 294
    inserting, 68-70, 408
    moving, 68, 69
    relative, 70
    searching for, 106
    types of, 66-67
Tabs & Returns option, 397
Tagged Image File (TIF), 305, 323
Task Manager, Windows, 402
Technical writing style, 346
Template defaults, setting, 221-223
Template directory, default, 203, 221-222, 394
Template files, backups of, 218
Template path, 393-394
Templates, 158, 201-202
    attached, 150, 202
    built-in, 225-226
    creating, 204-205
    default, 159, 222-223, 394
    deleting, 217-218
    editing a style in, 212-213
    including text in, 223-224, 369-371
    including when moving files, 150
    moving styles to, 210-211

INDEX

name, 205
and page layouts, 215-217, 220
selecting, 203-204, 394-395
switching, 218-220
Temporary margins, 65
10-pitch (pica) typeface, 251
Text
    aligning, 55-56, 145, 156
    assigning a style to, 161-162
    associated, 88, 100
    blocks of, 41-48
    cut off on screen, 409-410
    deleting, 31-32
    entering, 27-29, 31-32
    in frames, 286-288
    importing, 133-140
    including as part of template, 223-224
    introductory, for paragraphs, 193-194
    inverting, 325-326, 328
    large size, 368
    normal, 252
    rotating, 325-326, 328
    scrolling through, 18-19
    sending in E-Mail, 354
    transferring between documents, 131-132
Text attributes, 49, 252
    assigning, 50-52, 53, 172-173
    changing, 99-100, 104, 107
    undoing, 51-52
Text boxes, 14-15, 64
Text cursor, 6, 29-31
Text files, DOS, 133
Text flow, in newsletters, 377
Text frames, 296-297, 298-300, 325. *See also* Frames
Text menu, 50
Text spacing. *See* Line spacing; Text tightness
Text tightness, 179-182
Text/Spacing option, 367
Thesaurus, 94-96
Thesaurus icon, 390
TIF format, 305, 323
Times Roman typeface, 52, 249
Title bar, 7
TO: List dialog box, 352
Today's date insert variable, 117
Toggle, 4
Trackball, 2

Tractor feed, 256
Transparent frame, 296-297
Troubleshooting, 408-410
TYP, for typeover, 32
Type size, 172-173, 251
Type-generating software, 406-407
Typefaces, 52, 249-250. *See also* Fonts
    scalable, 173, 257, 259-261
    selecting, 172-173, 365
    serif and sans serif, 250-251
Typeover edit mode, 32
Typing Replaces Selected Text option, 392

U

Underline attributes, 49
Underline Text icon, 53, 390
Undo, 115-116
    and attributes, 51-52
    and block deletions, 47-48
    clearing the memory of, 116
    from the Edit menu, 47
    setting the number of levels, 400
    speed key, 48, 116
Undo icon, 48, 116, 390
Units of measure, for indentation, 177
Unmatched paragraph style name, 219
Uppercase, attribute, 51
User names, in E-Mail, 354

V

Variables, insert, 117-118
VEAMAB51.LEX file, 92
Vector graphics, 303-307
Vertical ruler, 73-74, 316
Vertical Ruler option, 396
Vertical scroll bars, 7, 18
View, default, 391
Views, 40-41

W

When Not at Break option, 180
Wildcard characters
    changing attributes with, 107
    locating and replacing text with, 104-105, 106
Windows, manipulating, 130-131
Windows Bitmapped format, 304, 323
Windows Clipboard, 42-43, 132-133, 280, 326
Windows Control Panel, 270-272, 402-403
Windows, Microsoft

    directory, 386
    installing printers under, 402-406
    screen fonts from, 263
    version required, 2
Windows Task Manager, 402
WMF (Windows Metafile format), 305
Word underline attribute, 49
Word Underline Text icon, 53, 390
Word-wrap, automatic, 28
WordPerfect (versions 4.2 and 5.x) file format, 141
WordStar 2000 file format, 141
WordStar file format, 141
Working view, 41, 391, 410
Working View Level option, 396
Writing style, in grammar checker, 345-347
WYSIWYG, 395

Get PC Magazine Now...and SAVE!

SPECIAL OFFER FOR READERS OF
GUIDE TO PROFESSIONAL WRITE PLUS

SAVE 54% on 22 Issues

SAVE 62% on 44 Issues

Subscribe now and get 2 Free Disks!

You purchased *PC MAGAZINE GUIDE TO PROFESSIONAL WRITE PLUS,* with one thing in mind—to get *THE MOST* from your system. Now, to keep vital information coming throughout the year, order *PC MAGAZINE,* the #1 resource for IBM— standard personal computing. 22 times a year, *PC MAGAZINE* delivers it all! Plus if you subscribe now you'll get the Best of PC Magazine's Utilities on a 2-disk set—guaranteed to enhance your DOS, Video and Printer capabilities—FREE with your paid subscription!

PC MAGAZINE delivers:
- More in-depth reviews than any other computer publication.
- Benchmark test reports on new products from our own PC Labs.
- A comprehensive productivity section for working faster and smarter.

Send in the SPECIAL SAVINGS CARD below:

YES! I want to take advantage of this SPECIAL OFFER. Please rush me the Best of PC Magazine's Utilities and **PC MAGAZINE** for:

☐ One year (22 issues) only $29.97. **I SAVE 54%.**

☐ Two years (44 issues) only $49.97. **I SAVE 62%.**

Name_____
(please print)

8S8S6

Company_____

Address_____

City_____

State_____ Zip_____

☐ Payment enclosed.   ☐ Bill me later.

SAVE UP TO 62%

Please add $32 per year for postage outside the U.S., U.S. currency only. Canadian GST included. Please allow 30 days for delivery. Disks will be shipped upon payment.

PC MAGAZINE

GUARANTEE YOURSELF NON-STOP SYSTEMS INFORMATION. ORDER PC MAGAZINE TODAY!

SAVE 54% when you order a one-year (22 issue) subscription.

SAVE 62% when you order a two year (44 issue) subscription.

MONEY-BACK GUARANTEE
If at any time you find that **PC MAGAZINE** does not provide you with the help and information you need, simply cancel your subscription for a *full refund* on all unmailed issues.

THIS IS A SPECIAL OFFER FOR GUIDE TO PROFESSIONAL WRITE PLUS READERS!

BUSINESS REPLY MAIL
FIRST CLASS MAIL   PERMIT NO. 66   BOULDER, CO

POSTAGE WILL BE PAID BY ADDRESSEE

PC MAGAZINE
P.O. Box 51524
Boulder, CO 80321-1524

NO POSTAGE
NECESSARY
IF MAILED
IN THE
UNITED STATES